Tatort Germany

Although George Bernard Shaw quipped that "the Germans lack talent for two things: revolution and crime novels," there is a long tradition of German crime fiction; it simply hasn't aligned itself with international trends. During the 1920s, German-language writers dispensed with the detective and focused instead on criminals, a trend that did not take hold in other countries until after 1945, by which time Germany had gone on to produce antidetective novels that were similarly ahead of their time. German crime fiction has thus always been a curious case; rather than follow the established rules of the genre, it has always been interested in examining, breaking, and ultimately rewriting those rules. This book assembles leading international scholars to examine today's German crime fiction. It features innovative scholarly work that matches the innovativeness of the genre, taking up the *Regionalkrimi*; crime fiction's reimagining and transforming of traditional identities; historical crime fiction that examines Germany's and Austria's conflicted twentieth-century past; and how the newly vibrant Austrian crime fiction ties in with and differentiates itself from its German counterpart

Studies in German Literature, Linguistics, and Culture

Tatort Germany

The Curious Case of German-Language Crime Fiction

Edited by
Lynn M. Kutch
and
Todd Herzog

CAMDEN HOUSE
Rochester, New York

Copyright © 2014 by the Editors and Contributors

All Rights Reserved. Except as permitted under current legislation, no part of this work may be photocopied, stored in a retrieval system, published, performed in public, adapted, broadcast, transmitted, recorded, or reproduced in any form or by any means, without the prior permission of the copyright owner.

First published 2014 by Camden House
Reprinted in paperback 2018

Camden House is an imprint of Boydell & Brewer Inc.
668 Mt. Hope Avenue, Rochester, NY 14620, USA
www.camden-house.com
and of Boydell & Brewer Limited
PO Box 9, Woodbridge, Suffolk IP12 3DF, UK
www.boydellandbrewer.com

Paperback ISBN-13: 978-1-64014-026-4
Paperback ISBN-10: 1-64014-026-3
Hardcover ISBN-13: 978-1-57113-571-1
Hardcover ISBN-10: 1-57113-571-5

Library of Congress Cataloging-in-Publication Data

Tatort Germany : the curious case of German-language crime fiction / edited by Lynn M. Kutch and Todd Herzog.
    pages cm.—(Studies in German literature, linguistics, and culture)
Includes bibliographical references and index.
ISBN 978-1-57113-571-1 (hardcover : alk. paper)—
ISBN 1-57113-571-5 (hardcover : alk. paper)
    1. Detective and mystery stories, German—History and criticism. 2. German fiction—21st century—History and criticism. 3. Austrian fiction—21st century—History and criticism. 4. Detective and mystery television programs—Germany—History and criticism. 5. Television crime shows—Germany—History and criticism. 6. Literature and history—Austria. 7. Identity (Psychology) in literature. I. Kutch, Lynn M., 1970– editor. II. Herzog, Todd, editor. III. Title. IV. Title: Curious case of German-language crime fiction.

PT747.D4T38 2014
833'.087209—dc23

2014023843

Contents

Acknowledgments   vii

Introduction   1
   Lynn M. Kutch and Todd Herzog

Part I. Place

1: *Vor Ort:* The Functions and Early Roots of German Regional Crime Fiction   23
   Kyle Frackman

2: Krimi Quo Vadis: Literary and Televised Trends in the German Crime Genre   41
   Sascha Gerhards

3: Plurality and Alterity in Wolf Haas's Detective Brenner Mysteries   61
   Jon Sherman

4: The Case of the Austrian Regional Crime Novel   81
   Anita McChesney

Part II. History

5: "Darkness at the Beginning": The Holocaust in Contemporary German Crime Fiction   101
   Magdalena Waligórska

6: Case Histories: The Legacy of Nazi Euthanasia in Recent German *Heimatkrimis*   120
   Susanne C. Knittel

7: "Der Fall Loest": A Case Study of Crime Stories and the Public Sphere in the GDR   139
   Carol Anne Costabile-Heming

8: What's in Your Bag?: "Freudian Crimes" and Austria's
   Nazi Past in Eva Rossmann's *Freudsche Verbrechen*   155
   Traci S. O'Brien

Part III. Identity

9: Layered Deviance: Intersexuality in Contemporary
   German Crime Fiction   177
   Angelika Baier

10: Girls in the Gay Bar: Performing and Policing Identity
    in Crime Fiction   200
    Faye Stewart

11: Eva Rossmann's Culinary Mysteries   223
    Heike Henderson

Works Cited   239

Notes on the Contributors   255

Index   259

Acknowledgments

THE EDITORS WOULD LIKE TO THANK the Camden House team, especially Jim Walker and Julia Cook, for their support and exceptional professionalism.

Cover photo credit: Peter Mackey (http://www.mackeyphoto.com).

Introduction

Lynn M. Kutch and Todd Herzog

Crime Fiction: Archetypes and Iterations

CRIME FICTION, FULL OF GENRE CONVENTIONS, well-worked formulas, and clichéd characters, rarely takes itself seriously. Why, then, should we as literature scholars take it seriously? Robert A. Rushing provides one answer in his 2007 study *Resisting Arrest: Detective Fiction and Popular Culture* when he enters into a scholarly dialogue with critic John Irwin, who had considered the possible incompatibility of crime fiction and high art; and had called into question the simple structure of the crime novel and the formulas it repeatedly employs. He suggests that readers' expectations of the genre could discourage the rereading that he deems an essential part of serious literary criticism.[1] Rushing argues, however, that the genre's basic structures, or what he calls the "central mechanism of detective fiction," are precisely those characteristics that *encourage* the reader, and we would argue the literary critic, to return to crime texts again and again in search of satisfying solutions.[2] Given the once persistent, even now seemingly unyielding differentiation in Germany between high and low art—or in this case, *Literatur* and *Schundliteratur*[3]—the interrogation that Rushing offers of Irwin's critique holds particular relevance for a volume on German-language crime fiction. Recent trends in scholarship confirm that academics have increasingly joined this search for solutions, which refers less to the one-time discovery of whodunnit and more to the careful rereading and analysis of how and why the author has led the reader to that point. Attending just one panel on crime fiction at an academic conference quickly leads to the discovery that crime fiction is a "guilty pleasure" for many scholars who otherwise spend their time with ostensibly higher-minded literature. And we as scholars of the genre are in good company: Walter Benjamin, Siegfried Kracauer, Bertolt Brecht, Ernst Bloch, and many other towering intellectual figures of the past century have been avid readers of crime fiction.

As the prominent German literary scholar Jochen Vogt has pointed out, the traditional philosophical split between high literature and crime fiction, the latter labeled as "primitives Lesefutter" and

"Verbrauchsliteratur" (2; primitive reading material and literature for the average consumer) has also traditionally extended into the scholarship of German crime fiction.[4] Vogt states in a 2007 article: "Bemerkens- und nachdenkenswert ist aber doch, dass Kriminalliteratur sowohl in der (deutschen) Literaturwissenschaft wie in der überregionalen Literaturkritik nicht oder eben nur gelegentlich 'stattfindet.' Im literaturwissenschaftlichen Studium ist das Thema Krimi inzwischen *möglich* . . ., bleibt aber marginal" (2; it is worth noting and thinking about the fact that crime literature in [German] literary studies as well as those outside Germany does not "take place," or if so only occasionally. Literary studies of the topic of the crime novel are *possible*, but remain marginal).[5] More recent evidence, such as the program for the April 2013 "Krimi-Symposium im Brecht Haus," which alternately highlighted discussions of crime fiction's potential for the *Verblödung* (dumbing-down) of literature as well as its literary value, strongly suggests that international scholarly study of German-crime fiction has indeed become more than marginally possible.[6] By offering literary critical readings of contemporary German-language crime fiction, the scholars showcased in this volume show that this developing genre, like its predecessors in innovative German literature since the 1960s, greatly enriches the literary landscape, and indeed asserts itself as a potentially viable part of the international genre.[7] In *Tatort Germany*, contributors analyze superficially entertaining yet deeply critical examples of current German-language crime fiction that test the increasingly flexible but still-present boundaries between high and low culture. In exploring specific ways that authors of contemporary German-language crime fiction exploit traditional formulas of literature and classic crime fiction in order to address local and global issues of the past and present, this volume demonstrates a professional advocacy for the genre's significance within conventional German literary scholarship.

German-speaking crime novelists, especially those who have published within the past two decades, have taken up the distinctly German challenge of injecting serious critical purpose into a perceived literature of pure entertainment. Although German-speaking crime fiction has a distinct personality, part of which involves reconciling the culturally defined split between the superficial and the intellectual, the texts nonetheless rely on an established crime-fiction narrative structure. John G. Cawelti has defined this general narrative formula as "a combination or synthesis of a number of specific cultural conventions with a more universal story form or archetype."[8] When he writes about the crime formula specifically, the main attributes he names, "the investigation and discovery of hidden secrets," could characterize crime fiction of nearly any society.[9] Thus, the word "universal" in his definition rightly suggests that the mechanism or the archetype, whether adventure, romance, mystery or melodrama, easily crosses borders. Indeed, the increasing prevalence of the crime genre worldwide evidences the crime formula's versatility and adaptability. In his discussion of these archetypal formulas, however, Cawelti also makes the important point that "in order for these patterns to work, they must be embodied in figures, settings, and situations that have appropriate meanings for the culture which produces them."[10] Given the recent, nearly frenzied, proliferation of crime fiction in German-speaking countries, Cawelti's comment inspires a critical look into the specific cultural and narrative strategies that contemporary German-language crime novelists employ. On the one hand, the recent works of German-language crime fiction treated here fit into a long tradition of crime fiction both within and outside German-speaking borders. On the other hand, they exhibit traits peculiar to the places in which they were produced. As we will argue in this volume, the selected works of crime fiction appropriate and adapt the basic formula, which Cawelti and many others have defined for decades, by focusing on the particularly German cultural products of place, history, and identity.

German-Language Crime Fiction and International Trends

Because this book examines German-language crime fiction[11] and crime-fiction scholarship at the beginning of the twenty-first century, it is important to regard it not only within the perhaps enigmatic and seemingly truncated German tradition of crime fiction, but also within recent international trends. Consequently, in addition to defining the distinct profile of German-language crime fiction, this volume aims to situate its current trends and scholarship within historical, international, and theoretical contexts. As such, it functions as a complementary next chapter in a series of critical works on crime fiction that have included treatments of German crime fiction, though often not exclusively. Other critical works to date have concentrated on novels from earlier time periods, on particular German, English, or international authors, or have structured their studies around the general aesthetics of global crime fiction.[12] In addition to these book-length studies, an increasing number of scholarly articles on German-language crime fiction have also appeared in recent years and point toward a growing interest in German crime fiction.[13] German-language crime fiction has traditionally displayed innovation within the larger genre, and, as we have mentioned, often concerns itself with peculiarities of German place and history and how these factors influence characters and plots. It has also, however, recently begun to align itself with international movements.

The individual contributions contained in this book differ greatly from each other in methodology and individual subject, but as a whole they present a snapshot of contemporary trends in German-language crime fiction and its scholarship, which draw connections to international movements in crime fiction such as placing crime fiction in the service of social critique and asking complex questions about identity and social interactions. In the 2009 volume *Investigating Identities: Questions of Identity in Contemporary International Crime Fiction* Marieke Krajenbrink and Kate M. Quinn illuminate such "points of common interest that exist within the genre at an international level," and highlight contemporary texts that "shed light on processes of adaptation and appropriation of the genre to specific national, regional, or local contexts."[14] It should not be surprising that German crime fiction does this, as indeed this has been a hallmark of the German style of the genre since at least the 1920s. In the recent edited collection *The Millennial Detective: Essays on Trends in Film and Television, 1990–2010,* Malcah Effron cites global influences such as scientific advancements and the rise of terrorism and argues that authors have increasingly used the genre to respond to societal change and incorporate into their textual responses a range of critical techniques such as cultural geography and feminist studies.[15]

Seen in a broader context, textual treatments of current societal conditions in German-language crime fiction certainly correspond to international trends in and adaptations of the genre in the twenty-first century. But at the same time, we would argue along with William W. Stowe that understanding a work of crime fiction must take into account its position as a product, a representation, and a critique of a particular time and place, and that it therefore demands a closer investigation of the peculiarities of those times and places that inspire and shape a text.[16] While German-language crime fiction of the twenty-first century does not inhabit a space completely isolated from global examples of the genre, it does, however, exhibit a specific set of historical and aesthetic conditions, as the volume's three parts articulate. Each of the parts takes up a marked element of recent German crime fiction: the first part, "Place," regards the blossoming of German regional crime fiction in a period of increasing globalization; the second, "History," takes up the always contentious topic of victims, perpetrators, and guilt during and after the Third Reich; and the third, "Identity," examines the ways in which crime fiction has become a means to examine and subvert questions of identity.

The Contradictory Nature of German-Language Crime Fiction

Before we turn to more in-depth explanations of how these three distinct categories define contemporary German-language crime fiction, it is necessary to address the ostensible contradictions in its development.

When combining traditional crime-fiction formulas, culturally defined attitudes toward high and low culture, and twentieth-century German history, the present profile of German-language crime fiction may indeed appear quite incongruous. On the one hand, Germany's history, the distinctiveness of its literary industry, and pointed international criticism of German crime fiction could lead to the conclusion that German-language writers have not been consistent and viable contributors to the larger genre. In fact, scholars and readers both within and outside of Germany have often concluded that crime fiction is simply "kein deutsches Genre" (not a German genre).[17] At many junctures, it has seemed to lag behind the genre's dynamism outside German-speaking borders. On the other hand, we would argue, German-language crime fiction has not only reexamined, reconfigured, and rewritten conventional and established rules of the genre, but has also been an innovator of trends, even anticipating tendencies in international crime fiction. Today, as this volume's contributors demonstrate, German-language crime fiction is largely in step with the major trends in international fiction, although it still remains largely unrecognized outside of Germany, largely due to the lack of published translations.

The neglect of German-language crime fiction on the international stage is nothing new. The Germans have frequently been maligned for their alleged lack of facility with the crime genre: in the 1920s Willard Huntington Wright pronounced German efforts at the genre "abortive and ponderous"[18] and George Bernard Shaw once quipped that "the Germans lack talent for two things: revolution and crime novels."[19] In his history of the continental detective story, published in 1947, Howard Haycraft does not expand the map of continental Europe beyond the borders of France, arguing that "continental contributions to the detective story, aside from the French, have been so few, so indirect, and so unimportant that there would be no sensible object in discussing them here."[20] Even the nationalistic Austrian crime writer Edmund Finke complained that the "German crime novel is somewhat of a sad case."[21] Despite these unequivocally negative comments, in some cases, advancements in German-language crime fiction preceded similar developments elsewhere. During the Golden Age of English-language detective fiction in the 1920s—when the two main branches of detective fiction (the British analytic detective story and the American hard-boiled detective story) became firmly established—German-language writers dispensed with the detective altogether and focused instead on criminals. Only after the Second World War would international crime fiction take up this trend. By then, however, German-language writers were producing anti-detective novels that were similarly ahead of their time.[22]

Progressive crime fiction's proliferation during certain time periods suggests a certain assertiveness, often critically neglected, of German-language crime-fiction texts. Questions still arise, however, about the difficulty of tracing a continuous history of the German crime novel, which is, to use Arlene Teraoka's fitting formulation, a "mystery worthy of detective work."[23] As we have mentioned, two distinctly German factors have contributed to the perceived lack of or delay in development: the cultural divide between high and low culture and the peculiarities of twentieth-century German history, particularly the experience of National Socialism. These two distinctly German elements have in fact evolved into primary literary themes that have in turn generated critical theoretical questions. For example, ideological conflicts located in the National Socialist past have produced an ethical dilemma for that contemporary branch of German-language crime fiction that relies on events of the Holocaust for its plot. At the same time, authors have made progress in closing the gap between high and low art by producing works closer in style and purpose to conventional literary fiction. The peculiarly German twist to German-language crime-fiction trends and the key factors that have influenced its development and shape its current direction are related to the three areas mentioned above, which we will elaborate now: regionalism defined heavily by the German cultural concept of *Heimat*; the country's twentieth-century past; and twenty-first-century definitions of identity.

Tatorte: German-Language Crime Scenes

"Throughout its history," as Mark Lawson has argued, "crime literature has operated as a sort of imaginative travel agency."[24] The idea of leisurely travel to various locations certainly corresponds to the implicit entertainment value of crime fiction, and perhaps more automatically to the televised variety. If we think of the German word for crime scene, *Tatort*, any German reader who has sat in front of a television set in Germany at 8:15 on any Sunday evening since November 29, 1970, will think of what is arguably the most important German contribution in any medium to the genre of crime fiction: the long-running and much-celebrated television series of the same name. Now numbering over eight hundred episodes, *Tatort*'s storylines are inextricably tied to its regional settings and marked by a vérité style that emphasizes recognizable regional spaces, customs, and accents as well as identifiable cases and events. It is plausible that this German popular-culture association of the term "crime scene" with any crime story has even contributed to the current German crime novel's emphasis on place, which resonates particularly in post–World War II Germany. Because the German-speaking locations to which readers travel encompass specific cultural and historical markers, the notion of place in crime fiction demands—and has received—much scholarly attention. Eva Erdmann traces an international trend toward heightened specificity of location in which "the heinousness of crime is increasingly being replaced by the search for more colourful settings and, by means of a specific local connection, the crime novel takes on the function of a new type of *Heimatroman*."[25] The comparison with the *Heimatroman*—a conservative German genre that typically paints an idyllic picture of timeless rural life and an unproblematized, unchanging German identity—is surprising and, we suspect, deliberately provocative.[26]

At first glance, nothing could be further from the typically urban, messy, and often cynical genre of crime fiction than the *Heimatroman*. But Erdmann's point—and it is a crucial one—is to alert us to the importance of place, often quite specific and intricately detailed, in German-language crime fiction. Melanie Wigbers, in her study of German crime fiction across many time periods, *Krimi-Orte im Wandel*, emphasizes the importance of settings and touches on the intertwined threads of place and history as especially problematic for German-language crime fiction, calling for a critical reevaluation of place, and reminding us of the historical determinacy of setting.[27] In his 2013 study *Das Milieu im Fernsehkrimi*, Björn Otte not only examines the growing significance of milieu as it relates to the television crime drama, but he also reinforces the notion of place-determined interactions between characters and location when he argues "Zusammenfassend bezieht sich der Begriff des Milieus auf eine Umwelt, die vom Akteur nicht völlig unabhängig ist. Wenn vom Milieu die Rede ist, spielt das Zusammenwirken der Akteure, welches das Handeln jedes Einzelnen beeinflusst, eine große Rolle" (33; in sum, the term milieu refers to an environment that is not fully independent of the actor. When talking about milieu, the interactions of the actors, which influence the actions of the individuals, also play a large role).[28]

Similar to current offerings in German-language crime fiction, targeted investigation of place enables focused social critique, as Otte emphasizes when he writes that milieu and society appear in the foreground while the actual crime slips into the background.[29] Indeed, specificity of place, social critique, and a deemphasis of the actual crime characterize much of contemporary global as well as German-language crime fiction. A potentially paradoxical feature of the German-language variety, and what distinguishes it sharply from the *Heimatroman*, is that these site-specific stories could potentially enjoy popularity well beyond their described locations because of their implementation of the basic and expected elements of crime fiction. The fact that nearly all of the works studied in this volume have not been translated, however, significantly hinders popularity beyond German or Austrian borders. Like its Scandinavian counterparts that find success through the combination of literary factors and political or socioeconomic observations, contemporary German-language crime fiction likewise has the potential for expanded critical appeal because of its original adaptations of narrative formulas that are then influenced by specifically German cultural factors as well as historical impulses.

Regional Crime Fiction for a Global World

Part 1, "Place," focuses on discussions of setting in the regional crime novel (in German: *Regiokrimi*),[30] a popular subgenre that K. D. M. Snell has succinctly defined in a study of British and Irish regional novels as "fiction that is set in a recognizable region, and that concerns itself with the culture of the area and the lives of its people."[31] By presenting an interplay between an area's regionality and internationality, texts belonging to regional fiction show that they are grounded in the local community, but are "simultaneously relevant to larger issues of both national and international significance."[32] In his contribution to the present volume, "*Vor Ort*: The Functions and Early Roots of German Regional Crime Fiction," Kyle Frackman links the notion of regional fiction that emerges from and emphasizes a distinct culture and area with increasingly more complex understandings of identity. Tracing the literary-historical beginnings of German-language regional crime fiction, he not only discusses the genre in its present context, but also argues that regional crime fiction exhibits structural similarities to eighteenth- and nineteenth-century *Fallgeschichten* (case studies). With this comparison, Frackman addresses important questions about the public interest throughout several centuries in narratives that intriguingly combine the familiar or realistic and the fantastic or mysterious. Frackman's essay considers the essential questions of how crime develops at a certain time and in a certain place, and how social issues relate to and influence criminal events. He further shows how this specificity of time and place can be transcended and made relevant for readers in other times and other places. Frackman's study weaves together two main analytical threads of place and identity that form a crucial critical pair throughout this volume.

In "Krimi Quo Vadis: Literary and Televised Trends in the German Crime Genre," Sascha Gerhards takes a dual-media approach to tracking the progression and future direction of German regional crime fiction. At the center of his discussion lies the enduringly popular series *Tatort*. Gerhards argues that, despite the typically German reliance on elements associated with *Heimat*, both the screenwriters of *Tatort* and contemporary German crime-fiction authors veer far from the traditional politics of *Heimat* stories but instead use regional crime fiction as a vehicle for social critique. By way of a detailed analysis of a 2011 *Tatort* episode that relocates a portion of the action from inside the German borders to geographically far-removed Morocco, Gerhards identifies a deliberate authorial shift away from the established regional crime-fiction formulas and the related notion of *Heimat*, and theorizes that screenwriters have begun to globalize their topics, albeit not always to the audience's liking. Picking up on a critical line of thought that the *Tatort* television series has increasingly become an instrument of social messaging and a mouthpiece for discussion of current political topics, Gerhards reads *Tatort*'s aesthetic approaches along a continuum of change in the German regional crime-fiction formula, which has particular consequences for German identity.[33] He also incorporates a reading of recent regional crime novels that recast the genre as a way to renegotiate twentieth-century German history. Gerhards coins the term *Verarbeitungskrimi* for crime fiction that is set in the past and renegotiates the formation of political identity as manifested in the present. With his multimedia approach to crime-novel scholarship, the author intertwines common thematic threads of place, the past, and identity, and raises questions about how the interaction of these factors changes as the relationship to place, traditionally associated with *Heimat*, changes.

The final two chapters in this section expand the critical discussion's geographical reach beyond the borders of Germany to examine contemporary Austrian crime fiction. Jon Sherman presents a reading of Wolf Haas's Simon Brenner mysteries as a type of landscape painting of modern Austria, in which Haas functions as a portraitist of sorts of modern Austria. Sherman argues that Haas is an unconventional crime novelist in that he does not adhere to traditional conventions of the crime-fiction formula to produce his novels. For example, Haas's novels do begin with a murder, but that is not the crime that Brenner investigates. Instead, the seven Simon Brenner novels provide detailed snapshots of the society in which the crimes take place. Sherman provides a thorough analysis of exactly how Haas shapes his mystery into a social critique of contemporary Austria. In this respect, Haas might be seen as fitting in with the strong critical trend in contemporary Austrian literature, although his style differs significantly from the aggressively critical tone of Thomas Bernhard. Responding to the same critical questions that Frackman raises about ways that crime relates to national identity, and social issues relate to criminal events, Sherman demonstrates how contemporary crime fiction prioritizes a study of the society in which the crimes take place, and not necessarily the crimes, or the criminals, themselves.

In her examination of the regional Austrian crime novel, Anita McChesney also argues for the significance of place and social critique in the novels that she analyzes. She argues that recent Austrian crime fiction, of which Haas's work is a prime example, consciously subverts and challenges traditional images of Austria. While she concentrates on the regionality of crime fiction, McChesney also broadens the critical scope of relationships between identity and place to include not only Austrian self-assessment of identity but also external perceptions of the country as an idealized vacationland. When the familiar place is the idyllic Austria of postcards and movies, and when crime takes place in a location where it is generally perceived to be unlikely, then the setting works, as McChesney argues, as an ironic tool to showcase hidden problems behind the facade.

McChesney views Haas as working more within the traditional conventions of the crime novel than Sherman, but both are ultimately united in seeing the subversive critical message behind the genre-fiction facade.

These four explorations of place in regional crime fiction show that whether the scene of the crime is set in the mountains of western Austria or the lowlands of northern Germany (or anywhere in-between), this subgenre displays a remarkable coherence. Hyperlocal customs, locations, and speech-patterns combine with global concerns to form a potent mix that locates these novels both specifically and universally. Crimes that are typically seen as disrupting the otherwise unproblematic course of everyday life are, in fact, revealed to be symptoms of much larger and less dramatic conflicts and problems. These *Regiokrimis* indeed adopt many of the conventions of the traditional *Heimat* story, but, with their concentration on crime and disorder in society, ultimately subvert the typically conservative and nostalgic politics of that tradition.

The Historical German Crime Novel: Past Crimes and Persistent Guilt

Tatort Germany's second section, "History," examines the fictional treatment of historical themes, focusing on the traumatic legacy of two periods in Germany's twentieth-century history: the Third Reich and the German Democratic Republic. When crime writers treat topics such as German totalitarianism, and thus combine its related crimes with a perceived genre of entertainment, ethical questions emerge and are even magnified.[34] Magdalena Waligórska's essay on the Holocaust in crime fiction considers precisely this problem, focusing on the literary and critical consequences when crime fiction thematizes some of the most horrific true cases of criminality of the twentieth century. Through her close readings of Holocaust-themed crime fiction written between 2006 and 2011, Waligórska gestures toward larger critical concerns about discussing crimes against humanity in a crime-fiction format. She also, however, confronts ethical issues and matters of reception that relate specifically to German authors and their attempts to establish narrative order in events that are ultimately beyond full comprehension.

Susanne C. Knittel also addresses the legacy of National Socialist crimes. She begins her essay with a description of Grafeneck, a former National Socialist "euthanasia" center, which today houses a memorial to the victims killed there, while also being a home for people with mental and physical disabilities. This site provides the setting for two recent local crime novels. Knittel explores the potential and the limitations of crime novels that deal with weighty historical topics, but that do so in a manner that she calls "hyperlocal." This emphasis on precisely localizing events in actual places ties in with the discussions in the first part of this volume, thus reminding us that the terms that we have used to organize this volume—place, history, and identity—are inextricably bound together. Places, perhaps quite obviously, are sites of history and provide a physical setting for memory work. Knittel argues that *Krimis*[35] themselves similarly perform memory work. When the victims and perpetrators of these fictional crime stories are linked with real people and crimes from Germany's National Socialist past, the stories necessarily move beyond the conventional boundaries of detective fiction and deal with more weighty questions of memory, repression, and collective guilt. In this way, Knittel argues, these novels are able to increase public awareness about and interest in a repressed and still-marginalized aspect of German history.

Carol Anne Costabile-Heming turns to a different moment in German history and investigates the East German novelist Eric Loest, who published crime fiction under a pseudonym beginning in the 1950s. Place once again assumes a prominent role in Costabile-Heming's study as she looks at the mobility of the author, and his ability to navigate private and public spheres. Loest's settings encompass a number of international venues, from Wembley Stadium to Nigeria, far outside the borders of the GDR to which most of its citizens were confined. On the one hand, Loest made use of these foreign places in order to comment on contemporary political issues and depict elements of corruption within capitalism, as he does with his African novel *Das Waffenkarussel* (1968). But since neither he nor his intended readers had ever visited these places, they become fantasy versions based on East German locations. Loest imagines London, for example, to resemble Leipzig. If we return to Cawelti's theoretical requirement that formulaic novels must also incorporate "specific cultural themes and stereotypes" and culturally appropriate places and characters in order to have an authentic appeal[36] (a formula that we have seen put to use many times in the texts discussed in this volume), then Loest's crime fiction begs us to consider how to understand novels containing real places reconceived as fantasy locations. Costabile-Heming's chapter also invokes a historical period in which even popular crime fiction was taken seriously by the governing authorities as political statements, and authors such as Loest had to negotiate a treacherous political situation.

In the final chapter of this section, Traci S. O'Brien turns to Austria's attempts to confront—or avoid confronting—its historical legacies in her analysis of Eva Rossmann's 2001 crime novel *Freudsche Verbrechen*. O'Brien emphasizes the methodological connections between psychoanalysis and detection: both aim to uncover a truth that is hidden beneath a veil of mystery. The connections between psychoanalysis and history are also important to O'Brien's analysis and Rossmann's novel: just as memories lie buried beneath layers of repression, the past lies buried beneath the contemporary reality of 1990s Vienna. O'Brien's reading of Rossmann's text emphasizes a convergence of the three threads of place, history, and identity as they relate to contemporary Austria, dealing on an ironic level with the legacy of Freud and on a more serious level with the legacy of Austria's involvement in National Socialism.

By focusing on German and Austrian historical events and their fraught legacies, the chapters in this second section demonstrate the ability of crime fiction to address controversial political topics and present them in critically meaningful and productive ways. The genre of the crime novel, with its emphasis on uncovering hidden truths, offers a powerful means by which to negotiate the complex relationship between present and past crimes, between everyday and state crimes, and between guilt and innocence.

Transforming Identities

The contributions in part 3, "Identity," explore the contemporary German crime novel as an instrument for commenting on culturally specific, gendered identity politics over the past twenty years. Angelika Baier connects the topic of intersexuality to the larger tradition of crime fiction, asserting that a focus on nontraditional gender categories continues the genre's concern with the links between perceived corporeal and psychological deviance and crime. In her analysis of popularly perceived similarities between intersexed individuals and serial killers, Baier demonstrates the ways that the texts she analyzes both align with the historical development of crime fiction, in particular with what Mark Seltzer, following Foucault, has identified as the "shift in focus from the criminal act to the character of the actor,"[37] and break with that tradition by introducing an unlikely perpetrator. Where definitions of serial killers and deviance often overlap, Baier demonstrates how these definitions are extended in this innovative genre of crime fiction to include intersexed individuals.

Lesbian detective fiction is another subgenre that has emerged over recent decades and has treated identity politics within the frame of the crime novel.[38] Generally, readings of both lesbian novels in general and lesbian crime novels in particular have involved taking methodological cues from queer theory in order to reveal "the mechanisms by which the texts produce, naturalize, interrogate, and destabilize categories of identity."[39] Faye Stewart's essay returns readers to the notion of place in her analysis of sexual identity. In particular, she brings place and identity together by interrogating accepted notions of space and gender roles in her chapter on female detectives as active investigative agents in the male gay bar. The space she examines is not the small town or the metropolis of most crime novels, but rather the interior space of the bar, and more specifically, the German gay bar scene. Stewart's study focuses on the female detective who masquerades as a man and thereby allows for an examination (and complication) of gender roles and sexual identities. She compares two contemporary German novels that involve a female detective's professional activity in a male gay bar, in order to offer an innovative interpretation of alternative geographies located in crime fiction. In Stewart's reading, the classic boundaries between law and outlaw become blurred and everyone shares guilt for participating in oppressive structures.[40]

Also taking up the topic of gender relations and introducing yet another subgenre, Heike Henderson's study invites readers to explore Eva Rossmann's culinary crime fiction. She focuses in particular on how Rossmann's culinary mysteries recast the basic formula yet again to offer, through her narrative reevaluation of cooking and crime fiction, a critical examination of gender roles in contemporary Austria. Only recently has the culinary crime story entered the discourse of crime-fiction criticism.[41] In Rossmann's novels, setting once again directly affects identity. This time the setting is not small-town Austria or a German gay bar, but rather the domestic space of the kitchen, which works to transform the identity of the detective. Although few spaces have as much global reach as the kitchen, Henderson highlights the typically Austrian elements of Rossmann's culinary crime fiction and articulates ways that Rossmann advances specifically Austrian social criticism. Rossmann relocates the setting of her crimes to restaurants and supermarkets, allowing her to magnify her social critique of associated issues such as traditional stereotypes about women and minorities. Henderson not only presents to a wider audience this Austrian subgenre that features a nonprofessional detective with culinary aspirations, but she also demonstrates ways in which trends in Austrian crime fiction both parallel those of international crime fiction in their basic structures and break away from them through their cultural specificity.

At its most basic level, the crime story is about identities: the detective's task is to identify the criminal.[42] These texts play with this fundamental element in order to throw the very notion of identity into question. Identities—gender, sexual, national, even criminal—are shown to be fluid, rather than fixed. If the classical detective story ends with the identification of an individual as deviant and criminal in order to separate him or her from society, these stories end with a refusal to differentiate "deviance" from the norm. They thus turn the most basic hallmark of the genre around, which is itself by now a well-established formula of the genre.

Making the Curious Case for German Crime Fiction

Despite the literary merits and innovation that the studies in this volume ascribe to German-language crime fiction, its international reach remains limited.[43] As this volume attests, however, we can—and should—look to Germany for pioneering, engaging, and even enjoyable crime fiction that deserves more scholarly and popular attention both within and outside the German-speaking countries. The contributions to this volume point toward lively, innovative, and powerful applications of the genre of crime fiction in the service of social critique. The regional crime novel evokes local customs, characters, and places in order to question and subvert nostalgic notions of *Heimat* and draw connections between the order of everyday life and the disorder brought on by the criminal and his or her crimes. The historical crime novel, in turn, draws troubling connections between the traumatic past and the present that pretends to have left that past behind. And crime novels that focus on gender and sexual identity work to upset commonly held distinctions between these identities and to present identity as complex, fluid, and, similar to the German-language crime novel itself—often contradictory. Place, history, and identity all play roles in these texts and none of these terms escapes with a stable, unproblematic meaning.

Taken as a whole, this volume offers a snapshot of a newly vibrant German-language crime fiction at the turn of the twenty-first century. The texts that make up this dynamic scene are diverse in their styles and subjects, but they share common themes: the importance of place, history, and identity, along with the desire to investigate critically the complex layers of meaning associated with each of these terms. The essays also call into question common assumptions about what those terms connote. On the one hand, these texts offer their readers expected entertaining narratives full of colorful characters and mysterious actions. But at the same time they share with less accessible texts a critical edge that seeks to unsettle cultural assumptions and blur the boundaries between deviance and the norm, the past and the present, and the local and the global. Like other examples of innovative pop fiction that have been subject to the typically German high vs. low divide, they demand to be (and indeed are) taken seriously. And, as the chapters that follow show, they reward serious attention by offering engaging and thought-provoking questions and perspectives on important elements of German and Austrian culture—and beyond.

Notes

[1] See John Irwin, *The Mystery to a Solution: Poe, Borges, and the Analytic Detective Story* (Baltimore, MD: Johns Hopkins UP, 1994), 1. Irwin's subsequent reading of Poe's *Purloined Letter* suggests that the critical questions he raises are rhetorical, and that he does in fact see the literary value of crime fiction. Nonetheless, his guiding question provides a springboard for subsequent critics such as Rushing.

[2] Robert A. Rushing, *Resisting Arrest: Detective Fiction and Popular Culture* (New York: Other Press, 2007), 3.

[3] Jörgen Schäfer has labeled the dichotomy in German culture between high and low literature as something that has been consistently handed down (*tradiert*). This tradition reaches back to the 1960s when the view of popular literature as a sign of a decay of quality (*Qualitätsverfall*) in the literature industry remained largely uncontested partly because of the industry's elitism and partly because of the repercussions of Horkheimer and Adorno's theories of the culture industry. Since the 1980s, new German pop authors who have entered the scene still endure the occasional claim that their literary products are not literature, but they paradoxically also count among the most significant new authors. "'Neue Mitteilungen aus der Wirklichkeit': Zum Verhältnis von Pop und Literatur in Deutschland seit 1968," in *Text + Kritik: Pop-Literatur*, ed. Heinz Ludwig Arnold and Jörgen Schäfer (Munich: Richard Boorberg Verlag, 2003), 10–12, 23.

[4] The full quotation reads: "Gleichzeitig wird 'der Krimi' aus 'hochkultureller' Perspektive, also von Literaturkritik und Literaturwissenschaft, aber auch von zahlreichen 'literarischen' Leser/inne/n weiterhin als primitives Lesefutter und reine Verbrauchsliteratur bewertet und näherer Betrachtung für unwert gehalten" (2; At the same time, the crime novel is assessed from a "high culture" perspective, that is one of literary criticism and literary studies, as primitive reading material and purely literature for the average consumer. Upon closer examination, it's deemed worthless). Jochen Vogt, "Krimi—international," *Der Deutschunterricht: Beiträge zu seiner Praxis und wissenschaftlichen Grundlegung* 2 (2007): 2–6.

[5] Vogt, "Krimi—international," 2.

[6] View the archived program here: http://www.lfbrecht.de/event/2013/4/ (accessed August 2, 2013).

[7] German-language crime fiction, as evidenced in this volume's analyses, shares many characteristics with the internationally popular and critically successful Scandinavian crime fiction, such as their offering "sociopolitical insights" and a more complex picture of the region. Additionally, they "dig below the engaging surface of popular fiction" to elevate the crime novel above "entertainment status." Barry Forshaw. *Death in a Cold Climate: A Guide to Scandinavian Crime Fiction* (Basingstoke: Palgrave Macmillian, 2012), 2, 4. Despite these overlaps, German-language crime fiction remains largely untranslated and undistributed to English-speaking readers. This could have something to do with the persistent divide between German high and low culture, as discussed in this volume, and the related perceived unmarketability of the works beyond German-speaking borders.

[8] John Cawelti, *Adventure, Mystery and Romance* (Chicago: U of Chicago P, 1976), 6

[9] Cawelti, *Adventure*, 43.

[10] Cawelti, *Adventure*, 6.

[11] Throughout this volume, we have tried to remain consistent with terminology as it relates to the larger scholarly field of genre fiction. For example, throughout the collection we have decided to use "German-language crime fiction" to designate the primary sources that the contributors discuss. As the essays make clear, several other subgenres exist within this far-reaching category; and some are even peculiar to the German-speaking realm. At times, individual contributors have chosen their own terms when that advances the argument in a particular way.

[12] See, for example: Peter Morris-Keitel, *Die Verbrechensthematik im Modernen Roman: Untersuchungen und Analysen zur Motivstruktur in der Deutschsprachigen Literature nach 1970 anhand kriminologischer Theorien* (1989); Jochen Vogt, ed., *Der Kriminalroman: Poetik, Theorie, Geschichte* (Stuttgart: UTB, 1998) and *Medien Morde: Krimis intermedial* (Paderborn: Fink, 2004); Mary W. Tannert, *Early German and Austrian Detective Fiction: An Anthology* (2007); and Björn Otte, *Das Milieu im Fernsehkrimi*. (Marburg: Tectum Verlag, 2013).

[13] See, for example, Helen Chambers, "'Bestialisch dahingeschlachtert': Extreme Violence in German Crime Fiction." in *Violence, Culture and Identity: Essays on German and Austrian Literature, Politics and Society*, ed. Chambers (Oxford: Peter Lang, 2006), 401–15; Doreen Bollmann, "Deutschsprachige Kriminallliteratur im Wandel der Zeit," in *Lesekultur: Populäre Leststoffe von Gutenberg bis zum Internet*, ed. Petra Bohnsack and Hans-Friedrich Foltin (Marburg: Universitätsbibliothek Marburg, 1999); Christopher Jones, "Images of Switzerland in Swiss Crime Fiction," in *German-Language Literature Today: International and Popular?*, ed. Arthur Williams, Stuart Parkes, and Julian Preece (Oxford: Peter Lang, 2000), 85–98.

[14] Kate M. Quinn and Marieke Krajenbrink, *Investigating Identities: Questions of Identity in Contemporary International Crime Fiction* (Amsterdam: Rodopi, 2009), 1–2.

[15] Malcah Effron, *The Millenial Detective: Essays on Trends in Crime Fiction, Film and Television, 1990–2010* (Jefferson, NC: McFarland, 2011), 6.

[16] William W. Stowe, "Critical Investigations: Convention and Ideology in Detective Fiction," *Texas Studies in Language and Literature* 31, no. 4 (1989): 571.

[17] Wolf Dieter Lützen, "Der Krimi ist kein deutsches Genre. Momente und Stationen zur Genregeschichte der Krimiunterhaltung," in *Der neue deutsche Kriminalroman: Beiträge zu Darstellung, Interpretation und Kritik eines populären Genres*, ed. Karl Ermert and Wolfgang Gast (Rehburg-Loccum: Evangelische Akademie Loccum, 1985. = Loccumer Kolloquien 5), 162–81.

[18] Willard Huntington Wright, *The Great Detective Stories: A Chronological Anthology* (New York: Charles Scribner's Sons, 1927), 30.

[19] Qtd. in Jürgen Roland, "Time doesn't move forward . . .," in *Out of the Dark: Crime, Mystery and Suspense in the German Cinema 1915–1990*, trans. Leslie Ann Pahl (Munich: Goethe Institut, 1992), 5.

[20] Howard Haycraft, *Murder for Pleasure: The Life and Times of the Detective Story* (New York and London: D. Appleton-Century Company, 1947), 110. He does allow that "the police novel is reported to have made new strides in the Scandinavian nations" (110).

[21] Edmund Finke, "Über den Kriminalroman," *Das deutsche Wort* 12 (1936): 419.

[22] Truman Capote's 1965 work of creative nonfiction, *In Cold Blood*, which is often credited with offering "a totally new idea in detective stories," has strong precedents in a series of true crime stories from mid-1920s Germany "Außenseiter der Gesellschaft" (Outsiders of Society). See: Truman Capote, In Cold Blood (New York: Random House, 1965); Tom Wolfe, "Mauve Gloves & Madmen,

Clutter & Vine" in Wolfe, *Mauve, Gloves & Madmen, Clutter & Vine and Other Stories, Sketches, and Essays* (New York: Picador, 1990), 163–64; and Todd Herzog, *Crime Stories* (New York: Berghahn Books, 2009), 34–56. Friedrich Dürrenmatt's "requiem for the detective novel," *Das Versprechen*, appeared in 1958 (Zürich: Verlag der Arche).

[23] Arlene Teraoka, "Detecting Ethnicity: Jakob Arjouni and the Case of the Missing German Detective Novel," *German Quarterly* 72, no. 3 (1999): 266.

[24] Mark Lawson, "Crime's Grand Tour: European Detective Fiction," *The Guardian*, 26 October 2012, http://www.guardian.co.uk/books/2012/oct/26/crimes-grand-tour-european-detective-fiction.

[25] Eva Erdmann, "Nationality International: Detective Fiction in the Late Twentieth Century," in *Investigating Identities: Questions of Identity in Contemporary International Crime Fiction*, ed. Mareike Krajenbrink and Kate M. Quinn (Amsterdam: Rodopi, 2009), 15–16.

[26] For further discussion of this comparison by key figures in the contemporary German language crime-fiction industry, see Thomas Fitzel "Heimatroman mit Leichen: Regional-Krimis verkaufen sich ausgezeichnet," *Deutschlandradio Kultur*, April 12, 2013, http://www.dradio.de/dkultur/sendungen/fazit/2072786/.

[27] "Aufwertung der Handlungsorte." Melanie Wigbers, *Krimi-Orte im Wandel: Gestaltung und Funktion der Handlungsschauplätze in Kriminalerzählungen von der Romantik bis in die Gegenwart* (Würzburg: Königshausen & Neumann, 2006), 16, 18.

[28] "Zusammenfassend bezieht sich der Begriff des Milieus auf eine Umwelt, die vom Akteur nicht völlig unabhängig ist. Wenn vom Milieu die Rede ist, spielt das Zusammenwirken der Akteure, welches das Handeln jedes Einzelnen beeinflusst, eine große Rolle." Björn Otte, *Das Milieu im Fernsehkrimi: Am Beispiel der Krimi-Reihe "Tatort"* (Marburg: Tectum Verlag, 2013), 33.

[29] Otte, *Milieu*, 268–69.

[30] For more in-depth discussion of the term *Regiokrimi* and its definitions, please see Frackman's, Gerhards's, McChesney's, and Sherman's essays in this volume. The editors understand the term to mean any crime novel that relies on references to and exact descriptions of local places, traditions, or customs to not only build the crime story but to boost the appeal to local readers. Given the propensity within the German tradition to conflate *Regiokrimi* and *Heimatroman*, or even the hybrid term *Heimatkrimi*, the editors would also like to make the point that, in their view, the terms are not interchangeable. Although the *Regiokrimi* and the *Heimatkrimi* do share many common characteristics, *Heimatkrimi* is not, for example, used for marketing purposes, due to the negative connotation of *Heimat* (see in particular Gerhards's chapter in this volume for a discussion of that aspect).

[31] K. D. M. Snell, "The Regional Novel: Themes for Interdisciplinary Research," in *The Regional Novel in Britain and Ireland. 1800–1900*, ed. K. D. M. Snell (Cambridge: Cambridge UP, 1998), 1.

³² Susan Mandala, "Crime Fiction as Regional Fiction: An Analysis of Dialect and Point of View in Sheila Quigley's *Bad Moon Rising*," *Style: A Quarterly Journal of Aesthetics, Poetics, Stylistics, and Literary Criticism* 46 (2): 178.

³³ Most notably, Michelle Mattson has argued that television is a mechanism that allows for a "social distribution of meaning," and most importantly that the series offers a "televisual mediation of political reality to the German public" on a large scale. Michelle Mattson, "Tatort: The Generation of Public Identity in a German Crime Series," *New German Critique* 78 (1999): 162, 164.

³⁴ In his general discussion and analysis of formulas found in detective fiction, Robert A. Rushing argues that the reader of crime fiction engages in "forgetting real violence in favor of a spectacle manufactured for his passive enjoyment" (Rushing, *Resisting Arrest*, 126). In her iconic *Talking about Detective Fiction*, P. D. James makes a similar point about the "entry to a familiar and reassuring world in which we are both involved in violent death and yet remain personally inviolate both from responsibility and its terrors." P. D. James, *Talking about Detective Fiction* (New York: Alfred A. Knopf, 2009), 14. Although neither James nor Rushing refers specifically to works that situate the experiences of the Holocaust in a fictional frame, a subsequent comment by James encapsulates the ethical criticism that could arise when a crime novelist takes up this historically linked subject matter.

³⁵ In terms of terminology, Knittel views *Heimatkrimi* as synonymous with *Regiokrimi*.

³⁶ Cawelti, *Adventure*, 6.

³⁷ Mark Seltzer, *Serial Killers: Death and Life in America's Wound Culture* (London: Routledge, 2004), 158.

³⁸ See, for example, Anna Wilson, "Death and the Mainstream: Lesbian Detective Fiction and the Killing of the Coming-Out Story," *Feminist Studies* 22, no. 2 (1996): 251. Rather than simply as a deviation from the established narrative forms of crime fiction, Wilson defines lesbian crime fiction as a subdivision of the lesbian novel genre.

³⁹ See Anna Faye Stewart, "Queer Investigations: Genre, Geography, and Sexuality in German-Language Lesbian Crime Fiction," PhD diss., Indiana U (2007).

⁴⁰ Because of its setting, the traditional spy story "almost inevitably brings political or social attitudes into play since conflicting political forces are an indispensable background for the antagonism between the spy-hero and his enemy," Cawelti, *Adventure*, 31.

⁴¹ See, for example, Nieves Pascual Soler, *A Critical Study of Female Culinary Detective Stories: Murder by Cookbook* (Lewiston, NY: Mellen, 2009).

⁴² For a more in-depth discussion of the terms crime fiction and detective fiction, please see Anita McChesney's and Jon Sherman's essays in this volume. McChesney, for example, cites Julian Symon's use of the crime novel to refer to the broad category of novels dealing with crime and detection. See Julian Symons, *Bloody Murder: From the Detective Story to the Crime Novel: A History* (Harmondsworth: Viking, 1985). Sherman cites Richard Alewyn's differentiation between a *Kriminalroman*, in which murder is at the center, and the detective novel

(*Detektivroman*), in which the clarification of the crime is at the center. Richard Alewyn. Richard Alewyn, "Anatomie des Detektivromans," in *Der Kriminalroman II*, ed. Jochen Vogt (Munich: Fink, 1971), 52–72.

[43] In an article entitled "Why German Crime Fiction Fails to Thrill US Readers," an Icelandic publisher seeks to pinpoint the reasons behind the perceived lack of appeal of German crime fiction for an international audience: "We look to other countries for suspense, but for quality literature, we look to Germany." Susan Stone, "Why German Crime Fiction Fails to Thrill US Readers," *PRI's The World: Global Perspectives for an American Audience* (December 28, 2012). http://www.theworld.org/2012/12/why-german-thrillers-are-not-popular-in-us/.

Part I. Place

1: *Vor Ort*: The Functions and Early Roots of German Regional Crime Fiction

Kyle Frackman

THE IDEA THAT LOCATION WOULD BE IMPORTANT to the production and reception of crime fiction is not new.[1] Since their earliest existence, *Kriminalliteratur* and *Kriminalerzählungen* have been bound to a certain necessity of place.[2] In some ways, the concept is basic, especially if one considers that one of the very functions of the wider genre is to situate a particular crime in a particular place. This often requires a detective or some investigatory figure to examine the scene of the crime (the *Tatort*, an element so obviously important that it became the title of one of Germany's most successful and long-lasting television series).[3] The setting of a mystery or crime story is often one of its primary defining characteristics: Sherlock Holmes's London, Agatha Christie's enclosed manor houses and train compartments, Kurt Wallander's Scania or Sweden more generally, V. I. Warshawski's Chicago, Inspector Morse's Oxford. The subject of this essay, crime fiction native to and reflective of particular regions in Germany, represents in a way a hyperextension of the importance of location, in which the various settings of these stories become their creation myths or existential foundations. This essay argues that German regional crime fiction is both a modern development and simultaneously a recollection of crime fiction's journalistic and literary beginnings. I will demonstrate that regional crime fiction has connections to eighteenth- and nineteenth-century *Fallgeschichten* (case stories) that fascinated a developing reading public and satisfied readers' taste for sensational details with a more local flavor. In what follows, I maintain that reader interest has helped to define the genre, and I track the literary-historical beginnings of this literature.

This essay will demonstrate that the regional subset of the crime-fiction genre fits in with the genre's modern genesis. By referring to modernity, I aim to situate these developments in reading behavior among the technological, social, and class-related changes taking place especially after the early nineteenth century. Emerging from the sensational interests of a burgeoning reading public, crime narratives serve, in the sense defined above, an essentially modern function of investigation and enlightenment, a quest in which identity has been crucial.[4] Marieke Krajenbrink and Kate M. Quinn argue that the solving of a crime, possibly the primary function of detective and crime fiction, leads ipso facto to the question of identity, which has gradually become more complex as the genre has evolved. Instead of focusing merely on establishing a criminal's identity and motives, the works within this subgenre thematize greater problems in society in general, including questions of what "crime" actually is, how social issues relate to criminal events, and what conclusions one might draw about the ordered foundations of society.[5] Eva Erdmann maintains that crime fiction has shifted away from its original task of focusing on a crime per se to that of showcasing a place, the setting, and the characters' attachment to it (or lack thereof).[6] Indeed, crime stories can also become "chroniclers for the settings of their plots," presenting detailed examinations of these areas.[7] The narratives, she writes, become more widely relevant and appealing (i.e., to people beyond those who might live in those particular localities) by employing certain motifs that engage the story's location. Attempts to express an atmosphere can include "cultural stereotypes and clichés that are affirmatively used, ironically used or problematized."[8] Although Erdmann's argument focuses on national characteristics, the observation can include the regional variety, some examples of which are discussed below. Moreover, this signals the importance of location for these stories, showing a characteristic also discussed below—namely that readers not from that region can explore someplace new and locals can live their own familiarity.

Discussing a topic that has wider popular appeal and a broad critical reach is not without its perils, since untold critics, theoreticians, and writers of all varieties have worked in and around the field of crime fiction for many decades, including the scholars in this volume. Before proceeding to what this essay will do, I must explain what it will not do. I will not endeavor here to advance a new definition of crime fiction, the crime story, the detective story, mysteries, or thrillers. Many critics have already and repeatedly argued about these concerns.[9] Nonetheless, I would like to underscore characteristics of crime stories that are central to my examination.

While the portrayal of unknown settings could appeal to readers' imaginations, realism is an essential element of crime fiction, regional crime fiction included. Some critics maintain that this approach leads to bloated texts, overburdened with details that are not universally appealing.[10] In his oft-quoted *Murder for Pleasure*, Howard Haycraft opines, however, that

> the *less* exotic the scenes, the better they will serve the essential interest of verisimilitude. [Writer G. K.] Chesterton remarked somewhere

that the detective story is at its best when it "stays at home"—or words to that general effect.... Most successful are those backdrops known to the average reader, yet "touched up" by artful brushwork; for it is the "semblance of reality" which is desired, rather than reality itself.[11]

The approximation of reality that regional crime fiction employs is ideally situated in well-known or seemingly familiar surroundings, allowing for the reader's identification with the narrative. The potential draw for readers who wish to find lifelike portrayals of scenery with which they are acquainted is understandable. Interestingly, the local connections and flavor have deeper genealogical roots that reach back to a perhaps more elevated purpose, as we will see: journalistic reportage. Before proceeding, however, some "geographic" boundaries must be drawn around the subgenre of regional crime fiction.

Definitions are important to some degree, as the focus of this essay is a particular subgenre, a smaller offshoot of the German *Krimi* branch of the world's crime literature tree (to use Julian Symons's metaphor): the *Regionalkrimi*.[12] Lynn Marie Kutch writes that "regional crime fiction exhibits crime fiction's traditional elements, but the plot's perhaps disproportionate emphasis on the relationship between the protagonist and his [sic] surroundings reflects the thematic concentration on local place and its bearings on global identity, and by extension the problematic relationship between author and text."[13] Stefanie Rahnfeld of the Cologne-based Emons Verlag explains, "Ein echter Regionalkrimi ... *lässt sich nicht* an einen anderen Ort verlagern" (emphasis added; A true regional crime story *could not* be relocated to another place).[14] In other words, while we can grant that location is important for crime fiction in general, it becomes *essential* for regional crime fiction, not only for definitional reasons of the subgenre's name, but rather for one of the main goals that the subgenre has: to evoke vividly the place in which the story occurs.

For the present analysis, an awareness of *why* we are reading is slightly more important than a circumscription of a genre definition (*what* we are reading). The former question is crucial and illuminating for an examination of mystery and detective fiction more generally, but also for regional crime fiction specifically. The genre and its subgenres rely on appeals to interested readers' expectations of what they will encounter in the narrative. Even literary great Friedrich Schiller acknowledged this in his preface to the popular "Pitaval" collection of stories (discussed below), conceding that many people read awful stories that they should not, or works that do little to contribute to the readers' moral edification.[15] Indeed, one of the reasons the body of detective literature and mysteries is often placed under the rubric of "trivial literature" has to do with its effect on the reader: it gives the reading public what it wants or what it will buy.[16]

Crime fiction enjoys great popularity in the German public. The crime novel is second in popularity only to the classic fictional novel.[17] As a trade secret, exact sales and publishing statistics are difficult to come by, but it would seem that, in the first few years of the twenty-first century, crime fiction has increased in popularity. Among the crime novels that Germans read, however, crime fiction from German-speaking lands has been decreasing in prevalence in recent years, losing out to English-language works that are then translated and sold in the German market.[18] If the trend continues, as it is likely to do, the future of specifically German regional crime fiction is not completely clear. At the very least, it will become even more of a niche subject as stories that are written elsewhere (in the United States or the United Kingdom) overtake their popularity.[19]

Contrary but related to the stories that situate a mystery or crime narrative in a metropolis or other urban setting, regional crime fiction can be characterized by its tendency to locate narratives in more rural, less-trafficked locations. One of the first regional crime novels in German, Jacques Berndorf's *Eifel-Blues* (1989), and its subsequent stories place their protagonist in the region of Germany that gives the series its name, the Eifel, making the location arguably more important to the series than the investigator.[20] Unlike the gritty city that may play a prominent locational role in a noir detective story, the Eifel is a sometimes romanticized, hilly area in western Germany that overlaps the states of North Rhine-Westphalia and Rheinland-Palatinate and counts vineyards among its most important agricultural features. Certainly, following the popularity of Berndorf's Eifel stories, German regional crime fiction has expanded to include most, if not all, local regions in Germany. From Swabia and the Bavarian Allgäu in the south to the island of Sylt and the Baltic coast in the north, almost every region and subregion in Germany now has its own category of this literature. As Eckart Baier reported in the *Börsenblatt*, the weekly trade publication of German bookstores, "Egal, ob Bamberg oder Bielefeld, Eifel oder Herrgottswinkel: Kaum ein Flecken auf der Deutschlandkarte, an dem nicht geraubt, entführt oder betrogen wird—wenn auch nur zwischen zwei Buchdeckeln. Der Regionalkrimi boomt und hat sich mittlerweile als moderne Form der Heimatliteratur etabliert" (44; It doesn't matter if it's Bamberg or Bielefeld, the Eifel or Nowheresville: there's hardly a fleck on a map of Germany where there isn't stealing, kidnapping, or betraying—even if it's just between the covers of a book. The regional crime story is booming and has established itself as a modern form of home literature). When regional festivals and local customs can play a role in a murder, the consequences of location become even more apparent. Local and real problems, like unemployment and urban planning, can lend the stories a vital element of credibility.[21]

As in other genres and subgenres, there is a great deal of diversity in the form and kinds of narratives within German regional crime fiction.

Examples of novels include the aforementioned Eifel stories, Jürgen Reitemeier and Wolfram Tewes's stories in and about Lippe, and Sibylle Baecker's and Klaus Wanninger's Swabian crime novels. Regional fiction has also thrived in shorter forms, with numerous short story collections, such as Gudrun Weitbrecht and Nessa Altura's anthologies (also discussed below), giving more exposure to a wide range of authors and styles of writing. With respect to time period, these narratives also represent a remarkable variety, ranging from the Middle Ages to the present.[22] If one expands the genre's definition to include television and film, the rubric could encompass locally focused episodes of the long-running *Tatort* series, as well as the ZDF series *Mörderischer Norden* (Murderous North), which showcases murder mysteries on Germany's Baltic coast.

The crime fiction formula can depend on a unilateral (or unidirectional) relationship between an author and a reader. From one perspective, the author has control, creates a story according to an exact template, and transmits it to the naïve reader, who supposedly should know better than to read artless literature or who is being taken in by the opportunistic author's desires for "easy" financial gain. From another perspective, it is the demanding and genre-addicted reader who drives the production of the text, somehow manipulating the author (and the publisher) in the narrative creation. Each of these views has valid elements. It is more productive, though, to try to explain the subgenre's continued success with a bilateral model that acknowledges the roles of both the reader and the author. No one can doubt that detective and similar crime stories are written to follow a particular recipe. On the surface, one might be tempted to think that they are read for the thrill of uncovering the solution at the end of the mystery. That is certainly one component, and many mystery readers might assert as much. As Umberto Eco describes it, however, this genre presents the paradox that it is supposed to deliver something "unforeseen" or "sensational" (a mystery and its solution), but it is popular because it can be "taken for granted, familiar, expected."[23] Eco's observation can extend to the nature of regional crime fiction. This subgenre's success depends not on the potential to introduce or explore unfamiliar terrain, but rather on the interest, both the reader's and the author's, in functioning within severely limited boundaries.

Despite the presupposed nature of the subgenre, some critics posit that a kind of organic relationship exists between author and reader. Wolfgang Iser, a proponent of reader-response theory, understood there to be an interplay between a reader and the text (as separate from the author), as the reader uses her or his own experiences to develop an interpretation of the text.[24] Literary theorist Hans Robert Jauß described a "horizon of expectations" that helps to define a text from the outset when a reader encounters it. As George N. Dove writes, referring to Jauß's concept, "A book, although it may be new to a given reader, does not really present itself as something absolutely new but predisposes its audience to a specific kind of reception; it awakens memories of that which was already read and so enters the reader's horizon of expectations."[25] Dove's study deals specifically with detective fiction, but it could be applied more broadly to crime fiction and mysteries. He argues that reading this kind of fiction is different from reading most others, in that most readers are willing to operate within the accepted formulaic structure of these stories; in some ways, they know what to expect.[26]

The relationship between the author or the text and reader is deepened by reliance on the repetitive conventions inherent in the subgenre of regional crime fiction. In part of his semiotic study of *The Role of the Reader*, Eco analyzes detective and popular fiction, arguing that an author of such texts will include numerous "redundant" narrative devices that remind the reader of the characters' constitution and their roles in the stories. These can be plot elements as well as character traits. In English-language fiction, for example, one can think of Sherlock Holmes's difficult personality or Hercule Poirot's dandy fussiness. According to Eco, readers can "find an old friend in the character portrayed."[27] Indeed, for Eco, what brings readers back to these stories *is* their reliability; that is, the reader can count on knowing what to expect. "The attraction of the book . . . lies in the fact that, plopped in an easy chair or in the seat of a train compartment, the reader continuously recovers . . . what he [*sic*] already knows, what he wants to know again: that is why he has purchased the book."[28] Reader expectation, then, is dependent on what the author delivers and what the reader returns.

In beginning to explain the existence and popularity of regional crime fiction, one can place it on a historical timeline of the public's interest in its surroundings. Both literate and nonliterate people are greatly interested in their immediate environment, as local happenings would likely be of greatest relevance to their daily lives. Just as former US Speaker of the House Tip O'Neill declared that "All politics is local," one could argue that all crime is local, and that all crime has both local implications and local origins.

According to Peter Nusser's analysis of the crime novel, the foundation of this genre must lie in the eighteenth and nineteenth centuries for reasons of class and society.[29] First, there had to be a social infrastructure, or some kind of law enforcement, for the identification and investigation of crime. Indeed, there needed to be categories of *crime* itself. Secondly, there had to be a group or class of people relatively safe and educated enough to read about it and to be concerned about its possible spread into their lives: primarily the bourgeoisie. For these and other reasons, the economic, educational, and civil developments of the eighteenth century are requisite for the kinds of fiction with which we now concern ourselves in this volume. Documenting some of these changes,

Nusser presents the argument that fears of an assault on nascent state authority helped to reinforce the interest in crime fiction: the people demanded a criminal justice system on which they could depend.[30] The late eighteenth and mid-nineteenth centuries witnessed a reform of criminal codes and the creation of criminal justice institutions, which aimed to protect the burgeoning civil society.[31]

Already in the eighteenth century, creators and publishers of "sensational" literature began to cultivate a public interest in local "true crime," tapping into readers' curiosity and local concern. Likely the first incarnation of this was François Gayot de Pitaval's (1673–1743) stories, which presented accounts of actual criminal cases. These texts, documenting crimes in early modern France, offered descriptions of real cases that served as inspirational material for some writers who incorporated events and characters from these texts into their own work.[32] Pitaval, originally a theology student and eventually an attorney, studied old court files and used his own court experience to deliver remarkable cases, and published his first of twenty-two volumes in 1734 as *Causes célèbres et intéressantes, avec les jugements qui les ont décidées* (Famous and Interesting Cases with their Deciding Judgments), focusing on cases involving aristocratic as well as bourgeois individuals. Pitaval's texts were reworked and translated in various editions, including a nine-volume German version published in Leipzig between 1747 and 1768. In 1792, Friedrich Schiller wrote the aforementioned preface for one German translation, in which he recommends the text for readers interested in issues of criminal justice as well as the nature of humanity.[33]

In the mid-nineteenth century, in 1842, *Der neue Pitaval* (The New Pitaval) appeared, edited and rewritten by Julius Eduard Hitzig and Wilhelm Häring in its first edition. Hitzig and Häring made important changes in their presentation of new material, in that they changed Pitaval's original style in order to focus on the sensational and to build suspense.[34] Both the original and the later reworked *New Pitaval* stories consciously grounded their events by means of a journalistic listing of the location, time, and manner of the crime as well as the customary revelation of the guilty party.[35] We can connect these stories based on their subject matter and, more importantly, their nature as realistic, straightforwardly situated tales. We can be certain, though, that Hitzig and Häring aimed to make these stories more widely available to a readership that extended beyond the educated expert in order to include the educated layperson.[36]

After 1850, these kinds of stories saw wider circulation in German *Familienzeitschriften* (family periodicals). In publications like *Unterhaltungen am häuslichen Herd* (Conversations around the Hearth), *Das Familienblatt* (The Family Journal), *Daheim* (At Home), and *Die Gartenlaube* (The Arbor), numerous authors delivered serial narratives, spread over weeks or even an entire year.[37] The omnipresence of criminal stories in these publications further testifies to the important role that crime, whether a mere awareness or an actual fear of it, played in Germany at that time, especially after the revolutions of 1848–49.[38] Some of these stories present specific details about their setting; others allude to distant locales. Still others tantalize the reader by following the German convention of abbreviating proper names, as when businessman B. loses something of importance on the train between stations R. and K. in the story "Auf der Eisenbahn" (On the Train).

An issue of the *Münsterberger Wochenblatt* (Münsterberg Weekly) from 1839, for instance, gives evidence of the smattering of local flavors that these publications could offer. The opening pages of this first issue of the year saw the beginning of a captivating serial story, "Der Staatsgefangene und seine Tochter" (The State Prisoner and his Daughter), a melodramatic moral tale, along with notices from local citizens of houses for sale, grain prices, and, interestingly, a police blotter or *Chronik*, which offered statistics about the year that had just passed.[39] We learn that nine people had met unfortunate deaths, including the detail of their locations, by, for example, being run over, falling from a barn, or burning to death after clothing caught fire.[40] Also noted were suicides, dog bites with and without the presence of rabies, and the appearance of smallpox and hoof-and-mouth disease. Part of the popularity of these stories must have relied on the alienation effect created by their combinations of familiar surroundings and unfamiliar happenings.[41] The *Berliner Gerichts-Zeitung* (Berlin Court Newspaper) provides another example of a story in which a man enters a local establishment and orders schnapps, only to receive a glass of acid instead and be put in "Lebensgefahr" (mortal danger).[42]

These kinds of matter-of-fact, sometimes transcript-like depictions testify to a public interest in realistic narratives—an interest which is in line with literary developments of the mid- to late nineteenth century.[43] In regional crime fiction, we see a modern adaptation and intensification of this verisimilitude. Regional crime fiction's oft-maligned tendency to ground its narratives in local minutiae is a recent continuation of this style that established itself in the eighteenth century. Moving into the nineteenth and twentieth centuries, attitudes toward crime changed and one wanted assurance that crime, local or otherwise, would stay where it should be, beyond middle-class existence. As Symons explains, those "who have a stake in the permanence of the existing social system" sympathized with law enforcement officers, to the extent that the latter existed, as part of a desire to maintain what was locally good and remove what was locally bad.[44]

Contemporaneous with the increase in social and civil preoccupation with questions of crime and criminal justice was a dramatic growth of journalism.⁴⁵ Daily newspapers, weeklies, and periodicals proliferated in Europe and North America. The German *Berliner Gerichts-Zeitung*, established in 1853, for example, notes in its first issue that the public has "ein unverkennbares Interesse, zu erfahren, einmal, welche Wege das immer studirter auftretende Verbrechen einschlägt; sodann, welche Mittel von Richter und Recht, von Gesetzgebung und Verwaltung aufgewendet werden, um dasselbe kenntlich zu machen, um es einzuschränken und seine traurigen Wirkungen und Einflüsse so viel als möglich zu neutralisiren (an unmistakable interest in learning, first of all, which forms the ever-more-capable crime may take; then, which means of legislation and administration the judges and the law might use to make the same [the crime] recognizable, to limit it, as much as possible, to neutralize its sad effects and influences).⁴⁶ These "effects and influences" play out in the pages of each issue of the newspaper, describing local, regional, and national circumstances. In the same first issue, the reader learns of a court session of September 27:

> Ein großes Interesse bot die heutige Sitzung . . . dar, weil sie uns die nicht unbedeutende Zahl von 11 Personen auf der Anklagebank vorführte, die beschuldigt sind, wiederholte Diebstähle zur Nachtzeit und in Gemeinschaft verübt, oder als Hehler an den Vortheilen dieser Diebstähle Theil genommen zu haben. Dieser Fall mahnt um so mehr das Publikum zur Vorsicht, als die Diebe in 10 Fällen die Schaufenster, welche jetzt in der Regel durch hölzerne Rouleaux geschlossen werden, mit überraschender Gewandtheit erbrochen haben.⁴⁷

> [Today's session was of great interest, because it presented us with the not insignificant number of eleven persons in the defendants' chairs, who are charged with repeated thefts together and at night or with having received stolen goods from these thefts. This case exhorts us all the more to caution, as the thieves in ten cases broke open the shop windows, which are usually covered with wooden blinds, with surprising dexterity.]

These reports relay an image of a Berlin and its surroundings that, first, are in want of journalistic coverage for the good of the public according to the newspaper's editors, and, second, are witnessing increases in crime or developments in types of crime that now spread across class boundaries.

Moving out of Berlin, we can see accounts in the *Heidelberger Zeitung* (Heidelberg Newspaper), for example, of the always-sensational topic of alleged infanticide:

> Ein sonst sehr gut beleumundetes, erst 20 Jahre altes, hübsches Mädchen, *Rosine Stößer* von Bruchhausen, Amtsgericht Ettlingen, stand heute vor den Schranken des Gerichts unter der Anklage, ihr neugebornes Kind vorsätzlich getödtet zu haben. Während die

Angeklagte in der Voruntersuchung die Hauptsache geläugnet hatte, legte sie heute das offene, reumüthige Geständnis ab, daß sie am 6. Februar i. J., Nachmittags, im Ettlinger Gemeindewald ihr Kind umgebracht, indem sie ihm einen großen Pfropf von Moos und Gras in den Mund stopfte, es sodann im Boden verscharrte und einen schweren Ast darauf legte. Wenn der heutige Fall mitunter das Gefühl des Mitleidens hervorrufen konnte, so machte doch mit Recht der großh. Staatsanwalt *Haaß* in seiner Anklagebegründung darauf aufmerksam, daß das Verbrechen des Kindsmords seit einigen Jahren in erschreckender Weise zunehme, wie denn im Mittelrheinkreis allein während des letzten Halbjahres sechs Fälle von Kindsmord vorgekommen seien.[48]

[An otherwise well-regarded pretty girl, *Rosine Stößer* of Bruchhausen, jurisdiction of Ettlingen, stood today before the bench, having been accused of premeditatedly killing her newborn child. While the accused had denied as much in the preliminary inquiry, today she made the rueful confession that on the afternoon of the 6th of February this year in the Ettlingen forest, she killed her child by shoving a wad of moss and grass in its mouth and then hurriedly burying it and placing a large branch over it. While today's case could arguably summon forth a feeling of compassion, the ducal prosecutor *Haaß* in his justification for the charges called attention to the shocking increase in the crime of infanticide over the past few years, as in the Middle Rhein District alone during the past half-year there have been six cases.]

The account goes on to describe some of the young woman's familial circumstances before eventually describing the dramatic *in camera* consideration by the judges and the eventual sentence.

These reports serve a number of purposes, depending on one's perspective and position in the reading public. Some of these periodicals and their stories catered to overlapping audiences: on the one hand, to those well-versed in the ways of the criminal justice system of the time and, on the other hand, to the lay public, fascinated by a need to know about legal and criminal developments in the region or around the corner. The editorial stance in the prospectus at the start of the first issue of the *Berliner Gerichts-Zeitung* points to another goal of these accounts—namely, the altruistic and enlightening perspective of serving a public good, delivering details of law and order to members of the public, who wish to know who their fellow citizens are, with whom they are jostling about in a growing, bustling city.[49] Finally, these reports can fan the flames of sensationalism, sometimes imitating the melodramatic serial stories that graced their pages.

Regional crime fiction provides the reader with an addictive combination of the normal and the abnormal, the probable and improbable, the realistic and fantastic. Such a mixture helps to explain the subgenre's steady increase in appeal. It helps to deliver to readers a new insight into or view of their surroundings. Like the journalistic accounts of crime, the reader is treated to perpetrators' traits and moral failings, the details of the crime (including location and method), and the social means used to uncover and punish the criminal acts. Just like the aforementioned serial characters that elicit identification in readers' recognition, regional details similarly facilitate readers' entrance into the fictional crime narratives. I will provide two different examples from the subgenre, each from a different form but located in the same region: first, from Klaus Wanninger's novel *Schwaben-Ehre* (Swabian Honor, 2009) and, second, from Gudrun Weitbrecht's collection *Mörderisches Ländle* (Murderous Swabia, 2008), specifically Gunter Gerlach's short story "Keine Tränen" (No Tears).[50] Both the novels and the short stories use the strategy of appealing directly to readers' regional ideas in their titles. They also offer favorable examples of crime literature that resembles its forebears.

Klaus Wanninger has written a popular and long-lasting series of regional crime novels set in southwest Germany, primarily in and around Stuttgart. Although his productivity expands beyond this, between 2000 and 2011 Wanninger wrote fifteen novels with permutations of the title above, among them *Schwaben-Rache* (Swabian Wrath, 2000), *Schwaben-Herbst* (Swabian Autumn, 2007), and *Schwaben-Liebe* (Swabian Love, 2011). His novels in this series, which are arguably the most prominent of the *Schwaben-Krimis*, have sold over half a million copies according to the publisher's website and feature two investigators from the *Landeskriminalamt* (state police) in Stuttgart, a male-female team: Steffen Braig and Katrin Neundorf.[51]

Schwaben-Ehre begins with the discovery of a corpse in the men's room at the Stuttgart Liederhalle, a locally respected venue for conferences and cultural performances in the Swabian area, the so-called *Ländle* (8). Wanninger proceeds in a series of sentences, consisting of extended modifiers of extended modifiers, to give the subgenre's customary background on the crime scene's broader location, either for the benefit of non-Swabian readers or to strengthen the narrative's local or regional bona fides: "Der mitten im Zentrum Stuttgarts gelegene Komplex war in den fünfziger Jahren des vergangenen Jahrhunderts als weltweit gelobte Meisterleistung der Architektenkoryphäen Rolf Gutbrod und Adolf Abel anstelle des 1864 erbauten und 1944 durch Bombenangriffe zerstörten Vorgängergebäudes als deutlich von expressionistischen Strukturen geprägtes Konzerthaus errichtet und 1991 durch einen vom Gutbrod-Schüler Henning kreierten Neubau ergänzt worden" (8; The complex, situated right in the center of Stuttgart, was built in the 1950s, a concert hall clearly influenced by expressionist structures, and praised worldwide as a masterpiece by architectural luminaries Rolf Gutbrod and Adolf Abel, is on the site of the preceding building—which was built in 1864 and destroyed by bombs in 1944—and was expanded with an addition by Henning, a pupil of Gutbrod).

In a brief textual interlude before the investigation continues, the reader goes on another geographic trip as Braig thinks of the long, pleasant weekend just past, listing people and places that really exist in this part of Germany. He remembers going to a concert by his most-loved folk rock band, the real Wendrsonn, at the Staufer School Center in Waiblingen. The lead singer, Biggi Binder, performed his favorite song and drove away his work-related stress. The next day, Braig went to a classical organ concert at the *Stiftskirche* in the town of Backnang (9). In addition to the surroundings, the narrative includes elements of daily life in this environment with which readers from across Germany could potentially be acquainted but which local initiates or experts might be especially keen to see.

Shortly after his own arrival at the crime scene, Braig is irritated by the early appearance of a new prosecutor, who is quick to make observations about the crime and apparently does not operate in the usual manner. The prosecutor, Söderhofer, a transplant to Swabia who speaks with a Bavarian accent, nonetheless takes ownership and proves his affiliation with the region: "Und das ausgerechnet in unserer Liederhalle!" (13; And in our Liederhalle of all places!). Söderhofer's accent is complemented by the introduction of another character common to crime stories: the surly forensic scientist. After arriving at the crime scene, Helmut Rössle further contributes to the geographic flavor as he barks in Swabian dialect not easily conveyed in translation: "Alle Idioten von Sindelfinge, der Sparrefantel scho wieder. Ihr hent mir hoffentlich nix agrührt" (13; All idiots from Sindelfingen, the crotchety one again. Hopefully you all haven't touched anything). Further, Rössle provides dialectal comic relief after Söderhofer's departure: "Zum Glück sind mir den überkandidelte Großkotz los. Dem hent se net nur oi Mol ins Hirn gschisse" (24; Luckily we're rid of that over-the-top bigshot. He's got less than shit for brains). Thus far, the novel's narrative has inserted itself into the life of the reader, all the more so if the reader is familiar with or aware of these places. These strategies continue throughout this and Wanninger's other novels, facilitating immediate recognition for locals and supporting vivid imagination for nonlocals.

Gunter Gerlach's short story "Keine Tränen" takes a slightly different approach to ingratiating itself with readers. This story is one in the collection *Mörderisches Ländle* (2008), which, like Gudrun Weitbrecht's preceding anthology *Tödliche Kehrwoche* (Deadly Cleaning Week, 2007) and the following *Tod unterm Tannenbaum* (Death under the Christmas Tree, 2012), presents entertaining and short crime stories that usually have tongue firmly planted in cheek.[52] That the second and third collections were published attests to the success of the first.

In its appeal to readers' knowledge about the region, Gerlach's short story resembles Wanninger's novel. Unlike Wanninger, however, Gerlach does not entice the reader with renditions of Swabian idiom; instead, he situates the action of the story at a popular festivity that might be similarly familiar to the reader—the annual Esslingen *Zwiebelfest* (Onion Festival). Every summer since 1986, area residents, known as *Zwiebeln* (Onions) or *Zwieblinger*, along with tourists, gather to taste culinary specialties from local restaurants. According to legend, Esslingen residents are known as "Onions" because a market woman spotted the devil in disguise when he asked her for an apple, and instead gave him an onion. This shocked the devil and prompted him to name Esslingen residents "Onions." This act of biting into a whole onion also features in Gerlach's story and unites with the humorous title.

In the story, Hannes plans to murder his acquaintance Ulrich when they find themselves in a quarrel over a woman, Brigitte. Hannes, whose eyes do not have functioning tear ducts, proposes a contest in which they both bite into a whole onion; the first to cry loses Brigitte. Hannes has brought two onions with him: one poisoned, one not. Ulrich, a bodybuilding outsider who lives in Stuttgart and only works in Esslingen, enters into the bet, ordering himself and Hannes a regional specialty: *Maultaschen* (large Swabian ravioli). The story does not end as Hannes might have intended, but he is still able to whisper to Ulrich's corpse, "Siehst du. . . . Keine Tränen" (13; You see? No tears).

In these regional crime stories, location takes on a role that moves beyond basic plot and the delivery of mundane contextual details. In definite ways, the reader becomes a part of the narrative's locality as either a new initiate or an experienced local. When discussing criminal or mystery stories, we must consider the extent to which the reader or viewer is familiar with the material presented by the author and what the goal of the author and narrative might be. This degree of readers' familiarity contributes to the plausibility or novelty of the narrative. What reality does not allow—especially in locales like small Esslingen or parts of Swabia (to continue with the aforementioned examples)—we are able to do in crime-fiction narratives, as Edgar Marsch observes.[53] Wherever the story takes us, the reader gains impressions that are alluringly ordinary and exotic.

As we have seen, the subgenre is not universally well-received. The local insight can lead to narratives that are groaning under the weight of details that could be easily found in a travel guide. By contrast, they can include subtle allusions to their environment that may not distract from the broader goal of the larger genre of the crime story. Such a variety attests to the likely on-going vitality of the subgenre, as readers find that different styles meet different needs. Berndorf's Eifel stories reach a public that may not overlap with Gerlach's or Wanninger's. It is a truism that readers will receive a narrative and find things in it dependent upon their own personality and style. Nonetheless, this bilateral relationship between reader and author could contribute to the categorization of regional crime fiction (and nonregional versions) as trivial literature.

Although regional crime fiction has suffered from poor critical reception, the connections we can draw between it and its journalistic and early literary beginnings remain intriguing. Just like the eighteenth- and nineteenth-century case histories discussed above, regional crime fiction attests to a reading public's curiosity about its environment, the social and legal issues it faces, and the ways in which the extraordinary can enter one's daily life.

Notes

[1] Earlier versions of parts of this essay were presented in a related talk at the 2012 meeting of the Northeast Modern Language Association. I would like to thank Shuo Liu and the Centre for Student Involvement and Careers at the University of British Columbia; James Kelly, librarian at the University of Massachusetts Amherst; Mary Luebbe, librarian at the University of British Columbia; Corinna Norrick-Rühl, research associate at the Institute for Book Studies at the Johannes Gutenberg University of Mainz; and Hermann Staub of the Archiv und Bibliothek des Börsenvereins des Deutschen Buchhandels at the Deutsche Nationalbibliothek for invaluable research assistance in preparing this essay.

[2] *Kriminalliteratur* refers to the early collections of these stories (sometimes called *Criminalliteratur* or *Criminalgeschichten*). See, for example, Julius Eduard Hitzig and William Häring, *Der neue Pitaval: Eine Sammlung der interessantesten Criminalgeschichten aller Länder und Völker* (Frankfurt am Main: Insel Verlag, 1986).

[3] For an extensive investigation of this German television cultural phenomenon, see Sascha Gerhards's essay in this volume.

[4] In their chapters in this volume, Faye Stewart and Angelika Baier in particular interestingly connect this identity-forming or -revealing function of crime fiction to sex, gender, and sexuality.

[5] Marieke Krajenbrink and Kate M. Quinn, "Introduction: Investigating Identities," in *Investigating Identities: Questions of Identity in Contemporary International Crime Fiction*, ed. Krajenbrink and Quinn (Amsterdam: Rodopi, 2009), 1.

[6] Eva Erdmann, "Nationality International: Detective Fiction in the Late Twentieth Century," in *Investigating Identities*, ed. Krajenbrink and Quinn, 12.

[7] Erdmann, "Nationality International," 15.

[8] Erdmann, "Nationality International," 22.

[9] Peter Nusser, for example, differentiates between *Verbrechensliteratur* (literature of crime) and *Kriminalliteratur* (crime fiction). The former attempts a literary explanation for the roots of crime, the mindset of the criminals, and the nature of punishment (1). He offers the examples of *Oedipus Rex* and Dostoyevsky's *Crime and Punishment*. Crime fiction, on the other hand, spends more time providing an exposition of how the crime is discovered, investigated, and eventually how the

mystery is solved. British crime writer and critic Julian Symons remarked, "rigid classifications simply don't work in practice" (3). He continued, however, to write that "Of course this is not to say that there are no distinctions to be made.... The tree is sensational literature, and these are among its fruits" (4). See Julian Symons, *Bloody Murder: From the Detective Story to the Crime Novel* (New York: Mysterious Press, 1992).

[10] One of the most common critiques of regional crime fiction is what some, like Ulrich Baron, see as the tendency to emulate—or replace—travel guides. Ulrich Baron, "Markt & Totschlag: Regio regiert (nicht)," *CULTurMAG* (May 21, 2011) http://culturmag.de/crimemag/markt-und-totschlag-regio-regiert-nicht. Another complaint is that this subgenre's entire creation and subsequent boom are all ploys by publishers to cash in on the same customers who would otherwise buy locally focused coffeetable picture books or other regional memorabilia. Eckhart Baier, "Mord in der Heimat," *Börsenblatt* no. 27 (July 5, 2007): 44–46. The defining characteristic of this subgenre, then, is certainly not universally appealing. For example, Rutger Booß of Grafit-Verlag, publisher of one of the first series of regional crime fiction, echoes widespread criticism of many crime and detective stories in general when he says that, with these regional stories, any small press can make their way into the market without respect for the quality of the books produced (qtd. in Baier 45).

[11] Howard Haycraft, *Murder for Pleasure: The Life and Times of the Detective Story* (New York: D. Appleton-Century Company Inc., 1941), 242.

[12] See Anita McChesney's chapter in this volume for a discussion of the Austrian regional crime novel.

[13] Lynn Marie Kutch, "'Die lange blutige Literatursitzung': Veit Müller's Interrogation of the Writing Process in Regional Detective Fiction," *Modern Language Studies* 41, no. 2 (2012): 37.

[14] Qtd. in Baier, "Mord in der Heimat," 45.

[15] Friedrich Schiller, "Vorrede zur Pitaval-Ausgabe von 1792–1795," in *Schillers Pitaval: Merkwürdige Rechtsfälle als ein Beitrag zur Geschichte der Menschheit, verfaßt, bearbeitet und herausgegeben von Friedrich Schiller*, ed. Oliver Tekolf (Frankfurt am Main: Eichborn Verlag, 2005), 75–76.

[16] Michael Dunker, *Beeinflussung und Steuerung des Lesers in der englischsprachigen Detektiv- und Kriminalliteratur: eine vergleichende Untersuchung zur Beziehung Autor-Text-Leser in Werken von Doyle, Christie und Highsmith* (Frankfurt am Main; New York: Peter Lang, 1991), 11. Attempts at explanations of crime fiction's popularity are multiple and diverse; Julian Symons divides them into two main categories, the psychological and the social (Symons, *Bloody Murder*, 5, 13).

[17] Tina Klinkner, "Der deutsche Regionalkrimi," *media mania*, n.d., accessed July 10, 2012, http://www.media-mania.de/index.php?action=artikel&id=51.

[18] Almuth Heuner has observed the disparity between incoming translations into German and outgoing translations of German into other languages (especially English). She does not offer a satisfactory explanation for the deficit, noting only (and surprisingly) that "German mysteries are different.... There is more realism, probably because Germany is not a homogeneous country [*sic*]." Heuner,

"Germany's Crime and Mystery Scene," *World Literature Today* 85, no. 3 (2011): 16.

[19] The question remains why German crime fiction, despite its large quantity within the German-speaking countries, has not experienced the same kind of boom that, for example, Scandinavian crime literature and its film and television adaptations have. This engages questions unfortunately too large to be addressed here in detail, like external perspectives on German fiction, the translatability of the German language and its literature, and the latter translatability particularly with respect to German regional attributes and regional humor. There is wide circulation among the German-speaking countries, but language seems to be one of the barriers to further transmission of the German-speaking area's large number of mysteries and crime stories. See Heuner (previous note), who also mentions the translation issue.

[20] For a discussion of this, see Melanie Wigbers, *Krimi-Orte im Wandel: Gestaltung und Funktionen der Handlungsschauplätze in Kriminalerzählungen von der Romantik bis in die Gegenwart* (Würzburg: Königshausen & Neumann, 2006), 12.

[21] Anita McChesney's chapter in this volume offers another engagement with defining characteristics of this genre in the Austrian tradition. Paul Cobley criticizes the genre's adherence to what he sees as an overly conservative approach to realism: "The Reactionary Art of Murder: Contemporary Crime Fiction, Criticism and Verisimilitude," *Language and Literature* 21, no. 3 (2012): 286–98.

[22] For different time periods, see, for example, Gudrun Weitbrecht, ed., *Henker, Huren, Mordgesellen: historische Schwabenmorde* (Mannheim: Wellhöfer, 2009).

[23] Umberto Eco, *The Role of the Reader: Explorations in the Semiotics of Texts* (Bloomington: Indiana UP, 1979), 120.

[24] Wolfgang Iser, "Indeterminacy and the Reader's Response," in *Twentieth-Century Literary Theory*, 2nd ed., ed. K. M. Newton (New York: St. Martin's Press, 1997), 196–97.

[25] George N. Dove, *The Reader and the Detective Story* (Bowling Green, OH: Bowling Green State University Popular Press, 1997), 9.

[26] Dover, *The Reader*, 23–24.

[27] Eco, *Role*, 118.

[28] Eco, *Role*, 119.

[29] Peter Nusser, *Der Kriminalroman* (Stuttgart: Metzler, 2009).

[30] Nusser, *Kriminalroman*, 70.

[31] Examples include the Prussian *Kriminalkommissare* after 1822 and Berlin's *Kriminalpolizei*, the so-called "Department IV," in 1830. What followed was the gradual professionalization of police officers and detectives, a process I will not describe here. See Nusser, *Kriminalroman*, 71.

[32] Edgar Marsch, *Die Kriminalerzählung: Theorie, Geschichte, Analyse* (Munich: Winkler, 1972), 119.

[33] Other similar texts and collections include August Gottfried Meißner's *Skizzen* (1778–96, Sketches) and Paul Anselm Ritter von Feuerbach's *Aktenmäßige*

Darstellung merkwürdiger Verbrechen (1828–29, Documentary Portrayal of Remarkable Crimes). For more on the relation between factual and fictional crime stories, see also Jörg Schönert, "Kriminalgeschichten in der deutschen Literatur zwischen 1770 und 1890: Zur Entwicklung des Genres in sozialgeschichtlicher Perspektive," in *Der Kriminalroman: Poetik, Theorie, Geschichte*, ed. Jochen Vogt (Munich: Fink, 1998), 322–27.

[34] Marsch, *Kriminalerzählung*, 123–24.

[35] Hans-Otto Hügel, *Untersuchungsrichter, Diebsfänger, Detektive: Theorie und Geschichte der deutschen Detektiverzählung im 19. Jahrhundert* (Stuttgart: Metzler, 1978), 84. There is debate about whether the earlier stories could have led directly or eventually to "detective stories" because of, for example, their preemptive disclosure of the murderer or thief. See Hügel, *Untersuchungsrichter, Diebsfänger, Detektive*; Marsch, *Kriminalerzählung*.

[36] Julius Eduard Hitzig and Wilhelm Häring, eds., *Der neue Pitaval: Eine Sammlung der interessantesten Kriminalgeschichten* (Frankfurt am Main: Insel Verlag, 1986), 9–10.

[37] Hans-Otto Hügel, *Die Leiche auf der Eisenbahn: Detektivgeschichten aus deutschen Familienzeitschriften* (Darmstadt: Luchterhand, 1981), 199–200.

[38] Hügel, *Die Leiche auf der Eisenbahn*, 201; Nusser, *Der Kriminalroman*, 70.

[39] "Der Staatsgefangene und seine Tochter," *Münsterberger Wochenblatt*, January 4, 1839, 1st ed., Staatsbibliothek zu Berlin Preußischer Kulturbesitz, http://zefys.staatsbibliothek-berlin.de/list/zdb/24335642.

[40] "Zur Chronik des Kreises Münsterberg," *Münsterberger Wochenblatt*, January 4, 1839, 1st ed., Staatsbibliothek zu Berlin Preußischer Kulturbesitz, http://zefys.staatsbibliothek-berlin.de/list/zdb/24335642.

[41] Richard Alewyn, "Anatomie des Detektivromans," in *Der Kriminalroman: Poetik, Theorie, Geschichte*, ed. Jochen Vogt (Munich: Fink, 1998), 67–68.

[42] "Miscellen," *Berliner Gerichts-Zeitung*, October 1, 1853, Nr. 1 edition, sec. Beilage zur Berliner Gerichts-Zeitung, 6, Staatsbibliothek zu Berlin Preußischer Kulturbesitz, http://zefys.staatsbibliothek-berlin.de/list/title/zdb/24332471.

[43] Again, see Cobley, "The Reactionary Art of Murder."

[44] Symons, *Bloody*, 10–11.

[45] For an analysis of journalism's relationship to the rise of sensationalism, see Joy Wiltenburg, "True Crime: The Origins of Modern Sensationalism," *The American Historical Review* 109, no. 5 (2004): 1377–1404.

[46] "Prospect," *Berliner Gerichts-Zeitung*, October 1, 1853, Nr. 1 edition, 1, Staatsbibliothek zu Berlin Preußischer Kulturbesitz, http://zefys.staatsbibliothek-berlin.de/list/title/zdb/24332471.

[47] "Schwurgericht," *Berliner Gerichts-Zeitung*, October 1, 1853, Nr. 1 edition, 3, Staatsbibliothek zu Berlin Preußischer Kulturbesitz, http://zefys.staatsbibliothek-berlin.de/list/title/zdb/24332471.

[48] "Bruchsal, 26. Juni," *Heidelberger Zeitung*, 152, July 2, 1861, http://digi.ub.uni-heidelberg.de/diglit/hdtz1861a/0001?sid=b599a5bbaac33b93cc37869c7b3aefe1 (accessed August 4, 2012).

[49] *Berliner Gerichts-Zeitung*, 1.

[50] Klaus Wanninger, *Schwaben-Ehre* (Hillesheim: KBV, 2009); Gudrun Weitbrecht, ed., *Mörderisches Ländle* (Stuttgart: Theiss, 2008); Gunter Gerlach, "Keine Tränen," in *Mörderisches Ländle*, ed. Gudrun Weitbrecht (Stuttgart: Theiss, 2008).

[51] "Klaus Wanninger," http://www.kbv-verlag.de/autorendetail.html?id=64, *KBV-Verlag* (accessed January 5, 2013).

[52] Gudrun Weitbrecht, ed., *Tödliche Kehrwoche* (Stuttgart: Theiss, 2007); Gudrun Weitbrecht, ed., *Tod unterm Tannenbaum: Weihnachtskrimis aus dem Ländle* (Stuttgart: Theiss, 2012).

[53] Marsch, *Kriminalerzählung*, 40.

2: Krimi Quo Vadis: Literary and Televised Trends in the German Crime Genre

Sascha Gerhards

THE OPENING SEQUENCE TO A RECENT EPISODE of a German television crime series presents the audience with a panning shot of a bustling market square. The camera captures small and large booths, tents, and cars scattered about the square. Tourists and flâneurs, intermingled with women in headscarves, populate the location. Superimposed text informs the viewer, "Marrakesch, Marokko," followed by a tracking shot into the arcades of the city's souks, or outdoor marketplaces. The camera follows a young man in his mid-to-late twenties, moving deeper into the heart of the city. His demeanor indicates that he fears detection. After repeatedly checking to see if someone has been following him, he enters an Internet café and starts a video call with a man in Arabic, only to switch to German a few sentences into the conversation. When asked about a certain wedding, the young man responds, "Ja, ich hab die Hochzeit gesehen. Ich weiß jetzt, wie 'ne Hochzeit geht" (Yes, I saw the wedding. I know how a wedding works now). Then he adds more aggressively, "Wir werden unser Fest feiern" (We will have our celebration).[1] Shortly thereafter, three men enter the Internet café. Flustered by their presence, the young man leaves the café toward the restrooms, located across a courtyard in the back of the building and he enters one of the three stalls. The men who have followed him identify themselves as policemen and start searching the stalls. They see a picture of a young girl on the floor of one of the stalls, and when they open the stall door, there is a young man holding a hand grenade, which explodes only seconds later. After a long shot of the destroyed building, the film cuts to the next scene.

Described here is the first scene of the *Tatort* episode "Der Weg ins Paradies," which premiered in December 2011. The popular *Tatort* television series began its run in 1970 on the public ARD network (Arbeitsgemeinschaft der öffentlich-rechtlichen Rundfunkanstalten der Bundesrepublik Deutschland, Consortium of public broadcasting institutions of the Federal Republic of Germany). Similar to the *Regiokrimi*,

Tatort has also consistently emphasized regional specificities and local customs, with teams of detectives based in various German cities such as Hamburg, Cologne, Munich, Leipzig, Münster, and Stuttgart. "Der Weg ins Paradies," however, indicates a crucial difference between the regionally distinct *Tatort* productions filmed from the 1970s through the end of the millennium and the more recent episodes. Rather than focusing exclusively on regional specificities, many episodes from the past three years offer new concepts for the genre such as transnationalism. Similarly, the literary crime genre has also deemphasized regionalism established by the New German Crime Novel (*neuer deutscher Kriminalroman*) of the 1970s in favor of a particular kind of historicity. In this chapter, I intend to examine recent trends in the German crime-fiction genre, both television and print, that indicate an abandoning of established concepts of the genre or its subgenres, such as regionalism.[2]

Terminology: *Krimi*, *Regiokrimi*, and the Problem of *Heimat*

Traditionally in Germany, the culturally intertwined literary and televisual crime genres have exhibited formulaic commonalities, and the term *Krimi* is commonly used to refer to crime stories in both genres.[3] This established intersection of genres allows me to highlight the overlaps in developing trends in the televisual and literary subgenres, while also showing how recent trends diverge from these decades-old, well-worn recipes. Elsewhere, I have employed the term *Regiokrimi* for the classic crime novels and *Tatort* productions that rely on distinct regionalism.[4] Other contributors to the current volume use *Regionalkrimi* exclusively to designate crime novels. Because I examine both literary and televisual subgenres, and to maintain consistency in my publication record, I will continue to use the term *Regiokrimi* when discussing regionalism in these works. In my comparison of established formulas and recent trends, I will focus particularly on the complex relationship of German crime authors and screenwriters to the concept of *Heimat*. In so doing, I attempt to explain the shift away from the *Regiokrimi*'s specificities such as the depiction of local customs and the use of recognizable rural settings and regional dialects.

The term *Heimat*, often associated with nation building and the establishment of a new national identity after the Second World War, especially spawned controversy with respect to the postwar *Heimatfilm*.[5] This genre of film features rural settings and a tendency to avoid problematic social contexts in favor of a notion of *heile Welt* (safe and sound world).[6] The *Heimatfilm*'s ostensible avoidance of socially relevant topics stands in stark contrast to the profile of the established *Krimi*:

both authors of the New German Crime Novel and the creators and screenwriters of the *Tatort* series implement the *Krimi* as a vehicle for social critique. Despite this difference, recent German *Krimis* have incorporated certain elements linked to the term *Heimat*. Interestingly, the function of the term *Heimat* that links to nation building stands in contrast to the post-1945 idealized national image in Austrian crime fiction that Anita McChesney highlights in this volume. The dichotomy in recent trends in German-speaking *Krimis* invites closer examination of the direction in which the genre is progressing.

Readers and audiences, both local and national, have favored the *Regiokrimi* for its focus on distinctly German regional specificities, and trends in scholarship have matched the enthusiasm for the subgenre.[7] The commercial success of the *Tatort* series and growing scholarly interest, manifested in the increasing number of publications and conference panels that have centered on regional crime novels and *Tatort* episodes, reaffirm this notion.[8] The trend toward the inclusion of national specificities lasted well into the new millennium; but in several recent *Tatort* episodes, virtually all of the regional characteristics that scholars have traditionally assigned to the *Krimi* are missing, as the opening sequence described above has indicated. The episode could take place in any German city or even in any given country of the Western world. It does not focus on regional problems, recognizable local settings, or *Lokalkolorit,* a term used to refer to regionally specific customs, dialects and the like. Because it eschews distinct national genre specificities in favor of a much more global theme, "Der Weg ins Paradies" represents a new subgenre of the *Krimi*.

Kriminalität und Klamauk: Genre Life-Cycles in the *Krimi*

Both *Tatort* and the New German Crime Novel have significantly influenced German concepts about the genre for more than four decades. Thus the current formulaic shift in filmed *Krimis* from regional to global aspects of crime could be seen as an expected progression in the *Krimi* genre's life-cycle. The same holds true for a shift of emphasis in the novelistic *Krimis*, where novels that map Germany on a historical scale have complemented the *Regiokrimi*'s geographical or horizontal mapping. In this vein, Franco Moretti even argues for the implementation of literary maps as preparation for text analysis.[9] The various regions that the *Regiokrimi* covers, by contrast, function like the pieces of a puzzle: when combined, they represent an integral map of Germany as a whole. Theorist John G. Cawelti argues for a life-cycle of genres in an analysis of Roman Polanski's neonoir crime film *Chinatown* (1974).[10]

He identifies four stages of a genre's life-cycle with an "initial period of articulation and discovery," a second stage where audiences and artists become conscious and self-aware of genre specificities, followed by a third stage where people grow tired of a genre's predictability. He then concludes that at this point of a genre's life-cycle, elements of parody and satire proliferate, before, eventually, new subgenres gradually replace their well-worn predecessors (208). Similarly, Moretti investigates the reason for a genre's life-cycles, concluding that certain subgenres eventually become extinct.[11] I have argued elsewhere that the German crime genre has once before in its postwar history reached a point where new genres were established—this took place when the New German Crime Novel and the *Tatort* television series emerged shortly before the end of the extremely successful series of Edgar Wallace film comedies (1959–72).[12] The Wallace films were crime comedies set in England but produced in Germany. When *Tatort* and the New German Crime Novel emerged in the early 1970s, audiences turned away from the well-worn Wallace concept. Several recent developments indicate that the crime-fiction formula might soon undergo a similar metamorphosis. Contrary to Cawelti's and Moretti's theories of genre evolution, the recent addition to the crime-fiction formula acts as a countertrend and complements existing subgenres. Established formulas and new trends continue to coexist at the same time in the *Krimi*.

The *Tatort* episodes located in Münster and starring Jan Josef Liefers and Axel Prahl frequently reach the highest audience ratings in the entire series.[13] Several critics have associated the Münster team's success with the comic talent of Liefers and Prahl, which reaffirms Cawelti's theory on increasing irony at the end of a genre's life-cycle.[14] Similar to the comical Münster *Tatort* productions, two new, regional crime series have been exceptionally successful with audiences in the recent past. Established in 2007, *Mord mit Aussicht* (Murder with a View) has been produced for the ARD public television network and is currently in its third season. In October 2011, the ARD introduced the first season of the series *Heiter bis tödlich* (Sunny to Deadly; this is a word play with the weather expression *heiter bis wolkig*, meaning mostly clear, cloudy at times). Both series reemphasize regional or even rural specificities. As is the case with *Tatort* episodes from Münster, the deliberate inclusion of comic elements and the resulting success with German audiences also confirm Cawelti's theory on the lifecycle of genres. The episodes of *Heiter bis tödlich* and *Mord mit Aussicht* demonstrate an increased use of comic elements, and yet, they share a distinct quality that critics, scholars, and audiences alike have attributed to the modern *Krimi*: both *Mord mit Aussicht* and *Heiter bis tödlich* emphasize regional specificities and must therefore be categorized as *Regiokrimis*,[15] although they showcase some stylistic mutations as suggested by Moretti.[16]

Regionalism and the Avoidance of *Heimat*

One could argue that the *Regiokrimi* relies on regionality while rejecting *Heimat* terminology. Translated as "home" or "homeland," *Heimat* carries the implication of the familiar, a place where we feel comfortable, cozy, and secure. But *Heimat* also carries a much more complex undertone in Germany, suggesting a continuing discourse in German society "about the proper relation between the locality and the nation, the particular and the general, the many and the one."[17] Although not always explicit, this debate has shaped the mostly negative connotation of the term in postwar Germany, which might explain the avoidance of the term in the *Krimi*. In *No Place Like Home—Locations of Heimat in German Cinema*, Johannes von Moltke offers a detailed analysis of the term's complexities in postwar Germany, adding postwar film to the ongoing *Heimat* debate. Although he writes about film criticism, von Moltke's theories resonate here because of the inextricable relationship of the literary and visual crime media in Germany. Furthermore, Germany did not have a national crime genre in the immediate postwar years, which legitimizes the inclusion of film. In his analysis, von Moltke approaches the *Heimat* discourse in postwar film both from a genre-based as well as a historical perspective. Ultimately, he identifies the cinematic construction of *Heimat* as a "refuge from modernity."[18] I would argue that this observation bears some significance for the analysis of *Heimat* in—and even its absence from—the *Krimi*. The *Heimatfilm* has been negatively perceived as a refuge from modernity, partially, but not exclusively due to its focus on regional and rural settings, its depiction of closed communities, and its general portrayal of the outsider as a *Störenfried* (mischief-maker). Based on these characteristics, the emphasis on regional specificities and *Lokalkolorit* represents a conspicuous parallel to the *Heimatfilm*. But contrary to the *Heimatfilm*, both literary and televisual manifestations of regional crime fiction contribute to the German crime genre's self-assigned engagement with social issues. Consequently, I would argue, regional crime fiction and film represent progressive, rather than conservative, genres.

Similar to von Moltke, Celia Applegate states in her analysis of the *Heimat* movement that, after the Second World War, "Germany, in short, was rebuilt from the regions outward and upward."[19] This makes *Heimat* a prominent concept when analyzing postwar Germany and the attempts at nation building and a reestablishment of national identity. And yet, crime authors of the New German Crime Novel have refrained from using the term *Heimat* despite the role that folkloric elements play in their novels. Jochen Vogt has emphasized the connection: "Das Erzählmuster der Detektivgeschichte ... wird hier sehr wirkungsvoll mit der folkloristischen Bilderwelt verschmolzen: Landeskunde als Thriller" (The detective story's narrative pattern is effectively combined with folkloristic imagery: Applied cultural studies as a thriller; 117).[20] Instead of evoking *Heimat*, the *Regiokrimi* relies on terms such as *Region* and *Provinz*.[21] For instance, Emons Verlag, one of the biggest German publishing houses specializing in crime fiction, markets its *Regiokrimi* novels as *regionale Meister* (regional masterpieces) and with the seeming contradiction *weltweit regional* (globally regional). Like Emons, publishing house Gmeiner avoids the term *Heimat* in its advertisements, using the term *Lokalkolorit* instead. The term *Heimat* is also absent from *Tatort* episodes and novel titles, for instance in Jacques Berndorf's successful Eifel-Krimi series, Felix Huby's Ernst Bienzle novels,[22] or the Ruhrgebiet *Krimis* of various authors that became popular when the region was awarded the prestigious title *Kulturhauptstadt* (cultural capital) in 2010. Deliberate or not, *Regiokrimi* authors and screenwriters also refrain from the use of the term *Heimat* despite the distinct regional characteristics defining the novels and television episodes. The primary focus on *Region* and *Provinz* in postwar Germany underscores the success of the *Regiokrimi* to some extent. Yet, the question as to why the term *Heimat* itself seems absent, even from the *Regiokrimi*, still remains unanswered, especially with respect to the genres' similarities. Although *Heimatfilme* were not crime stories, both genres share commonalities, and the absence of *Heimat* terminology from the contemporary *Krimi* indicates a progression in the genre.

The focus on regional, and even rural, customs is but one example of the striking parallels between the *Heimatfilm* and the literary and televisual regional crime genres. Of the various other traits that the *Heimatfilm* shares with the crime-fiction formula, the detectable mapping of Germany is one of the most prevalent. As von Moltke states: "Unsurpassed in popularity at the time, the genre of the *Heimatfilm* provided a site where 1950s (film) culture negotiated central concerns with home, space, and belonging in the ongoing process of national reconstruction. In this context, the *Heimatfilm* came to function as a veritable (if selective) map to a postwar national space."[23] With their deliberate regional focus and concern for sociocultural aspects of home, the televisual and literary regional crime genres present a map of Germany very much like the *Heimatfilm*. The distinctly leftist political motivation of German crime authors and screenwriters as well as their deliberate engagement with social problems, however, indicates the most significant difference between the two genres. Renowned representatives of the *Regiokrimi* have reaffirmed this notion time and again. For instance, author and screenwriter Felix Huby describes himself and his colleagues as leftist social democrats and communists, united in their goal to provide social critique.[24] Gunter Witte, creator of *Tatort*, emphasizes the series's engagement with factual events, "auf der Basis von tatsächlichen Vorkommnissen" (based on true events).[25] Likewise, author H. P. Karr mentions self-referentiality, and the depiction of demographic change in the Ruhrgebiet in particular, as his primary motivation.[26] While the *Heimatfilm* was mostly (and maybe incorrectly) perceived as a *heile Welt* phenomenon, *Krimi* authors and screenwriters deliberately engage with sociocultural issues in various German regions. By mapping Germany, and providing insight into social strata, both the *Heimatfilm* and the crime genre negotiate German obstacles, albeit taking completely opposite approaches. While the *Heimatfilm* focuses on rural, close-knit communities, the *Regiokrimi* presents an analysis of the influence of internal and external factors, such as crimes, on these very communities.

Regional novels, films, and television episodes have dealt with such diverse topics as child trafficking,[27] illegal organ trade,[28] German soldiers suffering from post-traumatic stress after returning from Afghanistan,[29] an assassination plot against Bill Clinton during the world economic summit in Cologne in 1999,[30] and terrorism targeting the world-famous Cologne Cathedral,[31] to name but a few. While the crimes have an internatonal aspect, the setting and subplots are distinctly German with a heavy emphasis on regional characteristics and folklore (unlike the Wallace films). I would argue that despite the obvious *Heimat* characteristics found in regional crime genre, authors avoid the term precisely because of the negatively nationalistic characteristics associated with the *Heimatfilm* as suggested by von Moltke. Conscious or not, this avoidance represents a crucial difference between the two genres. Some authors and screenwriters have even moved away from regional specificities and *Lokalkolorit* altogether. This shift, in fact, is a bipartite one. First, *Tatort* episodes with a transnational focus form a new subgenre that deserves attention. I would like to call this trend *Weltkrimi*, which suggests a shift in emphasis away from the region to globalization. Second, literary authors have offered crime novels that historicize Weimar and Nazi Germany. To delineate them from historical crime novels (*Historischer Kriminalroman*), I suggest *Verarbeitungsroman* or *Verarbeitungskrimi* (coming-to-terms-with-the-past novels/crime novels) as a name for this new subcategory. Interestingly, the two new subgenres also break with a tradition in the German *Krimi* that I have continuously emphasized in the discussion so far: in the past forty years, crime novels and television productions have shared multiple similarities and distinct genre traits. By contrast, *Weltkrimi* and *Verarbeitungskrimi* take the genre in entirely different directions.

A Televised Trend: The *Weltkrimi*

Especially the *Tatort* episodes from Hamburg (2008–11), starring Mehmet Kurtuluş, a German actor of Turkish heritage, present high-profile, Hollywood-style cinematography rather than a focus on

Lokalkolorit that has typified the series. After the opening sequence to "Der Weg ins Paradies" discussed in the introduction to this chapter, the episode returns to Hamburg, but regional specificities are mostly neglected. As the plot unfolds, the audience learns that both men seen in the opening sequence are members of a German terrorist cell. The audience quickly realizes that the conversation about the wedding in the above-mentioned dialogue serves as some kind of code between the men. After the German-Moroccan man's death, the remaining members of the group become even more radical. To prevent a terrorist attack, the Bundeskriminalamt (Germany's Federal Police Agency) sends undercover cop Cenk Batu to infiltrate the terrorist cell. During his investigation, he focuses on the leader of the cell, the convert Christian Marschall. Under his new name Al Malik, Marschall, an *über*-intelligent son of a rich family, plans to plant a bomb in Hamburg and bring about an explosion similar in its dimension to the 9/11 terrorist attacks in New York City. The episode displays topicality with respect to actual political events and thus reaffirms *Tatort*'s self-assigned function as a source of social commentary. By engaging with the political threat of a terrorist cell consisting of converts, the episode directly renegotiates the media discourse on the Sauerland-Gruppe, a terrorist cell that German authorities uncovered in 2007. Its members, mostly Germans who had converted to a form of radical Islam, were preparing a bomb attack in Germany when they were arrested the same year.[32]

Contrary to other *Tatort* productions, "Der Weg ins Paradies" avoids references to regional specificities such as dialects, customs or local places. For instance, one of the very few landmarks shown in the episode is Hamburg's harbor. The producers do not, however, exploit the harbor to evoke folkloristic sentimentality, but rather to position the episode's locale vis-à-vis other urbane settings. Few aerial shots, and a focus on indoor scenes as well as close-ups reaffirm this impression and create, at the same time, a constant feeling of uneasiness throughout the episode. The *heimelige* (homelike, homey) atmosphere that other *Tatort* episodes evoke to contrast with the threat presented by the crime is completely absent in "Der Weg ins Paradies." Mention of the rather famous *Schanzenviertel* and a few shots of Hamburg's infamous Reeperbahn presented in the background during a car ride cannot belie the utterly global threat presented here.

Similar to "Der Weg ins Paradies" with its opening sequence from Morocco, the last episode with Kurtuluş in 2012, "Die Ballade von Cenk und Valerie," though exclusively set in Hamburg, again lacks any of the regional specificities previously associated with *Tatort* productions. The episode presents Hamburg in a way that makes it interchangeable any other metropolis in Germany or even in the Western world. With its depressing, gloomy, and powerful cinematography, "Die Ballade von

Cenk und Valerie" almost completely redirects the series's emphasis away from the region and toward the increasingly globalized world. Although the crime revolves around an attempted assassination of the German chancellor, the episode really centers on the cold-hearted, deliberate stock manipulation of investment bankers in an international context. Thus "Die Ballade von Cenk und Valerie" still engages with social issues by commenting on the collapse of the world financial system, but it does so on a global or transnational rather than on a regional or national level, effacing nearly any mention of local specificity.

In "Der Weg ins Paradies," "Die Ballade von Cenk und Valerie," and other *Tatort* episodes starring *Hauptkommisar* (chief inspector) Cenk Batu, the investigator also differs from the more established *Tatort* colleagues. He is presented as an undercover cop who, equipped with a false identity and vitae, infiltrates criminal organizations. In "Die Ballade von Cenk und Valerie," an autistic contract killer kidnaps Batu's pregnant girlfriend in an attempt to force him to assassinate the German chancellor. Batu realizes that he has been trapped, and in the course of the narrative, he tries to save his girlfriend's life while at the same time informing the German secret service about the assassination. With the news cameras rolling, he suggests staging an assassination of the the chancellor, but the service's agents refuse to play along. Concerned for his girlfriend's life, Batu takes the chancellor hostage and is shot dead by a police SWAT team at the end of the episode.

Despite its impressive cinematography, top-shelf actors, and stellar reviews, "Die Ballade von Cenk und Valerie" was not successful with German audiences, receiving a mere seven-million-viewer rating.[33] Similarly, "Der Weg ins Paradies," though celebrated by critics, fared poorly with audiences, which led the German weekly *Der Spiegel* to conclude: "Mehmet Kurtuluş und der Hamburger 'Tatort' sind gescheitert? Vielleicht. Aber wie großartig sie dabei doch aussahen!" (Mehmet Kurtuluş and the Hamburg *Tatort* have failed? Maybe. But, oh, how excellent they looked when failing!).[34] It seems that the absence of regional specificities as well as the unusual investigator contributed to the lack of success for a new *Tatort* concept. As audience ratings and critical reviews suggest, *Tatort* viewers seem too accustomed to the series' decade-long focus on regionalism and its emphasis on local customs combined with criminal cases of sociocultural relevance.[35]

A Literary Trend: The *Verarbeitungskrimi*

The transnational *Tatort* episodes from Hamburg represent a prominent recent trend in the German *Krimi*. They almost completely diverge from the focus on regional specificities, local customs, and dialects, which were significant traits of the genre since the 1970s. Instead of continuing a social mapping of Germany, their focus lies on transnational topics and on localities that are neither regionally nor even nationally charged. But a trend in contemporary crime literature—the *Verarbeitungsroman* or *Verarbeitungskrimi*—contributes to the new *Krimi* even more successfully. The *Verarbeitungskrimi* owes its debt to the *Historischer Kriminalroman* (historical crime novel), a series of novels negotiating history before the turn of the century.

Frank Schätzing's *Tod und Teufel* (1995, republished 2006) only foreshadowed a wave of historical crime novels that has appeared over the past eighteen years in Germany. By the end of the new millennium's first decade, bookstores stocked a variety of *Historische Kriminalromane*, whose authors followed the trend in British and American crime novels,[36] and whose plots spanned several centuries, from the middle ages (Schätzing) to the mid-nineteenth century.[37] In addition to a general boom in crime fiction, Barbara Korte and Sylvia Paletschek have documented a growing interest in readerships in historical topics: "Die Entwicklung partizipiert also gleich an zwei aktuellen Trends: dem großen und wachsenden Interesse an Kriminalliteratur sowie dem gegenwärtig zu beobachtenden Geschichtsboom" (The development takes part in two different current trends: the great and growing interest in crime fiction as well as the presently noticeable history boom).[38] Historical crime novels deploy history in a manner that is distinctly different from the previously discussed *Regiokrimi*, with its focus on regional specificities and regional social obstacles. Instead of functioning on a horizontal, geographical level by focusing on regions, they employ temporality on a vertical level in a historical chronology. Nevertheless, like regional novels, the *Verarbeitungsroman* represents an important contribution to the negotiation of social aspects, "da Kriminalliteratur generell mit dem Anspruch auftritt, die Handlung und deren gesellschaftlichen Kontext möglichst realistisch und mit zahlreichen Details der Alltagswirklichkeit zu entwerfen" (because crime literature generally lays claim to framing the plot and its social context as realistically and detailed as possible) (11). With respect to the future of the German *Krimi* and its engagement with social change, it must be emphasized here that even historical crime novels contain references to social norms and values. In their analysis of classic historical crime novels, Korte and Paletschek successfully and rightfully defend the *historischer Kriminalroman* against critics who reproach it as a textual manipulation of history. While this is important for the historical crime novel in general, it becomes particularly important with respect to the *Verarbeitungsromane*.

Unlike the typical *historischer Kriminalroman*, the subgenre *Verarbeitungsroman* tends to focus on three specific eras of twentieth-century German history—the Weimar Republic on the verge of National Socialism, the period of the Third Reich, and immediate postwar

Germany. It therefore engages eras from which very few or no original crime novels are still available. This is not to say that crime novels were not read or written in Germany during these times. Among others, Volker Neuhaus[39] and Hans-Otto Hügel[40] have shown that, contrary to common belief, crime fiction did exist in Germany in the nineteenth and early twentieth century. Other historical literary genres have also addressed this dark era of German history, but the *Verarbeitungsroman* fills a gap in the otherwise complete history that has been written by the modern *Krimi*. It renegotiates aspects of German history that crime novels have not previously addressed, and it creates scenarios, "deren Details in der Regel ebenso genau—wenn nicht noch genauer—recherchiert wie bei Texten, die in der Gegenwart spielen" (whose details are researched as precisely— if not more precisely—than those of novels taking place in the present) (Korte and Paletschek, 12). This aspect of attention to detail makes the *Verarbeitungsroman* a particularly relevant genre by which to gauge the future of the *Krimi*. The *Verarbeitungsroman*, I argue, contributes to one of the most important aspects of the German crime genre: the recontextualization of German social history from the perspective of crime fiction. It combines fictional plots and plausible stories with historical detail and accuracy, enabling the reader to relive genuine German history through thrilling fictional crime plots.

Of the three time periods that the novels fictionalize, *Verarbeitungsromane* set in the Weimar Republic and during National Socialism seem particularly interesting.[41] Like the German crime-fiction formula of the past decades, the *Verarbeitungskrimi* reaffirms the genre's subliminal encounter with social and historical realities: "Historische Kriminalromane dienen nicht explizit und intentional der Vermittlung historischen Wissens, doch sie transportieren quasi als Nebeneffekt ihres kriminalistischen Plots mehr oder weniger gesichertes Wissen über die Vergangenheit, vor allem wenn die Textgestaltung durch Detailreichtum oder gar Glossare den Eindruck sorgfältiger Recherche erweckt" (Historical crime novels do not explicitly and intentionally convey historical knowledge but they transport more or less reliable knowledge about the past as a kind of side effect of their crime plots, especially when the textual composition suggests thorough research though richness of detail or even glossaries).[42] Almost by definition, historical crime novels involve controversial historical moments. Contrary to critics who have disparaged the entire subgenre of historical crime novels for their historical inaccuracy, I would argue that this side effect (*Nebeneffekt*) of historical facts makes the *Verarbeitungsroman*, after all a kind of historical novel, a strong representative of a crime history. This is not to suggest that these novels revise or rewrite history; instead they embed a fictional crime plot in an accurate and factual depiction of the past. Rather than constructing the crime narrative out of actual historical circumstances, the *Verarbeitungsroman* builds its narrative by recontextualizing factual events and political facts. The novels add a fictional dimension to history, offering a very detailed analysis of Weimar and National Socialist societies, much like Anita McChesney has shown for Gerhard Roth's *Der See* in this volume. Volker Kutscher confirms his interest in the historical development from the Weimar Republic to National Socialism. He describes as one of the most fascinating facets of the era the general assumption that the Weimar Republic inevitably led to Fascism. Contrary to this perception, he argues for a rereading of historical circumstances with fresh eyes. When approached from the point of view of a Weimar citizen, says Kutscher, Nazi Germany was only one of several options in Germany's political future.[43]

Volker Kutscher's Gereon Rath Novels

Kutscher set the first novel of his bestselling series, *Der nasse Fisch* (2007, The Wet Fish), in 1929 Berlin. Gereon Rath, a young and ambitious commissioner in the vice squad becomes involved in a case of the city's homicide division, and uncovers a network of local cliques that are involved in criminal activity. Kutscher's second novel, *Der stumme Tod* (2009, Silent Death) once again features commissioner Rath and presents the reader with the death of a silent movie star. Rath begins his investigations in the film business and finds himself in the midst of a rapidly changing industry. With the four novels *Der nasse Fisch*, *Der stumme Tod*, *Goldstein* (2010, Goldstein), and *Die Akte Vaterland* (2012, The Fatherland File), Kutscher has developed a series that facilitates the longer-term and more in-depth development of the detective figure and the rapidly changing historical events the character has to face.[44] In addition, the *Verarbeitungsroman* conveys an epochal renegotiation of historical circumstances to the reader, and thus resembles its genre forerunner, the *historischer Kriminalroman*: "Die dargestellten Epochen mögen weit von der Lebenswelt der Leser entfernt oder auch kulturell fremd sein, über alltagsweltliche Details werden aber trotzdem Anknüpfungspunkte für die Leser geschaffen und die Vergangenheit wird so zugänglich gemacht" (The depicted epochs might be far away from the readers' living environment, and even culturally different, but by providing everyday details, links for the readers are established. In so doing, the past becomes accessible).[45] A new subgenre of the historical crime novel, the *Verarbeitungsroman* by definition embeds its plot in historical circumstances, providing the reader with cultural details and missing links.

Documentaries such as the *Hitlers*...[46] series by controversial historian Guido Knopp have offered similar connections to the Weimar and Nazi eras, providing audiences with details about the political and social circumstances at the time. The availability and commercial success of the

Hitlers . . . series differentiate the position of the *Verarbeitungsroman* from that of historical crime novels: the wide availability of these documentaries and an ongoing cultural discourse on Nazi Germany equip potential readers of the *Verarbeitungsroman* with ample information about National Socialism and Weimar Germany. Complementing the nonfictional documentaries, the *Verarbeitungsroman* significantly contributes to this discourse through its fictional engagement with Weimar and National Socialist politics. I would argue that the *Hitlers* . . . series and similar documentaries account for the upsurge in popularity of novels that treat this subject matter. In addition to the characteristics the *Verarbeitungsroman* shares with the historical documentaries, the interplay and inner conflict of the investigators and other characters add to the fictional negotiation of history. Investigators such as Gereon Rath in Volker Kutscher's novels, Tom Sydow in Uwe Klausner's *Walhalla-Code* (2009), and Eugen Goltz in Bernward Schneider's *Spittelmarkt* (2010) showcase an inner conflict of Weimar citizens emotionally torn between the controversial political currents present in Germany.

In Kutscher's *Der nasse Fisch*, Rath has been transferred from Cologne to Berlin in response to a fatal shooting in his hometown. After his arrival in Berlin, Rath experiences severe problems with authorities, but also displays his true sense of justice. Both these tendencies develop throughout the four novels. Exposed to the political struggles of the late Weimar years, Rath clearly manifests a negative attitude toward the authoritarian currents afoot in 1929 Berlin. Kutscher skillfully weaves Rath's inner conflict into the plot by having a third-person omniscient narrator lead the readers through the narrative. For instance, Rath despises the Prussian architecture of the Berlin police headquarters: "Hinter den Bauzäunen des Alexanderplatzes hob sich das Präsidium dunkel in den Nachthimmel. *Rote Burg* nannten die Berliner den mächtigen Backsteinbau, der den Preußen größer geraten war als das Stadtschloss, aber im Gegensatz zum Schloss immer noch eine Funktion hatte. Die Kollegen nannten ihren Arbeitsplatz einfach nur Burg. . . . Aber die Preußen schafften es, auch aus filigranen Renaissancemotiven eine abweisende Zwingburg zu machen" (*Der stumme Tod* 53; Behind the construction fences of the Alexanderplatz, the headquarters rose dark into the night sky. The Berliners called this mighty brick building Red Castle; this building that the Prussians had erected to be bigger than the royal palace. But contrary to the palace, it still had a purpose. The colleagues simply called their workplace Castle. . . . But the Prussians even managed to turn the building's delicate renaissance motifs into a cold fortress).

Rath's conflict with Prussian authority is represented architecturally in this chapter of *Der stumme Tod*, while his resistance to political manipulation manifests itself through statements and actions at various points of the narrative. For instance, when Rath's direct superior orders him to observe the funeral of Horst Wessel, Rath hesitates to attend this politically charged event, and instead continues to investigate the case from which he has been withdrawn. On another occasion, Rath is traveling through Berlin when he encounters a street sign for Stresemannstraße. Here, Kutscher's narrator reports:

> Obwohl Politik ihn wenig interessierte, hatte er gespürt, dass etwas zerbrochen war, dass mit diesem Mann mehr gestorben war, als der Außenminister. Dieser Mann war Deutschland ein strenger, aber liebevoller Vater gewesen, und weit und breit sah Rath niemanden, der an seine Stelle treten könnte, einen starken Politiker, der sein Land wirklich liebte und nicht nur dieses hohle Pathos verbreitete, mit dem vor allem die Deutschnationalen ihre Minderwertigkeitsgefühle überspielten, oder die Großmäuligkeit, die Goebbels' Nazis mit Patriotismus verwechselten. (Kutscher 139)

> [Although he was hardly interested in politics, he had felt that something had broken; that more had died than this man, the secretary of state. This man had been a strict, yet loving father for Germany and, far and wide, Rath did not see anyone to replace him; a strong politician who really loved his country and who neither spread the hollow pathos used by the German National People's Party to mask their sense of inferiority, nor acted like a loudmouth, which Goebbels's Nazis seemed to mistake for patriotism.]

Although the omniscient narrator claims that Rath is apolitical, Kutscher assigns certain political characteristics and intellectual curiosity to the character. Rath is presented as a witty, intelligent, and mindful character who observantly, yet at times reluctantly, notices the social and political changes afoot in Germany.

Time and again, Kutscher has Rath reflect on political issues, and especially the case of Horst Wessel resurfaces throughout the plot of *Der stumme Tod*. After Rath had initially ignored his superior's order to attend Wessel's funeral, Kutscher has him brood about the growing influence of the National Socialists in German politics, and on the role of martyr the Nazis assigned to Horst Wessel:

> Ein Schuss, der ihn zum Märtyrer der Völkischen macht. Ein komischer Heiliger, dieser Wessel. Ein junger Pfarrerssohn, der in kürzester Zeit die SA in Friedrichshain auf Trab gebracht hatte. Sich dann in eine Nutte verliebt hatte und seine SA seither schmählich vernachlässigt hatte. Das war Goebbels gleichgültig, für Berlins Obernazi gab der Sturmführer einen prima Märtyrer ab. Ein Glück jedenfalls, dass Wessel seinen Verletzungen dann doch noch erlegen war, womöglich wäre der Vorzeigenazi am Ende noch aus der NSDAP ausgetreten. (Kutscher 204)

[A shot had made him a martyr for the *Völkisch* movement. A strange saint, that Wessel. A young son of a priest, he had jolted the SA in Friedrichshain into action. He then had fallen in love with a prostitute and started to neglect his SA ignominiously. Goebbels did not care. For Berlin's high-ranking Nazi officer, the *Sturmführer* made a prime martyr. Fortunately, Wessel had finally succumbed to his injuries; otherwise, chances were that the German model Nazi would have eventually left the NSDAP.]

Not only is Rath skeptical of the Nazis' political influence, he is also depicted as someone who is morally torn between his own standards and the social standards of the time. On the one hand, he despises Wessel for his two-faced lifestyle; on the other hand, he himself accepts bribes from shady characters, and consumes drugs on various occasions. The novel relates history in a narrative "from below," where people who do not usually get a voice become the center of attention.[47] Kutscher's Rath fulfills this function in *Der stumme Tod* and makes the character even more credible. The actions and statements Kutscher interweaves into the plot further reaffirm the observation that historical crime novels do not tend to narrate major historical events. Instead, they focus on the point of view of bystanders, of simple men and women who represent society at large. To add even more variety and detail, some of these people are depicted as the "good Germans," while others outspokenly sympathize with the imminent rise of the National Socialist Party. This "view from below" explains the appeal of the *Verarbeitungsroman* to readers. Instead of being elevated to the intellectual, god-like level of the classic investigator as suggested by Siegfried Kracauer,[48] readers find their own social strata and conventions in the novels' texts and subtexts.

Conclusion

The German *Krimi* has recently seen two trends that diverge drastically from the established genre traits of regionalism and the resulting geographical mapping of Germany. Even more important than the growing number of comic elements in the literary and audiovisual regional crime genres, the move away from the popular and commercially successful regionalism attests to the negatively charged perception of *Heimat*. Potentially caused by international flows of global capital and media saturation, the televised *Krimi* especially seems to stress the intrusion of the global into the local, as the discussion of the Hamburg *Tatort* productions has shown. A second, literary trend indicates a retreat from the geographical dimension altogether. Instead, authors offer a reengagement with twentieth-century German history. Barbara Korte and Sylvia Paletschek suggest that historical crime novels inevitably choose epistemological problems of writing history as their topic due to the crime genre's distinct history and conventions.[49] Set in the past, the *Verarbeitungskrimi* renegotiates the formation of a political identity in postwar Germany from a literary perspective. While regional crime novels and television productions had presented Germany on a geographical scale, the *Verarbeitungskrimi* does so on a historical scale. In other words, the regional genres have provided an exclusively horizontal map of Germany, with the *Verarbeitungskrimi* adding to that a vertical or historical level.

In a way, this vertical mapping represents a new approach to the *Heimat* concept. Further research will have to interpret the audience reception of the new idea of *Heimat* that manifests itself in the nationally specific crime-fiction formula. I would conclude that the inclusion of *Heimat*-related aspects by way of a historical scale explains the success and critical acclaim of the *Verarbeitungskrimi*. After all, German audiences and readers have embraced the idea of *Heimat* since the end of the Second World War, albeit ambiguously. This could also explain why audiences disliked the globally oriented *Tatort* episodes starring Mehmet Kurtuluş despite critical acclaim. Reviews such as the ones quoted here from *Der Spiegel* reinforce this impression. The turn away from concepts such as *Region* and *Provinz* and from regionally specific characteristics in the Hamburg *Tatort* episodes marked the absence of any local color. Once again in the history of the crime genre, audiences and readers seem to prefer nationally specific contexts to global topics and settings. In evolutionary theory, the vertical and horizontal axes in reality are "the two dimensions of the same tree," Franco Moretti argues.[50] Following this line of thought, space and time are essentially the same. The discussion of place (or the lack of place) in the Hamburg *Tatort* productions, and of history in the *Verarbeitungskrimi*, leads me to conclude that the recent *Krimi* bridges spatial and historical topics and offers the reader a kind of vicarious tourism with valuable political, social, and historical instruction.

Notes

[1] All translations in this essay are my own, except where otherwise credited.

[2] In Germany, the literary and audiovisual media are uniquely intertwined. A prime example is Felix Huby's detective Bienzle from Stuttgart, who not only appears in a series of some twenty or so novels, but also as a detective in *Tatort* episodes from Stuttgart. I have shown elsewhere how publishing houses and the ARD television network deliberately advertise the genre as regionally distinct. See also Sascha Gerhards, "Nation and Region—Regionalism in the German *Krimi*," in Gerhards, "Zeitgeist of Murder: The *Krimi* and Social Transformation in Post-1945 Germany," PhD Diss., U of California, Davis (2013), 112–49. These cultural formulas in the German crime genre seemed to have worked: especially the

Tatort series has proven to be exceptionally successful. With close to 900 episodes (891 episodes as of July 2013) in feature-film length, it is the most successful German television broadcast after the newscast *Tagesschau*, according to Jochen Vogt. For a complete list of *Tatort* episodes, see: http://www.daserste.de/unterhaltung/krimi/tatort/sendung/index.html (accessed July 1, 2013). Jochen Vogt has also rightfully called *Tatort* "der wahre deutsche Gesellschaftroman" (the true German social novel) in: Jochen Vogt, "Tatort—der wahre deutsche Gesellschaftsroman. Eine Projektskizze," in *Medien-Morde: Krimis intermedial*, ed. Jochen Vogt (Munich: Wilhelm Fink, 2005), 112–29.

[3] The ARD and ZDF public television networks advertise their crime shows as *Krimi* and *Sonntagskrimi* respectively. See, for instance, "Auch Joachim Król verlässt den 'Tatort,'" in *Die Welt*, May 28, 2013, http://www.welt.de/vermischtes/article116588474/Auch-Joachim-Krol-verlaesst-den-Tatort.html; Klaus Bassiner and Berit Teschner, "Wir arbeiten für gute Krimis," *2DF Jahrbuch* 2006, http://www.zdf-jahrbuch.de/2006/programmarbeit/bassiner_teschner.html.

Likewise, publishing houses refer to crime novels using the term *Krimi*. For instance, Gmeiner advertises its portfolio as "Gmeiner—Der Krimi-Verlag" (http://www.gmeiner-verlag.de/), and dtv markets its crime novels with the phrase "Krimi und Spannung" (http://www.dtv.de/krimi_und_spannung_22.html) (accessed July 1, 2013).

[4] Gerhards, "Zeitgeist of Murder."

[5] For a detailed discussion of the genre and related controversies, please see Johannes von Moltke's *No Place Like Home: Locations of Heimat in German Cinema* (Berkeley: U of California P, 2005).

[6] Von Moltke defines the Heimatfilm as a "genre that for almost a century has circled obsessively around the questions of home and away, tradition and change, belonging and difference inscribed in the German term *Heimat*," *No Place*, 3. He also offers a series of useful associations with the term *heile Welt*, which has become commonly accepted in the German language to mean a "welcome lie about an intact world," or an "undisturbed idyll," von Moltke, *No Place*, 80.

[7] See Kyle Frackman's extensive discussion of the regional crime-fiction genre in this volume.

[8] See, for instance, Jochen Vogt. "Alles total groovy hier—Oder: Wie das Ruhrgebiet im Krimi zu sich selbst kam," *Der Deutschunterricht* 2 (2010): 20–28; Björn Bollhöfer, *Geographien des Fernsehens—Der Kölner Tatort als mediale Verortung kultureller Praktiken* (Bielefeld: Transcript Verlag, 2007); Juliaka Griem, ed, *Tatort Stadt—mediale Topographien eines Fernsehklassikers* (Frankfurt: Campus, 2010).

[9] Franco Moretti, *Graphs, Maps, Trees—Abstract for a Literary History* (London: Verso, 2005), 53.

[10] John G. Cawelti, "*Chinatown* and Generic Transformation in Recent American Films," in *Mystery, Violence & Popular Culture* (Madison: The U of Wisconsin P, 2004), 193–209.

[11] The reasons for genre extinction as analyzed by Moretti are manifold. When examining the British competitors to Sir Arthur Conan Doyle's Sherlock Holmes,

for instance, Moretti shows that the absence of clues in the work of Doyle's contemporaries determined the end of certain subgenres, leaving Sherlock Holmes as the epiphany (70–78). And yet, Moretti concludes, "'A Scandal in Bohemia' becomes just one leaf among many: delightful, of course—but no longer entitled to stand for the genre as a whole" (*Graphs*, 76).

[12] Sascha Gerhards, "Ironizing Identity: The German Crime Genre and the Edgar Wallace Wave of the 1960s," in *Generic Histories of German Cinema: Genre and Its Deviations*, ed. Jaimey Fisher (Rochester, NY: Camden House, 2013), 133–55.

[13] *Tatort* Münster reaches an average 11.38 million viewers, followed by Hannover with 9.49 million and Frankfurt with 9.19 million people. (http://de.statista.com/statistik/daten/studie/169503/umfrage/durchschnittliche-einschaltquote-der-tatort-ermittler/.)

[14] Critics in magazines such as *Der Spiegel, Der Stern*, and *Focus* criticized the Münster productions for their slapstick comedy, while at the same time acknowledging their success. See, for instance, "Fast zwölf Millionen schauten 'Hinkebein,'" *Stern.de*, March 12, 2012, http://www.stern.de/kultur/tv/einschaltquote-fuer-tatort-muenster-fast-zwoelf-millionen-schauten-hinkebein-1798669.html; "Fast zwölf Millionen Zuschauer sehen 'Hinkebein,'" *Focus Online*, March 12, 2012, http://www.focus.de/kultur/kino_tv/tatort/fast-zwoelf-millionen-schalteten-ein-monster-quote-fuer-muenster-tatort_aid_723121.html; "Rekord-'Tatort': Quote wie in den goldenen Neunzigern," *Spiegel Online*, May 2, 2011, http://www.spiegel.de/kultur/tv/rekord-tatort-quote-wie-in-den-goldenen-neunzigern-a-760062.html.

[15] *Heiter bis tödlich: Fuchs und Gans* [Sunny to Deadly: Fox and Goose]: "Die Badende" [The Bathing Woman] (episode 7); "Sternschnuppen" [Falling Stars] (episode 8). *Mord mit Aussicht* [Murder with a View]: "Das nennt man Camping" [This is Called Camping] (episode 23); "Ein krummer Hund" [A Villain] (episode 24).

[16] Moretti, *Graphs*, 91.

[17] Celia Applegate, *A Nation of Provincials: The German Idea of Heimat* (Berkeley: U of California P, 1990), 6.

[18] Von Moltke, *No Place*, 13.

[19] Applegate, *A Nation of Provincials*, 229.

[20] Vogt, "Tatort—der wahre deutsche Gesellschaftsroman," 117.

[21] I offer a detailed analysis of the *Regiokrimi's* use of *Region* and *Provinz*, and the absence of *Heimat* terminology in "Nation and Region—Regionalism in the German *Krimi*."

[22] Many of these were later rewritten as screenplays for *Tatort* episodes.

[23] Von Moltke, *No Place*, 23.

[24] Eike Wenzel, "Sieben Herdringe: Interview mit Felix Huby," in Wenzel, ed., *Ermittlungen in Sachen TATORT—Recherchen und Verhöre, Protokolle und Beweisfotos* (Berlin: Bertz Verlag, 2000), 216.

[25] Eike Wenzel, "Das scharfe Schwert der Realitätsbezogenheit: Interview mit Gunther Witte," in Wenzel, ed., 26.

[26] Joachim Wittkowski, *Auf Streife im Revier—Der Krimi im Ruhrgebiet* (Bottrop: Verlag Henselowsky Boschmann, 2009), 68.

[27] *Tatort*, "Arme Püppi" (episode 386, 1998).

[28] *Tatort*, "Das Dorf" (episode 819, 2011), "Leben gegen Leben" (episode 792, 2011).

[29] *Tatort*, "Heimatfront" (episode 789, 2011), "Fette Hunde" (episode 841, 2012).

[30] Frank Schätzing, *Lautlos* (Cologne: Emons, 2000).

[31] Edgar Franzmann, *Der Richter-Code* (Cologne: Emons, 2011).

[32] See, for instance, Kai Bierman, "Terrorismus hausgmacht," *Die Zeit Online*, September 6, 2007, www.zeit.de/online/2007/37/Konvertiten.

[33] "Kurtuluş verabschiedet sich mit schwacher Quote," *quotenmeter*. July 24, 2012. www.quotenmeter.de/n/56540/kulturus-verabschiedet-sich-mit-schwacher-quote.

[34] "'Tatort über deutsche Islamisten'—Ich, der Schläfer," Spiegel Online, 16 December 16, 2011, http://www.spiegel.de/kultur/tv/tatort-ueber-deutsche-islamisten-ich-der-schlaefer-a-803539.

[35] The investigator Cenk Batu further reinforces this impression. The character does not carry the characteristics typical for the established German investigator. He does not represent the setting through his fictional biography, a sine qua non for successful *Krimi* investigators like Horst Schimanski (the quintessential Ruhrgebiet character) or Ernst Bienzle (famous as a literary as well as televised investigator from Stuttgart). Likewise, Batu's background as an undercover cop alters the well-established focus on a police commissioner.

[36] "Die Liste der Geschichtskrimis ist lang und wird immer länger, wobei das Genre international von britischen und amerikanischen Autoren und Autorinnen dominiert wird." Barbara Korte and Sylvia Paletschek, "Geschichte und Kriminalgeschichte(n)—Texte, Kontexte, Zugänge," in *Geschichte im Krimi: Beiträge aus den Kulturwissenschaften*, ed. Barbara Korte (Cologne: Böhlau, 2009), 13.

[37] See, for example, Silvia Kaffke's *Das rote Licht des Mondes* (Hamburg: Rowohlt Taschenbuch Verlag, 2000).

[38] Korte and Paletschek, "Geschichte," 7.

[39] Interview conducted in 2009 at the University of Cologne, Germany.

[40] Hans-Otto Hügel, *Untersuchungsrichter, Diebesfänger, Detektive. Theorie und Geschichte der deutschen Detektiverzählung im 19. Jahrhundert* (Stuttgart: Metzler, 1978).

[41] In addition to Volker Kutscher's serial *Der nasse Fisch* (2007; set in 1929), *Der stumme Tod* (2009; 1930), *Goldstein* (2010; 1931), and *Die Akte Vaterland* (2012; 1932), other novels engaging with this time period are Gunnar Kunz's *Dunkle Tage* (2006; 1920), the follow-up *Organisation C.* (2007; 1922), *Inflation!* (2011; 1923), and his latest novel *Zeppelin 126* (2013; 1924); Gabriele Stave's *Gefährliches Terrain* (2011; 1923); Wilfried von Serényi's *Janus* (2011; 1930); as well as Jan Zweyer's *Franzosenliebchen* (2007; 1923) and *Goldfasan*

(2009; 1943). These *Krimis* are evidence of an increasing authorial interest in negotiating Germany's past via crime novels. This parallels a growing scholarly interest in criminal cases, and the role of the police, in Weimar and Nazi Germany.

[42] Korte and Paletschek, "Geschichte," 10.

[43] Lutz Feierabend and Tobias Kaufmann, "Ich bin kein Wanderprediger—Interview mit Volker Kutscher," *Kölner Stadtanzeiger*, Sept. 2011, http://www.ksta.de/kultur/volker-kutscher--ich-bin-kein-wanderprediger-,15189520,12066410.html.

[44] Kutscher's Gereon Rath novels not only successfully represent the new trend of the *Verarbeitungsroman*, but they also reaffirm character development as a crucial element of the crime-fiction formula.

[45] Korte and Paletschek, "Geschichte," 16.

[46] Knopp's multiepisode TV documentaries specifically focus on early twentieth-century German history. His *Hitlers* ... series is divided into several subtopics such as "Hitlers Helfer," "Hitlers Krieger," "Hitlers Kinder," and "Hitler's Frauen." In addition to the *Hitlers* ... series, Knopp's documentaries span from the political preconditions of National Socialism in Weimar Germany (e.g., "Die Machtergreifung") to the postwar aftermath of Nazi Germany (e.g., "Die Nürnberger Prozesse").

[47] Korte and Paletschek, "Geschichte," 16.

[48] Siegfried Kracauer, *Der Detektiv-Roman—Ein philosophischer Traktat* (Frankfurt am Main: Suhrkamp Taschenbuch Wissenschaft, 1979), 50–64.

[49] "Geschichtskrimis können aber darüber hinaus—und dies erklärt sich über die Entstehungsgeschichte und die Konventionen des Genres sowie die häufig behauptete Parallelität von historischem und detektivischem Ermitteln—erkenntnistheoretische Probleme von Geschichtsschreibung thematisieren" (Moreover, historical crime novels can thematize epistemological problems of historiography—and this can be explained with their evolutionary history, genre conventions as well as the frequently suggested parallels between historical and criminal investigation). Korte and Paletschek, "Geschichte," 20.

[50] Moretti, *Graphs*, 69.

3: Plurality and Alterity in Wolf Haas's Detective Brenner Mysteries

Jon Sherman

LIKE MOST PEOPLE, former police inspector Simon Brenner has some skeletons in his closet. Readers of the Austrian novelist Wolf Haas's (1960–) Brenner mysteries, however, are unaware of the detective's youthful transgression until the sixth novel in the series, *Das ewige Leben*.[1] The revelation of the detective's crime in the "last" mystery (Haas intended to end the series but wrote one more Brenner novel six years later) coincides with a number of important disclosures. The first is that *Das ewige Leben* finally reveals the identity of the narrator of Haas's novels. It is also the first of the Brenner mysteries with a more overt focus on race and ethnicity. And, as mentioned above, *Das ewige Leben* finally narrates the events of a bank robbery that took place long before *Auferstehung der Toten*, the first novel in the series.

Das ewige Leben reveals that when Simon Brenner was in the police academy, he and three other police cadets had robbed a bank. While studying various alarm systems, they began planning the robbery of the Raiffeisenkasse, a bank in Graz, as an intellectual exercise. The heist was scheduled to take place during *Fasching* (carnival), when intoxicated and costumed celebrators will help conceal the robbers' escape. Interestingly, the four police cadets decide to disguise themselves in traditional Austrian dress: "Der Saarinen hat gesagt, mit den Trachtenanzügen halten sie uns auf der Straße für verkleidet, aber in der Raiffeisenkasse halten sie uns für normal angezogen und auf der Flucht wieder für verkleidet, praktisch perfekte Tarnung" (44; Saarinen said that with the *Trachten* [traditional costumes] people on the street will think we are costumed, but in the bank they will think we are dressed normally and during our escape, again, as disguised, practically the perfect camouflage).[2]

So, chronologically speaking at least, the first crime in the Brenner mystery series is committed by none other than the protagonist Simon Brenner, a police cadet turned robber wearing a traditional Austrian *Tracht*: an Austrian masquerading as an Austrian. Although the reading audience is not aware of Brenner's criminal act until the sixth novel, viewed against the backdrop of police officers robbing a bank and

Austrians disguised as Austrians, Haas's mysteries can be read as an exploration of identity in a diverse and pluralistic society.

Haas has written seven mysteries that feature detective Simon Brenner. The first, *Auferstehung der Toten*, was published in 1996 and was awarded the Deutscher Krimi Preis. Two additional Brenner mysteries, *Komm, süßer Tod* and *Silentium!*, have also been recognized with this award. Three of the novels, *Komm, süßer Tod* (2000), *Silentium!* (2004), and *Der Knochenmann* (2009), have been adapted into successful films starring Josef Hader as detective Simon Brenner.[3] As the awards and interest in film adaptations imply, Haas's novels are entertaining mysteries; but they have also captivated audiences with their language, unique narrative voice,[4] and their exploration of "contemporary Austrian issues."[5] The Brenner mysteries are all set in Austria, though in different parts of the country, and they are, as Laura Detre has stated, "unabashedly Austrian in both tone and subject."[6] Long after the dissolution of the Habsburg Empire, modern Austria is still a multiethnic, multilingual, and multireligious society, and the popularity of Haas's novels is in no small part due to the author's ability to capture and describe the diversity and variety of contemporary society.

The Brenner mysteries, therefore, can be viewed as a portrait of modern Austria. Haas depicts the pluralistic and multicultural nation in which he lives, but unlike some of his contemporaries, he is less a critic than a portraitist. In interviews, Haas even avoids questions about specific issues, and claims not to judge the society he depicts.[7] Unlike the "aggressiven österreich-kritischen Ton" (aggressive, Austria-critical tone) found in some of Thomas Bernhard's work,[8] the style of Haas's novels imply that he is merely an observer. Detective Simon Brenner interacts with both the rich and the homeless. He visits brothels, the theater, abortion clinics, churches and art galleries. Brenner interviews actors, doctors, a transvestite, a shoe-saleswoman, Eastern European soccer players, and a fortune-teller. In short, the novels depict the plurality of a complex and multifaceted nation and are as interested in Austria's marginalized groups as they are in the veneer of homogeneity of the dominant culture.

Haas and the *Detektivroman*

The focus of the Brenner novels on contemporary Austrian society is perhaps even evident in the author's approach to the mystery genre. There are certain expectations associated with detective fiction and Haas's mysteries seem disinclined to follow even the most basic of these, placing his novels in a singular position in the category of crime fiction.[9] Richard Alewyn argues that murder is the core of both the crime novel (*Kriminalroman*) and the detective novel (*Detektivroman*), and claims that the difference lies in how the narrative is presented: "Der Kriminalroman erzählt die

Geschichte eines Verbrechens, der Detektivroman die Geschichte der Aufklärung eines Verbrechens" (The crime novel tells the story of a crime, the detective novel the story of the clarification of a crime).[10] Crime fiction traces the events chronologically from the crime's inception up the point where it is committed, and a detective novel begins at the crime and works backwards: "Wenn man sie mit dem zeitlichen Ablauf des erzählten Geschehens vergleicht, kann man die eine Form des Erzählens progressiv nennen, die andere invertiert oder rückläufig" (If you compare them with the chronological course of narrative events, you can call the one form of narrative 'progressive,' and the other 'inverted' or 'regressive').[11] The job of the detective is not to predict outcomes from a given scenario, but to unravel the facts that led up to an event, or as the great sleuth himself described it to Dr. Watson:

> Most people, if you describe a train of events to them, will tell you what the result would be. They can put those events together in their minds, and argue from them that something will come to pass. There are few people, however, who, if you told them a result, would be able to evolve from their own inner consciousness what the steps were which led up to that result. This power is what I mean when I talk about reasoning backward, or analytically.[12]

In both crime fiction and detective fiction, the crime, usually a murder, is the focus of the narrative. Although all seven Brenner novels contain a murder, and often more than one, the murder is, in most cases, not the crime that the detective first investigates. In fact, with the exception of the first two novels,[13] it is fair to say that this initial crime in the Brenner mysteries is of secondary significance. Peter Plener even calls the initial crime in *Silentium!* an "Ablenkung" (distraction)[14] and this crime is actually left unresolved as Brenner uncovers other, more disturbing truths. As Eike Muny has pointed out, the essence of the Brenner novels is not the mystery itself, but the way the mystery is presented.[15]

Haas's detective is also difficult to position in the traditional mystery genre, as he does not exactly fit into either of Helmut Heißenbüttel's detective types: "Es gibt bei den Detektiven ein klassisches Gegensatzpaar, den einen, der im rauhen bis rüden Einsatz so lange Gegner zusammendrischt (und natürlich zwischendurch auch selber zusammengedroschen wird), bis er heraus hat, wer es gewesen ist, und den anderen, der durch eine Mischung aus Faktenermittlung und kombinatorischer Rätselraterei das zunächst Verworrene und Undurchschaubare in plausible Zusammenhänge bringt und durchschaubar macht" (Regarding detectives there is a classical opposition: the one who continues to hammer opponents [and of course sometimes gets beaten himself] with his raw and abrasive efforts until he finds out who did it, and the other type, who through a mixture of factual investigation and computational puzzle-solving transforms what is at first convoluted and inscrutable into plausible context and makes it transparent).[16] Simon Brenner lies somewhere between these two poles. He is clearly not the Sherlock Holmes-type detective who is the "entspannter Darsteller der Ratio" (calm representative of rationality.)[17] Brenner often overlooks the obvious and his investigative method is even described by the narrator as being oddly circular and often unfocused. Brenner's only real claim to the keen, rational intellect one expects from a Hercule Poirot or a Miss Marple, is actually quite unusual. His powers of observation are, surprisingly, unconscious. The detective's subconscious mind works independently on the cases and provides him with, often overlooked or misunderstood, hints to help with the investigation.[18] Although Brenner shares a number of traits with hard-boiled detectives like Sam Spade, he is also not left solely to the obstinate plodding and brute-force battering that characterizes this type of investigator. As an investigator, Simon Brenner is an anomaly, which further shifts Haas's novels out of the conventional mystery genre.

The positioning of Haas's novels outside of the conventions of standard detective fiction is, however, not instantly apparent. Each of his mysteries, as the genre dictates, begins with a murder, or at least a dead body. Brenner, however, is not necessarily engaged in discovering the killer, and the initial death, even the central murder, is often less important than subsequent crimes and discoveries. The fifth Brenner novel, *Wie die Tiere*, illustrates this nicely. The novel begins with the death of Manu Prodinger, an animal lover who is ironically killed by a dog. Her death, however, is not thought to be foul play, nor is it later discovered that she was murdered. Prodinger's death, of course, plays an important role in the mystery, but it is entirely accidental. *Wie die Tiere* is not, therefore, a murder mystery in the strictest sense, until midway through the novel when Frau Hartwig, who disappeared, is discovered dead. More importantly, it is never Brenner's job to discover who killed her, although he does. Brenner is actually hired to find out who is leaving malicious surprises for the dogs in Vienna's Augarten. The detective solves the mystery he is hired to investigate halfway through *Wie die Tiere*. Brenner confronts Mali, an angry teenager who was maimed by a dog as a child, and his work is essentially completed, but during his investigation, the detective has also uncovered other unpleasant truths, which lead to his confrontation with Frau Hartwig's killer.

After the first Brenner novel, each subsequent mystery begins "Jetzt ist schon wieder was passiert" (once again something has happened),[19] which, if referring to a murder, furnishes the ideal beginning for a detective novel. As mentioned above, however, Haas plays with genre expectations and, in *Komm, süßer Tod*, for example, this statement refers to a run-over cat.[20] A similar disregard for the conventions of crime fiction can be found in the novel *Silentium!*, where Brenner is hired to investigate accusations of child molestation by a priest. When the now-adult accuser, Gottlieb, is found murdered, Brenner's job shifts into an entirely different investigation. Before the novel concludes, the detective uncovers corruption in the Salzburger Festspiele, extortion, prostitution, and human trafficking, and he investigates a number of subsequent murders. In the end, however, the priest and the molestation charges are essentially forgotten and the reader is left uncertain if Gottlieb was actually abused or not. Haas's novels are less concerned with the crimes the detective investigates than with the society in which these crimes take place.

The Setting

In a general sense, location and the crime scene itself are central elements in detective fiction, as Kyle Frackman has pointed out in this volume. Similarly, the setting of Haas's mysteries also plays an important role in positioning the Brenner novels to explore issues of Austrian identity. Haas's mysteries are set in locations that "represent the stereotypical tourist-Austria which is marketed all over the world."[21] Each location is described in detail with easily identifiable sites and landmarks.[22] Individually, the settings of the seven Brenner novels are quite specific, but taken as group, they create a geographic cross-section of modern Austria from the smallest rural towns to the capital of the former Habsburg Empire. The opening scene in *Auferstehung der Toten* takes place at a ski resort, the quintessence of Austria marketed abroad. The TV commentator's description of the town Klöch in *Der Knochenmann* reads like a tourist brochure advertising something out of *The Sound of Music*.[23] *Komm, süßer Tod* begins with an ambulance racing across Vienna along specific and recognizable streets: Plötzleinsdorfer Straße, down Gersthofer Straße onto Währinger Straße and finally onto Währinger Gürtel, before it arrives at the Allgemeines Krankenhaus (5, 8, 9, 10). Like *Der Knochenmann*, the novel *Silentium!* has a number of descriptions reminiscent of travel brochures, this time of Salzburg: "Mitten in der Stadt die zwei Berge, du stehst am Mönchsberg, von drüben schaut der Kapuzinerberg herüber, und im Tal dazwischen tausend Kirchen und Klöster aufgefädelt am grün blitzenden Salzachfluß, das mußt du dir vorstellen wie ein funkelndes Edelsteinkollier" (In the middle of the city [are] the two mountains, you stand on the Mönchsberg, and from across the way the Kapuzinerberg overlooks the scene, and in the valley between them thousands of churches and monasteries interwoven along the shining green Salzach river, you have to imagine it like a shining, bejeweled necklace).[24]

The locations and the circumstances of most of the Brenner novels (except *Das ewige Leben*) correspond to Haas's own biography, as Sigrid Nindl has pointed out.[25] Haas's birthplace, Maria Alm, is mere kilometers from Zell am See where *Auferstehung der Toten* is set.[26] Haas attended the Borromäum Gymnasium in Salzburg, which is reminiscent of the Marianum, the school in which Gottlieb's body is found in *Silentium!* Frequent trips to the Steiermark, his mother's birthplace, during his childhood provided background for the town Klöch in *Der Knochenmann*.[27] But the choice of settings for each of the Brenner novels is far more significant than Nindl's observation about the correlation between Haas's biography and the locations of his mysteries. With the seven Brenner novels Haas has created a portrait of modern Austria. Helga Schreckenberger's claim that "more important than the murders themselves is their setting"[28] is not an exaggeration. The allure of Haas's works is often found more in his descriptions of places and people than in mystery.

Like the setting of each novel, Brenner's living situation and current occupation in each mystery provide additional opportunities for the author to depict a cross-section of contemporary Austrian society. In the first novel, Brenner, like a typical ski tourist, is staying at a hotel in Zell am See for the course of his investigation.[29] In *Der Knochenmann*, Brenner is put up in the workers' quarters of the *Grillstation*, the restaurant he is hired to investigate. In *Komm, süßer Tod*, Brenner lives in the dingy barracks used by the ambulance drivers. The detective is housed in the prefects' wing of the boarding school in *Silentium!*, and in *Wie die Tiere*, he stays in an apartment above a brothel owned by his new employer, which he shares with a Polish prostitute. In the sixth and supposedly final Brenner novel, when the detective returns to his hometown of Graz, he temporarily moves into his deceased grandfather's house. And in the seventh and final Brenner mystery, the detective is working as a chauffeur in Vienna and living in the Kressdorf's employee quarters. When he is fired for incompetence, he essentially becomes homeless and spends his nights with a girlfriend. As Schreckenberger indicates: "Brenner lives on the margins of society. He has no fixed address or regular income, but constantly moves around taking on odd jobs to make ends meet."[30]

Simon Brenner's changing occupations in the seven novels—police officer, private detective, ambulance driver, mall security officer, and chauffeur—also allow him to interact with various strata of Austrian society.[31] Dr. Watson's comment in *A Study in Scarlet* that Sherlock Holmes "had many acquaintances, and those in the most different classes of society"[32] could also be applied to Simon Brenner. He begins his career as a police officer in Salzburg. At the outset of the first novel, however, Brenner resigns from the Kripo (Kriminalpolizei) and returns to Zell am See as a private detective working for an insurance company. Brenner's job frequently forces him into "eine für ihn ungewohnte Umgebung" (an unusual environment for him),[33] allowing him to hobnob with Austria's elite at the Salzburger Festspiele in *Silentium!*, share an apartment with a prostitute in *Wie die Tiere*, interview an artist in a brothel in *Der Knochenmann*, and take a beating at the hands of street thugs in *Brenner und der liebe Gott*. His lack of a permanent residence and his frequently changing occupation allow Haas's mysteries to depict both a geographic and social cross-section of modern Austria.

Language and Linguistic Outsiders

Das klingt natürlich fürchterlich, wenn du es von einer Zigeunerin gesagt kriegst.

—Wolf Haas, *Das ewige Leben*

The success of the Brenner novels can be attributed in part to the unique narrative voice that permeates them. The narrator is perhaps a more tangible presence than the protagonist himself.[34] In *Das ewige Leben*, this narrative presence solidifies into a character, transitioning from an extradiegetic narrator to a diegetic one.[35] When the narrator speaks directly to the reader, often repeating the phrases "Pass auf" or "Ob du es glaubst oder nicht" throughout the series of novels, the audience can almost hear his voice.[36] When he criticizes Brenner's decisions or comments on Austrian society, a distinct personality emerges. The narrative voice in Haas's mysteries blends eloquent literary language with slang and colloquialisms, and mixes standard High German with Austrian dialect[37] in a way that creates immediacy and a feeling of connection between the reader and the storyteller. Even before the revelation of the narrator's identity in *Das ewige Leben*, the reader has a sense of him as a person.

This unique narrative voice and the importance of language as a stylistic device in the Brenner novels are not surprising. Haas studied linguistics at the University of Salzburg and graduated with a dissertation on the linguistic foundations of concrete poetry.[38] Nindl even argues that the language of the Brenner novels is more important than the plots: "Die Handlung ist jedoch nicht das Wesentliche in den Simon-Brenner-Romanen, sondern dient vielmehr als Rahmen für die sprachliche Stilisierung" (The plot, however, is not the essence of the Simon Brenner novels, but serves more as a frame for the linguistic stylization),[39] an assertion that Florian Sänger echoes.[40] But as a linguist, Haas was not only concerned with language as a medium to create his mysteries, but he was also interested in the role it plays within them. Language is an essential element in identity creation, and this is especially true in Austria. Similar to religion, politics and social class, language is a marker of inclusion in or exclusion from a group, and the characters in Haas's novels (not just the nonnative speakers) are identified in part by their ability to speak German. Lying in a hospital bed at the end of *Der Knochenmann*, Brenner explains to Jacky the role language plays in the perception of people: "Wenn heute ein Mensch deine Sprache nicht kann, glaubst du automatisch, daß er ein bißchen blöd ist. Aber der Milovanovic alles andere als blöd" (150; If someone today cannot speak your language, you automatically assume, that he is a little slow. But Milovanovic [was] anything but slow).

Haas's personal interest in language is mirrored in the linguistic awareness of both his protagonist and narrator. Brenner, out of principle, attempts to speak only "korrektes Deutsch" with children and foreigners, an effort that is humorously contrasted with his own linguistic shortcomings. A conversation in *Der Knochenmann* between Brenner and the Klöch goalie Milovanovic illustrates that the detective has given some thought to the topic, even if he is inconsistent in his efforts:

> "Gestern sind Sie ja gewaltig in Form gewesen," sagt der Brenner. Weil er ist der Meinung gewesen, man muß mit Ausländern ordentliches Deutsch reden, sonst lernen sie es nie.
> "'tschuldige?"
> "Gestern. Gewaltig in Form gewesen!"
> "'tschuldige, nix gut Deutsch."
> "Gratuliere! Nix Tor gekriegt gegen Oberwart!" sagt der Brenner, und da siehst du, wie schnell ein guter Vorsatz zerbröstelt. (20)
>
> ["Yesterday you were in top form," Brenner said. He was of the opinion that one should speak proper German with foreigners, otherwise they would never learn.
> "sorry?"
> "Yesterday. Top form!"
> "sorry, no good German."
> "Congratulations! Not goal scored against Oberwart!" Brenner said, and there you see how quickly the best intentions evaporate.]

A similar comment is made in *Brenner und der liebe Gott*, when the narrator points out that Brenner more consistently applies the same theory to the two-year-old Helena as well: "'Ich bring dir eine Schockolade mit,' hat er beim Aussteigen gesagt, weil nie 'Schoggi' oder irgendwie Babysprache, sondern der Fahrer immer korrektes Deutsch mit der Helena, aus Prinzip" (11; "I will bring some chocolate back for you," he said as he got out, because [he never said] chocki or any type of babytalk; instead the driver always used correct German with Helena, out of principle).

His good intentions regarding language aside, Brenner himself is, as this evidence from *Der Knochenmann* testifies, "nicht besonders begabt für Fremdsprachen" (19; not particularly talented with foreign languages), and occasionally has a difficult time with the grammar of his native tongue. In *Auferstehung der Toten*, when the journalist Mandl refers to Brenner as a police officer, even though he is no longer with the police, the detective asks "Zu was soll das sein, daß du immer Polizei zu mir sagst?" (20; What do you keep saying "police" to me for?). In his response, Mandl not only avoids answering Brenner's question, but persists in addressing him as a police inspector, and instead focuses on Brenner's grammar: "Wozu, Inspektor! Es heißt: wozu. Weil zu was haben wir eine Grammatik?" (20; Why, inspector, it should be: why. For, what do we have grammar for?)

Brenner's awareness of language is also evident in his ability to hear different accents in nonnative German speakers and to recognize various Austrian dialects. His conversations with the Polish prostitute Magdalena in *Wie die Tiere* provide one example. Brenner and Magdalena share an apartment above a brothel in Vienna. Although Magdalena plays a relatively small role in the novel, she is central to the successful solution of Brenner's case and their morning coffee is not only a humorous parody of married life,[41] it is essential to Brenner's investigative process. But Brenner is also always conscious of the fact that Magdalena is speaking Polish-German while the narrator reminds the audience that they are from vastly different geographic, and thus linguistic, backgrounds: "Der Brenner aus Puntigam und Magdalena aus Polen haben sich die kleine Wohnung über dem *White Dog* geteilt" (71; Brenner from Puntigam and Magdalena from Poland shared the small apartment above the White Dog). Magdalena's questions and comments reflect the type of language that a nonnative speaker of German would produce: "ich glaube nicht, dass du bei die Mütter viel findest" (131; I don't think that you will find much with the muther [*sic*]) or "Warum rufst du nicht endlich Kollege an?" (132; why don't you finally call friend?). And in the course of their friendship, Brenner "ist aufgefallen, dass die Magdalena gute Fortschritte mit ihrem Deutsch gemacht hat" (130; noticed that Magdalena's German was improving). Brenner and the narrator are acutely aware of language. Especially their interest in and reflections on how people speak redirects the readers' focus toward issues of language and identity, and often away from the actual mystery.

Language and accent also play an important role in Brenner's ability to hide his identity by disguising his voice. In *Wie die Tiere*, when Brenner needs to ascertain if someone is at home, he uses an "alte[n] Trick, anrufen und Entschuldigung, falsch verbunden" (138; old trick, call and apologize, wrong number). For this trick, the detective often disguises his voice by using a foreign accent: "Er hat sich im Laufe der Jahre ein, zwei Stimmen zugelegt, die für ein kurzes 'tschuldigung' gereicht haben. Oft hat er noch zusätzlich ein bisschen den jugoslawischen Akzent verwendet, 'tschuldige, nix richtige Nummer', dann natürlich perfekte Tarnung" (139; Over the years he had acquired one or two voices, which sufficed for a quick "sorry." In addition, he often used a Yugoslav accent, "sorry, not right number," then naturally the ideal deception). At one point, he disguises his voice by imitating Magdalena's Polish accent: "Er hat es ja so gut im Ohr gehabt, wie die Magdalena redet, jetzt Idee: Probiere ich es einmal polnisch statt mit Jugo-Akzent" (139; The way Magdalena spoke was still so clear in his mind, he thought, I will try it with a Polish, instead of a Yugoslav, accent). And just as Brenner is able to imitate foreign accents, he is also adept at recognizing Austrian dialects. In *Brenner und der liebe Gott*, the detective opens a conversation with an important witness by impressing her à la Sherlock Holmes. Instead of greeting her or introducing himself, he guesses she is from Südtirol based on one word she said while buying cigarettes (78–79). The idea of linguistic identification is even addressed with regards to the Austrian-born children of nonnative speakers of German. Again in *Brenner und der liebe Gott*, Frau Doktor Kressdorf comments on one variety of *Ausländer-Deutsch*: "Ich weiß wirklich nur ihren Vornamen. Und den hat sie mir in diesem Ausländer-Wienerisch gesagt. Wie die Kinder reden, die schon hier geboren sind, aber daheim wird noch eine andere Sprache gesprochen" (141; I really only know her first name. And she told it to me in that foreigner-Viennese. The way the children speak who were born here, but speak another language at home).

Language plays an even more salient role in social identification in *Das ewige Leben*. Not only does Brenner have the expected linguistic difficulties in his interactions with the various Roma he encounters, but language is also one focus of the hate-group's anti-Roma rhetoric.[42] The leader of the *Initiativ Grazer Sicherheit* (the city of Graz's security initiative) is concerned that so few people on the streets of Austria speak German—that is, that there are too many foreigners in the country. In the past, he claims, things were better "weil es eine gemeinsame Sprache noch gab, weil man nicht einen Passanten auf der Straße, den man um eine Auskunft bitten wollte, zuerst fragen musste, sprechen Sie Deutsch . . . weil eine Frau, ein Kind auf offener Straße nicht dreisprächig um Hilfe rufen musste, damit es vielleicht doch einmal verstanden wird" (148; because there was still a common language, because one didn't need to ask a person on the street if he spoke German first, before asking him for information . . . because a woman, a child on a public street did not have to yell in three languages for help, so that it could perhaps be understood).

Against the backdrop of hate speeches, Brenner's interaction with the Roma palm reader is almost humorous. Before she can even open her mouth, Brenner assumes that she does not understand much German: and this time he is actually correct. When she answers the door, he says "Handlesen" (palm reading) and then explains his one-word utterance with "Zukunft! Vergangenheit!" (86; future! past!). Brenner even talks about language to make conversation. The woman is singing to herself (*"Te me pijav laches rosnes"*) while she reads his palm and Brenner asks what the words mean, hoping to establish a bond through their shared language difficulties. She teaches him the words and then explains their meaning. The woman translates the line, understandably, into poor German: "Wenn ich mir betrinken tu, ich viel traurig" (89; When I get drunk, I much sad). Brenner connects these words to the Puntigamer beer jingle "Lustig samma, Puntigamer," the first words he uttered when he woke up from his coma. As Brenner mumbles "traurig samma" (89; we are sad), the woman repeats his words "weil sie hat geglaubt, der Brenner will ihr Deutsch verbessern" (89; because she thought that Brenner wanted to correct her German). The Roma woman displays the typical expectation and response of a nonnative speaker when interacting with a native speaker. She is aware that her German is not that good and perceives the meanderings of Brenner's mind as the expected correction of her grammar. Her confusion is perhaps mirrored in the narrator's unusually uninformed[43] description of her language as "zigeunerisch" (89; Gypsy), rather than Romani.

This scene further highlights the significance of language through another humorous misunderstanding, this time on Brenner's part. After examining his palm, the woman says, again in poorly pronounced German, "Brena abgraz ibermorgen" (92; Brena away day after tumoro). Brenner misunderstands and believes she is predicting his death. The narrator's ambiguous comment, "Das klingt natürlich fürchterlich, wenn du es von einer Zigeunerin gesagt kriegst" (92; That, of course, sounds horrible, when a Gypsy says it to you) could relate to the content of her statement (as Brenner perceives it) or to the way it was said—that is, to the language. Brenner finally understands when she elaborates and says "Zug" (train), but by this point Brenner begins to have an elastic and associative approach to language and decides that "'Zug,' ein hässliches Wort. Nur drei Buchstaben. Vorne ein 'Z' und hinten ein 'g.' Und in der Mitte ein 'u.' Eine gewisse Ähnlichkeit mit dem Wort 'Tod'" (94; *Zug* [train], an ugly word. Only three letters. At the front a 'z' and at the end a 'g.' And in the middle a 'u.' A certain similarity to the word *Tod* [death]). The Roma woman has limited German skills. Although Brenner recognizes accents, he is, somewhat surprisingly, not that adept at understanding nonnative speakers of German. More interestingly, Brenner's brain has taken his initial misunderstanding of her poor German and forced his later, correct understanding to mirror it. Language in Haas's mysteries plays a central role not only in identity formation, but also in the perception and understanding of others.

Ethnicity

Like modern Austria, Haas's mysteries are filled with a vast array of people with diverse cultural traditions and varied ethnicities. In most of the novels, this is not overtly thematized, but is simply part of contemporary society.

Milovanovic and Ortovic, two soccer players in *Der Knochenmann*, are nonnative speakers of German and foreign nationals living and working in Austria. As discussed above, Milovanovic's German is a focus of Brenner's ruminations on language and perception, but little attention is accorded to ethnicity or the related issues of intolerance and *Ausländerfeindlichkeit* (xenophobia). Hints of societal prejudices and fears are, however, present. Goran Milovanovic is first introduced in the novel as "der Jugo" (the Yugoslavian) by Herr Löschenkohl (9), and is not actually named until significantly later. The first murder victim in the mystery was a mercenary from the former Yugoslavia. Like Goran Milovanovic and Helena Jurasic, a prostitute from Eastern Europe, Ortovic is also from the former Yugoslavia and is an abusive boyfriend and an extortionist. Although *Der Knochenmann* does not focus overtly on Austrian fears of foreigners immigrating from the East, many Slavs in the novel are associated with drugs, prostitution, gun smuggling, and other scandals. Coupled with the dehumanization of Goran Milovanovic inherent in the designation "der Jugo," *Der Knochenmann* hints at some of the racial and ethnic tension that will become more prominent in *Das ewige Leben*.

In *Silentium!*, another minority group plays a significant role in Brenner's murder investigation. Women from the Philippines are being used to service the wealthy clientele of the Salzburger Festspiele in a prostitution and human trafficking ring. Brenner's initial investigation of the child-molestation accusations is quickly transformed into a murder case after Gottlieb's mutilated body is found in the boys' shower in the Marianum. As the detective examines Gottlieb's life, his trail leads him away from a church scandal and, eventually, places him in contact with a woman from the Philippines who worked on the cleaning staff of the boys' dorm during Gottlieb's school years. When she is murdered, Brenner uncovers a connection between the Philippine women, nominally imported as cleaning staff but forced into prostitution, and the Salzburger Festspiele. At the conclusion of *Silentium!*, the sexual abuse and church cover-up are forgotten in light of the multiple murders committed to protect the human trafficking ring. Similar to the depiction of Slavs in *Der Knochenmann*, the role of the Philippine women—both their forced prostitution and their working conditions—is of tertiary significance in the novel, but once again hints at prejudices and societal tension relating to ethnicity.

In each of the Brenner mysteries, the central crimes become progressively more convoluted and Haas's later mysteries move further away from the standard detective-novel format. The first crime in *Das ewige Leben*, the sixth of the Brenner novels, seems to be the shooting of Simon Brenner, which turns out to be a self-inflicted, drunken suicide attempt. The subsequent murder of the detective's friend, Köck, slowly becomes the core of Brenner's investigation. Two Roma, who were seen near the crime scene, are wanted by the police for questioning. Law enforcement's attempt to ascertain if the Roma witnessed anything is used by an overly patriotic, xenophobic group, the IGS (*Initiativ Grazer Sicherheit*), to incite xenophobia, and the group transforms these potential witnesses into murder suspects. Brenner's search for the two men and the information they might possess is in the end fruitless, but this story-line allows *Das ewige Leben* to develop a more concrete focus on stereotypes, ethnicity, and societal intolerance than the earlier Brenner novels.

The IGS desires an Austria free of foreigners. They use hate speech directed at the inability of *Ausländer* (foreigners) to speak German as a battle cry to incite fear and distrust of outsiders. They also blame the foreigners residing in the city of Graz for the city's high crime rate, and claim that the city used to be a better place because formerly "noch nicht an jeder Kreuzung ein Drogenhändler, ein Bettler, ein Zigeuner, ein Neger gestanden ist" (149; there wasn't a drug dealer, a beggar, a Gypsy, an African at every street corner). The group is not taken seriously by the police, who consider it marginal and without public support, but this position becomes questionable when the two Roma are found murdered. As is often the case in Haas's mysteries, the death of these two men has nothing to do with racial prejudices as Brenner first assumed, but his suspicions, and therefore the reader's, make xenophobia and intolerance an important, if in the end unrelated, aspect of the crimes in *Das ewige Leben*.

Gender Identity and Sexuality

Another identity issue as topical in modern Austria as elsewhere in the world is that of gender and sexuality. As with the other social issues that Haas addresses in his mysteries, these never become the focus of the narrative. Instead, Haas incorporates them into his novel as part of the mosaic that is contemporary society. The fact that the missing artist in *Der Knochenmann* has been dressing as a woman and working as a waitress for almost a year comes as a surprise to Brenner, but nothing more.[44] The detective's room in the workers' quarters of the *Grillstation* is adjacent to the waitress's, and he wakes up one morning realizing that he heard the missing artist Horvath in her room: "Wie der Brenner am nächsten Morgen aufgewacht ist, hat er zuerst natürlich geglaubt: Traum. Weil wenn der Mensch etwas nicht wissen will, dann hofft er zuerst einmal, es ist nur ein Traum. Aber nein, es ist kein Traum gewesen, daß er im Zimmer der Kellnerin den Horvath gefunden hat" (97; When Brenner woke up the next morning, he naturally first thought: a dream. Because when a person does not want to know something, he first hopes that it was only a dream. But no, it wasn't a dream that he had found Horvath in the waitress's room). As Brenner's investigation proceeds, the detective interviews the artist Palfinger to find out more about the missing artist

Horvath. Brenner does not uncover Horvath's whereabouts, but is told that Horvath was bulimic: "Er [Horvath] hat ja an dieser Freßsucht gelitten. Fressen, kotzen, fressen, kotzen, fressen, kotzen" (104; He suffered from bulimia. Binge, purge, binge, purge, binge, purge) and Brenner's first thought is "das haben doch normal nur Frauen" (104; normally only women do that). Suddenly Brenner realizes that he did not hear two people in the waitress's room the night before, and he then wonders if Palfinger knew about Horvath: "Oder hat er es wirklich nicht gewußt, daß der Horvath seit fast einem Jahr als Kellnerin in der Grillstation Löschenkohl gearbeitet hat" (105; or did he really not know that Horvath had been working for almost a year as a waitress in the Grillstation Löschenkohl). At this point Brenner also begins to realize what has happened at the *Grillstation* although he is unaware of the identity of the first murder victim and is still uncertain of the killer. He suspects the waitress Horvath, in part because she has a secret, but Brenner hopes she is not the killer: "Sicher, die Kellnerin ist ihm [Brenner] sympathisch gewesen. Mir [the narrator] auch sympathisch, das gebe ich ehrlich zu" (109; Brenner certainly liked the waitress. Me too, I readily admit). Brenner confronts the waitress in the dining area of the *Grillstation* and she voices what she thinks are Brenner's suspicions: "Ein Mann, der sich als Kellnerin ausgibt, mit dem muss was nicht in Ordnung sein" (113; A man who pretends to be a waitress, something has to be wrong with him), to which Brenner answers "Nicht unbedingt" (113; not necessarily). Although Brenner is initially surprised by his discovery, in the end he is not troubled by a man dressing as a woman. The waitress decides to tell Brenner her story and leaves to change. Horvath returns in Brenner's clothing, which she borrows from his room: "Ich habe kein Männergewand mehr gehabt" (114; I no longer have any men's clothing), reinforcing the idea that she has now entirely abandoned her life as a man.

The waitress takes Brenner to a nearby workshop where she grew up and tells him: "Wie ich siebzehn Jahre alt gewesen bin, habe ich meinen ersten Freund gehabt . . . wir haben uns jede Nacht hier in der Werkstatt getroffen. Die Leute haben ihn fast erschlagen wie es aufgekommen ist." (120; When I was seventeen I had my first boyfriend . . . we met every evening here in the shop. The people in town almost beat him to death when they found out). Horvath's boyfriend returned to the workshop while the family was at church and turned on the band saw "so hat er sich vorbereiten können. Weil in den Himmel kommst du ja nicht, wenn du dir selber den Hals abschneidest" (120; thus preparing himself. Because you can't go to heaven, if you cut your own throat), implying that Horvath's family killed him. Brenner's discovery of Horvath's secret, Horvath's revelation of her childhood love, and the hate-crime committed against her boyfriend play no further role in the mystery. At the end of *Der Knochenmann*, the killer—the owner of the *Grillstation*—is brought to justice. Horvath's life and the fact that she is a cross-dresser are not further addressed. She is simply one of the many diverse individuals living in a complex and varied modern Austria.

Wolfgang Murnberger's film *Der Knochenmann*, cowritten with Wolf Haas, further emphasizes this theme. Haas, Hader, and Murnberger's cinematic adaptation includes a description and photos of Horvath's impending gender-reassignment surgery, which is never mentioned in the novel. Additionally, Brenner's rather sexist Casanova-like friend Berti is not only curious about the cross-dressing waitress, but sexually interested. To an even greater extent than the novel, the film not only avoids judgment of Horvath's choices, but reintegrates her into the narrative by providing a potential love-interest. This does not significantly change, nor diminish, the characterization of the waitress in the novel, but within the film's condensed story, serves to draw even more attention to Horvath's character.

Conclusion

What is perhaps most telling about the author's intent with the Brenner novels is the gradual loss of interest throughout the series in what is usually the focus of crime fiction: the initial crime. The first Haas mystery, *Auferstehung der Toten*, follows a more traditional detective-story formula. The novel begins with a murder. A detective investigates the murder. And in the final pages of the narrative, the detective confronts the killer, his questions are answered, and the murderer is taken away by the authorities. A case could be made that the murder slowly becomes secondary for most of the narrative, but the formula is essentially that of most detective novels. *Der Knochenmann*, the second Brenner mystery, however, is a different story. Like *Auferstehung der Toten*, the novel begins with a murder, which is followed by a number of additional killings committed to cover up the first death. During the investigation, however, Brenner uncovers human trafficking, Eastern European women who are forced into prostitution, multiple soccer scandals, drug-dealers, a kidnapping, father-son conflicts, genital-mutilating war injuries, an extortion scandal, a cross-dressing waitress, and a homophobic murder, all of which are completely unrelated to the first murder. By the time Brenner confronts the killer, the reader has almost forgotten the initial crime. In *Der Knochenmann*, the classic detective-story scene, in which the investigator reveals all, does not even mention the first death (150–52). Not until page 131 does Brenner realize who the killer is. The first murder is mentioned, but the comment is brief and no details or motivations are provided. Only at the very end of the novel, long after realizing that Löschenkohl was the killer, does Brenner actually understand the motivation for the mercenary's death; and this revelation occurs while the detective is being attacked by a meat-cleaver wielding Löschenkohl. The waitress Horvath knew all along that her boss Löschenkohl was the killer, but she would not give up her dream of leading a normal life as a waitress for some shady mercenary: "Außerdem hat es der Horvath verstehen können, daß sein Chef, der selber mit sechzehn in den Krieg gehetzt worden ist, aus dem Söldner-Vermittler Fleisch gemacht hat" (137; and moreover Horvath could understand that his boss, who himself was drafted at sixteen, made hamburger meat out of the mercenary recruiter). This brief explanation, given while Brenner is being attacked, is all Haas chooses to provide his audience. And *Silentium!*, the fourth Brenner mystery, does not even resolve the initial crime, the question of Gottlieb's molestation.

Wolf Haas's Brenner mysteries are less preoccupied with the traditional issues central to most crime fiction and instead explore the vast array of people, value systems, religions, languages, ethnicities, sexualities, and gender identities characteristic of modern Austria. Characters and their backgrounds are more fully developed than their compatriots in more traditional detective stories; as Gunther Martens has commented, "Einblick in die Innenwelt von Nebenfiguren ist im Krimi relativ selten, da diese üblicherweise noch als mögliche Täter in Betracht kommen und deshalb möglichst rätselhaft bleiben sollten" (Insight into the inner workings of supporting characters is seldom provided in detective stories, because they are potential suspects and should therefore remain mysterious);[45] but these *Nebenfiguren* are the core of Haas's narratives. While the traditional detective story "seems to discourage the unlimited rereading associated with serious writing,"[46] Haas's mysteries merit multiple readings. Initial crimes are left unsolved, investigations are abandoned, and new truths about people and places are uncovered. Social issues currently of concern in Austria—including many not discussed in this essay—are examined in greater detail than, for instance, the motivation for the initial murder in *Der Knochenmann* or the kidnapping in *Brenner und der liebe Gott*. Along with themes of identity, these issues play important roles in Haas's novels. The Nazi past is discussed in connection with the *Staudamm* in *Auferstehung der Toten*.[47] Religion and homelessness are repeatedly addressed in *Silentium!*, and abortion is initially believed to be the reason for the kidnapping in *Brenner und der liebe Gott*. The focus of the seven Simon Brenner novels is not the crimes the detective investigates, but the diverse and pluralistic society in which these crimes take place.

Notes

[1] Wolf Haas has written seven novels featuring detective Simon Brenner. In order of publication they are *Auferstehung der Toten* [Resurrection] (Reinbek bei Hamburg: Rowohlt, 1996); *Der Knochenmann* [The Bone Man] (Reinbek

bei Hamburg: Rowohlt, 1997); *Komm, süßer Tod* [Come, Sweet Death] (Reinbek bei Hamburg: Rowohlt, 1998); *Silentium!* [Silence] (Reinbek bei Hamburg: Rowohlt, 1999); *Wie die Tiere* [Like Animals] (Reinbek bei Hamburg: Rowohlt, 2001); *Das ewige Leben* [Eternal Life] (Hamburg: Hoffmann und Campe Verlag, 2003); and *Brenner und der liebe Gott* [Brenner and God] (Hamburg: Hoffmann und Campe Verlag, 2009).

[2] Haas, *Das ewige Leben*, 44.

[3] There were also plans to film *Das ewige Leben*, but at the time this essay was written, the project was unconfirmed and without a fixed release date.

[4] Gunther Martens, "'Aber wenn du von einem Berg springst, ist es wieder umgekehrt.' Zur Erzählerprofilierung in den Meta-Krimis von Wolf Haas," *Modern Austrian Literature* 39, no. 1 (2006): 66, and Sigrid Nindl, "Jetzt wird schon wieder was analysiert . . .," in *Gesprochen—Geschrieben—Gedichte* (Berlin: Erich Schmidt Verlag, 2009), 103–15.

[5] Helga Schreckenberger, "The Destruction of Idyllic Austria in Wolf Haas's Detective Novels," in *Crime and Madness in Modern Austria*, ed. Rebecca S. Thomas (Newcastle upon Tyne, UK: Cambridge Scholars Publishing, 2008), 429.

[6] Laura A. Detre, "Wolf Haas: The Weather Fifteen Years Ago (Review)," *Modern Austrian Literature* 43, no. 3 (2010): 112.

[7] "sich nicht als 'Kritiker' der von ihm geschilderten 'Milieus' (Rotkreuz, Klosterschule, . . .) eingeschätzt wissen oder sich von realen und medienwirksamen Affären eingeholt sehen will." Martens, "Aber wenn du von einem Berg springst," 78.

[8] Manfred Mittermayer, "Das Schweigen der Salzburger: Zur Verfilmung des Romans *Silentium!* von Wolf Haas durch Wolfgang Murnberger," in *Gegenwartsliteratur* 7 (2008): 140.

[9] Florian Sänger, *Literatur und Film im Feld narrativer Theorien* (Aachen: Shaker Verlag, 2009), 73.

[10] Richard Alewyn, "Anatomie des Detektivromans," in *Der Kriminalroman II*, ed. Jochen Vogt (Munich: Fink, 1971), 375.

[11] Alewyn, "Anatomie des Detektivromans," 374.

[12] Sir Arthur Conan Doyle, *Sherlock Holmes: The Complete Novels and Stories*, vol. 1 (New York: Random House, 1986), 115–16.

[13] Even in the first Brenner novel *Auferstehung der Toten*, which more or less follows the genre-established pattern of murder-investigation-resolution, the secondary crimes and scandals are surprisingly complex and almost overshadow the initial crime. See also Anita McChesney, "The Case of the Regional Austrian Crime Novel" in this volume.

[14] Peter Plener, "404 Ding. Über die Kriminalromane von Wolf Haas," in *Neues: Trends und Motive in der (österreichischen) Gegenwartsliteratur*, ed. Friedbert Aspetsberger (Innsbruck: StudienVerlag, 2003), 123.

[15] Eike Muny, "Erzählen ohne Ewigkeit: Strategien der Aussparung bei Wolf Haas," in *Schrift-Zeichen: Poetologische Konstellationen von der Frühen Neuzeit bis*

zur Postmoderne, ed. Jan Broch and Markus Rassiller (Köln: Kleine Schriften der Üniversitäts- und Stadtsbibliothek, 2006), 225.

[16] Helmut Heißenbüttel, "Spielregel des Kriminalromans," in *Der Kriminalroman II*, ed. Jochen Vogt (Munich: Fink, 1971), 356.

[17] Siegfried Kracauer, "Detektiv," in *Der Kriminalroman II*, ed. Jochen Vogt (Munich: Fink, 1971), 345.

[18] This unconscious hint usually takes the form of a song, which the detective finds himself whistling, only to realize later that the lyrics explain a connection or clue on which his mind was currently focused. This revelation, however, tends to happen after other information has also pointed him towards a similar conclusion.

[19] *Auferstehung der Toten* begins "Von Amerika aus betrachtet, ist Zell ein winziger Punkt" (5; Viewed from America, Zell is a tiny dot). The seventh Brenner novel, *Brenner und der liebe Gott*, which takes place after the death of the narrator, begins "Meine Großmutter hat immer zu mir gesagt, wenn du einmal stirbst, muss man das Maul extra erschlagen" (5; My grandmother always said to me, when you die, they will have to kill your mouth separately). *Der Knochenmann; Komm, süßer Tod; Silentium!; Wie die Tiere;* and *Das ewige Leben* begin as mentioned with the almost infamous "Jetzt ist schon wieder was passiert."

[20] Moritz Baßler, *Der deutsche Pop-Roman* (Munich: C. H. Beck Verlag, 2006), 192.

[21] Schreckenberger, "The Destruction of Idyllic Austria," 427.

[22] Sigrid Nindl devotes a chapter to "Österreichisches Lokalkolorit" in *Wolf Haas und sein kriminalistisches Sprachexperiment* (Berlin: Erich Schmidt Verlag, 2010), 286–94. See also McChesney's essay in this volume.

[23] Schreckenberger points this out in regard to the contrast between the idyllic setting of the town Klöch and the gruesome murders that have taken place there. Schreckenberger, "The Destruction of Idyllic Austria," 427.

[24] Haas, *Silentium!*, 26. Manfred Baumann's description of Salzburg in *Zauberflötenrache* also includes the Kapuzinerberg, Mönchsberg, churches, and the Salzach River, which he describes as a *Silberband*. The similarities are not so striking as to indicate a common source, but instead point to both authors' familiarity with travel brochure language: "Der Kapuzinerberg ist einer der beiden dominierende Stadtberge in Salzburg. Er liegt gegenüber dem Mönchsberg, an dessen Fuß sich der Festspielbezirk erstreckt. Zwischen den beiden Stadtbergen schlängelt sich das Silberband der Salzach. Die Stadt mit ihren Häusern und Kirchen, Straßen und Plätzen schmiegt sich in den geschützten Raum zwischen den Flanken der Erhebungen wie in ein Nest." Manfred Baumann, *Zauberflötenrache* (Pößneck, Germany: Gmeiner, 2012), 74.

[25] Nindl, "Jetzt wird schon wieder," 104; and Franz Haas, "Aufklärung in Österreich. Die erhellenden Kriminalromane von Wolf Haas," in *Mord als kreativer Prozess. Zum Kriminalroman der Gegenwart in Deutschland, Österreich und der Schweiz*, ed. Sandro Moraldo (Heidelberg: Winter Verlag, 2005), 127–28.

[26] Nindl, "Jetzt wird schon wieder," 104.

[27] Nindl also demonstrates biographical correspondences for the other Brenner mystery settings, except for Graz (*Das ewige Leben*), a city in which Haas never lived or worked. Nindl, "Jetzt wird schon wieder," 104. *Das ewige Leben* was commissioned by the city when Graz was celebrated as a Kulturhauptstadt. Nindl, *Wolf Haas*, 64.

[28] Schreckenberger, "The Destruction of Idyllic Austria," 426.

[29] Brenner begins the novel as a police detective investigating the murdered Americans and subsequently quits his job, but continues the investigation as a private detective working for the relevant insurance company.

[30] Schreckenberger, "The Destruction of Idyllic Austria," 430.

[31] Mittermayer, "Das Schweigen der Salzburger," 143.

[32] Doyle, *Sherlock Holmes*, 15.

[33] Mittermayer, "Das Schweigen der Salzburger," 138.

[34] Plener, "404 Ding," 107; and 115.

[35] Sänger, *Literatur und Film*, 77; and Martens, "'Aber wenn du von einem Berg springst,'" 75.

[36] Although Peter Plener demonstrates that Haas's grammar and diction are highly stylized and artificial, and therefore not "aus dem Alltag transkribiert worden" (directly transcribed from everyday life), the result for the reader is still a sense of everyday, colloquial speech. Plener, "404 Ding," 112.

[37] Nindl, "Jetzt wird schon wieder," 105.

[38] Arno Rußegger, "'Alte Regel, solange du liest, bist du nicht tot' Wolf Haas' *Silentium!* und die Didaktik des Kriminalromans," *Informationen zur Deutschdidaktik* 1 (2003): 75.

[39] Nindl, "Jetzt wird schon wieder," 103.

[40] Sänger, *Literatur und Film*, 77.

[41] Haas, "Aufklärung in Österreich," 129.

[42] The narrator (and many of the characters) in *Das ewige Leben* use the pejorative "Zigeuner" (Gypsy) to refer to the various Roma characters in the novel. I refer to the characters as "Roma," but have retained the word "Gypsy" in my translations where Haas uses the word "Zigeuner."

[43] Muny points out that the narrator makes the impression of not being particularly intelligent or educated, so it is not surprising that he refers to the fortuneteller's language as "zigeunerisch." Muny, "Erzählen ohne Ewigkeit," 233.

[44] The artist Horvath is introduced in the novel as a man, and the waitress, obviously, as a woman. There is no indication, at first, that they are the same person. The novel refers to Horvath with masculine pronouns and possessive adjectives (he/his) and to the waitress with feminine pronouns and possessive adjectives (she/her). In this essay I refer to the female-identifying Horvath with feminine pronouns, but the English translations reflect the language used in Haas's novel.

[45] Martens, "'Aber wenn du von einem Berg springst,'" 66.

[46] John T. Irwin, "Mysteries We Reread, Mysteries of Rereading," in *Detecting Text: The Metaphysical Detective Story from Poe to Postmodernism*, ed. Patricia

Merivale and Susan Elizabeth Sweeney (Philadelphia: U of Pennsylvania P, 1999), 27.

[47] Baßler points out that the Nazi past in *Auferstehung der Toten* and the embargo on Serbia in *Der Knochenmann* "wird nich verschwiegen, aber er wird niemals zum Sinnzentrum des Textes" (are not avoided, but never become the focus of the narrative). Baßler, *Der deutsche Pop-Roman*, 192.

4: The Case of the Austrian Regional Crime Novel

Anita McChesney

In 1994 Karl-Markus Gauss proclaimed that since 1980 every second Austrian novel masquerades as a *Krimi*.[1] Indeed, crime fiction dominates current bestseller lists in Austria as it does throughout the German- and English-speaking world.[2] A distinguishing feature of many bestselling Austrian texts is their regional focus. In these *Regionalkrimis* (regional, or provincial crime novels), the protagonists investigate crimes in rural Austria, which requires them to explore the area's culture along with the crime. Accordingly, the detectives' narratives emphasize both the ongoing case and distinctive features of the regional landscape, cultural traditions, and residents. These descriptions notably reference familiar stereotypes and clichés of Austria and Austrians. Depictions accentuate landscapes like the fruitful *Weinviertel* (wine region) in Lower Austria, scenic ski resorts in the Alps of Upper Austria, and lakeside tourist resorts in Burgenland. They also allude to familiar aspects of Austrian culture such as its celebrated café tradition, its monarchical past, and its theater. The novels also refer to characteristic traits of local inhabitants, including their honesty, hospitality, and peaceful nature. Yet by filtering these familiar images through the sinister context of crime, the texts undermine them. The investigation of the crimes reveals conflicts that underlie outward projections of a model culture and society. The novels thereby use the conventions of the crime genre to challenge traditional local and international images of Austria and to subvert those preconceptions.

Three contemporary authors who capitalize on the regional crime genre's critical potential vis-à-vis their native Austria are Alfred Komarek, Wolf Haas, and Gerhard Roth. The detective series by Komarek and Haas use the traditional narrative structure of crime novels to suggest secrets hidden behind images of a provincial idyll. Komarek's *Zwölf Mal Polt* (Twelve Times Polt, 2011) offers a sympathetic depiction of a province battling to maintain its cultural integrity against external influences, while Haas's *Auferstehung der Toten* (Resurrection of the Dead, 1997) gives a satirical commentary on the provincial idyll as a mere façade. Gerhard Roth's less conventional crime narrative *Der See* (1995; The Lake, 2000) complements these detective novels with its harsher critique of provincial Austria that leaves little of the traditional images intact. Roth depicts the provinces as the breeding grounds for the wanton violence, exploitation, and distortion that, for him, define Austria's past and present. This article examines the sociocritical function of regional Austrian crime novels as seen in these representative texts. Focusing on the depiction of iconic places and the interconnected cultural institutions and inhabitants, I show how the novels draw on familiar images to unsettle notions of the provincial Austrian homeland. These regional Austrian crime novels offer readers the pleasure of investigating mysteries and gaining cultural information about the provinces, yet utilize these structures to undermine beliefs in an ordered, rural Austrian society and in an Austrian cultural hegemony. These sociocritical images show Austria as anything but the proverbial "Land der Berge, Land am Strome" (land of mountains, land by the stream) touted in its national anthem.

Defining the Regional Austrian Crime Novel

The last thirty years have witnessed a boom in *Regionalkrimis* in German-language literature.[3] This subgenre of crime fiction, as the name already indicates, centers on provincial settings. According to Reinhard Jahn's definition, *Regionalkrimis* focus on provincial villages, larger rural regions, and areas around midsized cities rather than metropolises such as Los Angeles, London, Berlin, or Vienna.[4] The setting becomes the means to map out the country's rural character, including its geographical, linguistic, and social distinctions. *Regionalkrimis* began to dominate the Austrian literary scene in the late 1980s.[5] Locations include country regions such as the *Weinviertel* (wine quarter) or Styria, small tourist towns such as Zell am See and Neusiedlersee, or midsized cities like Salzburg or Graz.[6] In their basic structures and themes, regional crime novels maintain the familiar characteristics of the crime-fiction genre.[7] At the foundation of the genre is the search to resolve a mysterious crime that is replete with puzzles, suspense, and violence.[8] Ernst Bloch succinctly captures the three key structural attributes as the suspense of guessing, the act of detecting and revealing, and the untold event and its reconstruction.[9] The texts fill out this pattern with descriptions of distinct places and characters that enhance the sense of mystery that "etwas ist nicht geheuer" (something is uncanny), to use Bloch's words, and provide clues to solve the crimes.[10]

Suspense, detection, and the reconstruction of crimes are intertwined with the settings in regional crime novels. Moreover, since the novels center on actual, recognizable regions of a country, place descriptions take on increased import. The texts use detailed portrayals of places to promote the crime narrative and to communicate knowledge about that region. First, the select locations create the sense of the uncanny that advances the crime plot. As Colin Watson points out about classic British detective novels, murder scenes are often chosen to disturb and disrupt the reader's sense of security and thus are often set in familiar places associated with safety.[11] Similarly, in regional Austrian crime novels crimes occur in the apparent safety of the peaceful countryside and small villages with their cozy wine cellars, cafés and restaurants, and ostensibly welcoming inhabitants. The unsolved crimes transform these locales into places of suspicion and fear. Within this sinister setting, the narratives then describe or evoke actual locations with recognizable specificity so that readers can use the details to solve the crimes. Second, detailed place descriptions give readers knowledge about a specific area. In her study on regional Austrian crime novels, Katrin Giritzhofer points out that the descriptions must be realistic: "Besonders wichtig ist, dass die Umgebung—auch die fiktive Umgebung—realitätsgetreu und genau beschrieben wird, damit sich der Leser ein umfangreiches Bild davon machen kann. Teilweise finden sich so detaillierte Wegbeschreibungen, dass man anhand des Buches den angegebenen Ort finden würde" (It is particularly important that the surroundings—even the fictional surroundings—are described realistically and precisely, so that the reader can visualize the place extensively. In part, directions are described in such detail that one could use the book to find the specified place).[12] As Giritzhofer's comments indicate, the texts offer readers a type of travel guide to the area.[13] The details may not always be completely accurate, but they always give the appearance of authenticity. Moreover, naming actual roads and towns where people safely live and travel creates a sense of familiarity and security that the crimes will destroy.

Detailed descriptions of cultural traditions are part and parcel of the place descriptions in regional crime novels. Austrian texts convey the sense of a locale by highlighting general national traditions such as food, wine, and music, and particular regional events such as annual wine harvest festivals and theater productions. By intertwining place and culture, regional crime novels present an ethnographic and anthropological reading of a place and become a medium for cultural exploration.[14] Critics have even suggested that the crime novels take on the function of a new type of *Heimatroman* (homeland novel) or *Anti-Heimatroman*, which respectively glorify or vilify a home region and its culture, including its architecture, traditional clothing, customs and values, and dialect.[15] In regional crime novels, extended descriptions of the fictional characters are interconnected with the represented place and culture. Since the figures are usually native to the location, they personify their surroundings and thereby give readers a richer sense of the area.[16] In regional Austrian crime novels the character portraits—like the related place and cultural descriptions—serve a dual purpose: the details advance the pursuit for answers to mysterious crimes and at the same time they portray a sense of what is Austrian by projecting familiar images that will subsequently be called into question.

The striking boom in *Regionalkrimis* in the last two decades raises the question of their distinction vis-à-vis other subgenres of crime novels. Critics have suggested that the novels fulfill readers' desire to identify with what is described. Readers like to read about murders that take place at their own front door, so to speak, and they like to recognize real streets, bars, and butcher shops.[17] The genre's popularity, however, exceeds local audiences. In "Nationality International," Eva Erdmann observes that *Regionalkrimis* also draw worldwide fascination. She suggests that the explicit descriptions of the region, its culture, and inhabitants serve as a travel guide to regions otherwise inaccessible to outsiders.[18] Speaking of German crime novels, Jochen Vogt similarly suggests that the genre of recent decades has become a means of ethnographic exploration, a transcultural genre, and even a type of travel literature. These tendencies mean that *Regionalkrimis* help define a region's identity on both the local and international stage.

Contemporary Austrian *Regionalkrimis*, however, are not glossy travel guides that describe the provinces' unique culture and society in order to reaffirm locals and to attract international readers to the area. The details uncovered by the investigations lead natives to question the hidden secrets in everyday life around them, and they offer nonnatives an alternative, and considerably more thrilling, sense of a region they might know only through general stereotypes. For both local and international readers, the novels' primary goal is to peel away the touristic sheen as a way to unsettle familiar associations with the region. Austrian crime novels base their critical views on actual geographic and social conditions and on Austrian self-perception. The settings of Austrian *Regionalkrimis* reflect the country's heavily rural geography. Between 2010 and 2012, 32 percent of the country's total population still lived in rural areas, a number that remained relatively unchanged from the 33 percent in 1980 to 1982.[19] Moreover, the images of the Austrian countryside, culture, and people in the regional novels correspond to statistical data on Austrians' self-image. According to a 1987 study conducted by Albert F. Reiterer, et al., central national symbols of identification are the beautiful landscape, the welcoming, peaceful residents, and cultural accomplishments.[20] Subsequent surveys reinforce the same key traits at the regional level. According to a 1993 study, the most important identification symbols in the provinces were: (1) climate, weather, landscape, and nature; (2) lifestyle and neutrality (quiet, peace, friendliness, and congeniality); and (3) cultural identification figures, including buildings, works of art, sites, productions, and personalities.[21] Foreign views of Austria mirror native images. According to Ernst Bruckmüller, Austria is internationally known for its classical music tradition, its winter sports like skiing, and its rich cultural traditions, from its coffeehouses to its theater. The notion of the "culture-state" Austria is one of the most frequently self-proclaimed and foreign-cited images.[22]

Austrian *Regionalkrimis* noticeably draw on these local and international stereotypes and alter the images by using them within a literary genre that promotes suspicion and fear. Through a mixture of fiction and fact, the crime investigations draw attention to real social conditions in the provinces today. Contemporary Austrian *Regionalkrimis* can be described as a critical society novel, a term Jochen Vogt uses to describe the stated intent of the New German Crime Novel since the 1970s.[23] Beatrix Kramlovsky and Giritzhofer see social criticism as the trademark of Austrian crime novels since the 1990s.[24] As Kramlovsky notes, Austrian crime novels combine "crime, local color, and a detailed representation of the social situation" to challenge ordered structures.[25] The crime novels of Komarek, Haas, and Roth exemplify the sociocritical character of contemporary Austrian *Regionalkrimis*. Their novels feature places that clearly reflect the country's image as a cultural tourist retreat, yet they also render them mysterious through the crimes. The investigations rupture the idyllic settings heralded for their unspoiled beauty and culture to show the hidden side of provincial Austria. The authors thereby use the genre's narrative structure as the catalyst to reflect on deeper sociohistorical issues.

Defamiliarizing the *Weinviertel*: Alfred Komarek's *Zwölf Mal Polt*

Alfred Komarek sets his Simon Polt series in Brunndorf and Burgheim, small wine-growing villages in the fictional Wiebachtal Valley in the *Weinviertel* (wine region). Austria's largest wine-growing area, the *Weinviertel* is located in the northeast corner of Lower Austria on the Slovakian and Czech borders. The author is well-versed in the region and its culture, having lived in Lower Austria and written several nonfiction books on the region and on Austria's wine culture. In his six Polt novels, Komarek interweaves crime with portrayals of the region's landscape, culture, and citizens. Komarek's most recent volume, *Zwölf Mal Polt* (2011), captures the novels' sociocritical tinge. The twelve short stories span the years of the five previous novels, from Simon Polt's first day as a police detective to his later years in retirement when he continues to investigate out of curiosity and his desire to help local citizens. The stories depict crimes ranging from murder, attempted murder, and accidental death, to missing persons, petty theft, and human smuggling. Polt always solves the crimes and extracts a confession from the guilty, but he metes out justice with a soft hand. The criminals often choose their own punishment, such as promising to turn themselves in to the police or seek psychological help, and Polt always respects their desire for privacy, often remaining silent about some or all aspects of the crimes.

Predominant throughout all of the novels are descriptions of the wine cellars that show two sides of the Lower Austrian province. On the one hand, the narratives openly praise the beauty and cultural importance of the wine culture represented by the layout of the press houses and wine cellars. In "Roter Oktober" (Red October), the narrator describes the layout of Kellergasse (Cellar Street):

> Die Kellergasse von Burgheim war eine der längsten im Lande. Weit über hundert kleine, weiß gekalkte Pressehäuser standen dicht aneinander gereiht. Darunter verbargen sich große Weinkeller. Dort, wo die Kellergasse endete und sich bis zur Grenze zu Tschechien hin unverbautes Hügelland dehnte, stand ein zwischen Büschen und Bäumen fast verborgenes Presshaus. Polt hatte es vor einigen Jahren gekauft, obwohl er kein Weinbauer war. Es machte ihm einfach Freude, so etwas sein Eigen zu nennen. (57–58)[26]

> [Cellar Street in Burgheim was one of the longest in the country. Well over a hundred small, whitewashed press houses stood close together. Large wine cellars lay hidden beneath them. There, where Cellar Street ended and the unspoiled hill country stretched clear to the Czech border, a press house stood almost hidden between the bushes and trees. Polt had bought it a few years back although he was not a vintner. It just gave him pleasure to call something like that his own.]

The narrator describes the Kellergassen as the topographical and cultural entrance to the region, and as central to local pride. The village's carefully cultured external image also centers on its wine cultivation. After retiring, Simon Polt declares it his goal to make the wine culture renowned, and the local residents share Polt's zeal to advertise the region. In the story "Roter Oktober," residents promote the area's wine culture to a passionate group of visiting Japanese wine connoisseurs. One of the wine growers, Franz Jagenteuefel, describes wine as the very essence of local culture:

> Dunkel ist das Geheimnis des Weines. Im Mittelpunkt strahlt der Genuss. . . . Wieder einmal ein Grüner Veltliner. Frisch, jung, ein Musterknabe: der Duft nach sonnensatter Reife, herrlich frischer Traubengeschmack, voluminös im Mund, diskret am Gaumen, verspielt und verführerisch im Abgang. Aber was rede ich: Sie haben den Herbst und die Weinlese hierzulande ja erlebt, mit allen Sinnen. Nehmen Sie diese schönen, leichtsinnigen Erfahrungen und gewinnen Sie daraus die dichteste Essenz. Mit diesem Wein können Sie davon kosten, immer und immer wieder. (65–66)

[The mystery of wine is deep. Pleasure radiates at its core.... Again a Grüner Veltliner. Fresh, young, an ideal: the scent of sun-filled ripeness, glorious fresh grape flavor, voluminous in the mouth, discrete on the palate, a playful and seductive aftertaste. But what am I talking about: you yourself experienced autumn and the grape harvest in this region with all your senses. Take these beautiful frivolous experiences and draw from them the most concentrated essence possible. With this wine you can taste that essence again and again.]

The concentrated essence of local beauty and sensory enjoyment that Jagenteuefel attributes to the wine also informs the narrator's descriptions of the regional landscape.[27] In "Eine Ewigkeit Belichtungszeit" (An Eternity of Exposure Time), the German tourist Babsi, for example, refers to the area as "Eine Landschaft zum Träumen" (33; a landscape to dream of). The picturesque landscape, like the superb wine culture, gives inhabitants a sense of well-being year round, as the narrator emphasizes, particularly when describing the detective's sense of ease ("Sich-Wohlfühlen," 127, 176).

The descriptions of wine cellars and landscapes in Komarek's novels read at first glance like a tourist advertisement for the region and its culture. The narratives give readers a geographical and ethnographical introduction to the *Weinviertel* as a place of beauty, solitude, and even escape from the burdens of the outside world. Yet on the other hand, these detailed descriptions of an idyllic setting and culture exist in sharp relief to the crimes that also center on the region's wine culture. The description of the Kellergasse and Polt's press house in "Roter Oktober" contrasts with the detective's reason for retreating to his refuge to review facts about the murder of a Japanese tourist. Franz Jagenteufel's enthusiastic portrayal of wine and culture in the same story becomes eerie when readers discover at the end of the story that his performance was intended to detract attention from Mr. Sato's body lying in his wine cellar. In *Zwölf mal Polt*, as in all of Komarek's texts, the famous wine cellars provide the settings and motives for crime. Victims and perpetrators are found in the press houses and wine cellars. Causes of death include toxic poisoning in the cellars and accidental deaths or suicides under the influence of alcohol. Polt's interrogations take place almost exclusively in the wine cellars and attached *Wirtshäuser* (inns), and the solutions to the crimes also lie in the region's wine culture. Motives for committing or concealing crimes include ensuring wine profits, maintaining the region's and inhabitants' untarnished reputation, and covering up alcoholism.

As Polt investigates the crime scenes and talks with the related parties, the narratives construct a tableau of village life with the beauty and pitfalls of the area, culture, and inhabitants. In his analysis of Komarek's novels, Ernst Kretschmer calls the texts a *Sittengemälde* (a study of a region's milieu) similar to nineteenth-century crime stories such as *Die Judenbuche* (The Jew's Beech) and *Unterm Birnbaum* (Under the Pear Tree).[28] Komarek's novels give readers a contemporary *Sittengemälde* of provincial Lower Austria.[29] Using the structure of a crime novel, Komarek peels away stereotypical images of an idyllic Austrian tourist region to reveal a countryside also struggling to maintain its cultural integrity. While the characters and events are fictional, Komarek's novels paint a tableau of actual circumstances in the *Weinviertel*. The narratives show problems with changing conditions over the past fifty years, such as a mass exodus of the young people to the cities and the decline in industry with the resulting economic recession. In the end, however, the novels seem to suggest that the problem is more with change than with tradition. The novels present crime as an external disturbance—victims and perpetrators are often from outside the village—that disrupts the order of life. Particularly the old-fashioned detective Polt embodies the fight to maintain the regional way of life against the onset of modernity. Through Polt's successes, Komarek implicitly advocates fighting to maintain traditional, provincial life. Komarek's crime novels offer a soft social critique that includes the positives and negatives of the Austrian provinces. They paint an image of regional village life replete with an exemplary wine culture, landscape, and sense of well-being, but also plagued by crime, tourism, alcoholism, and resistance to change. The detective's work underscores the region's celebrated beauty and the problems beneath the village's idyllic façade.

Defamiliarizing Zell am See: Wolf Haas's *Auferstehung der Toten*

Wolf Haas's Simon Brenner novels similarly use descriptions of places to evaluate Austria, yet his sarcastic tone renders a more explicit critique of deep-seated problems in the provinces. Each of Haas's seven novels features an iconic Austrian location, including the popular ski resort Zell am See, a *Backhendlstand* (grilled chicken eatery) in beautiful Eastern Styria, a Catholic boarding school in Salzburg, and the Austrian cultural capitals Vienna and Graz. The author, born Wolfgang Haas, writes about regions where he has lived. His crime novels give readers an inside introduction to these familiar places with a twist. As Helga Schreckenberger notes in her analysis of Haas's novels, each of his settings has been chosen "to challenge conventional images of Austria."[30] What makes Haas's critique particularly poignant is that the fictional texts all include references to actual, contemporary issues in Austria. These include the harmful effects of ski tourism, Austria's largest income provider, on the environment; the rise in the fast-food industry and ensuing loss of local food culture; and sex scandals in the Catholic Church. Through his mixture of fiction and fact, Haas's provincial crime novels interweave crime with the region's landscape and its cultural and social character to suggest the hidden problems behind the idyll.

Haas's first novel, *Auferstehung der Toten*, exemplifies this critique of the Austrian provinces. The novel is set in the tourist town Zell am See, which is located in the state of Salzburg and is renowned as a ski resort in winter and a lakeside resort in summer. The plot revolves around the murder of an elderly, wealthy American couple who are also the in-laws of the wealthiest man in the village, Vergolder Anstetter. The couple visits Zell am See to celebrate their anniversary with the traditional *Vormachen*, a small play performed about a bride and groom's life, but then their frozen bodies are found suspended on a chairlift. By the time detective Simon Brenner solves the case ten months later, two more people have died.

The contrast between the idyllic tourist setting and the shocking crimes emphasizes the disparity between the village's external image and internal reality. Those contrasts first emerge in the descriptions of the provincial setting in the novel's opening lines: "Von Amerika aus betrachtet, ist Zell ein winziger Punkt. Irgendwo mitten in Europa. Aber vom Pinzgau aus gesehen, ist Zell die Hauptstadt des Pinzgaus. Zehntausend Einwohner, dreißig Dreitausender, achtundfünfzig Lifte, ein See. Und ob du es glaubst oder nicht. Zwei Amerikaner sind letzten Dezember in Zell umgebracht worden. Aber jetzt paß auf" (5; Seen from America, Zell is a miniscule dot. But seen from Pinzgau, Zell is the capital of the Pinzgau region. Ten thousand inhabitants, thirty mountains of over three thousand meters, fifty-eight ski lifts, one lake. And believe it or not: two Americans were killed last December in Zell. Now listen up).[31]

Similar descriptions of Zell am See begin chapters 2 and 4. This tongue-in-cheek description begins like a tourist advertisement that emphasizes stereotypical regional highlights, much like Komarek's portrayal of Austria's *Weinviertel*, yet ends as a murder scene. This first passage in *Auferstehung der Toten* signals Haas's characteristic tone. The narrator's language is colloquial and punctuated with at times humorous and at times biting commentary on the region. Through this narrative tone, Haas suggests here that the double murder and not the ski industry is the town's main attraction, and already at the beginning he signals the discrepancy between the image of an idyllic resort town and its more sinister side.[32]

Subsequent depictions of the village's landscape and buildings in *Auferstehung der Toten* give readers a deeper sense of two contrasting sides of the region's topography, culture, and inhabitants. Typical attractions include the *Hirschenwirt* hotel; the café *Feinschmeck*; the reservoir, which locals call the "Symbol der Republik" (32; symbol of the republic);

the church in the town center; the ski slopes; and the lake. Wolf's novel also describes local traditions such as *Vormachen*. As a long-time resident, "die Deutsche" (the German), explains the ceremony to Brenner: "Die Brautleute kommen aus der Kirche, und am Kirchplatz spielen ihnen die Einheimischen kleine Theaterszenen vor. Anekdoten aus der Vergangenheit des Bräutigams und der Braut. Wie sich das Paar kennengelernt hat. Sehr komisch und oft ganz schön. . . . Ich lache jedesmal Tränen beim Vormachen" (52; The bridal couple comes out of the church and on the church square locals act out small theater scenes for them. Anecdotes from the groom's and bride's past. How they met. Very funny and often quite beautiful. . . . I laugh myself to tears at each *Vormachen*). An additional cultural highlight is the town's *Heimattheater* (home theater), which is advertised as an old custom but, as the narrator tells readers, was actually founded in the middle of the 1960s by the tourist association. As Brenner investigates the case, residents are rehearsing the latest performance on regional history.

Similar to the opening description, Haas uses each of these depictions to expose the provincial Austrian idyll as a carefully crafted image, in particular by using the narrator's humorous undertone to turn each potentially positive description of the region's culture into a critique.[33] When "die Deutsche" ends her description of *Vormachen* with the comment "Sehr komisch und oft ganz schön . . . Ich lache jedesmal Tränen beim Vormachen" (52; Very funny and often quite beautiful . . . I laugh myself to tears at each *Vormachen*), Haas's narrative leaves readers with the sense that the provincial tradition is more "komisch" than "schön," more a source of amusement than respect. Similarly, advertising the newly established *Heimattheater* as ancient points to the distinction between the town's projected cultural image and the less glorious reality.

Haas's depiction of the citizens reinforces the view that all is not as the outward image suggests. The duplicity of the people is particularly evident in the exaggerated tales locals tell about their town to attract tourists:

> Zum Beispiel mit dem Schnee. Immer wieder haben sie die Geschichte ausgegraben, daß es früher, vor zwanzig, ja noch vor ein paar Jahren, viel mehr Schnee gegeben hat. Und der Lift Lois hat natürlich am besten gewußt: kein Wort wahr. Das Gerücht ist nur von den Lift- und Pensionsbesitzern in die Welt gesetzt worden. . . . Und natürlich—die Schitouristen nicht zufrieden, sparen das ganze Jahr im Ruhrgebiet und sitzen dann in ihrem Hotelzimmer. (6)

> [For example with the snow. Time and again they dug up the story that in the past, twenty or even just a few years ago, there had been a lot more snow. And of course Lift Lois knew best: not a word was true. The rumor was only started by the lift and guesthouse

owners. . . . And naturally—the ski tourists are dissatisfied, they save up all year in the Ruhrgebiet only to then sit in their hotel rooms.]

Brenner's investigation uncovers further evidence that the citizens are prone to evoke the appearance of tradition to gloss over a contradicting reality. Readers discover that the ostensibly welcoming tourist town has a long history of exploiting tourists and locals and of silencing the truth. This tendency is the source of the crimes committed by Frau Anstetter, referred to previously as either "die Deutsche" or "die Handlose" (the handless person). Brenner discovers that she is a native of Zell am See who fled the village after an affair with her brother, Vergolder Anstetter, left her pregnant and alone at seventeen. According to Frau Anstetter, the village's stony silence determined the downward spiral of her life. She was forced to give up the child and then lost her hands after an unsuccessful suicide attempt. She returns to the village fifty years later for public revenge by murdering her brother's American in-laws.

Haas's novel presents the circumstances of these crimes as typical of life in a provincial Austrian village. In the novel, Zell am See has a long-standing history of crimes such as incest. Also typical of the provinces is the inclination to ignore and forget such crimes. When Brenner wonders how no one in the village, including the brother, recognized her, she responds: "'Vergessen ist eine Gnade, müssen Sie wissen. Und diese Gnade hat der liebe Gott den Zellern im Übermaß erwiesen.' 'Und Ihr eigener Bruder? Sie sind ihm doch begegnet?' 'Wie gesagt: eine Gnade'" (141; "Forgetting is a blessing, you must understand. And the loving God has bestowed this blessing on the Zell citizens in abundance." "And your own brother? You ran into him too?" "As I said: a blessing"). Brenner's investigations also reveal that the village has a long history of blessedly forgetting, or at least conveniently revising, the truth. Brenner discovers that the town's celebrated reservoir was constructed in part by prisoners of war (95). Thus, the central public symbol of local cultural pride is rooted in exploitation, murder, and silence. The fictional "Symbol der Republik" in Haas's novel corresponds to Kaprun, a real dam in Upper Austria, with a nearly identical history. Construction on the dam began in the 1930s, was efficiently continued by the Nazis in the late 1930s and early 1940s, and relied heavily on prisoners of war in the late 1940s before construction was finally completed in 1959.[34] Haas's novel embellishes historical facts with numerous fictional elements, yet veiled references to an actual dam and its history contribute to a larger critique of Austria and its past. This is particularly apparent when Haas's narrator first describes the landmark's historic unveiling. "Symbol der Republik ist in der Zeitung gestanden, das war 1951. Jetzt kann man natürlich in sechs Jahren keinen Hochgebirgsstausee bauen, oder vielleicht könnte man es heute, aber damals nicht. Die Politiker haben natürlich kein Wort darüber verloren, daß er—aber ich möchte jetzt auch nicht wieder mit der Nazizeit anfangen" (32; Symbol of the Republic was printed in the newspaper, that was 1951. Now of course one can't build a dam in a high mountain range in six years, or maybe one could do it today but not then. Of course the politicians didn't waste any words about the fact that it—but I don't want to start up again with the Nazi period). The offhand reference to the "Nazizeit" as the real explanation for the dam's efficient construction, which the narrator quickly silences, suggests that the history of the fictional Zell am See can be seen as a larger commentary on Austria's external image. The idealized representation of the reservoir in local history implicitly parallels Austria's reconstructed national image after 1945 around the myth of being Hitler's first victim, rather than a participant in National Socialism.

In *Auferstehung der Toten*, crimes and their concealment are the source and motive for Frau Anstetter's murders and they shape her chosen methods. She carefully stages the spectacular murders to make the hidden past public. She entices the American couple onto the chair lift in the middle of a frigid winter night as part of the *Vormachen* ceremony she promised them for their anniversary. The suspended bodies become a public performance of their life, but one that twists the local celebratory custom into a horrifying death scene. Moreover, Frau Anstetter constructs her entire plan to be a living performance of the village's secret history. When Brenner confronts Frau Anstetter in the dénouement, she is rehearsing the annual play for the town's *Heimattheater*. But as Brenner insightfully notes, she has already completed the true performance: "Aber sie haben keine Gnade gekannt. Ihr Heimattheater, das haben Sie nicht im Theater aufgeführt" (But you knew no mercy. Your homeland play, you didn't perform it in the theater), to which she adds, "Sondern in der Heimat" (141; But rather in the homeland). Simon Brenner's investigations expose the beautiful performances and the underlying secrets of this "Heimat."

Wolf Haas's *Auferstehung der Toten* shows the definitive traits of all his crime novels.[35] The author uses the suspense of the genre and the mixture of fiction and fact to peel away the celebrated beauty and culture to expose the hidden side of rural Austria. In contrast to Komarek, Haas depicts crime as a result of silence and past cover-ups. The texts criticize the image Austrians cling to and outwardly portray at all costs; they offer an alternative view of an area that needs change.

Defamiliarizing Neusiedler See: Gerhard Roth's *Der See*

Gerhard Roth's *Der See* (1995) offers a counterpoint to the series by Komarek and Haas. While the latter maintain characteristic narrative structures of detective fiction, Roth plays with the familiar models to critique the Austrian provinces. The novel is set in Neusiedler See, which is located in the easternmost Austrian province, Burgenland, on the Austro-Hungarian border. The lake region is internationally renowned as a UNESCO World Heritage Site and nationally known as a rural retreat for the Viennese. The plot follows protagonist Paul Eck, who travels to the lake to meet his father for the first time after thirty years. The night he arrives, a devastating storm hits the region and the father and his sailboat disappear without a trace. In contrast to traditional crime narratives, like Alfred Komarek's and Wolf Haas's, the protagonist is neither a detective nor even a skilled observer; indeed, he is psychologically fragile and he is a drug addict who often struggles to comprehend the events around him. *Der See* also foregoes the prototypical dénouement that explains all puzzling events. The father's disappearance is never fully resolved, although the novel suggests he drowned in the storm. Yet like Komarek and Haas, Roth uses the investigation into the mystery and the suspenseful search for clues to contrast idyllic images of the Austrian region with a sinister side.

Roth's place descriptions underscore these distinctions. Detailed portrayals of the lake show pollution and exploitation and not a beautiful, natural, national-heritage site. These contrasts are most apparent when Paul flies over the lake with a local pilot to look for his father's sailboat. From a distance, the landscape still seems as pristine as depicted on the glossy tourist brochures. As he describes their approach, "Am Horizont dehnte sich der See als ein schimmerndes Band aus. Als sie den Schilfgürtel überflogen, schienen sie sich über einer grünen Fläche zu verlieren" (40; On the horizon, the lake stretched out like a shimmering ribbon. When they flew over the reed marsh, they seemed to be lost above a green surface, 26).[36] Eck continues to describe the distant aerial view of water and land as a beautiful geometrical painting with mysterious black arms and white and blue dots. A closer look at these beautiful, yet imprecise features soon reveals the truth. The waterways are black from rotting leaves; the white dots are a discarded truck radiator, ship hull, cans, and rubble; and the blue dot is an electric boat (40–41; 26–27).

Similarly, each place Eck visits during his investigation bears a sinister side, particularly vis-à-vis Austrian history. He begins his trip in Trieste where he visits Schloß Miramare, built for the Austrian Archduke Ferdinand Maximilian and later Archduke of Mexico, and the so-called rice factory, Risiera di San Sabba, which was a Nazi extermination camp. The airstrip in Trausdorf at Neusiedler See was built by the Nazis, and Eck also visits a Jewish cemetery where he meets a Holocaust survivor. Even more so than the other regional crime novels, Roth's critique here extends beyond the context of the crime plot to refer to actual regional conditions and national historical realities. In her analysis of *Der See*, Krajenbrink notes that Eck's investigations in the region become a journey through Austrian history past and present, from the Empire and the Second World War to current political struggles in the border regions of Eastern Europe.[37] All of the renowned cultural sites Eck visits are national icons and monuments to the nation's repressive monarchical and National Socialist past. This select portrayal of local sights introduces readers to Austria's negative history, which, it suggests, fuels present chaos. Roth's novel uses the fabricated story of crime and investigation around historical facts to suggest the danger of maintaining actual historical patterns—here, specifically, the inevitable, negative effect of heralding cultural artifacts and ignoring the history they conceal.

As Eck interacts with local residents in his investigations, Roth's narrative reveals that the destruction hidden behind the landscape and culture also defines the citizens. Gratuitous violence and cruelty are prevailing regional attributes. Before Eck even arrives at Neusiedler See, he is attacked and his money and driver's license stolen; on his first visit to the lake, a young hunter shoots at him; suspicious neighbors at his camping site turn out to be bank robbers and experience a bloody demise; and body parts discovered in the lake point to multiple murders, including that of a vicious mercenary from the Bosnian War. Eck's own family history, he discovers, is full of violence. His Hungarian grandfather was a militant monarchist, and his father was involved in illegal international arms trade during the Yugoslavian War, and had business ties to a former Gestapo agent and a known Serbian assassin (217; 153–54). Eck eventually repeats the violence that characterizes his family and native region. At a political rally, Eck is so overcome with hatred against the radical right-wing Austrian politician called "der Hoffnungsmann" (185–88; the man of hope, 129–30), that he attempts to shoot him. The plan fails only because the revolver jams at the last minute. In this scene, Roth confronts readers with another obvious reference to Austria's actual political scene, as the politician unmistakably resembles Jörg Haider (1950–2008), long-time leader of the national-conservative Austrian Freedom Party (FPÖ). Roth's depictions of Neusiedler See paint provincial Austria as a place defined not by solidarity, security, and cultural richness but rather by violence, subversion, manipulation, and distortion. For Roth, these attributes are most visible in but not limited to the provinces. As the provocative title of the motto found in the preface of the book, "Im Land der Mörder" (In the Land of the Murderers), indicates, his critique includes all of Austria. Austria's celebrated beauty and culture, the novel suggests, are only blurry, distant, perhaps even nonexistent, images.

Conclusion

The crime novels by Alfred Komarek, Wolf Haas, and Gerhard Roth represent a spectrum of possibilities for using *Regionalkrimis* as a medium of social critique. They offer readers the adventure of investigating mysteries while also showing the hidden side of the familiar images of Austrian culture. Speaking of the international popularity of regional crime novels, Erdmann concludes that they enhance the readers' interest through their treatment of national images: "The thematization of national characteristics becomes even more interesting when well-known stereotypes are observed from a new perspective and well-known clichés updated."[38] Regional Austrian crime novels make their unique mark by updating the customary and hackneyed images of tranquil Austrian provinces to show the dark secrets they conceal. In Austrian *Regionalkrimis*, detection reveals crimes buried beneath the provinces' idyllic projection that tarnish familiar images long after the cases have been closed. Indeed, the novels suggest that the idyll never did exist.

Notes

[1] Richard Donnenberg, "Kurze Geschichte des österreichischen Krimis," http://www.krimiautoren.at/geschichte_krimi.html, last modified 2005 (accessed December 15, 2012).

[2] For contrasts between German-language and Anglo-American crime fiction, see Almuth Heuner, "Germany's Crime and Mystery Scene," *World Literature Today* 85, no. 3 (May–June 2011): 16–17. For a brief contrast between Austrian and Anglo-American crime fiction, see Arno Russegger, "Ortspiele. Wortspiele. Aspekte kriminalistischen Erzählens in der österreichischen Literatur," in *Mord als kreaktiver Prozess*, ed. Sandro M. Moraldo (Heidelberg: Universitätsverlag Winter, 2005), 75–98.

[3] Volker Meid speaks of "eine ausgesprochene Regionalisierung" (a pronounced rise in regionalism) in recent decades. Volker Meid, *Sachwörterbuch Zur Deutschen Literatur* (Stuttgart: Reclam, 1999), 287.

[4] For Jahn's full definition of *Regionalkrimis*, see Reinhard Jahn, "Was ist ein Regionalkrimi" (presentation, Thomas Morus-Akademie, Bergisch-Gladbach, Bensberg, January 9, 2000). Republished online at *Krimiblog*, September 29, 2009, http://krimiblog.blogspot.com/2009/09/was-ist-ein-regionalkrimi-eine-autopsie.html; and Franziska Gerlach, "Der Boom der Regionalkrimis," Goethe Institute, http://www.goethe.de/kue/lit/aug/de8129560.htm and http://www.goethe.de/kue/lit/aug/en8129560.htm, last modified November 2011 (accessed December 15, 2012); and Katrin Giritzhofer, "Mörderisch und Kulinarisch: Eva Rossmanns Frauenduo Mira und Vesna zwischen Wien, Wein und Veneto" (MA thesis, University of Vienna, 2008), 23.

[5] Gerlach, "Der Boom der Regionalkrimis," Goethe Institute.

[6] Donnenberg, "Kurze Geschichte."

[7] For a good overview of categories of crime fiction and diverse subgenres in Austrian literature, see Donnenberg, "Kurze Geschichte." For a comprehensive overview of the diverse genres and subgenres in Anglo-American crime fiction,

see Stephen Knight, *Crime Fiction 1800–2000: Detection, Death, Diversity* (New York: Palgrave Macmillan, 2004).

[8] There has been much debate on the genre's names, in particular the difference between the detective novel and the crime novel (*Detektivroman* and *Kriminalroman* in German) and what they imply about differences and continuities in form. For the purpose of clarity, I follow Julian Symons's lead and use the term crime novel to designate the broad category of novels dealing with crime and detection. Julian Symons, *Bloody Murder: From the Detective Story to the Crime Novel: a History* (Harmondsworth: Viking, 1985).

[9] In Bloch's words, "die Spannung des *Ratens*"; "das *Entlarvende, Aufdeckende*"; and "sein *Unerzähltes* und dessen *Rekonstruktion*." Ernst Bloch, "Philosophische Ansicht des Detektivromans," in *Der Kriminalroman: Poetik, Theorie, Geschichte*, ed. Jochen Vogt (Munich: Fink, 1998), 41, 45.

[10] Bloch, "Philosophische Ansicht des Detektivromans," 38.

[11] Colin Watson, *Snobbery with Violence: Crime Stories and Their Audience* (London: Eyre and Spottiswoode, 1971), 169, quoted in Helga Schreckenberger, "The Destruction of Idyllic Austria in Wolf Haas's Detective Novels," in *Crime and Madness in Modern Austria: Myth, Metaphor and Cultural Realities*, ed. Rebecca S. Thomas (Newcastle upon Tyne: Cambridge Scholars, 2008), 427.

[12] Giritzhofer, "Mörderisch und Kulinarisch," 23. Unless otherwise noted, all translations are my own.

[13] In contrast to this positive association of the novels with travel guides, some critics suggest that regional crime novels are nothing more than exaggerated reports full of banal facts that readers could better get from actual travel guides or by visiting the place. Ulrich Baron, "Markt & Totschlag: Regio regiert (nicht)," *Crimemag, Kolumnen und Themen* (blog), May 21, 2011 (7:12), http://culturmag.de/crimemag/markt-und-totschlag-regio-regiert-nicht.

[14] For more on regional crime novels as medium for cultural exploration, see Eva Erdmann, "National International: Detective Fiction in the Late Twentieth Century," in *Investigating Identities. Questions of Identity in Contemporary International Crime Fiction*, ed. Marieke Krajenbrink and Kate M. Quinn (Amsterdam; New York: Rodopi, 2009), 11–26; and Trisha Yarbrough, "The Cultural Work of Regional Mysteries," *Clues: A Journal of Detection* 22, no. 1 (2001 Spring–Summer 2001): 13–20. Both authors suggest that the genre's recent popularity is connected to this new role.

[15] For more on the *Regionalkrimi* as a *Heimatroman*, see Erdmann, "Nationality International," 15–16; Jahn, "Was ist ein Regionalkrimi?"; Donnenberg, "Kurze Geschichte"; and Beatrix Kramlovsky, "Show Your Face, oh Violence," *World Literature Today* 85, no. 3 (May–June 2011): 13. For more on the *Regionalkrimi* as an anti-*Heimatroman*, see Baron, "Markt & Totschlag." For more on the tradition of anti-*Heimat* novels in Austria in general, see Karl Konrad Polheim, ed., *Wesen und Wander der Heimatliteratur am Beispiel der österreichischen Literatur sein 1945* (Bern: Peter Lang, 1989).

[16] Giritzhofer also points to this essential connection between character and place descriptions in Austrian *Regionalkrimis*. Giritzhofer, "Mörderisch und Kulinarisch," 23.

[17] Gerlach, "Der Boom der Regionalkrimis," Goethe Institute; Jahn, "Was ist ein Regionalkrimi?"

[18] See Erdmann, "National International" for a comparative look at national settings in detective fiction from around the globe.

[19] "Rural Population," World Bank, http://data.worldbank.org/indicator/SP.RUR.TOTL/countries, last modified 2013 (accessed March 24, 2014).

[20] Albert F. Reiterer, ed., *Nation und Nationalbewusstsein in Österreich* (Vienna: Verband der wissenschaftlichen Gesellschaften Österreichs, 1988), 117.

[21] Ernst Bruckmüller, *The Austrian Nation: Cultural Consciousness and Socio-Political Processes* (Riverside: Ariadne Press, 2003), 90–93; 112–14.

[22] Bruckmüller, *The Austrian Nation*, 119–22.

[23] Jochen Vogt, "'Alles total groovy hier,'" *Der Deutschunterricht* 2 (2010): 21.

[24] Giritzhofer, "Mörderisch und Kulinarisch," 19; Beatrix Kramlovsky, "Show Your Face, oh Violence," 13–15.

[25] Kramlovsky, "Show Your Face, oh Violence," 13. Kramlovsky specifically differentiates Austrian from German crime fiction, in that the former commonly breaks, varies, or satirizes the genre's rules.

[26] Alfred Komarek, *Zwölf mal Polt: Kriminalgeschichten* (Innsbruck: Haymon, 2011). Subsequent references will be by page numbers in parentheses in the text.

[27] This essence is also what sets the provinces apart from the city. For more on the depiction of the Viennese in Alfred Komarek's regional crime novel, see Ernst Kretschmer, "Abgründe in der Provinz. Alfred Komareks Kriminalromane," in *Mord als kreativer Prozess*, ed. Sandro M. Moraldo (Heidelberg: Universitätsverlag Winter, 2005), 111–26.

[28] Kretschmer, "Abgründe in der Provinz," 119–22.

[29] For more on the struggle between tradition and modernity in Komarek's novels, see Kretschmer, "Abgründe in der Provinz," 117.

[30] Schreckenberger, "The Destruction of Idyllic Austria," 426.

[31] Wolf Haas, *Auferstehung der Toten* (Reinbek bei Hamburg: Rowohlt, 2007). Subsequent references will be by page numbers in parentheses in the text. Unless otherwise noted, all translations are my own.

[32] Jon Sherman offers a contrasting understanding of the iconic locations in Haas's mysteries. He reads the stereotypical tourist settings as elements in a geographic and social portrait of modern Austria rather than a critique as I suggest. See his "Plurality and Alterity in Wolf Haas's Brenner Mysteries" in this volume.

[33] For more on Wolf Haas's use of narrative voice as critique, see Schreckenberger, "The Destruction of Idyllic Austria," 434–39.

[34] "1950 bis 1959: Mythos Kaprun und Ybbs-Persenbeug," VERBUND, http://www.verbund.com/cc/de/ueber-uns/unternehmensgeschichte/1950-1959-mythos-kaprun, last modified 2013 (accessed June 6, 2013).

[35] See also Franz Haas, "Aufklärung in Österreich. Die erhellenden Kriminalromane von Wolf Haas," in *Mord als kreativer Prozess*, ed. Sandro M. Moraldo (Heidelberg: Universitätsverlag Winter, 2005), 130.

[36] Gerhard Roth, *Der See* (Frankfurt am Main: S. Fischer, 1995). Subsequent references will be by page numbers in parentheses in the text. Gerhard Roth, *The Lake*, trans. Michael Winkler (Riverside, CA: Ariadne, 2000). Subsequent references will be by page numbers in parentheses in the text following the English translation.

[37] Marieke Krajenbrink, "Unresolved Identities in Roth and Rabinovici: Reworking the Crime Genre in Austrian Literature," in *Investigating Identities*, ed. Krajenbrink and Quinn (Amsterdam: Rodopi, 2009), 243–60.

[38] Erdmann, "National International," 24.

Part II. History

5: "Darkness at the Beginning": The Holocaust in Contemporary German Crime Fiction

Magdalena Waligórska

> *A crime novel is an attempt at organizing chaos.*
> —Witold Gombrowicz, *Diary*, 1966

CRIME FICTION PROVIDES ENTERTAINMENT by focusing on the darkest sides of reality, such as violence, murder, and injustice, and the genre is often seen as the escapist genre par excellence. In the eyes of some of its theoreticians, crime fiction's appeal exists precisely in its capacity both to expose evil and to present the triumph of its counterpole: innocence and justice. W. H. Auden, a great "addict" of crime fiction himself, once stated: "The interest in the detective story is the dialectic of innocence and guilt."[1] "The magic formula," notes Auden, "is an innocence which is discovered to contain guilt; then a suspicion of being the guilty one; and finally a real innocence from which the guilty other has been expelled . . . by the detective who discovers the truth."[2] Crime fiction, in other words, has the cathartic function of confronting us with injustice and guilt and delivering what Auden termed a "magical satisfaction" by presenting us with a vision of the society that "re-establishe[s] its innocence anew."[3] What happens, however, when crime fiction takes evil of the greatest possible dimensions—genocide—as its theme? This essay examines the theme of the Holocaust in contemporary German-language crime fiction and the ways the genre forces the responsible society to confront its own historic wrong-doing.

The particular appeal of crime fiction is that it supplies readers with narratives of crime *and* punishment, presenting a utopia of social order that eventually triumphs over the disorder of crime. This formal characteristic has important implications when a crime novel features the ultimate Nazi crime, because the very incorporation of the Holocaust into the plot of a crime novel might imply that it is a crime that can be adequately punished or avenged. Furthermore, such crime fiction needs to reconcile the necessity to address the German complicity in the crime of the Holocaust with the genre's prerogative to offer a cathartic experience of relief from guilt. This essay analyzes five contemporary German crime novels that deal with the Holocaust and the National Socialist period, examining the ways in which this popular genre frames the Holocaust according to the paradigm of crime and punishment. Looking at Monika Buttler's *Dunkelzeit* (2006), Henrike Heiland's *Blutsünde* (2007), Dankwart Paul Zeller's *Das Geheimnis der Partisanen-Tora* (2008), Erich Schütz's *Judengold* (2009) and Volker Kutscher's *Goldstein* (2011), I will analyze how these five German crime authors position the Holocaust within their novel's plots, and how they use the structural elements and typical motifs of a crime novel to address the subject of National Socialism and the Holocaust.

Crime fiction constitutes the most important sector of the German fiction book market. In 2011, it comprised nearly a third of its sales.[4] According to surveys from 2009, 54 percent of Germans named the crime novel as their favorite genre.[5] Crime novels that feature Jewish motifs or deal with the subject of the Holocaust must be seen as an integral part of this literary landscape. The writers of the novels discussed here are mostly established crime authors; two of the novels make up part of detective series (*Goldstein* and *Dunkelzeit*) and three of them were in their second printing at the time of this writing. Given that crime fiction can be seen as *the* popular genre that perhaps best reflects the tastes, concerns, and anxieties of contemporary society, considering the way it handles the Holocaust can give us an insight not only into the sensibilities of the German readers, but also into the public demand to frame the nation's dark past in a popular format that is easily digestible.

In his book *Holocaust as Fiction*, William Collins Donahue argues that popular culture, in particular crime fiction, is a venue that "enables us to 'feel' at once engaged with the Holocaust while enforcing an absolute distance from its essential character of atrocity, fundamental criminality, and human suffering."[6] In his analysis of Bernhard Schlink's detective trilogy: *Selbs Justiz* (1987), *Selbs Betrug* (1992) and *Selbs Mord* (2001), Donahue puts forward the claim that "the very emplotment of Nazism within the detective genre provides all manner of ideological relief."[7] Analyzing this mechanism of relief, Donahue refers to Ernst Bloch's category of the "alpha" event or the unnarrated, "unsolved darkness [that] always precedes the rise of the curtain."[8] For Bloch, the "alpha" is the crime that takes place prior to the plot and is the "dark pre-lude"[9] to the actual story, the mystery that has to be brought to light by the detective. Utilizing this concept, Donahue argues that Schlink's trilogy, which is set in the post-1945 period, positions National Socialism and the Holocaust in the role of the "alpha" event. By relegating the Holocaust to the status of this Blochian "darkness at the beginning," crime fiction of this kind allows readers to distance themselves from this "great unknown foundational crime."[10] In this way, according to Donahue, the very structure of the crime novel creates conditions for an exculpatory perspective for the reader, who can detach herself from the narrated events.

Apart from the structural characteristics of crime fiction, it is also its status as *U-Literatur* (*Unterhaltungsliteratur* or entertainment literature) in Germany that underlines the genre's capacity to offer escapist narratives. Seen as belonging to the realm of so-called low culture, the popular assumption is that crime fiction merely provides entertainment. And even if it does actually address a difficult history, critics like Donahue believe that crime fiction will by definition be "significantly less sensitive to . . . [the] rigorous moral agenda of 'mastering the past.'"[11] According to Donahue, therefore, crime fiction, exempt from the constraints of political correctness and following its own agenda of reestablishing the readers' sense of innocence, is a medium in which the history of the Holocaust, if referred to at all, runs the risk of being particularly misrepresented.

The claim that the very conventions of the genre predestine crime fiction to produce only exculpatory visions of a nation's shameful past does not necessarily have to be true. As Claire Gorrara points out in her analysis of the motif of the Holocaust in recent French crime fiction, the genre can also offer a platform for writers and their audiences to engage in a critical reconstruction of the repressed past. Gorrara argues that, when it concentrates on the pursuit of truth and the reconstruction of events lying in the past, the genre offers the writer and the reader "a highly codified format in which to remember the past" and uncover the "missing" history.[12] This critical capacity of crime fiction to address difficult legacies and challenge the existing interpretations of the national past became manifest not only in France with its "thriller de la mémoire historique,"[13] but also in Poland, where Władysław Pasikowski's recent thriller *Pokłosie* (Aftermath, 2012)—based on the real events in Jedwabne, where 1941 Polish inhabitants killed hundreds of their Jewish neighbors, burning them in a barn—was the first feature film to address the infamous pogrom.[14] These examples, although not necessarily representative of the bulk of crime fiction, illustrate that the detective narrative, with its imperative to return to the past and locate "missing" memories, can also provide a medium to investigate the dark chapters of history.

Pursuing the question of whether contemporary German crime fiction provides an exculpatory vision of Germany's dark past or offers a critical investigation of the National Socialist period, I will look at two aspects in particular detail: the positioning of the Holocaust in the plot and the way the narration about the Holocaust is mediated by the conventions of the genre.

Holocaust as Source of Suspense

The Holocaust features in the plots of contemporary German crime novels in different ways, even if they are not set during the Second World War. A case in point is Volker Kutscher's *Goldstein*, whose action takes place in 1931 Berlin, but whose plot is permeated with a sense of foreboding about the approaching doom. The main protagonist of the novel, criminal inspector Rath, investigates a case that involves a Jewish American contract killer Abe Goldstein. The story of Goldstein, the "good gangster," unfolds against the background of increasing brutality and political radicalization of the 1930s. Visiting Berlin on a mysterious mission, he witnesses antisemitic violence firsthand and, in the closing episode of the novel, himself becomes the victim of a street riot initiated by an SA troop. Because of these interludes of proto-Nazi violence, the story of Berlin's rivaling gangs becomes framed in an atmosphere of impending catastrophe. Moreover, the last chapter of the novel, which is prefaced with an ominous quotation from W. H. Auden's "If I Could Tell You," is a clear prefiguration of future violence.

The main protagonists, Goldstein and Rath, are meeting for the last time before Goldstein's return to America, when they become trapped in a rampaging antisemitic mob led by the SA. And against this background, bidding farewell to Goldstein, Rath makes a prophetic statement: "'Immer glaubt man, schlimmer kann's nicht mehr werden mit diesen Idioten . . .' Er zeigte auf die Braunhemden draußen auf dem Trottoir. '. . . und dann wird's doch noch schlimmer'" (568; "You always think it can't get any worse with those idiots . . ." He pointed to the Brown Shirts outside in the street. ". . . and then it does get even worse").[15] The Holocaust thus overshadows the narrative, providing a "darkness at the end" of the story and serving as a source of additional suspense and a lens though which we read Kutscher's story.

Holocaust as Catalyst of Crime

Erich Schütz's *Judengold* could probably be classified as "thriller de la mémoire historique." Schütz's second crime novel is constructed around an investigation that unearths the complicity of the German and the Swiss states in the systematic appropriation of Jewish assets during the Holocaust, and their postwar reticence in restitution. The main protagonist of the novel, set in the German-Swiss borderland around Lake Constance, is investigative journalist, Leon Dold who, researching a mysterious case of contraband gold, tracks down the former NSDAP member, extortionist, and murderer Joseph Stehle. Back in his youth, working as train conductor of the Deutsche Reichsbahn, Stehle blackmailed and killed a female Jewish courier transferring to Switzerland money belonging to wealthy German Jewish families, and he appropriated the Jewish gold, placing it in nameless accounts in a Swiss bank. After the war, joining the militant Gladio organization, Stehle uses the Jewish money to finance weapons trafficking and right-wing terrorism. When one of the

Jewish heirs shows up to claim the family fortune, an escalation of violence is unavoidable.

The novel's cover features a bleak landscape of cloudy skies and a dark, sinister lake, cut by horizontal strings of barbed wire—the visual shorthand for the Holocaust. The Holocaust is never directly described, but it occupies a central position in the plot. The protagonists of the story are aware of the existence of the death camps and this knowledge generates their fear, determines their actions, and creates power relations. The Holocaust might be out of the spatial frame of this novel, but it makes part of the cause-and-effect chain in the plot and has long-term consequences for the protagonists. It serves therefore not only as the historical backdrop of the novel, but also appears as a criminogenic context, a situation that breeds crime and instigates criminal behavior in common people.

In Henrike Heiland's *Blutsünde*, National Socialism and persecution of Jews in the Third Reich likewise provide a frame for the investigation. As in *Judengold*, the first misdeed is also the appropriation of Jewish possessions, which later triggers a sequence of other (retributive) crimes. The plot of the novel starts in 1936 when, just before her family manages to leave Königsberg for Sweden, Hannah Simon, who is Jewish, entrusts Ernst Priebe, her non-Jewish boyfriend, with a set of valuable watercolor paintings by a "degenerate" artist. Priebe, who is also father of Hannah's unborn baby, changes his identity during the war, not only evading Hannah's efforts to find him, but also undeservedly enjoying recognition as a self-professed antifascist and helper of Jews. Although Heiland's treatment of historical facts is not necessarily accurate—she portrays, for example, a Jewish family in Königsberg as living in hiding as early as 1936 for no apparent reason—it is the persecution of Jews during National Socialism that serves here, again, as a criminogenic setting, which enables not only genocide, but also other forms of criminal behavior like fraud, theft, and appropriation of identity.[16]

Holocaust as Motive

Contemporary German detective stories feature the Holocaust not only as a context triggering criminality, but also as a motive for crime—an injustice that needs to be revenged. The figure of the Jewish avenger plays a key role in this kind of plot. Monika Buttler's *Dunkelzeit* illustrates this structure well. The novel, set in contemporary Hamburg, centers around a series of murders, the victims of which—all elderly, non-Jewish women—live in a neighborhood where many of the houses were in Jewish possession before the Second World War. Laura Flemming, journalist and, in private, girlfriend of the police inspector investigating the crime, suspects that revenge could have been the motive and is convinced that the murders are somehow connected to *Stolpersteine* (stumbling stones), small metal-coated stones with inscriptions commemorating deported and killed Jews, set into the pavements in front of the victims' houses.[17] The Jewish physician and practitioner of hypnosis, Philipp Palmer, is the therapist of one of the murdered women and quickly becomes the main suspect. We learn that his father was murdered in Auschwitz and that Palmer dreams of retributive justice. He has a private archive of clippings about prominent Germans whose Nazi past came to light, possesses a gun, and fantasizes about killing Hartmann, a retired university professor and former SS officer involved in human experiments in Dachau. And although Palmer eventually turns out to be a red herring—the murderer being a frustrated, unemployed librarian who had worked for each of the three ladies to supplement his meager social benefits—Palmer's will to avenge the death of his father turns out to be real. During a hypnosis session, he commands Hartmann's daughter, who also happens to be his patient, to commit suicide, although this is prevented at the last moment.[18]

Philipp Palmer thus embodies the figure of a Jewish avenger who seeks retribution for the crime of the Holocaust. We encounter variations of this figure in *Blutsünde* in the person of Rudi Baumgart, who punishes Ernst Priebe for his trespasses against Rudi's Jewish grandmother Hannah. In each of these cases, Jewish or Jewish-identified protagonists (Rudi Baumgart and Philipp Palmer, as we are expressly informed, are only partially Jewish) engage in acts of revenge that are criminal in nature. And although the avengers are one or two generations removed from the Holocaust, it is the loss or trauma they suffered as a result of the Holocaust that motivates their actions.

The crime novels addressed in this essay both employ the trope of the Holocaust as the context of the criminal investigations they narrate, and they narrate the Holocaust by means of the conventions of the genre. There are three typical crime-fiction themes that prove of key importance here: the motif of the curse of the past, the unmasking, and retributive justice.

Curse of the Past

The curse of the past has featured prominently in mystery fiction ever since Edgar Allan Poe, but it has a particular significance in the context of German crime fiction referencing the Holocaust. On the one hand, the trope of the curse of the past provides German readers with a framework to ponder the possibility of "inheriting" evil and collective guilt. On the other, it is a vehicle to fantasize about the Jewish revenge.

Thus *Judengold* and *Blutsünde* confront us with the question of whether the Nazi ideology can be transmitted transgenerationally within a family. Both novels address the problem of neo-Nazi violence in contemporary Germany, framing it in terms of "inherited evil." In *Judengold*, we meet Sven and Bernd, grandsons of a former NSDAP member, who become fascinated with the figure of their grandfather and join a neo-Nazi organization.[19] Likewise, in *Blutsünde*, we encounter Dirk Sass, a high-ranking neo-Nazi, who takes his Nazi grandfather as a role model because he is disappointed with his Communist father.[20] But if the third generation is portrayed as susceptible to the myth of their "heroic" Nazi grandparents, members of the second generation seek ways to distance themselves from the dark inheritance. Ernst Priebe from *Blutsünde* changes his identity into that of Karl Rohde to cut himself off from his Nazi father, whom he abhors.[21] In *Dunkelzeit*, an SS man's daughter Hedda Hartmann (also living under the new name of Rosita Gonzalez) goes to therapy to ease her sense of guilt for the crimes of her father.[22] In Zeller's *Das Geheimnis der Partisanen-Tora* we even witness an act of expiation by the actual perpetrator, a former Waffen-SS officer who decides, in the final scene of the novel, to reveal what he did during the war and ask for forgiveness in a synagogue, during Yom Kippur celebrations.[23]

In the framework of crime fiction, National Socialism takes the position of a "cursed past" that determines the fate of the characters. And regardless of whether the "inherited" dark past is presented as a source of guilt or fascination for the next generations, such a framing implies a certain lack of agency on the part of the protagonists who are "doomed" by the evil committed by someone else a generation or two before. Moreover, the idea of history as a burden applies not only to characters whose forefathers were implicated in Nazi crimes, but also to Jewish protagonists, who, as in the case of Rudi Baumgart and Philipp Palmer, are fated to commit crimes in order to restore justice.

Unmasking

If history is the key to present-day crimes, the measure of success of any investigator is to expose the hidden past. Ernst Bloch identifies "unmasking" as one of the key characteristics of a crime novel, while W. H. Auden speaks of a "concealment-manifestation formula" that necessitates both in the discovery of the culprit, and the unearthing of any other unknown facts about the rest of the protagonists.[24] In a classic detective story, it is usually the least-suspect figure whose mask falls as we discover that he committed the crime. In the novels discussed here, the motif of "unmasking," or the revelation of hidden identities, plays a central role even if it does not concern the person of the perpetrator.

The entire plot of *Blutsünde* is built around the exposure of the true identity of Karl Rohde as Ernst Priebe. The discovery, made by his grandson, Rudi Baumgart, provokes a series of deaths, as Rudi decides to take revenge on his unrepentant progenitor. But Rudi's own identity also undergoes a dramatic change as the plot enfolds. The crucial event that turns Rudi into an avenger is the discovery of the true identity of his father, which makes him realize that he is of partially Jewish descent. As soon as Rudi learns this truth, he begins to identify as Jewish, proclaiming pride in his "Jewish blood," and pledging revenge for the sufferings of his newly-found grandmother. At one point during Rudi's killing spree, when a hostage he takes challenges his Jewishness, Rudi explains his motives in the following way:

"Jeder, der eine jüdische Mutter hat, ist Jude. Da wird man nicht getauft."
"Also bist du keiner, oder wie jetzt?"
"Nein. Aber ich habe jüdisches Blut. Im Dritten Reich hätten sie mich ins KZ gesteckt," sagte er stolz. (276)

["Anyone that has a Jewish mother is a Jew. You don't get baptized there."
"So you're not Jewish, or what?"
"No. But I have Jewish blood. In the Third Reich they would have put me in a concentration camp," he said proudly.]

Given that crime fiction usually relies on stereotypes, generating figures without much psychological depth who have a rather "emblematic function"[25] to play, it is perhaps not surprising that the novels quoted here also rely on a very essentialist vision of identity. The focus on "unmasking" hidden Jewish identities is, nevertheless, remarkable in these novels, as is the number of antisemitic clichés that the description of such identity investigations sometimes entails.

A case in point is Monika Buttler's *Dunkelzeit*, whose main protagonist, investigative journalist Laura Flemming, discovers that the famous practitioner of hypnosis she wants to interview for her new book, Philipp Palmer, is Jewish and that his real name is Blaustein. Laura "unmasks" Palmer thanks to a *Stolperstein* located just outside of his studio commemorating Ernst Blaustein, Philipp's father. From that point on, she becomes obsessed with answering questions as to why Blaustein uses a pseudonym: "Sie musste mehr über diesen Philipp Palmer wissen, der in Wahrheit Philipp Blaustein hieß" (165; She had to know more about this Philipp Palmer, whose real name was Philipp Blaustein). She also asks herself: "Und warum nennt er sich Palmer, wenn er eigentlich Blaustein heißt? Vielleicht gibt es da einiges aufzudecken." (188; And why does he call himself Palmer, if his real name is Blaustein? Perhaps there was something to investigate there). The fact that Palmer changed his name makes him into a suspect, his partially Jewish identity now becoming his defining feature. Later in the text, the police inspector Danzik describes Palmer's true identity in yet more detail: "Philipp Palmer heißt richtig Philipp Blaustein und ist Halbjude. Oder sollte ich sagen: halbjüdischer Herkunft." (268; Philipp Palmer's real name is Philipp Blaustein and he is a half-Jew. Or should I say: of half-Jewish descent). But the final "unmasking" of Palmer's motives takes place pages later when another character asks Danzik: "Und er heißt in Wirklichkeit Blaustein. Warum hat er sich umbenannt?" (278; So he is really called Blaustein. Why has he changed his name?). To which inspector Danzik offers his insights into the "Jewish nature," replying: "Manche glauben, dass ihre Geschäfte besser laufen, wenn sie nicht gleich als Jude erkennbar sind. Manche wollen damit eine Art Normalität herstellen." (278; Some of them believe that it's better for business if they're not immediately recognizable as Jews. Some want to create a kind of normality). And thus the myth of the Jewish conspiracy, which implicitly accompanies the reader throughout the entire plot of the novel, becomes adopted as the ultimate heuristic tool.

Palmer's supposedly "hidden" identity—in fact, the physician never denies that he is Jewish—serves here to create an atmosphere of suspense. At the same time, the figure of the "mysterious Jew" is also used to project a set of other stereotypes about Jews. And thus we learn, for instance, that Palmer is not only rich, driving a spectral Porsche that he, apparently, did not earn honestly: "Der silbergraue Porsche, in dem die Tausender seiner verzweifelten Patienten steckten, wartete wie ein sprungbereitetes Tier" (24; The silvery Porsche purchased with the money of his desperate patients awaited him like a crouching animal), but also that he accumulated his fortune fraudulently, cheating his patients and prescribing them unauthorized medications (277). The stereotype of the rich Jewish exploiter reverberates in the novel with the other familiar myth of the Jewish superior intelligence.[26] When Laura meets Palmer for the first time, she finds him exceptionally smart, a feature she immediately identifies as a Jewish quality: "Sie dachte an die Juden, die ihr bisher begegnet waren: ausnahmslos brillante, geistsprühende Männer, deren Kopfpotenz sie erotisch fasziniert hatte" (110; She thought of all the Jews she had met in her life: they were all brilliant, scintillatingly witty men, whose intellect fascinated her in an erotic way). The daemonic Palmer is therefore an embodiment of all popular stereotypes about Jews, combining the old cliché of the Jewish usurer and dishonest capitalist with that of the Jewish genius and the Jewish sorcerer (hypnosis). At the same time, Palmer is a Jewish avenger who wreaks vengeance on the perpetrators of the Holocaust and their children. And this particular capacity seems to be a relatively new appearance among the Jewish archetypes in popular culture.

Retributive Justice

If the figure of a Jewish avenger challenges some of the popular stereotypes about Jews, especially those framing Jews as passive victims of the Holocaust, it caters at the same time to the demand for retributive justice that crime fiction is expected to satisfy. In his analysis of Schlink's detective novels, Donahue puts forward a claim that popular crime stories offer "the sense of completion and retributive justice missing from historical responses to the crimes of the Holocaust."[27] Gerhard Selb, Schlink's honest private investigator who kills a Nazi villain, embodies the self-appointed vigilante who takes justice into his own hands and thus fulfills the readers' desire to see the crimes of National Socialism punished. Notably, in the novels discussed here, this role of the avenging hero is delegated to the Jewish characters. And although most of the avenger figures are noble individuals, who often end up being victims of violence themselves—Abe Goldstein, the good Jewish gangster from Volker Kutscher's novel, falls victim to an intrigue by a group of Berlin policemen, and David Gloger from Erich Schütz's *Judengold* is eventually murdered by a neo-Nazi—all of these novels address the idea of a Jewish revenge.

In his remarks on Holocaust memory and revenge, philosopher Berel Lang notes that neither the phenomenon nor the topic of the Jewish revenge has been particularly prominent in "standard forms of historical writing" and the arts.[28] This lacuna existed "notwithstanding the expectation among the German populace that with the Nazi defeat, a fearsome revenge *would* be exacted."[29] In her analysis of Elie Wiesel's memoirs, Naomi Seidman observes that "the scandal of Jewish rage" has for a long time had the status of "the unsayable" in European literature, even in the writings of Holocaust survivors themselves.[30] And although one of the very first postwar German feature films, *Die Mörder sind unter uns*,[31] addresses the popular desire to avenge wartime crimes and discusses the admissibility of vigilante justice, it was more the exception than the rule. In the postwar era, questions of guilt and revenge did not occupy the German popular culture much. All the more interesting is the intertextuality of *Die Mörder sind unter uns*, which, as Todd Herzog observes, clearly alludes to Fritz Lang's 1931 crime thriller *M: Mörder unter uns*, thus using a reference to crime fiction to articulate a post-Holocaust yearning for retributive justice.[32] The potential of crime fiction to accommodate within its narrative frame also the moral aspects of retaliation in aftermath of violence and the almost-taboo subject of the "Jewish revenge" become of particular interest for the case study at hand.

Three of the novels discussed here feature the motif of the Jewish retaliation against Germans. In *Goldstein*, Abe beats up and humiliates SA men who have assaulted an Orthodox Jew in the street; in *Blutsünde*, Rudi Baumgart comes to claim appropriated Jewish possessions and repay

Karl Rohde for his disloyalty by killing his daughter and kidnapping his grandson; in *Dunkelzeit*, Palmer's attempt to bring Rosita to kill herself is a form of a Nazi hunt by proxy. Furthermore, Monika Buttler's novel introduces a discussion on the possibility of Jewish revenge into the dialogues of the protagonists. When Danzik's girlfriend Laura tries to convince him that the serial killer's motive might be revenge on the occupants of formerly Jewish houses, Danzik voices reservations. Laura tries to dispel his doubts by bringing up the story of the Jewish terrorist cell Nakam:

> "Vergeltung von jüdischer Seite? Das ist sozusagen nicht denkbar. Es ist politisch unkorrekt."
> "Du bist in der Schuldfalle gefallen. Lass diesen Gedanken doch mal zu. Tatsächlich waren die Juden nicht nur alles ertragende Lämmer. Es gab zum Beispiel eine Exil-Gruppe, die kurz nach Kriegsende in einem Lager der Alliierten, in dem SS-Leute interniert waren, das Brot vergiftet hat." (33)

> ["Revenge on the Jewish part? That is, so to speak, unthinkable. It's politically incorrect."
> "You've just fallen victim to the trap of guilty conscience. Give it a thought for a moment. In fact, Jews weren't just suffering lambs. There was an exile-group which, as the war ended, poisoned bread in an Allied POW camp, where SS men were interned."]

Nakam (Hebrew: vengeance), a group of former Jewish partisans under the leadership of Abba Kovner, remains the only known Jewish revenge group in the aftermath of the Holocaust.[33] Their plan to poison water supplies in four German cities in order to kill six million Germans in collective retaliation for the Holocaust eventually failed, resulting in the 1946 "Plan B" action that targeted a prisoner-of-war camp near Nuremberg, where several hundred inmates had to be hospitalized after they had been delivered poisoned bread.[34]

The story appears in *Dunkelzeit*, however, in a peculiar context. The information serves here to justify the accusations against Philipp Palmer and is used to call into question standards of political correctness that Laura refers to as a "Schuldfalle" (the trap of guilty conscience). The message of *Dunkelzeit* is therefore not a plea for recognition of the Jewish agency during the Holocaust, but a claim that Jews can also be perpetrators motivated by feelings of revenge. The figure of Philipp Palmer that embodies this vigilante potential of Jews reveals an attempt to subsume Jews into the category of perpetrators and criminals—an exculpatory strategy on the part of the author, who thus positions Germans and Jews in a category that could be called "individuals who committed crimes in the conditions of war." Such framing helps Buttler's German readers to distance themselves from the negative status of their national group as bearing the responsibility for the Holocaust.

Political correctness in Buttler's novel serves both as a rhetoric device and generates a specific language to speak about Jews. Laura, under the guise of challenging false political correctness, uses the notion to lend credibility to the figure of Palmer the avenger. On the other hand, Buttler's characters struggle to negotiate a language of speaking about Jews that would comply with what they understand as rules of political correctness. When Danzik calls Palmer a "halb-Jude," applying the language of the Nuremberg Laws, he quickly corrects himself, opting for what he believes a more appropriate expression: "halb-jüdischer Herkunft." Avoiding the word "Jew," Buttler's characters stigmatize the word as negatively charged—a relatively widespread practice in contemporary Germany, where politicians and the media often resort to awkward constructions like "jüdischer Mitbürger" (Jewish co-citizen) to avoid the word "Jew." Although the protagonists of *Dunkelzeit* seemingly question the rules of political correctness as they concentrate on Palmer as the main suspect, in reality they only recycle conventions that reveal the unconscious othering and prejudice underpinning the language of political correctness in Germany.

The preoccupation with standards of political correctness and the motif of the Jewish revenge explored by novels like *Dunkelzeit* raise the question of whether contemporary German crime fiction provides an alternative form of dealing with the past, where historical narratives about the Holocaust become transposed into what Donahue called "soothing fictions."[35] For Donahue, crime fiction does not operate within the limitations of political correctness, which enables the genre to articulate narratives that relativize the German guilt. Some of the novels considered in this essay, however, perform a similar function while retaining the (however superficial) patterns of political correctness recognized by the German society at large. But if crime fiction, with its investigative focus, can indeed offer a medium for addressing a traumatic past, does the genre actually venture into the areas of taboo or does it rather obscure that which standard forms of *Vergangenheitsbewältigung* have the obligation to speak about?

Crime Fiction and *Vergangenheitsbewältigung*

"Wer Geschichten vom Krieg und vom Faschismus erzählt, erzählt Kriminalgeschichten" (135; Whoever is telling stories of war and fascism, tells crime stories), states Dankwart Paul Zeller in the closing chapter of *Das Geheimnis der Partisanen-Tora*, marketed as a "theological crime story."[36] In fact, it is only this definition that permits a classification of Zeller's autobiographically based novel in the realm of crime fiction at all. Recounting the story of Zeller's alter ego, a pastor and theologian from

Tübingen, Theophil Böttcher, who organizes a fundraising campaign to provide the Jewish community in Petrosawodsk, Russia, with a Torah scroll, the novel does not feature any criminal case to solve. Instead, we witness an investigation that unearths the provenance of the old Torah, in the course of which we also discover the dark past of Böttcher's colleague, Ludwig Erler, a former SS man.

Zeller's is a *Vergangenheitsbewältigung* story that avails itself of some characteristic elements of crime fiction (the figure of the investigator, trying to solve a mystery; the "unmasking" of true identities of the protagonists). The plot is based on real events. In 1996, the Dietrich-Bohnhoeffer-Gemeinde in Tübingen did buy a Torah scroll for the Jewish community in Petrosawodsk, an act initiated by Dankwart Paul Zeller himself.[37] Zeller's fictionalized rendition of these events is, however, a disturbing narrative that foregrounds German benevolence toward Jews, refers to a German-Russian-Jewish community of suffering, and contains a series of exculpatory statements about the Waffen-SS.

In Zeller's narrative we encounter only good SS men. We hear, for instance, the story of Wadim, a young Ukrainian, arrested by the Germans after his father, a partisan, was shot in front of Wadim's eyes by a German patrol. The interrogation officer in Zaporozhye who questions the boy not only treats him in an extremely friendly manner, addressing him formally although Wadim is only sixteen, but also serves the prisoner coffee and breakfast. When Wadim is deported to Sachsenhausen, he likewise meets a friendly *Unterscharführer*, who saves his life during a selection, gives him SS chocolate and, when the boy falls ill, brings him cognac and medication.[38] Finally, we meet a Waffen-SS officer stationed in Rijeka who takes quarters in the house of the local rabbi and, having found out his hosts are Jewish, gallantly states:

> Herr Rabbiner, wenn ich jetzt kehr mache, dann wäre das nicht nur feige, sondern taktlos und ohne Anstand. Wir sind Soldaten, und Sie wissen sicher, dass die Waffen-SS etwas anders ist als die Gestapo und die politische SS. Wir wollen, zusammen mit der Wehrmacht, nur eines, den Krieg gegen den Bolschewismus gewinnen. Und wir können nur hoffen, dass uns Titos Partisanen hier in Ruhe lassen. (115)

> [If I turn back now, it would not only be cowardly, but it would also put my integrity in question. We are soldiers and, as you surely know, Waffen-SS is something else than the Gestapo or the political SS. Just like the Wehrmacht, we have only one objective: to win the war against Bolshevism. And we can only hope that Tito's partisans will leave us in peace.]

While the concentration of positive characters with SS affiliations is already striking, even more so are the passages where Zeller's protagonists recall at their pasts, relativizing the criminal nature of the SS. In one of the last scenes of the novel, Ludwig Erler, who has just been unmasked as the SS officer from Rijeka responsible for the destruction of the local synagogue, justifies himself in front of his friend Böttcher: "Im Kampf gegen die Partisanen gab es in diesem Krieg kaum einen Unterschied zwischen dem, was die Wehrmacht, und dem, was die Waffen-SS getan hat. Höchstens den, dass wir waghalsiger, oder sagen wir draufgängerischer waren und mehr eigene Opfer hatten" (135; In our fight against the partisans in this war there was hardly any difference between what the Wehrmacht and what the Waffen-SS has done. And if any, it was because we were more audacious or, let's say, more ballsy and we had more victims). Zeller features characters who not only whitewash the Waffen-SS but also, like Böttcher himself, identify themselves in the first place as victims of the war. While his whereabouts during the war are only briefly mentioned, Böttcher constantly emphasizes that he was a prisoner of war in Workuta. It is this experience of being a victim, not that of the perpetrator, that defines his identity, and by referring to the time of his imprisonment he builds his relationship with the Russian protagonists in the novel. During his visit in Petrosawodsk, when Böttcher tries to connect with the local Jewish community, he quotes his gulag experience to point to a universal community of suffering, in which he, as a former camp inmate, partakes. The scene, which features Böttcher and his Russian interpreter, university professor Valja, is emblematic of Zeller's portrayal of the noble German:

> "Du musst wissen, ich war vier Jahre Woina Plennji [*sic*] (Kriegsgefangener) in Workuta, und ich weiß wenigstens ein bisschen, was es damals bedeutete, Lagerhäftling zu sein, obwohl man Sachsenhausen nicht mit einem russischen Kriegsgefangenenlager vergleichen kann."
> Valja stutzte, war völlig verblüfft:
> "Du warst in Workuta und kommst hierher mit einem Hilfstransport!" ... Sie fiel Theophil plötzlich um den Hals und drückte ihn lange an sich, sie konnte nicht anders, egal, was ihre Studenten dachten. (77)
>
> ["You have to know that I spent four years in Workuta as a prisoner-of-war, so I know something about what it meant to be in a camp, even if you can't compare Sachsenhausen with a Russian POW camp."
> Valja started, and was fully taken aback:
> "You were in Workuta and now you come here with an aid convoy!"
> ... She impulsively threw her arms around Theophil and held tight for a long while, she couldn't help it, and she didn't care what her students would think of that.]

The former Wehrmacht soldier Böttcher is celebrated by both Russians and Jews as a benefactor, without anybody posing the question of what he did before he got into Russian captivity. Framed within the structure of a crime story, the novel is in fact a redemptive *Wiedergutmachung* (atonement) narrative about the Second World War that ponders the responsibility of those who participated in it as soldiers and offers mechanisms of relief to its readers.

German crime novels reference past events, reframe them, and also comment on the contemporary rituals of commemorating them. Monika Buttler's *Dunkelzeit* devotes particular attention to the initiative of the *Stolpersteine*. At the time of writing, there were over six hundred such stones, inscribed with names of Holocaust victims, located both in Germany and abroad.[39] And although the project has met with criticism from some Jewish organizations, which found the act of walking on the commemorative plaques to be disrespectful toward the victims, there has also been a lot of enthusiasm about this initiative.[40] In *Dunkelzeit*, the stumbling stones bring inspector Danzik to ruminate on the Holocaust-commemoration culture in Germany:

> Eine merkwürdige Aktion des Erinnerns. Stolpern und stehen bleiben sollte man auf dem Bürgersteig, um die Namen der Ermordeten zu entziffern, die vor ihrer Deportation in diesem Haus gewohnt hatten. Bei jedem Hinein- und Hinausgehen sollte man sich ihr Leid ins Gedächtnis rufen. Aber was taten die Vorübereilenden? Sie hielten nicht an, beugten sich nicht, um zu lesen, sie traten die Plättchen mit Füßen. War der Holocaust eine Sache, die man mit Füßen treten durfte? In Berlin turnten, turtelten und picknickten sie auf den Blöcken der neuen Gedenkstätte herum, anstatt sich still und respektvoll zu verhalten. Nein, man hatte es noch nicht geschafft, nichts war wirklich angemessen. (31)

> [It was a remarkable commemoration campaign. You were supposed to stumble and come to a halt to read the names of the victims who once lived in the house. People were supposed to remember their suffering every time they entered or left the house. But what were the hurried passers-by doing? They wouldn't stop, they wouldn't bend down to read, they trampled on the stones. Was the Holocaust something you should trample with your feet? Instead of keeping quiet and behaving respectfully, people jogged around, flirted and picnicked on the blocks of the new memorial in Berlin. No, we haven't made it yet. Nothing was really adequate.]

Commemorative interventions that, like the Memorial to the Murdered Jews of Europe in Berlin, bring the Holocaust into the urban space unsettle Danzik because they challenge the physical behavior expected of the passers-by. This anxiety about performing a disrespectful gesture in the context of Holocaust commemoration seems to bother Buttler's protagonists. At one point Danzik interrogates a witness, who reports that Ms. Westphal, one of the victims of the serial killer, attended a *Stolperstein* commemoration event. When a photographer urged the participants to kneel down for a group photo, Ms. Westphal intervened, crying: "Nicht in die Knie! . . . Haben Sie dann kein Gefühl dafür?" (100; Don't make them go down on their knees! . . . Don't you have any sensitivity for the situation?). Thinking of that scene makes the inspector conclude: "Danzik musste an den Begriff 'Philosemitismus' denken. Aber gleich korrigierte er sich. Nein. Kniende Juden, das passte nicht. Wer hatte gekniet? Willy Brandt in Warschau" [100; The term "philo-Semitism" crossed Danzik's mind. But he corrected himself immediately. No. Jews on their knees, that didn't fit. Who kneeled down? Willy Brandt in Warsaw.] Danzik initially interprets Westphal's reaction as exaggerated and philosemitic, then the aborted act of collective kneeling reminds him of Brandt's 1970 genuflection in the Warsaw ghetto. This disconcerting conflation of images of humiliation (reminiscent of Viennese Jews forced to scrub the streets in 1938) and German contrition (embodied by the *Kniefall* of Brandt) may, on the one hand, point to an anxiety about modes of Holocaust commemoration in public spaces; in a narrative that foregrounds a fantasy of Jewish revenge, however, it might also suggest a symbolic reversal of roles.

The Holocaust is not taboo in contemporary German crime fiction, nor does it play the role of "darkness at the beginning" that merely precedes the actual story. On the contrary, it features more prominently than just a backdrop to the narrated events. The Holocaust, its consequences, and its commemoration become integrated into the paradigm of investigation and unmasking that define crime fiction. This presence as "darkness at the center" of the story, however, does not exclude the possibility that the narratives featuring the Holocaust as a motif might have an exculpatory character.

If we consider crime fiction dealing with the Holocaust as an alternative form of coming to terms with the past, we see that the conventions of the genre can both foster and limit an honest engagement with history. On the one hand, crime fiction can bring difficult subjects, like the persecution, dispossession, and deprivation of Jews during the period of National Socialism to a wide readership. Crime novels also have the chance to formulate a clear message about the criminal nature of the Nazi ideology and to shed light on the failure of the system of justice regarding the punishment of Nazi criminals and the restitution of Jewish property. What is more, crime stories addressing the Jewish-German past may also comment on contemporary issues, including the rise of neo-Nazism, persisting antisemitism, or philosemitism. Despite their potential to inform, warn, and critique by inscribing the Holocaust into a plot of crime and punishment, however, novels of this kind may also be problematic.

Positioned in the plot as a source of suspense, a criminogenic context, or a motive for crime, the Holocaust as an instance of human evil becomes domesticated like any other kind of crime. By introducing Jewish avenging figures, or framing the Holocaust as a "curse of the past," crime novels may also create an illusion that evildoing is a question of fate rather than choice and that the Holocaust can be avenged. Attempts to relativize German guilt or portray Jews as perpetrators of crime point to a potential desire to alter the narrative of Germans as perpetrators. The genre of crime fiction serves in this case as collective memory's safety valve. It can be well-researched, based on historical facts, but it can also offer a literary niche for exculpating narratives, revisionist storytelling, and even antisemitic prejudice that would not be allowed to come to the fore in other kinds of officially sanctioned narratives about the Holocaust, like history textbooks, museum exhibits, or documentary films.

This leads to the larger critical question of whether crime fiction, by "rewriting" the Holocaust, reveals what Donahue called a "desire to substitute fiction for history."[41] Translating a difficult past into a popular genre, crime fiction does not readily fit into the realm of historiography, and I would argue that the crime genre is more accurately a product of memory. Certainly the theoretical categories of history and memory become extremely useful here to differentiate between a story whose main purpose is to document the past, and crime fiction, which is a popular form of engaging with the past. Essentially crime fiction that addresses difficult history is about how we order the chaos of the past into a narrative that satisfies our need to cast out evil and guilt beyond the perimeter of what we consider our community.

Notes

The author wishes to thank the Alexander von Humboldt Foundation, which generously supported the research this article builds upon.

[1] W. H. Auden, "The Guilty Vicarage: Notes on the Detective Story by an addict," *Harpers*, May 1948, available at: http://harpers.org/archive (April 12, 2012).

[2] Auden, "Guilty Vicarage."

[3] George Grella, "Murder and Manners: The Formal Detective Novel" *NOVEL: A Forum on Fiction* 4, no. 1 (1970): 48; Auden, "Guilty Vicarage."

[4] Statistics according to the Börsenverein des Deutschen Buchhandels, http://www.boersenverein.de/de/portal/Belletristik/189810 (accessed April 10, 2013).

[5] "D.A.CH.-Studie: Studie des Boersenblatts des Deutschen Buchhandels 2009," http://www.stiftunglesen.de/dach-studie (accessed February 7, 2014).

[6] William Collins Donahue, *Holocaust as Fiction: Bernhard Schlink's "Nazi" Novels and their Films* (New York: Palgrave, 2010), xii.

[7] William Collins Donahue "The Popular Culture Alibi: Bernhard Schlink's Detective Novels and the Culture of Politically Correct Holocaust Literature," *German Quarterly* 77, no. 4 (2004): 473.

[8] Ernst Bloch, "A Philosophical View of the Detective Novel," *Discourse* 2 (Summer 1980): 42.

[9] Bloch, "Philosophical View," 44.

[10] Donahue "Popular Culture Alibi," 473.

[11] Donahue "Popular Culture Alibi," 462–63.

[12] Claire Gorrara, "Reflections on Crime and Punishment: Memories of the Holocaust in Recent French Crime Fiction" *Yale French Studies* 108 (2005): 134.

[13] Gorrarra, "Reflections," 136.

[14] Władysław Pasikowski, *Pokłosie* (Aftermath, 2012), DVD.

[15] Volker Kutscher, *Goldstein* (Köln: Kiepenheuer & Witsch, 2011), 568. All translations from the German by the author.

[16] Henrike Heiland, *Blutsünde* (Bergisch Glattbach: Bastei Lübbe, 2007).

[17] This project of commemorating victims of National Socialism was initiated by German artist Gunter Demnig in 2003. See http://www.stolpersteine.eu/EN/home.html (accessed March 6, 2013).

[18] Monika Buttler, *Dunkelzeit* (Meßkirch: Gmeiner Verlag, 2006), 243.

[19] Erich Schütz, *Judengold* (Meßkirch: Gmeiner Verlag, 2009), 179–82.

[20] Heiland, *Blutsünde*, 162–63.

[21] Heiland, *Blutsünde*, 183.

[22] Buttler, *Dunkelzeit*, 162–64.

[23] Dankwart Paul Zeller, *Das Geheimnis der Partisanen-Tora: Eine Theologische Kriminalgeschichte* (Albstadt: C. M. Brendle Verlag, 2009).

[24] Bloch, "Philosophical View," 36; Auden, "Guilty Vicarage."

[25] Grella, "Murder and Manners," 39–40.

[26] Sander L. Gilman, *Smart Jews: The Construction of the Image of Jewish Superior Intelligence* (Lincoln: U of Nebraska P, 1996).

[27] Donahue "Popular Culture Alibi," 477.

[28] The Jewish revenge has inspired popular culture for a while, with Jewish avenger figures featuring, among others, in the highly popular comic series *X-Men*, where the Holocaust survivor Magneto discovers his latent supernatural powers, or on the silver screen, with Quentin Tarantino's 2009 "Jewish revenge fantasy" *Inglourious Basterds*. Indeed, it seems that superhero and alternate history genre have availed themselves here of the motif that so-called highbrow literature and historiography shunned for a long time.

[29] Berel Lang, "Holocaust Memory and Revenge: The Presence of the Past" *Jewish Social Studies* 2, no. 2 (1996): 1–2.

[30] Naomi Seidman "Elie Wiesel and the Scandal of Jewish Rage" *Jewish Social Studies* 3, no 1. (1996): 8.

[31] Wolfgang Staudte, dir., *Die Mörder sind unter uns*. (DEFA, 1946).

[32] Todd Herzog, *Crime Stories: Criminalistic Fantasy and the Culture of Crisis in Weimar Germany* (New York: Berghahn, 2009), 147.

[33] For the story of Abba Kovner, see, for example, Lang, "Holocaust Memory and Revenge" or Tom Segev, *The Seventh Million: The Israelis and the Holocaust* (New York: Henry Holt, 2000).

[34] The story of Nakam has already entered German popular culture. In 2009, Berlin-based American musician and songwriter Daniel Kahn recorded a song about the Abba Kovner group, "Six Million Germans," *Partisans and Parasites* (Oriente Musik).

[35] Donahue, *Holocaust as Fiction*, 51.

[36] Zeller, *Das Geheimnis der Partisanen-Tora*, 135.

[37] See the website of the Dietrich-Bohnhoeffer-Gemeinde in Tübingen: http://www.bonhoeffer-gemeinde.de/bilder/015/chronik.htm (accessed March 6, 2013).

[38] Zeller, *Das Geheimnis der Partisanen-Tora*, 50–51, 55, and 62.

[39] Stolpersteine Project Website, http://www.stolpersteine.eu/EN/home.html (accessed March 6, 2013).

[40] See Reimar Paul, "Kultusgemeinde kritisiert Stolpersteine" *Die Tageszeitung*, July 22, 2006. http://www.taz.de/1/archiv/archiv/?dig=2006/07/22/a0268 (accessed March 6, 2013).

[41] Donahue, *Holocaust as Fiction*, 55.

6: Case Histories: The Legacy of Nazi Euthanasia in Recent German *Heimatkrimis*

Susanne C. Knittel

> Deshalb übrigens . . . lesen die Leute so gerne Krimis. Man will die Geschichte hinter der Untat, oder irgendeine Geschichte. Denn dann erst ergibt das Böse einen Sinn. Wenn wir den Täter und sein Motiv kennen, wenn wir wissen, wann und wo und wie er es getan hat, dann weicht das Abgründige der Tat. Das beruhigt. Das festigt die Weltsicht. Aber das Böse *ist* in Wahrheit ein Abgrund.
>
> [That's why people like detective novels so much, by the way. People want to know the story behind the crime, or a story at least. Only then does evil make sense. If we know who the perpetrator is and what his motive was, if we know when and where and how he did it, then the deed no longer seems so abyssal. It's reassuring. It secures our perspective on the world. But evil really *is* an abyss.]
>
> —Rainer Gross, *Grafeneck*

Tucked away on a hill in the picturesque heart of the Swabian Alps in southern Germany is the baroque castle Grafeneck. Once a summer hunting residence of the dukes of Württemberg, the castle has been a home for people with disabilities since the late 1920s, run by the Lutheran Samaritan Foundation. More than one hundred residents live there currently; it is a lively community, a *Begegnungsstätte* (meeting-place), as the Samaritan Foundation calls it, which works toward the social integration of people with disabilities. Every Sunday Grafeneck hosts a café where residents and visitors can enjoy coffee and cake; annual concerts and summer parties are held; and many of Grafeneck's residents go to work in the surrounding towns. Grafeneck's history as a care facility, however, has not been entirely uninterrupted. During the National Socialist regime, the castle was expropriated and turned into the first of six institutions for the euthanasia program, committed to the extermination of people with supposedly hereditary illnesses in the interest of so-called racial hygiene. During the eleven months of its operation (January 18–December 13,

1940), 10,654 people were gassed and cremated there. In 1947 it was returned to the Samaritan Foundation and resumed its function as a care facility. In the 1990s a memorial was opened on the site, and in 2005 a documentation center was added. Since then, the number of visitors to the Grafeneck memorial has increased steadily, from about five thousand in 2005 to just under twenty thousand in 2010.[1]

This extraordinary increase in visitors to the Grafeneck memorial in recent years testifies to a growing awareness and interest regarding the history of Nazi euthanasia both locally and nationally. Ten years ago, the topic was still largely absent from debates about the commemoration of the National Socialist past. With the growing emphasis on non-Jewish victims of the Holocaust and within the context of the debates regarding German victimhood, the victims of Nazi euthanasia are beginning to gain a place within German memory discourse—not least because scholars, artists, and authors working in Germany have begun to challenge the de facto separation between the discourses about the euthanasia program and about the Holocaust. Memorials such as Horst Hoheisel and Andreas Knitz's *Monument of the Grey Buses* and reconstructed victim biographies such as Sigrid Falkenstein's *Annas Spuren* (Anna's Traces) have been highly successful in raising awareness of these forgotten victims of Nazi persecution.[2]

In the case of Grafeneck, however, it was another genre that contributed significantly to the increased interest in the site and its history: the perennially popular detective novel, or *Krimi*. A number of regional crime novels, all dealing with the Nazi euthanasia program and with the crimes committed at Grafeneck, have enjoyed vast popularity in Baden-Württemberg.[3] These *Regionalkrimis*, a subgenre of hyperlocal crime stories that has risen to prominence over the past decade, also perform memory work by combining revelations of past crimes with an exploration of questions of guilt, as well as local processes of coming to terms with repressed memories.[4]

In this essay I explore the potential and the limitations that these regional crime novels present for the process of *Vergangenheitsbewältigung*, especially with respect to marginalized memories. I will focus on two novels, *Grafeneck* (2007) and *Kettenacker* (2011), written by Rainer Gross, both of which deal explicitly with questions of memory and repression, collective guilt and responsibility, and the internal contradictions of *Heimat* associated with this concentrated sense of regionalism. The first of these two, *Grafeneck*, has won various prizes and was even chosen as an exam text in all Baden-Württemberg Realschulen (secondary school ending in tenth grade) for 2012. The latter contributed significantly to the increase in visitors to the Grafeneck memorial site.[5] A new generation of school children and other readers are being introduced to an aspect of their past about which they might otherwise have known little or nothing.

These *Krimis* can be seen as a form of popular historiography[6] that contributes to shaping collective memory by thematizing the ambiguity of concepts such as history and memory. They also point to the blind spots or taboo subjects of the official commemorative discourse.

Not only are these novels based on historical sources and historiographical materials, they also reflect on the process of reconstructing the past and thus potentially make the reader aware of the constructedness of *all* narratives about the past. To describe these novels, historian Achim Saupe has coined the term "retrospective historical detective novel." He characterizes such novels as pop-cultural contributions to the politics of memory that not only serve to popularize official and academic historiographical interpretations of the past, but also "offer a new, defamiliarized perspective on the Nazi past via the detective gaze."[7]

The popularization and new perspectives that such *Krimis* provide are especially important in the context of the Nazi euthanasia program, which has until very recently been decoupled entirely from the memory of the Holocaust. A key reason for this decoupling is the lasting assumption that the policies behind the euthanasia program were in some way justifiable from a medical standpoint. This assumption was reinforced by the fact that separate trials were held for the doctors and nurses responsible, and they invariably received very lenient sentences or were acquitted and continued to practice medicine after the war. The victims of euthanasia were excluded from any form of juridical or social acknowledgement or adequate financial recompense, as they were not considered part of the Nazis' racial, religious, or political persecution.[8] A national memorial and documentation center are currently under construction at Tiergartenstraße 4 in Berlin, the site of the headquarters of the euthanasia program.[9] To a large extent, however, commemoration has hitherto been the result of the work of small groups and individuals on a local or regional level. An additional reason is the fact that people with disabilities must still today contend with pervasive cultural prejudice and stigmatization. The tendency to evaluate a human life according to its socio-economic usefulness and the insistence on defining mental illness as a deviation from or as a threat to established norms contributes to a continuing marginalization of the disabled and an insecurity regarding interactions with them. The steadfast belief held by many that disability must be cured rather than accommodated tacitly affirms eugenicist notions that a disabled life is not worth living. All these attitudes and beliefs have made acknowledging the memory of the Nazi euthanasia program a considerable challenge, and have contributed to relegating the discussion and commemoration of these crimes almost exclusively to academic and professional circles.

Given the local, grassroots nature of the attention to Nazi euthanasia in Germany, the subject matter delivered within the genre of the regional crime novel, also referred to as the *Heimatkrimi*, delivers particularly compelling results. The local specificity of the setting makes it possible to illuminate different aspects of the history of the Nazi past and to look at it from different vantage points. These crime novels are situated not only at the intersection of history and family chronicle, but also of local and national history. The overwhelming popularity of *Heimatkrimis* throughout Germany means that the local histories and memories depicted in these novels reach a far greater number of readers who may be unfamiliar with this particular aspect of the Nazi past. The dissemination of these local histories and memories highlights the fact that this seemingly unique and specific local event in fact formed part of a national and even transnational campaign to eliminate people with supposedly hereditary illnesses. The *Heimatkrimis* not only individualize the Nazi crimes and the guilt, but also localize them, situating them within the small-town setting. This localization has several effects: it includes rather than deterritorializes the perpetrators; it shows the nuances of perpetratorship, thematizing the guilt and responsibility also of those who profited, collaborated or simply stood by; and it traces the motivations behind people's actions and interrogates their ability to make their own decisions. Finally, it also demonstrates the continuities between the Nazi period and the postwar period, and the oft-perceived seamless transition between the two. Above all, these *Heimatkrimis* are concerned with uncovering and questioning the familiarity and the security of the very concept of *Heimat*.

Heimat and the *Unheimlich*

At the root of the term *Heimat* lies the German word "heim," cognate with English "home." *Heimat* denotes a set of spatio-temporal relations between the subject and his or her surroundings. A person's *Heimat* is a place where he or she feels "at home," invested with an affective sense of belonging and rootedness, a point of orientation for a person's identity and self-conception. An inherently utopian space, *Heimat* acts as a screen onto which desires and longings (for wholeness, unity, safety, and belonging) are projected and which at the same time conceals anything that might undermine this idealized image. *Heimat* is thus essentially a defense mechanism against alterity, fragmentation, heterogeneity, and contingency. It is precisely for this reason that notions of *Heimat* become most important and pervasive in situations where these definitions are no longer self-evident. As Peter Blickle observes, "invocations of *Heimat* . . . always turn up where deep socioeconomic, ontological, psychological, and political shifts, fissures, and insecurities occur. *Heimat* buries areas of repressed anxiety."[10]

This repressive character links *Heimat* to another term derived from the root "heim": namely, *heimlich* and its dialectical opposite, *unheimlich*—specifically in the context of Freud's theory of the uncanny. As

Freud observes, the term *unheimlich* "is obviously the opposite of 'heimlich' [homely], 'heimisch' [native]—the opposite of what is familiar; and we are tempted to conclude that what is 'uncanny' is frightening precisely because it is not known and familiar."[11] Through a lengthy etymological investigation, Freud goes on to show how the word *heimlich* means *both* "what is familiar and agreeable," *and* "what is concealed and kept out of sight."[12] From this, Freud concludes that the semantic slippage between *heimlich* and *unheimlich* reveals something about the structure of the uncanny—namely, that it is "in reality nothing new or alien, but something which is familiar and old—established in the mind and which has become alienated from it only through the process of repression."[13] The idealized utopian *Heimat* might equally be regarded as the product of such repression, but, just as the word *heimlich* is shown by Freud to contain its opposite, so too is the uncanny forever lurking just below the surface of the *Heimat* itself.

The "return of the repressed" is a staple feature of the crime novel, which since its inception has been linked to psychoanalysis.[14] The detective, in pursuing his or her case, is like the analyst examining a patient. In the case of the *Heimatkrimi*, the criminal case under investigation bleeds into a psychological case in which the patient is representative of the entire local community. The memory work performed by the *Heimatkrimi* is thus the recovery of a repressed memory buried beneath the surface of the *Heimat* itself. In this, the genre can be seen as a cultural medium that testifies to the latest development in a series of transformations of the concept of *Heimat* over the course of the past century. As theorized by Celia Applegate and Alon Confino, *Heimat* functions as a mediator between the local and the national (or as a local metaphor for the nation), and it has done so in different forms, ranging from a defense mechanism of the local against the national in the late nineteenth century, to the reconciliation between *Heimat* and nation during the First World War, and the complete alignment of the two during the Nazi period.[15]

After the Second World War, *Heimat* assumed an escapist function, where an idealized, idyllic, traditional world substituted for the harsh postwar reality. This rehabilitative notion of *Heimat* was marked by a highly selective type of remembering, where the memory of German suffering overshadowed the memory of the crimes against people who did not fit in.[16] Only in the late 1970s and 1980s was this idealized notion of *Heimat* revised and critiqued: for example, in the form of the anti-*Heimat* narratives in literature and film, which uncovered the violence and repression that lurks beneath the idyllic surface. This is when the *Heimat* first turns into a crime scene.[17] It is this version of the *Heimat* that lies at the basis of the *Heimatkrimi*. Thus, it would be a mistake to dismiss the regional crime novels as being a mere throwback to the idealized *Heimatliteratur* of the past, since they are decidedly not interested in portraying the peaceful and morally impeccable small-town Germany. On the contrary: their primary focus consists in showing how the seeming order and structure of the local society and the silent consensus about the Nazi past are disrupted—and, what is worse, by someone from within their midst. As a genre, the *Heimatkrimi* thus operates with a quasi-Freudian sense of the "*unheimliche Heimat.*"

Readers recognize the villages, streets, or even people, which creates a sense of familiarity and mirroring, transforming the region itself into one of the protagonists. At the same time, however, this mirror estranges and distorts, as it presents the readers with a *Heimat* in which "the murderers are among us" and troubling continuities between the past and the present persist. The awareness of such continuities, of the way the past still haunts the present, is radically at odds with the harmony of *Heimat*, in which continuity between past and present is one of the most basic principles, but always in the sense of total homeostasis. The basic attitude of *Heimat* is nostalgic: everything was better in the past and that is why the past must be preserved at all costs. The very notion that the past might haunt the present presupposes that something bad happened in the past, which is incompatible with the precepts of *Heimat*, which is essentially a defense mechanism against the future, against the ravages of progress, change, and alterity. What it does not acknowledge is that it is also a defense mechanism against the past—or rather, against an intrusion from the repressed past. This dichotomy is ironically reflected upon in *Kettenacker*, where Mauser, the protagonist, is sitting at a local inn that used to make its own beer. He can still remember the label on the bottles: "*Bleibt Eurer Heimat treu.* Als wär man noch im Krieg. Im Krieg gegen das Fremde. Das hält heute fröhlich Einzug. Kein Nest ist heutzutage abgelegen, auch hier hat man seit März DSL, und die Schüsseln an den Hauswänden beten Astra an" (73; *Stay True to Your Heimat*. As if we were still at war. At war with otherness. Which today is merrily on the march. Not even the smallest village is truly remote anymore, even here since March they've had broadband, and the dishes on the houses all worship Astra). This war against otherness is waged against the outside world, but as Mauser discovers, the *Heimat* itself is always already "fremd" (strange, other).

The Return of the Repressed

Both *Grafeneck* and *Kettenacker* present a literalization of the return of the repressed, as bodies that have been buried for half a century resurface in the landscape of the *Heimat* like memories that have been buried deep within the subconscious. In his novels, Gross not only reveals the superficiality and unfinished nature of the process of coming to terms with the Nazi past, but also presents the Nazi euthanasia program and its memory as a lacuna within this process—a lacuna that is connected to ongoing misconceptions about disability, mental illness, and "deviant" behavior more generally. The setting is the picturesque village of Buttenhausen and its neighboring villages in the Lauter Valley near Castle Grafeneck in the southern part of the Swabian Alps. All of the locations exist in reality, and some of the characters are closely based on real historical figures, while others are purely fictional. Similarly, Gross draws substantially on the historical record, but the novels nonetheless contain fabrications or alterations of the facts, some of which are necessary on the level of plot, and others of which one is tempted to label as errors; an example of the latter is the statement that Mauser's sister was killed at Grafeneck in 1944, but Grafeneck was only operational as a killing center in 1940. (I will return to the issue of historical accuracy in the conclusion.) The novels are written in standard German but incorporate elements of the local Swabian dialect, especially in direct speech. This is a further indication of the way in which these *Krimis*, whilst emphasizing local color and authentic details, are nevertheless deliberately made accessible to a wider readership beyond Baden-Württemberg.

The protagonist of both novels is Hermann Mauser, a teacher at the local elementary school, who is also an amateur spelunker and archeologist. Mauser teaches *Heimatkunde* (sometimes translated as local history), a composite subject dealing with the geography and geology of the surrounding area, its flora, fauna, and agriculture, with an emphasis on pre- and ancient history. A nineteenth-century invention, *Heimatkunde*, as the name suggests, is characterized by a studied avoidance of difficult or unsavory aspects of local history, an essentially conservative and apolitical view of the traditional and enduring characteristics of the *Heimat*. In other words, *Heimat* and *Heimatkunde* are mutually reinforcing institutions.[18] Mauser is described as an "Eigenbrötler," a loner, who, even though he was born and raised in the village, likes to keep to himself. The slightly different status he has is also emphasized by the fact that he is not married like all the other villagers, but instead has a somewhat casual relationship with Veronika Baader, a potter, who moved to the village a few years earlier from Reutlingen, the district capital. In his spare time Mauser explores the landscape in search of remnants from the prehistoric and ancient times, searching for hidden caves in the karstic mountains and artifacts from the Stone Age, the Celtic, and the Roman periods. Instead he unearths bodies from the more recent past that compel him to confront the legacy of the Nazi period. Mauser reluctantly informs the police of his discoveries and a detective arrives from the capital to investigate. The detective, Stefan Greving, is originally from northern Germany and thus even more of an outsider in this region. The local population is not cooperative. Mauser decides to pursue his own investigation into the cases and soon uncovers well-kept secrets that not only shed new light on his own family's past, but also challenge the narrative that the people in the village have been telling themselves about the past.

"Es hat keine Nazis in Buttenhausen gegeben. Oder fast keine. Die kamen alle von außerhalb" (81; There weren't any Nazis in Buttenhausen. Or hardly any. They all came from elsewhere). This statement forms a refrain, repeated by all the characters in the novel *Grafeneck*. Before the time of the Third Reich, the village was home to a large Jewish population, and the current inhabitants pride themselves not only on the peaceful coexistence between Jews and Christians for more than two hundred years but also on the resistance with which the villagers met the Nazis' attempts to burn down the synagogue and deport the Jews. What actually happened in Buttenhausen during the Nazi persecutions, especially what happened in connection with the Grafeneck killing center, nobody talks about. In the neighboring town of Hundersingen, however, the story is a different one. They always say: "Frag doch die Buttenhäuser Busfahrer, die wissen wo's qualmt" (10; Go ask the Buttenhausen bus drivers, they know where the smoke's coming from), indicating that some of the inhabitants of Buttenhausen were involved in the deportation to Grafeneck of the mentally ill and disabled. What seems to be just a malicious rumor in the beginning, perhaps fueled by an old village rivalry, turns out to contain a certain truth in the end. On the surface, Buttenhausen seems to have dealt with its Nazi past: the village commemorates its Jews, cares for and conserves the old Jewish cemetery, and the village archivist has documented the names and fate of each Jewish family. This exemplary commemorative effort, however, has allowed another, undigested, aspect of the same past to be covered up entirely: the villagers' silent toleration of and even partial involvement in the euthanasia program. The two corpses that resurface force Mauser to acknowledge that the Nazi past is also part of *Heimatkunde* (21).

In *Grafeneck*, Mauser discovers in a mud-sealed cave the mummified and fully dressed corpse of a middle-aged man who was shot in the head before being hidden away in the cave. There is a chalk cross on the back of the suit jacket, and from the label in the suit Mauser concludes that the corpse has been there since the 1940s. Mauser's discovery is presented as almost preordained. The moment he enters the cave he thinks: "Hier ist etwas aufbewahrt worden. . . . Für mich. Eine Vergangenheit ist gegenwärtig, seit Jahrzehnten stumm, die jetzt zu sprechen anfängt" (12; Something has been kept here. . . . For me. A past is present here that has been silent for decades and is now beginning to speak). Instinctively he knows that this corpse has something to do with his father, who, as village policeman, "hat gekämpft, gelitten, standgehalten" (13; fought, suffered, stood fast) during the Nazi period. In Mauser's memory and the village lore, his father was a heroic resister who helped protect Buttenhausen's Jews, but somehow Mauser senses that this corpse will challenge his carefully constructed narrative about the past and about his father. The reader follows Mauser on this investigation that forces him to revisit traumatic events in his family history: the deportation of his mentally disabled older sister Therese (known as "Mutz") to Grafeneck and his mother's subsequent suicide. When Mauser finds with his metal detector the bullet that killed the victim and matches it to his father's old Luger P04 pistol, he begins to suspect that his father was the killer, causing his whole world to crumble. To make matters worse, the village archivist Heinrich Waltz informs him that the Nazis used the chalk cross to mark those who were selected for gassing in the euthanasia program. This discovery brings the question to the forefront of whether his father, who fought so hard for Mutz's life, could have murdered a disabled person and hidden the corpse in the cave.

This is so inconceivable to Mauser that he begins looking for an alternative explanation: "Es muß eine andere Erklärung geben. Einen Täter. Irgendeinen Fremden, der es getan hat, der in einer Geschichte vorkommt oder als Fahndungsfoto bei der Polizei, irgendein Fremder, den er nie gekannt hat und nie kennen wird" (114; There must be some other explanation. A perpetrator. Some stranger who did this, who exists in a story or as a police mug shot—some stranger whom he never knew and will never know). The perpetrator has to be someone from outside the village; it is impossible that it could be someone from the *Heimat*, let alone someone so close to home as his own father. Famously, there were no Nazis in Buttenhausen—ergo, any and all perpetrators must have been outsiders. The discovery in the cave is a loss of innocence for Mauser. *Heimat* is invariably connected to the imaginary space of childhood and the innocence associated with it.

For Mauser, childhood was the Nazi period, however, in which his family was victimized and destroyed, but from which he has salvaged the image of his father as a shining figure of courageous resistance against the external tyranny of the Nazis. This is why the suspicion against his father comes as such a blow. As Peter Blickle convincingly demonstrates, the feeling of being at home (in one's language, in one's memory, in one's identity) that is associated with *Heimat* is invariably also accompanied by a certain unawareness. A critical distance to the *Heimat* is not possible.[19] Thus, Mauser is unable to gain a detached, rational perspective on things because he realizes that he is invariably part of the history that he is trying to uncover: "Plötzlich steckt er mitten darin in den Geheimnissen und dem Dunkel der Zeit. Wir haben alle ein Höhlenauge, denkt Mauser. Ein Auge voll Dunkelheit, das in der Sonne blind ist. Wir können die Wahrheit nie sehen. Wir sind nie Beobachter. Wir sind immer Täter." (98–99; Suddenly he's right in the middle of these secrets and the darkness of time. An eye full of darkness, blinded by the sun. We can never see the truth. We are never observers. We are always perpetrators). The underlying message is that no one can escape responsibility.

In a last-ditch effort to keep the past at bay and the illusion of the neat and orderly *Heimat* intact, he goes to confront Fritz Hochstetter in Hundersingen, the doctor who diagnosed his sister's supposed hereditary illness and who sent her and many of his patients to their deaths in Grafeneck. Because of Hochstetter's involvement in the euthanasia program, Mauser thinks that he might be able to explain the chalk cross on the victim's back. Hochstetter hints that he knows about this incident and about Mauser's father's involvement, but tells Mauser to talk to Eugen Mattes, a farmer in Buttenhausen. Mauser confronts Mattes, who, it turns out, drove one of the grey buses used to deport patients to Grafeneck. But like Hochstetter, Mattes is unrepentant. Mauser is increasingly desperate for someone to blame, but both dismiss his admonitions that they confess their guilt, saying that it is not his place, and that he should look to his own past: "Glauben Sie, daß Ihr Vater ohne Schuld war? Glauben Sie, daß irgendeiner ohne Schuld gewesen ist?" asks Hochstetter (133; Do you think your father was innocent? Do you think anyone was innocent?). Mauser's attempts to identify the guilty party result only in ever-greater confusion as to who is responsible for these crimes. The further Mauser pursues his investigation, the more diffuse the responsibility for these crimes becomes, until ultimately the reader is forced to conclude that the entire community was implicated in one way or another. There may not have been any Nazis in Buttenhausen, but, as the Hundersinger have always claimed, the Buttenhausen bus drivers knew all about Grafeneck. There is a conscious irony in the fact that Hochstetter, the one unambiguous perpetrator figure, should live in Hundersingen, thus exposing the disingenuous nature of the villagers' finger-pointing. Their constant refrain is an indictment of the hypocrisy of the people of Buttenhausen, but it serves also to divert attention away from their own complicity.

In the end, it is detective Greving and modern technology that help solve the mystery of the body in the cave. Greving arranges for the facial features of the mummified corpse to be reconstructed and the dead man turns out to be Dr. Jürgen Schumacher, the director of the Grafeneck killing center. The victim, thus, is revealed to have been a perpetrator. Once the identity of the victim is established, the case is officially closed. The exact circumstances of Schumacher's death remain unclear, except to the reader, who is privy to Hochstetter's thoughts. Mauser's father and two other villagers had kidnapped Schumacher and Hochstetter, dressed the former up in the suit with the chalk cross on the back, and forced Hochstetter to shoot him, whereupon they let him go. After having "confessed" this to the reader—"Man hat mir die Waffe aus der Hand genommen. Mich laufen lassen. Ich sollte nur der Täter sein. Ich bin der Täter" (159; They took the gun from my hand. They let me go. I was just supposed to be the perpetrator. I am the perpetrator.)—Hochstetter dies of a heart attack.

Thus, the novel ends on a profoundly ambiguous and unsatisfying note; there is no classic denouement and no tidy resolution that would allow order to be reestablished. On the one hand, the crime committed against Schumacher is perceived to be far less serious than the crimes he himself committed and therefore there is no need to pursue the case further. When Mauser learns the identity of the victim from archivist Waltz, Mauser realizes that his father was a murderer after all, to which Waltz replies "Ein Nazi-Mörder. Das kann man doch verstehen, oder nicht?" (164; A Nazi-killer. That's understandable, don't you think?) and Mauser agrees. His father's guilt is thus mitigated because his victim was a perpetrator. On the other hand, the lack of a satisfying resolution to the case means that the uncanniness it brought to the surface persists. The *Heimat* remains forever tainted by these secrets and by this dark past.

The novel ends with a visit to the Grafeneck memorial site, where Greving and Mauser look through the memorial book with the names of the victims, including Mauser's sister. As they sit on a bench sharing a cigar, the conversation turns to the question of justice and of mercy. The case may not have been brought to a satisfactory conclusion, but Greving finds solace in his conviction that justice will be served at the Last Judgment. Greving is a deeply religious man, and indeed, religion plays a prominent role in the novel. The events in the novel take place over the Easter holiday and the idea of the resurrection functions as a leitmotif—only that it is the past that is resurrected and not the dead. Throughout the book, Mauser speaks repeatedly about the importance of having mercy and in his last conversation with Greving he says that he is not sure that he believes in justice, but that the most important thing is that people have mercy on each other.

The question of commemoration also plays a central role in *Grafeneck*. Earlier in the novel, Mauser and Veronika pay a visit to the Jewish cemetery in Buttenhausen. Mauser looks across the valley at the non-Jewish cemetery on the other side and thinks about the fact that his sister does not have a grave and that she is just a name in the book at Grafeneck. He thinks about the importance of having a place to go to commemorate the dead and considers making a grave for his sister next to those of their parents. For this reason, the novel can be seen as a more general commentary on commemoration in Germany where the victims of Nazi euthanasia still do not have a prominent place. Buttenhausen, with its conscientious commemoration of its Jewish heritage and the complacent belief that there were no Nazis in the village, forms a microcosm of *Vergangenheitsbewältigung* in all of Germany. The revelation of the local population's involvement in the Nazi euthanasia program serves as a reminder of all the unmourned victims of euthanasia. In this way, *Grafeneck* itself may be seen as a memorial commemorating the victims of Nazi euthanasia.

Lord Have Mercy

While *Grafeneck* is focused on the question of the perpetrator and can be read as a critique of the German commemorative landscape, *Kettenacker* centers on the victims of the euthanasia program, and questions some of the ongoing assumptions about its legitimacy from a medical standpoint. In *Kettenacker*, which is set in 2010, thirteen years after *Grafeneck*, Mauser is searching for Celtic artifacts with his metal detector when he comes across a silver pendant with the inscription "Gott schütze dich Kyrieleis" (May the Lord protect you kyrie eleison) buried in the earth along with a child's skeleton near the village of Kettenacker, about twenty-five kilometers southwest of Buttenhausen. He is tempted to cover up the corpse again and pretend he never found it, especially because the people of Buttenhausen have been avoiding and excluding him ever since he stirred up the uncomfortable past with the last corpse he found. But, like in *Grafeneck*, he suspects that this corpse has something to do with his family. His mother, we learn, was from Kettenacker and a cousin of Mauser's still lives there. Greving is called to the scene, and the investigation begins.

The corpse turns out to be of a little girl who was probably raped and killed in the early 1930s, at the beginning of the Nazi period. Mauser begins asking questions about the past in the village, which lead him to new insights about his late uncle, Heinz Mauser and his family. It turns out that Heinz had two children, not one as Mauser had always believed: in addition to his son Fidel, who is still alive but old and senile, he also had a daughter, Leisle, who disappeared one day in 1933 and was never seen again. Not only was this uncle a "Sozi" (a social democrat), and briefly imprisoned by the Nazis for his political beliefs, he was also a Spiritualist, which earned him the contempt of the village priest, Bonaventura Glattis. The priest and the Hitler Youth of the village spread the rumor that Heinz was a pedophile and that he had something to do with Leisle's disappearance. Mutz, Mauser's sister, visited these relatives often because Leisle was her favorite playmate. In the course of his investigation, Mauser realizes that in order to understand and solve this murder, he needs to understand more about his sister and her childhood. Reading his mother's diary, which he has kept in a box in the attic, Mauser finds out that Mutz was not always the withdrawn and "retarded" girl in need of constant care and assistance that he knew as a child.

The "strange" behavior began in May 1933, when she returned from a visit to Kettenacker silent and shaken. When Mauser realizes that "Leisle" is short for Kyrieleis, his cousin's real name, and that the word on the pendant is not an invocation to God (Kyrie eleison, Lord have mercy) but the girl's name, he concludes that the corpse in fact belongs to Kyrieleis Mauser. Whereas in the previous novel, Mauser had insisted on the importance of mercy, in *Kettenacker*, he discovers that "mercy" was raped and murdered during the Third Reich—by the village priest, Bonaventura Glattis. Moreover, Kyrieleis's disappearance coincides with Mutz's sudden "strange" behavior. Mauser suspects that Mutz must have witnessed Leisle's rape and murder and that she was traumatized by what she saw: "Vielleicht war Mutz gar keine Schwachsinnige. Würde das was ändern? . . . Vielleicht schon. . . . Sie war dann schon vor Grafeneck ein Opfer, ein Opfer des Lebens, ein Opfer von Menschen." (146; Maybe Mutz wasn't retarded after all. Would that change anything? . . . Maybe it would. . . . That means she was a victim even before Grafeneck, a victim of life, a victim of other people). Thus, the criminal case of Kyrieleis's rape and murder becomes interwoven with the medical case of Mutz's mental illness.

In order to find out what exactly happened to Mutz and who was responsible, Mauser begins piecing together his sister's story. He wants to find out how precisely "aus einem stillen, aber gesunden Kind ein Traumaopfer, eine Schwachsinnige und schließlich ein 'unwertes Leben' geworden ist. Ein einziger Mensch hat das vielleicht ausgelöst" (248; a quiet but healthy girl turned into a trauma victim, a retard and finally a "life unworthy of life." All because of a single person, maybe). The only document that can give him insight into Mutz's life besides his mother's diary is her patient file, which he gets from the medical archive in the regional capital. But reading the file, he realizes that there is a long chain of people who had a hand in Mutz's death in Grafeneck. These people include the family doctor who was the first to diagnose her "possible hereditary feeblemindedness," the public health official who concurred with the diagnosis, a professor at the university clinic in nearby Tübingen, who certified Mutz's "feeblemindedness" and had her sterilized. Because Mauser's mother thought that these doctors would help Mutz, she answered all the questions about her daughter's behavior without suspecting that with each answer she was sealing Mutz's fate. Finally, Mutz was deported, first to the nearby institution Zwiefalten, then to Grafeneck, where she was gassed and cremated. Mauser imagines Mutz's last minutes in the gas chamber, and they are far removed from the peaceful, "good" death implied by the word euthanasia.[20]

These revelations about Mutz's death prompt a reflection on the concept of "lebensunwertes Leben" (life unworthy of life), which guided the Nazi eugenics program. Over dinner, Mauser and Greving discuss the case, and Mauser tells Greving about Mutz's patient file. He expresses his indignation at the cold bureaucratic language and the fact that she was killed for not conforming to the standards of productivity. Greving responds that even today a person's worth is still measured according to her ability to perform: "Was heißt hier Menschenwürde? Ist die Würde eines Menschen abhängig von seinem Gesundheitszustand?

Oder von seinem Geisteszustand?" (302–3; What do we mean by human dignity? Is a person's dignity determined by her state of health? Or her mental state?). Mauser is especially outraged by the fact that all of these doctors were so quick to diagnose Mutz with "hereditary feeblemindedness" whereas in fact she was really suffering from post-traumatic stress and it was their job to help her. This realization goes to the heart of one of the enduring myths about the Nazi euthanasia program—namely, that it was in some way medically justified and predicated on humanitarian concerns: that it was ultimately an act of mercy in the face of incurable illness. In actual fact, however, the conditions that a large number of the victims of Nazi euthanasia were suffering from would not today be considered hereditary in any way and even if they were, that would not justify killing them en masse. The fact that Nazi euthanasia continues to be regarded as somehow separate from the Holocaust is indicative of the ongoing marginalization of people with disabilities and psychological problems in today's society.

The novel ends, just as *Grafeneck* did, without any clear resolution. The reader will not find out whether Mutz was also raped by Glattis, and Glattis's crime is not made public. Kyrieleis's corpse is buried and the village of Kettenacker can return to everyday life. In the last scene, Mauser and Greving again share a cigar. Mauser seems at peace. He has found out what he wanted to know, and has learned the true story of his sister. Now he seems reconciled with the fact that Mutz does not have a grave, "die hat ihr historisches Grab ... ganz offiziell.... Und ich weiß ja jetzt, wie's dazu gekommen ist" (358; she's got her historical grave ... completely official.... And, besides, I know what happened now). Thus, while the novel may lack a traditional or satisfying resolution, it nevertheless ends on a note of personal closure for Mauser that threatens to undermine any uncanny or unsettling effect such a lack of resolution might otherwise have created in the reader.

Stories and Histories

Grafeneck was initially conceived not as a *Krimi* at all, but rather as a more straightforward *Heimatroman*, with fictionalized names for the places and characters (Buttenhausen, for example, was to have been called "Lautlingen," and Grafeneck "Herrenwinkel"). Having tried unsuccessfully to publish earlier novels, Gross decided to write it as a detective novel in order to make it more attractive to the publisher and to a broader audience. It was his publisher who insisted that he use the authentic names of the locations and some of the historical figures. This genesis of the novel may provide an explanation for some of the historical inaccuracies: although the place names are now real, the plot remains the same. In its earlier incarnation, the novel was supposed to include an editorial note stating that while the persons and events depicted in the novel are fictional, the setting and historical background are based on fact. The note briefly outlined the history of the euthanasia program and alerted the reader to the fact that, while the novel places Mutz's death in Grafeneck in 1944, the victims there were actually killed in 1940.[21] This caveat was not included in the actual published novel, however. This is problematic since the authenticity of the setting now clashes with the inaccuracy of the historical facts presented and this is not acknowledged anywhere in the book. Thus, readers unfamiliar with the history of Nazi euthanasia will potentially get a false impression of historical details.

Certainly, a fictional text offers only one perspective on the historical past, which must not necessarily be "true-to-actuality" but should strive to be "true-to-meaning,"[22] assuming it seeks some historical credibility. In interviews, Gross has repeatedly justified his historical errors as "artistic license."[23] But this is a specious and highly problematic claim, particularly in light of the moral stance and commemorative ambitions of Gross's novels. As a genre, the *Heimatkrimi* is already constrained by a certain requirement of authenticity, and with the addition of a historical framework, particularly one as prominent as the Holocaust, the constraints to authorial freedom are even greater if the author wishes to maintain his or her historical credibility in the reader's eyes. And besides the historical "errors" there are numerous other internal inconsistencies that appear wholly unnecessary and unmotivated by "artistic license."[24]

The carelessness that Gross demonstrates with regard to the historical facts is all the more jarring given that the novels themselves consider the importance of getting the facts and knowing the truth. "Einer kann doch nicht mit einer erfundenen Geschichte leben," Mauser says to himself. "Mit etwas, das einer sich selber ausgedacht hat. Das geht nicht." (*Grafeneck*, 72; You can't live with a made-up story. With something you just thought up yourself. You just can't). But over the course of the two novels, Mauser gradually abandons this strict separation between historical fact and fictional narrative. In *Kettenacker* especially, his conversations with Greving repeatedly turn to the relationship between "Geschichte und Geschichten" (history and stories). Moreover, over the course of the investigation into his sister's death, he gains insight into the way our personal histories and biographies are connected to larger historical processes. This connection hits home with him when he reads Mutz's case history, which is itself a historical document. Thus, her personal history and her medical history are embedded in the larger history of Germany's Nazi past. "Der Mutz ihre Geschichte ist zu Geschichte geworden." Greving responds: "Geschichte und Geschichte hängen zusammen. . . . Wir sind es doch, die Geschichte erzählen. Wir Menschen! Wir erzählen uns dauernd Geschichten darüber, was wir für die Welt und für unser Leben halten" (*Kettenacker*, 303; "Mutz's story has become history."

"Stories and histories are connected. . . . We're the ones who recount history. We people! We're forever telling ourselves stories about what we call the world and what we call our lives"). History is equally a construct according to Greving, an attempt to make sense of the events that happen.

Especially an attempt to make sense of the bad things that happen, the stories we tell and the history books we write are, in Greving's view, ultimately a defense mechanism against the evil in the world, a reassurance that everything happens for a reason. Greving is less inclined to see his job as a detective as that of serving justice. In truth, he says, all he does is reconstruct the story behind a body, or rather, he adds, what he does is *construct* a reality: "eine lückenlose Realität in der sich das Böse mit Wissenschaft und Cleverness in ein durchschaubares Gefüge überführen lässt" (*Kettenacker* 92; a seamless reality in which evil can be placed in a transparent framework through science and cleverness). This, he says, is also the reason people read detective stories: "Man will die Geschichte hinter der Untat, oder irgendeine Geschichte. Denn dann erst ergibt das Böse einen Sinn. Wenn wir den Täter und sein Motiv kennen, wenn wir wissen, wann und wo und wie er es getan hat, dann weicht das Abgründige der Tat. Das beruhigt. Das festigt die Weltsicht. Aber das Böse *ist* in Wahrheit ein Abgrund" (*Kettenacker* 93; People want to know the story behind the crime, or a story at least. Only then does evil make sense. If we know who the perpetrator is and what his motive was, if we know when and where and how he did it, then the deed no longer seems so abyssal. It's reassuring. It secures our perspective on the world. But evil really *is* an abyss).

Given this typology of the detective novel, it is significant that neither *Grafeneck* nor *Kettenacker* has a traditionally satisfying conclusion. In the archetypal detective novel, it should always be unambiguous who the perpetrator is and who the victim is. The structure is invariably the same: some violent event exposes the dark underside of society (in Lacanian terms, the "Real" breaks through into the symbolic order): the detective arrives on the scene, pieces together the clues, and then in the classic denouement, gathers all the suspects in a room and reconstructs the events as they unfolded, ordering them all into a tidy, coherent narrative. In the end, the culprit confesses the crime and the symbolic order is reestablished.

In Gross's *Heimatkrimis*, by contrast, the culprits are usually dead, or else their guilt cannot be so easily established. Even after Mauser and Greving have reconstructed the events leading up to the victims' deaths and the cases are closed, the personal and communal wounds inflicted by these crimes remain open. Moreover, the responsibility for them is distributed throughout the community itself—the bus drivers, doctors, bureaucrats: the ordinary people who looked the other way. The symbolic order of the *Heimat* cannot be neatly reestablished. The bodies Mauser discovers may be those of Jürgen Schumacher and Kyrieleis Mauser, but the crime he is investigating is much greater. The body being autopsied is ultimately that of the *Heimat* itself.

Notes

Epigraph: Rainer Gross, *Grafeneck* (Bielefeld: Pendragon, 2007), 93.

[1] *Gedenkstätte Grafeneck*, "8. Grafenecker Brief: Gedenkstätte Grafeneck, Dokumentationszentrum. Fünf Jahre 2005 bis 2010. Rückblick und Bilanz" (2010), 4.

[2] The most prominent memorials are Horst Hoheisel and Andreas Knitz's *Monument of the Grey Buses* (2006) and Gunter Demnig's *Stumbling Blocks* (begun in 1994). Literary texts include Kerstin Schneider, *Maries Akte* (Frankfurt am Main: Weissbooks, 2008); Melitta Breznik, *Das Umstellformat* (Munich: Luchterhand, 2002); Helga Schubert, *Die Welt da drinnen. Eine deutsche Nervenklinik und der Wahn vom "unwerten Leben"* (Frankfurt am Main: Fischer, 2003); and Sigrid Falkenstein, *Annas Spuren: Ein Opfer der NS-'Euthanasie'* (Munich: Herbig, 2012). For academic scholarship on the memory of the Nazi euthanasia program, see in particular Sharon L. Snyder and David T. Mitchell, *Cultural Locations of Disability* (Chicago: U of Chicago P, 2006); Carol Poore, *Disability in Twentieth-Century German Culture* (Ann Arbor: U of Michigan P, 2007); and Stefanie Westermann, Richard Kühl, and Tim Ohnhäuser, eds., *NS-'Euthanasie' und Erinnerung: Vergangenheitsaufarbeitung—Gedenkformen—Betroffenenperspektiven*, Medizin und Nationalsozialismus (Münster: LIT, 2011). See also Susanne Knittel, "Beyond Testimony: Nazi Euthanasia and the Field of Memory Studies," *The Holocaust in History and Memory* 5 (2012): 85–101 and "Bridging the Silence: Towards a Literary Memory of (Nazi) Euthanasia," *Edinburgh German Yearbook* 4 (2010): 83–103.

[3] The two novels I will discuss in this essay are Rainer Gross's *Grafeneck* (Bielefeld: Pendragon, 2007) and *Kettenacker* (Bielefeld: Pendragon, 2011). Other prominent examples are Uta-Maria Heim, *Feierabend* (Meßkirch: Gmeiner, 2011) and *Wem sonst als Dir* (Tübingen: Klöpfer & Meyer, 2013), and Ulrich Ritzel, *Der Schatten des Schwans* (Lengwil: Libelle, 1999).

[4] On the representation of the Holocaust in German crime fiction, see also Magdalena Waligórska's contribution to this volume, in which she discusses the extent to which crime novels can provide a critical perspective on the past, rather than a merely escapist and exculpatory account, as has been alleged. In his contribution to the present volume, Kyle Frackman demonstrates how the recent popularity of regional and local crime fiction has its roots in the eighteenth- and nineteenth-century phenomenon of the journalistic case history (*Fallgeschichte*), which was a precursor to the genre as a whole.

[5] This increase was due in large part to the number of school groups visiting the site; between January and April, 164 school groups visited Grafeneck, compared to forty-six groups over the same period in the previous year. (Personal communication with Franka Rößner, May 2012.)

[6] Or, as Katharina Hall argues, even a version of *Alltagsgeschichte*. See Katharina Hall, "The Crime Writer as Historian: Representations of Natinal Socialism and Its Post-War Legacies in Joseph Kanon's The Good German and Pierre Frei's Berlin," *Journal of European Studies* 42, no. 1 (2012): 50–67.

[7] Achim Saupe, *Der Historiker als Detektiv—der Detektiv als Historiker. Historik, Kriminalistik und der Nationalsozialismus als Kriminalroman* (Bielefeld: Transcript, 2009), 266. My translation. See also Barbara Korte and Sylvia Paletschek, *Geschichte im Krimi. Beiträge aus den Kulturwissenschaften* (Cologne: Böhlau, 2009).

[8] There were at least 400,000 victims of coercive sterilization in addition to the more than 300,000 victims of Nazi euthanasia. They were originally excluded from the *Entschädigungsgesetz* of 1953 (Federal Law for the Compensation of the Victims of National Socialist Persecution) because they were not considered part of this specific form of racial, religious, or political persecution. It was not until 2011 that the German parliament decided to grant the victims of Nazi-euthanasia equal status to those of other Nazi crimes. See the website of the Bund der 'Euthanasie'-Geschädigten und Zwangssterilisierten, http://www.euthanasiegeschaedigte-zwangssterilisierte.de (accessed February 11, 2014).

[9] There is a virtual memorial online at http://www.gedenkort-t4.eu/en (accessed February 11, 2014).

[10] Peter Blickle, *Heimat: A Critical Theory of the German Idea of Homeland* (Rochester, NY: Camden House, 2002), 14. The body of scholarship on *Heimat* in German culture is vast. A good overview is provided by Friederike Eigler and Jens Kugele, *Heimat: At the Intersection of Memory and Space*, Media and Cultural Memory (Berlin: De Gruyter, 2012). See also Celia Applegate, *A Nation of Provincials: The German Idea of Heimat* (Berkeley: U of California P, 1990); Alon Confino, *The Nation as a Local Metaphor: Württemberg, Imperial Germany, and National Memory, 1871–1918* (Chapel Hill: U of North Carolina P, 1997); Elizabeth Boa and Rachel Palfreyman, *Heimat. A German Dream: Regional Loyalties and National Identity in German Culture, 1890–1990*, Oxford Studies in Modern European Culture (Oxford: Oxford UP, 2000); Johannes Von Moltke, *No Place like Home: Locations of Heimat in German Cinema* (Berkeley: U of California P, 2005); and Friederike Eigler, "Critical Approaches to Heimat and the 'Spatial Turn,'" *New German Critique* 39, no. 1 (2012): 27–48.

[11] Sigmund Freud, *Writings on Art and Literature*, ed. James Strachey, Meridian: Crossing Aesthetics (Stanford: Stanford UP, 1997), 195.

[12] Freud, *Writings*, 199.

[13] Freud, *Writings*, 217.

[14] See also Traci S. O'Brien's contribution in this volume, as well as Alfred Lorenzer, "Zum Beispiel 'Der Malteser Falke': Analyse der psychoanalytischen Untersuchung literarischer Texte," in *Der Kriminalroman: Poetik, Theorie, Geschichte*, ed. Jochen Vogt (Munich: Fink, 1998); Birgit Althans and Antke Tammen, "Das Begehren am Kriminalroman," in *Von Freud und Lacan aus: Literatur, Medien, Übersetzen. Zur "Rücksicht auf Darstellbarkeit" in der Psychoanalyse*, ed. Tanja Jankowiak, Karl-Josef Pazzini, and Claus-Dieter Rath (Bielefeld: 2006); Matthias Bauer, "Der unheimliche Fall der Psychoanalyse. Wie Sigmund Freud im

historischen Kriminalroman erst als Detektivfigur eingesetzt und dann des 'Seelenmords' verdächtigt wird," in *Geschichte im Krimi. Beiträge aus den Kulturwissenschaften*, ed. Barbara Korte and Sylvia Paletschek (Cologne: Köhlau, 2009), 59–76.

[15] Applegate, *Nation of Provincials*, and Confino, *The Nation*.

[16] Johannes von Moltke shows this in *No Place Like Home*, his analysis of the extremely popular genre of the *Heimatfilm* of the 1950s and 1960s; see especially 73–92. As an exception to this general amnesia of the *Heimatfilm* of the immediate postwar period, Moltke discusses *Rosen blühen auf dem Heidegrab*, which presents an example of "unheimliche Heimat." See Von Moltke, *No Place like Home*, 93–113.

[17] Von Moltke, *No Place like Home*, 203–7

[18] See also Applegate, *Nation of Provincials*, and Confino, *The Nation*.

[19] Blickle, *Heimat*, 65: "Heimat is the outwardly projected consolation of an identity's suppressed awareness of an inner anxiety that is conceived in the act of reflexivity itself."

[20] This scene is strongly reminiscent of Hans Ulrich Dapp's reconstruction of his grandmother's death at Grafeneck in his biography, *Emma Z. Ein Opfer der Euthanasie* (Stuttgart: Quell, 1990). Dapp's book was the first biography of a euthanasia victim to be published in Germany and set the tone for the ones that have followed, e.g., Falkenstein, *Annas Spuren*.

[21] Günther Gutknecht, Günter Krapp, and Cornelia Zenner, eds., *Grafeneck: Schülerheft* (Rot a. d. Rot: Krapp & Gutknecht, 2011), 51.

[22] See Nancy F. Partner, "Historicity in an Age of Reality-Fictions," in *A New Philosophy of History*, ed. Frank R. Ankersmit, and Hans Kellner (London: 1995), 38.

[23] See, for example, Maria Bloching, "Freiheit des Autors stößt auf Kritik," *Alb Bote*, Oct. 29, 2007.

[24] On page 254 of *Kettenacker*, for example, it says that Mauser's sister was thirteen years old when she was diagnosed with hereditary feeblemindedness, but two pages later she is said to be nine, which was her age when she witnessed the rape and murder of her friend Kyrieleis.

7: "Der Fall Loest": A Case Study of Crime Stories and the Public Sphere in the GDR

Carol Anne Costabile-Heming

THE TIME IS 1957; THE CITY IS LEIPZIG, German Democratic Republic (GDR). A successful author has been arrested for an alleged attempt to overthrow the government. In the fashion of a show trial, the writer is tried, convicted, and sentenced to seven years in prison. Prohibited from writing anything during his imprisonment, the author longs for the day of his release when he can begin writing again. But the authorities have other things in mind. Worried that the writer's loyal readers would become suspicious because of his seven-year absence, the authorities encourage the writer to adopt a pseudonym upon his release in 1964. To conceal his identity even further, the authorities permit him only to write crime fiction in the years immediately following his incarceration. Though these opening lines read like the description on a crime novel's dust jacket, it is the real life story of the GDR writer Erich Loest (1926–2013), and his fall from grace with the Socialist Unity Party (SED) in the GDR.

Crime fiction was a popular genre in the GDR, produced in large print runs. Because of their widespread availability, these texts reached substantially wider audiences than did the works of such famous GDR authors as Christa Wolf, Christoph Hein, or Volker Braun, whose often-controversial texts were available in more limited quantities. In this chapter, I undertake a case study of Erich Loest's crime novels. For my analysis of the publication histories of these works, I examine SED Party documents, secret police (Staatsicherheit or Stasi) files, and Loest's own autobiographical texts. These official documents establish that the SED, the Stasi, and editors at GDR publishing houses made a concerted effort to keep Loest and his critiques of the GDR out of the public sphere. Remarkably, however, Loest was able to access the public sphere through the genre of crime fiction. Nonetheless, even crime fiction was subject to the same types of censorship and manipulation at the hands of the SED. In this chapter I explore the publication practices within the GDR, focusing specifically on the ways that even nonmainstream fiction like crime fiction was viewed just as suspiciously as other forms of literature.

The GDR proudly proclaimed itself a *Literaturgesellschaft* and a *Leseland* (literature society; land of readers).[1] Despite this lofty ambition, it was not easy for readers to access books. Writers had to navigate a cumbersome process of requesting authorization in order to get their publications into the hands of readers. Censorship, programmed review, and the intervention of the Stasi strongly influenced the context of literature produced in the GDR, and controlled the distribution of very limited print runs to East German audiences. The tight control of publishing houses dates to the early days of the GDR. In September 1951, the Amt für Literatur und Verlagswesen (Office for Literature and Publishing Houses or ALV)[2] was founded to centralize and coordinate all aspects of literary production, and it also had the sole authority for granting licenses. The mere possession of a license, however, did not guarantee that a publishing house could indeed publish. First, the ALV had to approve the *Verlagsplan* (publishing house plan), and only those texts that were pre-approved in this way would be eligible for printing. Furthermore, the ALV was charged with raising the overall quality of literature produced: the publishing house was required to present all texts to the ALV for *Begutachtung* (evaluation).[3] In addition, the ALV served as the central coordinating point for all matters involving the development of literary texts, including providing direction and coordinating with other ministries, organizations, and institutions.[4] Thus, writers were forced to negotiate a rigorous *Drückgenehmigungsverfahren* (procedure for authorization to print) in order to get their books into print. As the 1950s progressed, the government paid increased attention to solidifying and centralizing all aspects of literary production, which resulted in publishing houses being subjected to the constraints of the Soviet-style planned economy. By 1956, all aspects of the publishing industry fell under the auspices of the ministry of culture.

Two events in the 1950s served as catalysts for the tightening of cultural policies. The June 1953 workers' uprising signaled a crisis point for the intellectual elite, who witnessed the tight reign that the Soviet Union had on the fledgling East German state. The year 1956 was a similar period of upheaval in the socialist world. The formation of the Petöfi circle in Budapest highlighted an intellectual movement that actually gave the GDR the opportunity to clamp down on writers and intellectuals who had strayed from the strictures of socialist-realist cultural policy. By the time of the Fifth Party Congress in 1958, the SED had tightened its grip on cultural production. In 1959 the Bitterfeld Conference attempted to solidify socialist realism for the writers and artists, to bring literary and artistic topics into the realm of the working class, and to encourage the emergence of a younger generation of writers, stemming in particular from the working class.

It is against this cultural-political background that I read Loest's biography.[5] Born in 1926 to a bourgeois family, Loest enlisted in the Hitler Youth, and later joined the German war effort. Following the capitulation of Germany, Loest settled in the Soviet Occupied Zone. He worked as a farmer's apprentice until the *Bodenreform* (agrarian reform). After that he went back to school and completed the *Abitur* (March 27, 1946) as part of the first graduating class after the fall of the Nazi regime. Four months later, he published his first journalistic article (July 26, 1946), moving eventually into the editorial team of the *Leipziger Volkszeitung*, an SED-controlled newspaper. As a matter of course, he became a Party member. Along with his editorial and journalistic duties, Loest developed a passion for writing fiction. His first attempts at fiction were successful, and several of his short stories appeared in newspapers.

His publications caught the attention of one of the editors at Verlag Volk und Buch, resulting in a contract for two books, *Nacht über dem See* and *Jungen die übrigblieben*, both of which were published in 1949.[6] *Jungen die übrigblieben* was a fictional account of some of Loest's experiences in the Second World War. Unfortunately, a review of this novel in the *Tägliche Rundschau* was less than complimentary, for the critique claimed that Loest had distanced himself too much from the events he was describing. The main character, Walther Uhlig, was, like Loest, just a teenager when called to take up the cause and fight for Hitler. The reviewer objected to the fact that, five years later, Loest was still portraying events so uncritically (such critiques would follow Loest throughout his career as a writer in the GDR). Among other things, Loest was accused of "Standlosigkeit," or an inability to maintain a consistent critical perspective.[7] As a consequence, he was fired from his position as editor for the *Leipziger Volkszeitung*.[8] Because of his bourgeois upbringing, so the Party reasoned, he could not understand the finer points of the proletarian class-consciousness, and he was sent to work in production in order to develop a sense of solidarity with the working class.

Because his job in production did not compensate him enough to pay the rent and support his wife and son, Loest turned to writing as a way to earn additional money. In his own words: "Er war *freier* Schriftsteller geworden wider Willen" (He became a *freelance* writer against his will).[9] He was an industrious writer, setting the goal of producing five pages daily. He was prolific and successful, despite his lack of formal training. His raw talent was easily recognizable to such well-known writers as Georg Maurer and Kuba (Kurt Barthel). Through their intervention and because the GDR so desperately needed to create a group of younger-generation writers, Loest was invited to attend a retreat in Bad Saarow. In the meantime, the publishing house Volk und Buch dissolved and Loest switched to the Mitteldeutscher Verlag in Halle.

In 1952 Loest was named head of the Leipzig section of the writers' union. This position brought him into contact with many of the GDR's important writers from the early 1950s and also required frequent travel to Berlin for meetings. As fate would have it, he was in Berlin on June 17, 1953, for a meeting, and thus witnessed the workers' uprising firsthand. Kuba suggested that the writers compose a statement for the press. Loest's contribution, "Mit Provokateuren wird nicht diskutiert" (We Do Not Discuss with Provocateurs) appeared in *Neues Deutschland* (June 21, 1953), the official Party newspaper. He soon realized, however, that blame for the troubles in June 1953 could not be attributed solely to Western agents, and lay instead with mistakes made within the Party and the GDR. This prompted him to write an article for *Börsenblatt für den deutschen Buchhandel* entitled "Elfenbeinturm und rote Fahne" (Ivory Tower and Red Flag) that was published less than three weeks after the violent uprising (July 4, 1953). Loest lamented the rift that had developed between the masses and the Party, arguing that organizations and ministries within the GDR, including the Party and the press, had made mistakes contributing to the uprisings. His attack against the press was particularly biting, for he argued that the newspapers had published only the "kritiklosen Jasager" (uncritical yes men) prior to June 17.[10] At first, Loest was harshly criticized. Wolfgang Böhme, chief editor of *Börsenblatt* practiced self-criticism and distanced himself publicly from Loest's article. Following the XV Party Plenum, many of the tensions died down, and in August, Loest and Erwin Strittmatter traveled to Hungary for a four-week tour.

Upon his return (September 21, 1953), Loest learned that he had been expelled from the writers' union. In his absence, it seems, there was considerable criticism leveled against the *Börsenblatt* essay, particularly in an article in the *Leipziger Volkszeitung* that portrayed Loest as a "faschistischer Provokateur" (fascist provocateur).[11] This sequence of events led to a special meeting of the Leipzig writers' union. The SED dispatched Party functionaries to the meeting who eventually convinced the district leadership to vote for expulsion. In the *Parteiverfahren* (Party proceedings) that followed, Loest received an official Party reprimand. In settling what became known as "Der Fall Loest" (the case of Erich Loest), meetings occurred in Berlin and in Leipzig. Following Kuba's advice, Loest displayed remorse, admitting that he never intended the article as an attack on the SED. Subsequently, Loest drafted a text entitled "Zu von mir begangenen Fehlern nach dem 17. Juni 1953" (On My Mistakes Following June 17, 1953) in which he readily discloses that he had misinterpreted the June events in Berlin. Such misunderstanding, he wrote, was attributable to his bourgeois background and his overall distance from the Party.[12] Though Loest emerged from this fight relatively unscathed, it proved to be the first of many battles with the likes of Siegfried Wagner, director of culture in the Leipzig district, and Paul Fröhlich, Leipzig's SED district secretary.

The GDR needed young writers with talent, and thus, despite his clashes with cultural functionaries, Loest was sent to study at the newly founded Literaturinstitut Johannes R. Becher, a school for aspiring writers. While studying in Leipzig, Khrushchev held his infamous speech at the XX Party Congress denouncing Stalin.[13] This led many East German intellectuals to hope for the possibility of change in the GDR. Modeled on the Hungarian Petöfi Club, the Donnerstag-Club in Berlin was but one example of the open dialogue that tried to emerge. But other events like the uprising in Hungary showed that democratization would not come to the East Bloc countries easily. This was a difficult time for Erich Loest, whose circle of friends included Gerhard Zwerenz and Conrad Reinhold. Both men were active in the Leipzig cabaret scene, and wrote a variety of sketches for the famous Leipzig Pfeffermühle.[14] Frequently, the performers and others from the cultural scene gathered at Loest's home, where they drank and debated, often into the early morning hours. These social get-togethers, which Loest never viewed as subversive or counterrevolutionary, proved to be his downfall in 1957. The precursor to Loest's second encounter with the Stalinist power structures and to his arrest occurred in autumn with the arrest of Wolfgang Harich in November.[15] Then cultural functionaries in Leipzig, among them Siegfried Wagner, began to take action against Gerhard Zwerenz for his outspoken criticisms; Loest was Zwerenz's only defender.[16]

Like many East German writers in the late 1950s, Loest was committed to socialism; he also had hopes for democratic reforms and openness. He defended controversial Western writers such as Kafka, Joyce, and Proust.[17] In addition, he was heavily involved in the establishment of a Klub der jungen Künstler (Young Artists Club). While Loest envisioned the possibility for an open discussion of cultural political issues of the day, the authorities, in particular the Stasi, viewed the establishment of this type of group as especially threatening. The authorities regarded an impromptu party at Loest's house (October 1956), at which a number of Polish dissidents were present, as the beginning of Loest's counterrevolutionary activity. Then, after Zwerenz fled to the West, the features editor of the *Leipziger Volkszeitung* demanded that Loest distance himself from Zwerenz publicly, but Loest refused. On November 11, 1957, Loest was expelled from the SED; his arrest by the Stasi followed on November 14, in Mittweida.[18] His wife Annelies was arrested the same day, and his in-laws were left to care for their three children. After five months, Annelies was released; Loest remained in prison.

After approximately six weeks in remand, he was certain that someone would wonder about his disappearance. In *Durch die Erde ein Riß* (A Rift in the Earth) he describes the lies and rumors that the Stasi spread about him. Heinz Sachs, head of the Mitteldeutscher Verlag, was informed that Loest had been arrested trying to cross the border into West Germany. At his trial, Loest was accused of violating §13: "Bildung einer staats- und parteifeindlichen Gruppe, die sich als Ziel gesetzt hatte, die Regierung der DDR zu stürzen und ein antisozialistisches System an ihrer Stelle zu setzen" (creation of a counter-revolutionary group, whose goal was to overthrow the GDR government and replace it with an antisocialist system).[19] His trial (December 19, 1958) was reminiscent of a show trial, for his attorney did not even attempt a defense. Loest was sentenced (December 23, 1958) to seven-and-a-half years in prison, and forced to surrender his savings. He served his time in Bautzen II from March 4, 1959, until September 25, 1964, earning an early release. Unfortunately, it was his success as a novelist prior to his arrest that served as justification for the long sentence. According to his prisoner's file, the Stasi viewed his publishing success as dangerous, for writing granted him access to the collective consciousness of the working class. Because he had the potential to affect the proletariat so directly, his counterrevolutionary activity was seen as all the more treacherous.[20]

The entire time that Loest was imprisoned, he was not allowed to write. Because GDR authorities did not want his readers wondering about his disappearance,[21] his earliest works were purged from public libraries, and Loest then disappeared from the public consciousness. His reemergence following his prison release was not immediate and occurred at a very difficult period for GDR writers and artists, after the XI Plenum resulted in the tightening of censorial control. In 1962, the Stasi Main Department IX/9 wrote a *Stellungnahme* (opinion piece) about Loest and his behavior in prison at that time. It depicted Loest as a problematic prisoner, who, because of his continued counterrevolutionary activity, had to be isolated from other inmates. Major Voigt recommended that the ministry of culture should not allow Loest to pursue his craft after his release, unless he changed his behavior during the remainder of his prison sentence. Moreover, Voigt suggested that Loest's demeanor would not permit him to perform his duties as a writer in raising the consciousness of the populace responsibly. In conclusion, Voigt also recommended that the Mitteldeutscher Verlag be informed of these measures.[22] Because the Mitteldeutscher Verlag was still interested in retaining Loest as a house author, this piqued the Stasi's concern. Indeed, in June 1963, the Stasi Main Department V saw this as an opportunity to keep a closer watch on Loest's contacts at the publishing house: "Es ist notwendig, mit operativen Mitteln zu überprüfen, inwieweit hier Verbindungen bestehen bzw. hergestellt werden sollen, die feindlichen Charakter tragen" (It is necessary to investigate with operational means the extent to which connections of a hostile nature exist or are to be made).[23] Following his prison release, the Stasi kept close watch on Loest (who was known as

"Operativer Vorgang Autor" or operative procedure author) and drafted frequent characterizations. One such portrayal depicted Loest as "in seiner Einstellung noch reaktionärer und der Partei feindlicher gesinnt als vor seiner Haftzeit" (his attitude is even more reactionary and his stance toward the Party even more hostile than before his imprisonment).[24]

Because Loest was not allowed to write while in prison (except for some short letters to Annelies), he had a tremendous backlog of ideas and stories that he wanted to develop. Before his imprisonment, he had begun two novels, one a satire about the Nazi Dr. Ley and another about the SS. Following his release, Loest assumed he would be free to develop these topics.[25] In *Der Zorn des Schafes* (The Sheep's Wrath) he describes a chance meeting with his *Lektor* at the Mitteldeutscher Verlag, Gert Noglik, who advised him to write crime stories.[26] Noglik suggested that the plots should take place outside the borders of the GDR and need not have political content, though "ein bißchen Anti-Imperialismus" (a little anti-imperialism) would not hurt.[27] Whereas place typically plays a key role in crime fiction, the suggestion to situate the plots at a geographic distance from the GDR meant that Loest's readers could not develop the same affinity to place as is typical of regional German crime fiction. Moreover, because Loest's readers were unfamiliar with the locations, the texts were able to take on the character of stereotyping about imperialism in the West, a tactic designed to underscore for GDR readers the negative aspects of life in the West.

Loest did indeed begin to write crime novels under the pseudonym Hans Walldorf and attained considerable financial success with his stories. In 1978 prior to leaving the GDR, Loest characterized his career as a crime novelist in a fairly positive light, explaining that "friends" had made the suggestion.[28] After the publication of *Der Zorn des Schafes*, Loest learned from Stasi files that Noglik had served not only as editor within the publishing house, but also as a Stasi *inoffizielle Mitarbeiter* (IM, or unofficial informant). The Stasi specifically instructed Noglik to suggest that Loest write crime novels under an assumed name.[29] Thus, the chance meeting of the two on the streets of Leipzig was not accidental after all. The political functionaries did not want Loest's name to be public again,[30] and the Party feared that Loest's loyal readers would begin to question why he had been silent for so many years, and they did not want to disclose information about Loest's arrest and imprisonment: "Ich kapierte bald: Für den Schriftsteller Loest war nur eine Auflage pro Jahr vorgesehen; er sollte nicht zu vehement auf sich aufmerksam machen. Buchhändler, Bibliothekare und Leser sollten nicht auf die Idee kommen zu fragen: Nanu, warum schwieg denn der so lange? Aber für einen Hans Walldorf war Papier vorhanden" (I soon understood: for the writer Loest, only one edition per year was planned; he shouldn't draw too much attention to himself. Booksellers, librarians and readers should not get the idea to ask: Hmmm, why has he been quiet for so long? But for Hans Walldorf, plenty of paper was available).[31]

The use of the pseudonym was known widely by the publishing houses, HV Verlage, and the Stasi. Political functionaries assumed that allowing Loest to write and publish anonymously would satisfy his desire to return to his calling. Indeed, because writers had constant contact with their publishing houses, it was easy for editors and Stasi IMs to surveil them. Thus, this official ruse to keep Loest writing also granted the authorities the means to keep close watch on him, a circumstance that was not known to Loest at the time.

Loest's career as a crime novelist spanned the years 1967 to 1975 and included twelve crime stories and three novels, but his fans remained unaware of the connection to Walldorf. Though the suggestion originated with his editor at the Mitteldeutscher Verlag, he only published four of his crime novels there. The majority of the detective stories appeared in the *Blaulicht* series published by the Verlag Neues Berlin. These were small pamphlets that cost approximately thirty-five East pfennigs and were distributed in print runs of more than one hundred thousand each. Thus, despite the cultural functionaries' desire to keep Loest's name out of the public view, they did not prevent him from reaching a substantial audience under the pseudonym.

Hilfe durch Ranke (Help from Twine, 1968), *Schöne Frau und Kettenhemd* (Pretty Woman and Chain Mail, 1969), *Gemälde mit Einlage* (Painting with Insert, 1969), *Erpressung mit Kurven* (Blackmail with Curves, 1970), *Oakins und der Elefant* (Oakins and the Elephant, 1972) and *Eine Kugel aus Zink* (A Zinc Bullet, 1974) all appeared in the *Blaulicht* series. Like all literature published in the GDR, these pamphlets were required to undergo the *Druckgenehmigungsverfahren*, a process that was in most cases not complicated and the authorizations were typically granted quickly. Ingeburg Siebenstädt, Robert Kündiger, and Marianne Kaufhold wrote many of the publishing house reviews. Siebenstädt, a mystery writer herself, was particularly complimentary, noting, for example, "Loests Erzähltechnik überragt das durchschnittliche Niveau der uns angebotenen Manuskripte" (Loest's narrative style tops the average level of the manuscripts we are offered).[32] Following Noglik's advice, the stories were set in other countries (England, Nigeria) and were thus reasonably nonpolitical. In the case of *Erpressung mit Kurven*, Loest did situate the plot in the GDR, occasioning an additional step in securing the authorization to print. In her review for the publishing house, Marianne Kaufhold noted that Loest took the idea for the case from the publishing house's catalogue. Blackmail was considered to be a serious crime in the GDR and one that happened infrequently. The publishing house provided the ministry of the interior with a copy of the manuscript, which then granted approval pending minor changes that Loest made.[33]

The detective stories that appeared in the *Blaulicht* series reached a different type of audience than literary texts. Such pamphlets were sold at kiosks or through subscriptions delivered by mail. This put Loest in contact with an entirely new readership. The substantial print runs underscore the fact that this type of literature was highly desired by the masses. The detective novels that the Mitteldeutscher Verlag published were both longer and more complex, two reasons that they also created more problems both for Loest and for the publishing house. The first, *Der Mörder saß im Wembley-Stadion* (The Murderer Sat in Wembley Stadium, 1967),[34] combined the genre of crime stories with Loest's passion for soccer. Set in England (and using a Scotland Yard inspector, Varney and his sidekick Oakins), Loest was able to construct highly apolitical characters, though Noglik did manage in his editor's review to mention the lack of integrity displayed by the British justice system.[35] Both Noglik and Carola Gärtner-Scholle addressed the wide readership that the book would earn, and a proposed print run of twenty thousand demonstrated that the publishing house was confident it could sell the books. Gärtner-Scholle remarked that this type of crime story "ist ein Krimi wie tausendmal gehabt" (is a crime story like a thousand others), which provoked some commentary from Meta Borst within the HV Verlage. Apparently, discussions were conducted with the Mitteldeutscher Verlag about the possible ramifications that publishing such detective stories could have for its overall profile, which up to this point had focused specifically on developing a canon of contemporary GDR literature.[36] The novel was a commercial success for Loest and, despite having been written under an assumed name, was a work in which he took great pride. After leaving the GDR, he finally was able to travel to London to visit the sites where his inspector Varney solved his crimes. Much to his dismay and shame, Loest learned that his assumptions about London were completely false, for he had imagined it to be much like the streets of Leipzig. Loest wonders why none of the editors or reviewers had bothered to point out the mischaracterizations, at least to the extent that they would have been aware of them.[37] Indeed, this misrepresentation of place seems to indicate that the editors also had little idea of what London was like, and that the ideological import of a book was of greater importance than its accuracy.

Loest situated his second crime novel, *Das Waffenkarussell* (The Weapons Carousel, 1968), in Nigeria, a location that allowed him to include an inherent critique of colonialism. As Cäcilia Friedrich, the external reviewer, described it, Loest sought to portray elements of corruption within capitalist power structures, specifically the smuggling of weapons. Because this novel took up very recent events in Nigeria (1966), the authorization process was slower and more careful. Friedrich's critique of the novel, though she still supported publication, rested on Loest's inability to portray adequately the origins of corruption in capitalist society. Clearly, she placed a much higher value on the social aspects and the potential pedagogical value of the text than did those reviewers working with the *Blaulicht* series stories, and was trying to move beyond mere *Unterhaltungsliteratur* (light fiction). Noglik, as Loest's *Lektor*, tried to characterize this more closely: "Er zeigt an dem bestürzend aktuellen Beispiel Nigeria den Kampf hinter den Kulissen. Dabei werden ebenso die kolonialen Raubgelüste Belgiens wie die Beteiligung alter Deutscher Nazis an der Ausbildung von Konterrevolutionären in die geschickt gebaute Handlung einbezogen" (He shows the fight behind the scenes using the topical example of Nigeria. Belgium's colonial plundering and the participation of old German Nazis in the training of counter revolutionary forces are built into the deftly constructed plot).[38]

The HV Verlage sent the manuscript out for additional review, this time to an expert in African affairs. This expert, noted simply as Meier in the files, disagreed to a certain extent with Noglik, stating that Loest resorts to superficial portrayals of the situation in Nigeria. He suggested that Loest needed to define the political and economic basis for the struggle in Nigeria: retarded economic development coupled with a feudal political system. Despite such critiques, the reviewer did not vote against publication, but rather suggested that the publishing house request revisions.[39] In an accompanying letter to Meta Borst, this reviewer also offered to confer with the publishing house and Loest directly. There is no additional information in the file to confirm that this did indeed occur. The HV Verlage did grant the authorization to print on November 16, 1967, approximately one month after manuscript submission. In a letter dated November 17, 1967, Eberhard Günther sent the authorization to print to Fritz Bressau, the head of the publishing house, with a request for the inclusion of additional background information: "Es würde den Wert dieses Kriminalromans, den Sie in 20.000 Exemplaren verlegen werden, erhöhen, wenn es dem Autor gelänge, eine Vertiefung des Nigeriakapitels vorzunehmen. . . . Wir bitten Sie, uns wissen zu lassen, wie diese Hinweise von Ihnen berücksichtigt wurden" (It would increase the value of this crime novel, which will be published in twenty thousand copies, if the author could deepen the Nigeria chapter. . . . We ask you to inform us how you will take these suggestions into consideration).[40] Bressau replied to Günter on December 15, 1967: "Für unsere Begriffe hat Walldorf, der sofort die Notwendigkeit einer klareren Darstellung der Fakten einsah, nun gerade diesen Hinweis sehr geschickt aufgenommen und verarbeitet. . . . Indem wir Ihnen nochmals für Ihre wertvollen Hinweise danken, dürfen wir Ihnen sagen, daß—soweit es im Rahmen eines Kriminalromans möglich ist—alle Möglichkeiten genutzt wurden, Ihre Anregungen zu verwirklichen" (From our perspective, Walldorf immediately recognized the need for a clear representation of the facts and incorporated this suggestion quite deftly. As we thank you once again for your valuable suggestions, we would like to tell you, that to the greatest extent possible within the context of a crime novel, all means were used to realize your suggestions).[41] This exchange illustrates that both writers and publishing houses attempted to comply with requests from reviewers for changes. The ultimate goal was for the book to be published, and this rarely occurred in the GDR without some form of compromise.

Loest's third crime novel, *Mit kleinstem Kaliber* (The Smallest Caliber, 1973) takes place in Czechoslovakia, where his two heroes Slavik and Karda solve the murder of a woman killed with a very-small-caliber weapon. According to Haaso Mager's external report, Loest pulled out all the stops and used all of the tricks in a crime novelist's repertoire. By this time, one sees that Loest was beginning to tire of the genre. Mager suggested a number of corrections to make the book more readable and thus sellable. Mager qualified this implied approval in his next sentence:

Andererseits kann ich eine Drucklegung des Manuskripts auch nicht ausdrücklich befürworten. Man kann nicht übersehen, daß der Autor in dem Bestreben, soviel äussere Sensation wie nur irgend möglich zu zeigen, die Realität, in der seine Handlung abläuft, weitgehend verzerrt, ja sie geradezu ins Unwirkliche transponiert. . . . Warum sollten kapitalistische Waffenschieber und deren professionelle Totschläger ihre Rechnungen ausgerechnet in einem sozialistischen Land austragen? . . . daß es sich hier um die Ermittlungsarbeit sozialistischer Kriminalisten dreht, daß hier die Realität eines sozialistischen Landes widergespiegelt wird . . . dieser Kriminalfall ist nicht im geringsten verflochten mit dem gesellschaftlichen Leben.[42]

[On the other hand I can't exactly approve the manuscript. One cannot overlook that the author, in his desire to incorporate as much sensation as possible, actually distorts reality, indeed transposes it into irreality. . . . Why should capitalist weapons traffickers and their professional hitmen settle their scores in a socialist country? . . . that it revolves around the investigative work of socialist detectives, that it represents the reality of a socialist country . . . this criminal case is not remotely interwoven into society.]

Mager furthermore quoted from a study on crime literature distributed by the ministry of culture that a detective novel "geht um die sozialistisch-realistische Aufhebung eines der wichtigsten Genres der Unterhaltungsliteratur . . . daß der Schriftsteller immer wieder neu seine Stoffe der gesellschaftlichen Realität entnimmt, aus ihr zugleich die ihnen gemäße literarische Struktur ableitet und seine Geschichten lebenswahr, parteilich und volksverbunden künstlerisch gestaltet" (reflects the socialist-realist elevation of one of the most important genres of light fiction . . . that the writer repeatedly draws his themes from societal reality, derives from it the appropriate literary structure and crafts stories that are realistic, partisan, and close to the people).[43] Mager closed his report with the damning conclusion that it appeared as if Loest had not even tried to emulate these goals.

Helga Duty's publishing house report polemicized against Mager's review, who in spite of his qualifications managed to ignore a number of factors that are essential to the social background of the text, and it accused him of misinterpreting the entire plot as it unfolded.[44] While rejecting Mager's criticisms, Duty also conceded that the manuscript was "kein besonderes literarisches Werk" (no special literary work).[45] Despite this confession, she closed her request for publication with a rather strong statement that this work represented: "Ein Kriminalroman, der in der sozialistischen Staatengemeinschaft spielt, die Gefahren, die von außen an uns herangetragen werden, aufzeigt und in einer spannenden Handlung zu verarbeiten weiß" (a crime novel that takes place in the socialist community of states, represents the dangers to which we are subjected from the outside, and wraps this all in a suspenseful plot).[46] In support of the text, the Mitteldeutscher Verlag also submitted an expert review from Paul Heinemann. He emphasized in particular the socialist setting, for it served as a lesson to readers that although criminal ideas may be born in imperialist countries, they could also be carried out in socialist ones. Heinemann found the story particularly exciting and suspenseful, with relatively few weak points. His main suggestion was to switch the citizenship of a married couple from East German to West because they were not portrayed as positive figures.

Such an example posed considerable problems for the HV Verlage in determining whether or not to grant permission to publish. Typically, the publishing houses sent a manuscript to external and expert reviewers first, and then, as can be seen clearly in Helga Duty's review, used the internal publishing house report as an opportunity to contradict criticisms that external reviewers had leveled. In this instance, Duty juxtaposed Heinemann's "expert" opinion against that of Mager in appealing for authorization. The HV Verlage, however, also sought advice from the reviewer Corinna Fuchas, who agreed with Mager on most points. Though the HV Verlage ultimately granted authorization, it first contacted Joachim Hottas at Mitteldeutscher Verlag to discuss weaknesses in the manuscript.

In *Rotes Elfenbein* (Red Ivory, 1975), the last crime novel Loest wrote for Mitteldeutscher Verlag, he takes his main character's love for soccer to the Federal Republic, where Varney accompanies the British soccer team for the 1974 World Cup. In her internal review, Helga Duty praised the manuscript, but noted at the end: "Wir wissen dabei zugleich—und hier teilen wir die Ansicht des Außenlektors—daß der Autor Loest mehr kann, als Walldorf leistet. Deshalb wird sich der Verlag bemühen, den Autor mit wesentlicheren Stoffen zu beschäftigen und ihm dabei eine intensivere

Gestaltung abzuverlangen" (We know—and here we share the opinion of the external reviewer—that the author Loest can do more than what Walldorf achieves. For this reason, the publishing house will strive to provide the author with more essential topics, and thus demand a more intensive style from him).[47] This signals the end of Hans Walldorf's career as a criminalist for the Mitteldeutscher Verlag.

One additional detective story, *Oakins macht Karriere* (Oakins Makes it to the Top, 1975), unites characters from several of Loest's crime stories. Because of its satirical elements, it found its home with the Eulenspiegelverlag.[48] Considerable time had passed since Loest's imprisonment and tensions between cultural functionaries and writers had eased somewhat following Erich Honecker's proclamation that there were no longer any taboo topics. Thus it was an opportune time for Loest to publish this crime story under his own name. Astute readers could finally make the link between Loest and Walldorf.[49] This, coupled with the Mitteldeutscher Verlag's willingness to work with Loest on more contemporary topics, would seem to indicate that Loest had finally overcome his problems with the GDR authorities.

Despite the openness that the 1970s promised, Loest's reprieve was shortlived. The Stasi was informed regularly about Loest's literary activities. Documents reveal that the IMs assigned to Loest came from his close circle of friends and confidants. These so-called friends exploited their relationship with Loest to gain access to manuscripts in progress, which they then turned over to the Stasi.[50] Although the Mitteldeutscher Verlag expressed a willingness to rehabilitate Loest, his texts from the late 1970s did not have as easy a time reaching print as the crime stories. And even though he was permitted once again to publish under his own name, his access to the public sphere decreased considerably following the publication of *Es geht seinen Gang oder Mühen in unserer Ebene* (It Goes Its Own Way, or Troubles in Our Rank, 1978).

Because of his repeated clashes with the Party, Loest serves as an illustrative example of how a prolific nonmainstream writer negotiated the public sphere in the GDR. While he got the authorization to print his earliest works fairly easily, his situation became more complicated following his release from Bautzen II in 1964. His first post-Bautzen publications highlight the tenuousness of Loest's access to the public sphere. In taking on a pseudonym and turning to the genre of crime fiction, Loest was once again formally and officially a writer. Because crime fiction was considered light fiction, it did not receive the same level of scrutiny as did texts that addressed everyday circumstances in the GDR. Once Loest's identity was revealed and he began writing about GDR topics again, he experienced increased surveillance and constant debates about his texts within the publishing community. Ultimately, Loest turned his back on the GDR, settling in the Federal Republic on March 20, 1981. In 1989, with his son Thomas and daughter-in-law Elke, Loest founded the Linden Verlag in Künzelsau, marking his entry into a new realm as publisher, granting him not only improved access to but also control of the public sphere. In April 1990 Loest finally was rehabilitated by the GDR. In that same year, he founded the Linden Verlag in Leipzig, and the family later dissolved the Künzelsau branch. Loest finally was able to reestablish his ties to his Eastern audiences.

Notes

Support for this chapter was provided by the American Council of Learned Societies and a Fulbright Research Grant.

[1] "Leseland DDR." Special issue, *Aus Politik und Zeitgeschichte* 11 (2009). The first culture minister, Johannes R. Becher, conceived of the GDR as a *Literaturgesellschaft*. It was the last culture minister, Klaus Höpcke, who coined the term "Leseland." See Höpcke, *Probe für das Leben. Literatur in einem Leseland* (Leipzig: Mitteldeutscher Verlag, 1982).

[2] Beginning in 1963, the agency became known as Hauptverwaltung Verlage und Buchhandel, or HV Verlage.

[3] SAPMO-BArch DR 1, 1270, "Verordnung über die Entwicklung fortschrittlicher Literatur vom 16. August 1951," 1–2, and SAPMO-BArch DR1, 1891, "Erste Durchfürhungsbestimmung zur Verordnung über die Entwicklung fortschrittlicher Literatur—Lizenzen," Dez. 13, 1951.

[4] SAPMO-BArch DR 1, 1270, "Verordnung über die Entwicklung fortschrittlicher Literatur vom 16. August 1951," 1–2.

[5] The biographical facts and information on historical background were collected during my work in three archives in Berlin: Akademie der Künste, das Bundesarchiv, and the Stasi Archiv.

[6] The latter carries the copyright of 1950, but was actually delivered in time for Christmas 1949. See Sabine Brandt, *Vom Schwarzmarkt nach St. Nikolai: Erich Loest und seine Romane* (Leipzig: Linden, 1998), 17.

[7] Erich Loest, *Durch die Erde ein Riß*, 4th ed. (Munich: dtv, 1990), 147.

[8] For more details, see Gunter Holzweißig, *Zensur ohne Zensor. Die SED-Informationsdiktatur* (Bonn: Bouvier, 1997), especially 152–54; and Ralf Bachmann, *Ich bin der Herr. Und wer bist du? Ein deutsches Journalistenleben.* (Berlin: Dietz, 1995), especially 103–27.

[9] Loest, *Riß*, 150.

[10] Loest, *Riß*, 217.

[11] Loest, *Riß*, 239.

[12] Loest, "Zu von mir begangenen Fehler nach dem 17. Juni 1953." Adk SV (neu) 313, Bl. 70–71.

[13] Years later Loest wrote: "Der 17. Juni 1953 und der XX. Parteitag im Februar 1956 schlugen Risse in mein Weltbild" (June 17, 1953, and the 20th Party

Congress in February 1956 ripped holes in my worldview). See "Der Verlag in der Wohnküche. Von Büchern, Autoren, Verlegern und Lektoren," in *Als wir in den Westen kamen* (Stuttgart: DVA; Leipzig; Linden Verlag, 1997), 103.

[14] Loest's prisoner file contains detailed information about the counter-revolutionary nature of the cabaret skits. Hl Au 23/59 Gefangenenakte Bl. 224.

[15] Along with Harich, Walter Janka, Heinz Zöger, Richard Wolf, and Gustav Just were also arrested. Many of these men have addressed the problems of the 1950s in a variety of works. See Wolfgan Harich, *Keine Schwierigkeiten mit der Wahrheit. Zur nationalkommunistischen Opposition 1956 in der DDR* (Berlin: Dietz, 1993); *Wolfgang Harich: Ahnenpass. Versuch einer Autobiographie*, ed. Thomas Grimm (Berlin: Schwarzkopf & Schwarzkopf, 1999); Walter Janka, *Spuren eines Lebens* (Berlin: Rowohlt, 1991); Janka, *Die Unterwerfung. Eine Kriminalgeschichte aus der Nachkriegszeit* (Munich: Hanser, 1994), Janka, *... bis zur Verhaftung. Erinnerungen eines deutschen Verlegers* (Berlin: Aufbau, 1993), Gustav Just, *Die fünfziger Jahre in der DDR* (Berlin: Buchverlag Der Morgen, 1990). Loest also provides an indepth look at the period in *Prozesskosten. Bericht* (Göttingen: Steidl, 2007).

[16] See Gerhard Zwerenz, *Der Widerspruch. Autobiographischer Bericht* (Frankfurt am Main: Fischer, 1974), especially 85–97.

[17] In the early 1950s, these writers had been defamed as formalist; socialist realist writing was to counter such tendencies.

[18] Brandt writes that Loest was aware that he had been under Stasi surveillance for some time. See Brandt, *Vom Schwarzmarkt*, 52.

[19] Quoted in Loest, *Riß*, 319. Ironically, the extension of this law, which led to Loest's conviction, was not passed until 11 December 1957, four weeks after his arrest. In *Prozesskosten* Loest explains that he never knew the real text of §13 until he already was serving his sentence.

[20] Hl Au 23/59 Gefangenenakte Bl. 233.

[21] According to Zwerenz, it took approximately one year before it was publicly known that Loest had been arrested, when a brief notice appeared on 24 December 1958 in *Neues Deutschland*. Zwerenz, *Der Widerspruch*, 93.

[22] Lpz. AOP 840/71 Bd. 2, Bl. 93–94.

[23] Lpz. AOP 840/71 Bd. 2, Bl. 99.

[24] Lpz. AOP 840/71, Bd. 3, Bl. 13.

[25] The first script Loest published after his release from prison was a story about the last two days of World War II in Slovakia, which Verlag Neues Leben released as an *Abenteuerheft* (adventure booklet) in 1965. This publication appeared to be an auspicious beginning because it reached a total print run of 156,000, a fact that belies the state's intent to prohibit Loest's works from reaching his readers.

[26] Loest, *Der Zorn des Schafes* (Munich: dtv, 1993), 45.

[27] Loest, *Zorn*, 45.

[28] See "Erich Loest," in *DDR-Schriftsteller sprechen in der Zeit. Eine Dokumentation, German Monitor* 27, ed. Gerd Labroisse and Ian Wallace (Amsterdam: Rodopi, 1991), 27.

[29] Conversation with Erich and Thomas Loest, Leipzig, March 2002.

[30] Prior to his arrest, Loest was a widely read author. According to some, his *Auflagenhöhe* (number of copies published) reached as high as 200,000, plus 100,000 in Russian translations. See Zwerenz, "Immer noch stalinistische Terrorjustiz. Zum exemplarischen Fall des Schriftstellers Erich Loest," *SBZ* Archivheft 2 (1959): 21 as quoted in Heinrich Mohr, "Spurensicherung. Erich Loests Versuch, die eigene Wahrheit zu schreiben," in *Probleme deutscher Identität. Zeitgenössische Autobiographien. Identitätssuche und Zivilisationskritik*, ed. Paul Gerhard Klussmann and Heinrich Mohr (Bonn: Bouvier, 1983), 14.

[31] Loest, *Zorn*, 46. Loest tried to circumvent the secrecy about his arrest. In the collection *Öl für Malta* Loest arranged the eight stories chronologically according to the year they were written. In that way, the eight-year gap from 1956 to 1964 would be readily apparent to readers. The HV Verlage succeeded in changing the order. See Lpz. AOP 840/71 Bd. 5, Bl. 54. In an interview with Carsten Gansel, Loest remarks that a typical print run for his texts in the Mitteldeutscher Verlag was 10,000 copies; by contrast, his crime novels reached as high as 40,000 copies. "'Hemingway ist eine Stilfrage, Fallada eine Inhaltsfrage' Erich Loest im Gespräch mit Carsten Gansel," in *Geschichte, die noch qualmt. Erich Loest und sein Werk*, ed. Carsten Gansel and Joachim Jacob (Göttingen: Steidl, 2011), 303.

[32] SAPMO-BArch DR 1,3627 (Bl. 93). Publishing house file for *Hilfe durch Ranke*.

[33] SAPMO BArch DR 1, 3628 (Bl. 171–72). Loest revised the story three or four times and still considers it to be the worst story he ever wrote. See "Erich Loest," in *DDR-Schriftsteller sprechen in der Zeit*, 32.

[34] A revised edition under Loest's name was published by Steidl in 2006.

[35] BA DR 1/2168a Bl. 403–4.

[36] BA DR 1/2168a Bl. 405–9.

[37] Loest, *Zorn*, 234.

[38] BA DR 1/2169b Bl. 649.

[39] BA DR 1/2169b Bl. 652–56.

[40] BA DR 1/2169b Bl. 646–48.

[41] BA DR 1/2169b Bl. 645.

[42] BA DR 1/2176a Bl. 327–36.

[43] BA DR 1/2176a Bl. 327–36.

[44] BA DR 1/2176a Bl. 340–42.

[45] BA DR 1/2176a Bl. 340–42.

[46] BA DR 1/2176a Bl. 340–42.

[47] BA DR 1/2178a Bl, 443–45.

[48] BA DR 1 3728a Bl. 312–13.

[49] In an interview, Loest described this as taking his leave of his crime-story past. See "Erich Loest," in *DDR-Schriftsteller sprechen in der Zeit*, 28.

[50] See, for example, Lpz AOP 840/71 Bd. 3, Bl. 96.

8: What's in Your Bag?: "Freudian Crimes" and Austria's Nazi Past in Eva Rossmann's *Freudsche Verbrechen*

Traci S. O'Brien

> Wie der Archäologe aus stehengebliebenen Mauerresten die Wandlungen des Gebäudes aufbaut, aus Vertiefungen im Boden die Anzahl und Stellung von Säulen bestimmt, aus den im Schutt gefundenen Resten die einstigen Wandverzierungen und Wandgemälde wiederherstellt, genau so geht der Analytiker vor, wenn er seine Schlüsse aus Erinnerungsbrocken, Assoziationen und aktiven Äußerungen des Analysierten zieht.
>
> [Just as the archaeologist builds up the walls of the building from the foundations that have remained standing, determines the number and position of the columns from depressions in the floor and reconstructs the mural decorations and paintings from the remains found in the debris, so does the analyst proceed when he draws his inferences from the fragments of memories, from the associations and from the behavior of the subject of the analysis.]
>
> —Sigmund Freud

In Eva Rossmann's detective novel, *Freudsche Verbrechen* (Freudian Crimes), the unconscious—or what we don't know we don't know—intrudes unexpectedly upon everyday reality.[1] As Mira Valensky, freelance "Lifestyle Journalistin" (5) and amateur sleuth, investigates the murder of a young woman in Vienna's Freud Museum, she uncovers connections between this contemporary crime and the theft of Jewish property after the *Anschluss* in 1938. The past, like the unconscious, is not only symbolically present in Sigmund Freud's psychoanalytic theory, but literally present in the contemporary reality of the novel—that is, Vienna in the late 1990s—nearly one hundred years after the publication of Freud's seminal work, *The Interpretation of Dreams*.[2] This novel, through its clever intertwining of history (*Geschichte*) and personal life stories (*Geschichten*), asks whether the repressed predictably returns and thus, as Slavoj Žižek would assert, "the letter always arrives at its destination."[3]

Valensky's quest to find out what happened to the young woman brings to light a piece of Austria's Nazi past and contemporary responsibility toward that past. The novel, like Rossmann's protagonist, questions the possibility of finding out the truth, bringing criminals to justice, and thus restoring the possibility of ethical relationships against the background of such contemporary and historical crimes. Rossmann creates a detective fiction fit for these complex historical tensions: Freud, a pioneer of postmodern suspicion, becomes the muse of a new kind of detective work, one that revises and updates his relevance in contemporary Austrian society but ultimately eschews the radical epistemological skepticism of "metaphysical" ways of detecting.[4]

When Valensky is called to the Freud Museum to help, it seems as if Freud were the butt of his own joke: he has been repressed so deeply that neither Valensky nor the homicide squad knows where to find the museum, located at Berggasse 19. This repression of Freud and his work has one very obvious ironic element: psychoanalysis began with Freud in Vienna. However, it was exiled, along with him, as a "Jewish science" in 1938.[5] Indeed, the second murder in the novel, of the psychiatrist, could be interpreted as the "murder" of Austrian psychoanalysis. A second bit of irony is that, as Ernst Bloch points out, the dynamics of crime detection parallel those of psychoanalysis, and the psychoanalyst also functions as a kind of detective, seeking out clues and interpreting their meanings.[6] Hanjo Berressem, echoing Bloch, identifies the "elective affinity" between detective fiction and psychoanalysis: each has a "knotty problem with death at its center."[7] Accordingly, the novel develops sympathy for Freudian structures in order to help recreate the narrative of the crime. Rossmann mines the parallels between psychoanalysis and detective fiction to have her sleuth uncover both the perpetrator and his motivations by negotiating a line between questioning traditional ideas of truth and generating knowledge in ethical ways.

Beginning with the murder in the Freud Museum, the references to Freud and his work abound. Freud's omnipresence seems to reflect a compromised enlightenment and thus to point out the limits of reason and truth in a postmodern, postwar reality. Rossmann investigates these limits even further as Valensky encounters Freud's infamous blind spots: Rossmann allows one of Freud's most famous analysands, "Dora," to tell her side of the story. Rossmann also cleverly refashions one of Freud's well-known symbols: the bag. While Freud viewed it solely as a symbol of female sexuality, the bags in this novel, from the murdered young woman's half-empty backpack to the old leather suitcase belonging to her grandmother (the contents of which set the whole chain of events in motion), are involved in acts of repression and discovery as well as questions of travel and exile.[8] Nevertheless, Valensky unpacks the bag, literally and figuratively: with the help of the letters she discovers in the grandmother's suitcase, she pieces together the victim's story, which actually precedes the beginning of the novel in time by sixty years. These letters, in turn, function as a kind of *Flaschenpost*, or message in a bottle, which calls the protagonist forth to ethical action.

Freudsche Verbrechen opens in Valensky's kitchen as she joyfully prepares an elegant meal for herself.[9] Interrupted in her cooking, she is called to the Freud Museum by Ulrike, an old school friend, with whom she has recently re-established contact. There, Valensky encounters the body of a young woman. Since the police have not yet arrived, Valensky investigates the scene with Ulrike in tow. None of the contents of the young woman's backpack indicate her identity or her purpose for being there. Moreover, the young woman's body is sitting on Freud's steamer trunk, "as if waiting for him" to return (7). In the chapters that follow, Valensky, with her cleaning woman, friend, and partner in crime-solving, Vesna Krajner, tries to discover, first, the identity of the young woman, and subsequently, precisely what had led her to Vienna and the Freud Museum. They are put onto the trail of the Bernkopf family by a slip of paper jutting out of a copy of the book *Freud's Women* that the young woman had been reading in the museum's library. Someone, presumably the young woman, had written "Birkengasse 14" on this slip of paper, currently the residence of the Bernkopf family.

The case gets more complicated when Ulrike's boyfriend, the psychiatrist Peter Zimmermann, who had had significant contact with the murder victim in the days leading up to the crime, is subsequently murdered. Convinced there is more to the story than meets the eye, Valensky and Krajner work together to establish a connection between the Bernkopf family and their house at Birkengasse 14, and the young woman. It turns out that the young woman, an American named Jane Cooper, was the great-granddaughter of the previous owners of the house, a fact that had been unknown to the Cooper family because its founding matriarch, the daughter of the original owners, had left Austria right before the *Anschluss* and had cut ties with both her homeland and her native language. As mentioned, Valensky discovers this history via letters hidden in an old suitcase. However, since the statutes governing the return of Jewish property have elapsed, there is no clear motive for the murders.

The novel initially suggests that Freud belongs to a thoroughly deconstructed tradition, one in which he remains as a kind of figurehead, but without anything of real value to say (even to psychoanalysts) in contemporary society.[10] However, the fact that the woman's body is found on Freud's steamer trunk suggests both Freud's absence as well as the idea that contemporary crimes could necessitate his return. Valensky first encounters Freud when she looks at "viele Bilder von alten Männern" (11; a lot of pictures of old men) on the museum's walls, and, while ostensibly musing on the choice of location, she could also be questioning any potential Freudian relevance: "Ich gebe zu, viel wusste ich nicht über Freud. Natürlich, er war 'der Vater der Psychoanalyse,' und es gab freudsche Versprecher, und er musste als Jude in der Nazizeit fliehen. In dieser Wohnung also hatte er gelebt und gearbeitet. Heute war in dieser Wohnung eine junge Frau ermordet worden. Ein Zufall? Oder hatte jemand den Ort bewusst gewählt?" (12; I admit I didn't know much about Freud. Of course, he was "the father of psychoanalysis," and gave us Freudian slips. And as a Jew he had to flee during the Nazi period. So, he lived and worked in this apartment. Today a young woman was murdered in this apartment. A coincidence? Or did someone consciously choose this spot?).

Rather than confirming Freud's irrelevance, Rossmann promotes an ironic sympathy for Freud's theories as the investigation develops. Indeed, the idea that human beings have motives and desires that are not transparent to themselves, or that repressed past trauma can perversely affect the present, belong to the cultural assumptions of postmodern reality. Moreover, Freud's sudden appearance in the life of her protagonist seems to validate the ideas of the unconscious: the morning following the murder, Valensky is suddenly awake at 5:00 a.m. bathed in sweat, heart pounding audibly, having had strange dreams and a panic attack. "Das macht der Tod," quips Krajner (22; Death can do that). She has several of these episodes throughout the novel.

Though Valensky is epistemologically and ontologically in the dark about the processes of her own psyche here, Rossmann handles the matter with a light, often humorous touch. It is not immediately clear what connection these intrusions of anxiety may have with the specifics of the murder, other than the fact that the confrontation with death has precipitated the crisis. But Rossmann cleverly inserts the Freudian unconscious—that is, the aspects of human existence inaccessible to the rational mind: the presence of the repressed (past trauma) or the presence of absence (anxiety brought on by confrontation with nonexistence)—alongside the presence of the ultimate irrational act—the murder of another—that is typical in the crime-fiction genre. Thus, the novel seems to suggest that Valensky's quest to find the murderer parallels a quest of self-discovery.

How does Rossmann have Valensky unpack the "bag" and resolve these issues involving the unknown? If, as Bloch phrases it, detective stories concern themselves with the attempt to shine an "in Untat hineinleuchtendes Licht" (a light into the atrocity), part of the mystery is discovering whence the beam of light or the source of knowledge comes.[11] In *Freudsche Verbrechen*, Rossmann juxtaposes the mystery to be solved—that is, the truth of the crime—with the ambiguity of signs and the distrust of overarching narrative that befits a postmodern novel. She foregrounds questions about who can know, what can be known, and how this knowable entity, or "truth," can be discovered: all of them relevant for the crime-fiction genre. One way that Valensky demonstrates faith in her ability to limit epistemological uncertainty is with good judgment of other people—her "Menschenkenntnis" (89). At first somewhat halfheartedly involved, Valensky becomes more engaged after the second murder. Ulrike comes under suspicion for both crimes, supposedly committed in acts of jealous rage. When Ulrike asks her for help, though Valensky has only recently seen her again after twenty years, Valensky is convinced that she could not possibly have committed the murders because of her reaction to the death of her boyfriend: "so gut kann sich kein Mensch verstellen," she says (90; No one is that good an actor).

Yet Valensky's faith in her perceptive abilities (which turn out to be confirmed) does not result in superhuman ability of the Sherlock Holmes, or even Freudian, variety to decode situations or read obscure signs. Rossmann's sleuth does not acquire knowledge by an investment in the ego's ability to know itself and the world, or by shutting out other possible interpretations in order to establish the one valid meaning. Instead, Valensky's status as freelance journalist, as well as amateur crime-solver, may give her a more flexible viewpoint as she gathers information: she is not beholden to either of these institutional behemoths (the news media or the police force). At the same time, her investigation stalls at key moments and Valensky is forced to admit that she may be wrong about the narrative of the crime she has been constructing. Thus, Rossmann endorses a kind of epistemological humility, one that recognizes the validity of other perspectives but—and this is important in a postmodern context—does not result in an overdetermined doubt or insecurity: Valensky carefully seeks out and reasonably integrates other viewpoints.[12] Enter Vesna Krajner, Valensky's cleaning woman and friend, whom Valensky calls: "im Gegensatz zu mir die geborene Abenteuerin" (22; In contrast to me, a born adventurer). This is not a crime-solving relationship of the Holmes-Watson type. Instead, they are co-archaeologists of the Freudian type, digging for clues and sifting through remains.[13]

After the identity of the murdered young woman is discovered—she is a twenty-two-year-old college student from the United States—it comes to light that this present-day murder could in fact be connected to the coerced sale of Jewish property after the *Anschluss*, and thus, in theory, to the events of Freud's life. The image of the crime scene, with the body of the young woman sitting on Freud's steamer trunk, could certainly suggest this connection to the reader: eighty-three years old and terminally ill with cancer, Freud was forced to flee Vienna when the Nazis came.

Valensky is drawn into the media fray about the case by her connection to Ulrike and her own investigation. As the reporting on the story of the two murders escalates, Valensky emphasizes her skeptical stance vis-à-vis the media's portrayal of "die so genannte Realität" and the potentially performative nature of truth (93; so-called reality). Valensky echoes this ambivalence toward stable definitions with her comments on the perspectival nature of "truth." While discussing Freud and the museum, for example, Valensky is schooled in psychoanalysis, "dass es wohl in erster Linie von unserem eigenen Standpunkt abhänge, was wir als verrückt betrachteten" (37; that what we define as crazy depends first and foremost on our own position). She herself brings up this same point later in a discussion with Droch, an older male colleague at the magazine, in defense of the potential merit of psychoanalysis, "dass die Frage, ob verrückt oder nicht, wohl in erster Linie vom eigenen Standort abhänge" (46; that the question, whether crazy or not, most likely depends first and foremost on one's own position). Later, as Valensky contemplates the change in her own viewpoint since she was the murder victim's age, she notes that "alles eben eine Frage des persönlichen Blickwinkels [ist]" (64; everything [is] just a question of personal perspective).

The idea that "everything" could be a matter of perspective seems to reflect the ultimate suspicion of enlightenment rationality as the sole (or even effective) path to the truth. Rossmann is clearly skeptical about overarching hierarchical notions of value and stable moral truths. This profound skepticism reflects other concerns about truth and justice in the novel. As Dagmar Lorenz points out, there is in Austrian crime literature since the 1980s, "a more pervasive, a more fundamental sense of disturbance," which connects the crimes of the present with those of the Nazi era and reenacts the profound sense of confusion as to categories of right and wrong.[14] Beyond the borders of Austria, the profound distrust of humanistic enlightened traditions (either as absolutist or as impotent in the wake of the Holocaust), and subsequent confusion about good and evil, has impacted crime fiction strongly in general. Susan Elizabeth Sweeney notes, for example, that postmodern investigation is so "overdetermined" that often "the private eye himself turns out to be the criminal he pursues."[15] Alternatively, as Hanjo Berressem claims in his Lacanian analysis of Polish author Witold Gombrowicz's work, one can refashion death by natural causes into murder. In both instances, no distinction is drawn between good and evil people or deeds. The obvious problem with such moral indeterminacy is that without some kind of defined value system, the number of potential viewpoints is limitless and could thus interfere with any kind of stable vantage point from which to solve the murder (whence Bloch's beam of light).

Later, Valensky is pushed into the role of "pacifistischen, antifaschistischen Feministin" by her colleagues in the media (203; pacifist, antifascist feminist); yet the reactivity of this position and its potential dogmatism are just as distasteful to her: "Selbstgerechtigkeit war mir ein Gräuel" (203; I had quite an aversion to self-righteousness). While this moment of ironic self-reflection may seem on the surface like another retreat into limitless perspective, there is evidence in the novel that Rossmann validates the human ability to know and discern truth. In another nod to Freud, in this case his definition of sanity, Valensky acknowledges the "real existente Umgebung" (203; actually existing environs)—in this case, the bartender polishing his glassware—that "brakes" or keeps her from going to extremes, precisely because it consists of a reality independent of her perspective. Such a reality could thus become an object of knowledge that is independent of a solely self-referential or perspectival version of truth.[16] In this way, Rossmann seems to be playing out the drama of Freud's own Nietzschean and romantic ambivalences toward enlightenment rationality and his very late affirmation of reason in *The Future of an Illusion* with the repeated call to "our God Logos."[17]

In my reading of this novel, Valensky is trustworthy precisely because she asserts from the very beginning the validity of certain distinctions, despite the instability of traditional categories; and the most basic of these is life and death. When she arrives at the crime scene, Valensky first perceives its staged, unreal quality. Then, she distinguishes between appearances and reality:

> Ich ging ganz nahe zu der jungen toten Frau hin. Eine unwirkliche Szene. Teil einer Inszenierung. . . . Blaue Flecken am schlanken weißen Hals, erst dann sah ich ihre weit geöffneten Augen. Braune Augen wie aus Glas. Mir wurde kalt, überdeutlich nahm ich wahr, wie sich an Rücken und Armen jedes kleine Härchen aufstellte. Der Eindruck des Unwirklichen war verschwunden. Realität war, dass diese junge Frau bis vor kurzem noch gelebt hatte. (8)

> [I went up very close to the dead young woman. An unreal scene. Part of a staged scene. . . . Blue blotches on her slender white throat, but only then did I see her wide-open eyes. Brown eyes as if made out of glass. I felt chilled, and I was hyperaware of how every little hair on my back and arms stood on end. The impression of the unreal had fled. The reality was that this young woman had been alive until very recently.]

This encounter with the reality of death, of murder, precipitates the suspiciously Freudian crisis in Valensky. For one thing, at this moment Valensky acutely experiences the mortal boundaries of human existence. This encounter with the uncanny, which in the intervening years has gone from "unheimlich" (Freud) to "ungeheuer" (Bloch),[18] at the very beginning of the novel causes the hair on her arms and neck to stand on end. The nearness of death as the negation of life, and potentially of meaning, returns throughout the novel in her frequent dreams and panic attacks at 5:00 a.m. On a subsequent visit to the office of psychiatrist Peter Zimmermann in order to determine the extent of his relationship with the murder victim, Valensky gets distracted by an ontological discussion of her attacks. She is deeply unsettled by his request that she define *who she is* (59).

Valenksy perceives but cannot really understand the boundary between life and death, and she cannot possibly know herself fully. Confronted with these epistemological and ontological questions, her "unconscious" repeatedly enters the narrative of detection to remind her (and us) that there is another side of the boundary between life and death, between the known and the unknown. However, rather than being paralyzed, Valensky responds to these incursions with increasing resolve to take ethical action and to discover the truth. In this way, Rossmann's first-person narrator, with her intuitive sense of certain boundaries, resonates with the hard-boiled ethic in which the sleuth is both self-contained and in possession of a moral compass.[19]

Rossmann's sleuth is able to find a stable vantage point from which to create a narrative of what happened. Based on the "signs" left by the unconscious, Valensky must, like Freud's analyst, "make out what has been forgotten from the traces which it has left behind or, more correctly, to *construct* it."[20] Yet the process of discovery is not an easy one: the full reach of the connection between Jane Cooper and the Bernkopf family refuses to reveal itself and, thus, blocks the sleuths' attempts to construct a reasonable narrative of the crime. Then, almost in a fit of free association, Valensky draws a parallel between investigating a person's life story and investigating the crime. She tells Krajner and Droch, "Wir haben uns viel zu wenig mit Jane Coopers Privatleben beschäftigt. . . . Wir müssen zurück zum Anfang" (123; We have paid too little attention to Jane Cooper's private life. We must go back to the beginning). Valensky decides to visit Jane's parents.

The novel's discreet placement of bags in the first part of the novel has suggested the importance of travel, dislocation and lost identity. Among them, both Freud's steamer trunk and the young woman's half-empty backpack did not actually contain anything of concrete value for the case. It is a different bag that will reveal the connection between the past and present and suggest a motive for the crime. Its contents correspond to Freud's "essential": it can be hidden but will eventually yield to analysis.[21] When Valensky exclaims that she must go "back to the beginning," this means finding the moment of Jane Cooper's involvement and the substance of her connection with the Bernkopf family. Valensky makes the discovery as she sits in the New York apartment where Jane had lived with her parents. Jane's mother knows about the letters but speaks no German and thus does not understand the full import of their content. She insists to Valensky that it all must be a case of mistaken identity since Jane had known no one in Vienna. As Freud would have it, the repressed returns. At this very moment, the image of the murder victim reenters Valensky's mind: "das Bild der jungen Frau, die wartend auf dem Überseekoffer Freuds gesessen hatte, stieg in mir auf" (134; the picture of the young woman, who was sitting on Freud's steamer trunk, waiting, arose in me).

Jane's mother tells Valensky how Jane had recently been to her grandmother's funeral and had brought back a suitcase. Jane's mother stands up, goes to the closet and takes out "einen abgeschabten dunkelbraunen Lederkoffer" (138; a well-worn dark brown leather suitcase).

In a detective story within the detective story, Jane's own discovery of the suitcase had precipitated the trip to Vienna in order to investigate the truth about her grandmother, Hanni Rosner, and the house at Birkengasse 14. With the help of some college German and a dictionary, Jane had decoded its contents: several letters and photographs that connect Rosner to the house in question. Rosner's parents, writing to their daughter in the months following March 1938, are initially hopeful that they are not in any serious danger. Over the course of the correspondence, however, the mood changes as her parents eventually relate how they have been forced to sell their house and are unsure about the future. At this moment, Valensky cannot know that the final letter written by Rosner's parents is missing. Though the remaining letters do not reveal their fate, Rosner's reaction indicates what happened: she cut all ties with her native country and her mother tongue and started over in the United States. Jane's father, Rosner's son, has heard nothing of his family history and also speaks no German, and thus could have had no way of knowing the reason behind his daughter's trip to Vienna. However, having inherited from his mother the idea that the past holds no value, he responds to his daughter's murder by urging his wife to try to look toward the future.

As they are sitting in her living room, Jane's mother asks Valensky the pivotal question: "Kann man für die Zukunft leben, wenn man mit der Vergangenheit nicht abgeschlossen hat" (137; Can you live for the future when you haven't really had closure with the past). Valensky has a few conversations with Jane's father (who seems more interested in recovering the house than in finding his daughter's murderer), during which he says: "Man muss in die Zukunft denken, das hat auch meine Mutter immer gesagt" (157; My mother always said, you have to think about the future). It is, of course, not as easy as that. Valensky replies: "Und trotzdem hat sie den Koffer aufbewahrt" (157; And even so, she still saved the suitcase). The past had been "bagged" but not eliminated, and thus it returned. As Valensky says simply: "Sie hatte diesen Koffer aufbewahrt, und Jane hatte ihn gefunden" (149; She had saved the suitcase, and Jane had found it).

If, as Freud suggests, it is the release of the repressed that restores the patient to psychological health, one might expect the case to be closed at this point.[22] In fact, however, though Valensky's suspicion is now completely fixed on the Bernkopf family, they still have no real proof.[23] After the discovery of the bag's literal contents, the remainder of the novel concerns itself with the attempt to restore the narrative of these lost lives and some contingent sense of justice. Valensky will chase down these leads in two ways: first, she attempts to recreate the Rosner family's lives (and their deaths) by literally walking in Jane's footsteps as she tracks down Hanni Rosner's friends (187, 189, 191); and second, she researches the Aryanization of Jewish property and how this impacted the Rosner family specifically. In this way, Rossmann integrates historical moments with personal history.[24] In both instances of "Geschichte," she shows that "die Vergangenheit . . . ihre Schatten, egal ob man wollte oder nicht, in die Gegenwart" (185; the past . . . threw its shadows into the present, no matter if you wanted it to or not).

The bag symbolizes both "baggage" from the past—that is, trauma—more generally as well as travel, forced exile, and deportation. Furthermore, it suggests both the reliability of the return of the repressed since the contents of the bag do not actually disappear, even if they are hidden from view, as well as the reliability of the connection between repression of trauma and perversion (in this case, murder). These are the shadows that the past throws into the present independent of human volition. At the same time, Rossmann's choice of metaphor has a wealth of other associations, which again are evocative of Freud's theories, yet deny them any kind of universal solvency.

Rossmann has a little fun with Freud via the symbol of the bag. The bag, specifically a woman's purse, evokes Freud's "Fragment of an Analysis of Hysteria" where the purse (as well as the jewelry case) is a symbol of female genitalia and women's sexuality.[25] Freud's disagreement with his patient about the symbol's meaning could have led to the failure of their therapeutic relationship. For critic Claire Kahane, Dora's case was a "representation of the master's failure, of his inability to complete the story."[26] Dora terminated her therapeutic relationship with Freud before she was, according to Freud, cured. Erik Erikson notes that the actual Dora, or rather Freud's report of her, "indicates that Dora was concerned with the *historical truth* as known to others, while [Freud] insisted on the genetic truth behind her own symptoms."[27] In *Freudsche Verbrechen*, Rossmann has Valensky side with Dora and thus "complete the story," as it is clear that historical circumstances are vital to understanding the contemporary crime. Valensky makes the acquaintance of this Dora, historian Dora Messerschmidt, through Ulrike's lawyer.[28]

As a historian, Dora Messerschmidt can help make sense not only of *Geschichte* but, in having an adequate sense of history, can also bring the *Geschichten* of individuals to light (229). The mystery of Jane Cooper's murder is not to be solved by delving into her personal history alone, but rather needs to be put into this historical context of crime and forgetting. Former friends and neighbors had coerced Hanni Rosner's parents into selling their home for a fraction of its value. It had been Mr. Bernkopf's father who had purchased the house at Birkengasse 14. Without the knowledge of these connections, people like Mr. Bernkopf can manipulate appearances to hide their complicity with the original crime (175).

Part of the moral of Dora's story is that a lack of historicity compounds the difficulty in discerning truth from fiction. Indeed, she asserts that the media avoid discussion of the systemic nature of these past crimes because many politicians in the postwar period had personally benefited from the confiscation of Jewish property. Instead, the recent uproar in the press about Austria's Nazi past has devolved into a superficial public dispute over money (221). Without background knowledge, the money at issue in these disputes becomes an empty, and ironically valueless, symbol that obscures the real nature of the relationships behind it. With her expertise, however, Rossmann's Dora can see through media tactics and notes—for example, "in gewissen Zeitungen werden Opfer schnell zu Tätern, wenn sie sich zur Wehr setzen. Österreich will seine Ruhe" (219; in certain newspapers, victims quickly become perpetrators when they defend themselves. Austria wants to be left in peace). However, it is not just the press that is invested in suppressing the real story. Dora continues, noting that the "proof" about dispossession of the Austrian Jews is still contained in official governmental files but remains unread, "weil es nichts gibt, was es nicht geben darf. In der Psychoanalyse nennt man das Verdrängung" (222; because things that mustn't be, aren't. In psychoanalysis, they call that repression). Finally, Dora reestablishes the connection between the history and the person. In response to Hanni Rosner's story, she says: "Es war für sie offenbar der einzige Weg, um leben zu können. Aber von Verdrängung kommt nichts Gutes. Und sie gelingt nicht vollständig. Denken Sie bloß an die Briefe, die sie aufgehoben hat. Wichtige Zeitzeugnisse für uns. Aber für Jane Cooper waren sie der Auslöser, um nach Wien zu fahren, um ganz allein nach ihren Wurzeln zu suchen. Und sie ist ermordet worden" (223; It was apparently the only way she could go on living. But nothing good comes from repression. And it also never is completely successful. Just think about the letters that she saved. Important historical documents for us. But for Jane Cooper they were the catalyst for her to come all alone to Vienna in search of her roots. And she was murdered). Though she validates Freud's notion of repression, with her fount of reliable, historical information, this Dora is the opposite of Freud's hysterical aphonic.[29] Dora's lengthy explanations illustrate, however, the necessity (and difficulty) of compiling a comprehensive historical narrative. At the same time, they remind us that historical truths are also connected to specific times and places.

Though there are many parallels suggested in this novel between psychoanalysis and crime detection, the "return" of the letters (that is, Valensky's discovery of them) does not devolve into a detective's solipsistic search for the truth about herself. Instead, Rossmann takes great pains to attach these letters to the concrete lived history of others. Sitting in Jane's bedroom in New York, Valensky remarks: "Das Ehepaar, dessen Fotos ich gefunden und dessen Briefe an die Tochter ich gelesen hatte, war ermordet worden. Millionen Juden waren ermordet worden. Durch den Blick in das Leben dieser zwei war diese Tatsache für mich nicht länger abstrakt, sondern ganz konkret" (148; the couple, whose photos I had found and whose letters to their daughter I had read, was murdered. Millions of Jews were murdered. Because of the glimpse into their lives, this reality was no longer abstract for me, but very concrete). The sleuth's quest to discover the truth requires confrontation with the reality of this experience.

Many contemporary analyses of crime fiction—in particular, of postmodern or metaphysical detective fiction—return to the "letter" (that is, the unconscious) and, in so doing, rely on Jacques Lacan's infamous analysis of Edgar Allan Poe's "The Purloined Letter."[30] Although one might be able to make an argument that the letters that had been hidden in Hanni Rosner's suitcase were symbolic debt coming home to demand payment (Žižek), these letters refuse to be made into the abstract representation of the "unconscious" (and therefore not contingent either individually or historically). Ultimately, one of the most refreshing things about Rossmann's story is its ability to find a line that is neither a postmodern devaluation of everything nor a feminist association of assertions of value with patriarchy.[31] In other words, alongside the flexibility of roles and perspectives, her sleuth embraces things that are part of the "real existente Umgebung," thus underscoring the novel's Freudian, rather than Lacanian roots.[32]

It is at this juncture that all three questions—namely, who can know, what can be known, and how this truth can be discovered—converge. Immediately following her discussion with yet another journalist who was unconcerned with the truth of the murders, Valensky affirms her own ethical stance: "an absolute Wahrheiten glaubte ich nicht. Aber ein paar Werte wollte ich hochhalten, höher als bisher" (203; I didn't believe in absolute truths. But I did want to uphold a few values, hold them higher than I had previously done). Valensky affirms values, such as friendship and dependability, which require others to make them real (115). *Freudsche Verbrechen* brings to mind a kind of revised Kantianism, with its "practical reason" as a foundation for an ethical stance, by both acknowledging the doubt that pervades postmodern attempts to establish stable knowledge, as well as positing the possibility of ethical commitments that reside outside the self.[33]

It is this concrete connection, in turn, rather than abstraction, which has the potential to inspire ethical commitments and acknowledgment of debt. Valensky says, "ich war es Jane und ihrer Großmutter schuldig, dass die Wahrheit herauskam. Viel zu lange war über viel zu viel geschwiegen worden" (281; I owed it to Jane and her grandmother that the truth came out. For too long there had been silence about too much). Compellingly, the very thing that brought about the end of humanism is the very thing that issues a call to think and act ethically. Similar to the way she feels beholden to her friend, Krajner, to try and know her *as she is* (237), Valensky invests that ethic here with greater historical importance: this victim must retain her own story.[34] Thus, Rossmann grounds stable ethical moments in the encounter between self and other—that is, in actual human relationship. Valensky's last panic attack occurs late in the novel:

> Meine Zähne klapperten. . . . Was bleibt von mir, wenn ich nichts tue, nichts schreibe, nichts recherchiere, für niemanden koche? Nicht einmal esse? Was ist dann? Was soll ich dann zählen, wenn mich niemand mehr wahrnimmt, habe ich den Psychiater gefragt. Er hat gesagt, dass es darum geht, zu begreifen, dass ich dann immer noch ich selbst bin. Es gilt, zu entscheiden, was ich wirklich tun will. Will ich wirklich diese Lifestyle-Geschichten schreiben? Will ich wirklich die Morde aufklären? Ich will Jane Coopers Geschichte wissen, ihre Geschichte, die den Anfang genommen hat in der Birkengasse 14, Jahrzehnte früher. Das will ich wirklich. (285)

> [My teeth were chattering. . . . What of me remains when I do nothing, write nothing, research nothing, cook for no one? Not even eat? What is then? I asked that psychiatrist what I should count for if no one perceives me. He said that the point is to understand that I am still always myself. I need to decide what I really want to do. Do I really want to write these "lifestyle" stories? Do I really want to solve the murders? I want to know Jane Cooper's history, her story which began at Birkengasse 14, decades earlier. I really do want that.]

Notable is, first, that the existential anxiety here triggers a commitment to another person's story. What had perhaps begun more as curiosity and professional interest has shifted to an ethical commitment to the story of another. Second, Valensky (and Rossmann) distinguishes again between a "story" (34, 36) as told by media (that is, the solely perspectival truth deployed for various wishes and desires but that has actually little in common with the "real" story) and "Jane Cooper's history, her story, which began at Birkengasse 14, decades earlier." She again emphasizes the situatedness of Jane Cooper's life and death.

If this is the case, then one must also deal with the possibility that some knowledge is possible, though difficult. At this moment, Valensky and Krajner know the following: the statutes enabling the recovery of confiscated property had expired several decades before and, thus, the Bernkopf family had never been in danger of losing possession of the house at Birkengasse 14. However, Valensky and Krajner also discover that thirty-year-old Michael Bernkopf, the Bernkopfs' son, had mortgaged half of the house in order to float the public launch of his internet-consulting business. Therefore, it was not the threat of losing the house, but the threat of a scandal about its past that endangered his company's stock bubble. Still, though they have suspicions, Valensky and Krajner do not have enough proof to hand the case over to the police. The investigation stalls for a second time. Valensky and Krajner return to the letters to figure out what they have overlooked.

The final clues as to the murderer's identity are revealed when the last two letters "arrive" and complete the narrative. The two sleuths are put on the trail of these letters by a careful rereading of the previous ones, especially one from Rosner's childhood friend: "Kannst Du Dich noch erinnern, wie wir unsere Botschaften und Schätzen in dem Loch in der Hausmauer versteckt haben?" (312; Can you remember how we used to hide our messages and treasures in the hole in the wall?).[35] Immediately, Valensky and Krajner set off to the house in Birkengasse 14 to see if there is, indeed, a hidden message in the wall.

Not surprisingly, Valensky and Krajner discover the letters and then retreat to the park directly behind the house to read them. In a moving scene that is filled with images of light and darkness (bringing us back to Bloch), the two sleuths read the letters out loud. The first (but written last) is from Jane to her grandmother, in which she pledges to win back the house and create a memorial center for all of the victims of the Nazi period. She also writes that she is off to the Freud Museum, a fitting venue, to meet the son of the owners of the house: "Vielleicht begreift er in dieser Umgebung leichter, worum es geht: nicht zu vergessen, weil man die grauenvollen Dinge, die im Krieg passiert sind, nur verdrängen, aber nicht vergessen kann. . . . Vielleicht wird er mir sogar bei einem Gedenkzentrum helfen. Das wäre ein schöner, versöhnlicher Akt" (317, ellipses in original; Perhaps he will understand the point more easily in these surroundings: not to forget because you can repress the horrible things that happened in the war but you can't forget them. . . . Maybe he will even help me with the memorial center. That would be a nice, reconciliatory act). Jane enclosed with this message to her deceased grandmother the final letter that Hanni Rosner's mother (that is, Jane's great-grandmother) somehow managed to send to her daughter in the United States from Auschwitz. This second letter (though preceding the first one by sixty years) contrasts brutally with Jane's youthful idealism and trust in the universal appeal of her values: "Die Bedingungen sind nicht gut. Vielleicht sehen wir uns nicht wieder. Eines möchte ich Dir mit auf den Weg geben. Hüte Dich vor zwei Dingen: vor Habgier und vor Fantasielosigkeit. Und hüte Dich vor allen, die habgierig und fantasielos sind. Sie können Dir alles nehmen. Das Haus und das Recht, zu leben, und sie werden sich dennoch keiner Schuld bewusst sein" (318; The conditions aren't good. Perhaps we won't see each other again. I want to give you one thing to take with you. Beware of two things: greed and poverty of imagination. And most importantly, beware of all who are greedy and poor in imagination. They can take everything from you. Your house and your right to live, and even then they will know no guilt).

This moment in the novel is important for several reasons (besides the obvious fact that we finally know who committed the murder and why). Now that all of the letters have been found, they can be read together as a "message in a bottle,"[36] one that engenders a redefinition of peace and reconceptualization of silence as reverence. Dora Messerschmidt had said in her discussion with Valensky that "Österreich will seine Ruhe." In contrast to this kind of "peace," which is the result of repression and active forgetting (which the Bernkopfs represent), a different and dynamic kind of peace descends on the scene as soon as Valensky reads these two letters (out loud) with Krajner: "Die Bäume rauschten leise im Wind. Der Weg war verlassen. Die wenigen Lampen warfen ein ruhiges Licht, so als ob sie immer schon geleuchtet hätten und immer weiterleuchten würden. Eine Zeit lang sagten wir nichts" (318; The trees were rustling quietly in the wind. The path was deserted. The few lamps shone a silent and steady light as if they had always been shining and always would. For a while we said nothing). Ironically, the contents of the bag seem to be at the intersection of historical contingency and Freud's preserved "essential": the letter has finally arrived at its destination.

What is the message? It becomes clear when Rossmann puts Mrs. Rosner and Mrs. Bernkopf into dialog. Valensky and Krajner go looking for Michael Bernkopf and find him exiting his parents' home. They split up as Krajner agrees to call the police, and Valensky tries to get him to confess. A scuffle ensues during which Bernkopf tries to strangle Valensky as he had strangled Jane. Unsuccessful, he is subdued and then hauled off by the police. At that moment, Mrs. Bernkopf comes flying out of the house. However, as Valensky reports: "sie stellte keine Fragen" (327; she asked no questions). Instead, Mrs. Bernkopf begins to scream.

In that last letter, Hanni Rosner's mother had warned her to avoid greed and poverty of imagination (*Habgier* and *Fantasielosigkeit*) as well as those who are greedy and poor in imagination, because they can take everything and still know no guilt. This letter, juxtaposed with Mrs. Bernkopf's final words, confirm how we should understand Rosner's warning and the ultimate "Botschaft," or message, of this novel. As her son is led away, insisting that his parents sent him to meet with Jane, Mrs. Bernkopf continues to scream: "Das ist alles nicht wahr, . . . er weiß nicht, was er sagt, . . . oh Gott, mein armer Sohn, ich weiß von nichts. Gar nichts. Ich habe keine Ahnung" (328; That is all just not true . . . he doesn't know what he is saying, . . . oh God, my poor son, I know nothing. Nothing. I have no idea). The penultimate chapter ends with Mrs. Bernkopf's unimaginative denial of knowledge.

Unlike other novels that might use events to "warn the reader away from the quest for knowledge,"[37] Rossmann's novel encourages the creative imagination (that is, *Fantasie*) as a way to confront the unknown—and the irrational—in an ethical way.[38] Such knowledge certainly takes effort; at the same time, Valensky's *Fantasie* allows her to recognize herself in the other person without turning the other's story into her own. Even if there is an essential difference there, imaginative effort is possible and can make up for the distances between people and in history. As Mrs. Bernkopf's claims to have known nothing echo through the final pages of the novel, the reader is reminded of the poignant irony of the epistemological concerns that followed the Holocaust: the radical impugning of the humanist tradition as well as the poststructuralist distrust of all stable forms of knowledge inevitably lead to a solipsistic subjectivity that crushes the integrity of the other. This can lead, in turn, to a kind of "poverty of imagination that can know no guilt." However, as Rossmann ingeniously shows with her detective novel—which has at its heart the imperative to make known the unknown—the pursuer of truth dare not allow the confrontation with the unknown to become a solipsistic investigation of self. Instead, to find any kind of justice, belated or otherwise, the sleuth must commit herself to definable human value(s) in order to form the framework of the investigation.

Notes

Epigraph: Sigmund Freund, *Konstruktionen in der Analyse: Studienausgabe. Ergänzungsband.* (1937; Frankfurt am Main: Fischer, 1982), 397. English translation: Sigmund Freud, "Construction in Analysis (1937)" in *The Standard Edition of the Complete Psychological Works of Sigmund Freud*, vol. 23, ed. and trans. James Strachey (London: Hogarth, 1964), 259.

[1] Rossman, Eva. *Freudsche Verbrechen* (Vienna: Folio, 2001).

[2] Sigmund Freud, *Die Traumdeutung* (1900; Frankfurt am Main: Fischer, 1991). Though the actual publication year was 1899, it bore the publication date of 1900 to coincide with the dawn of the new century. See Ludy T. Benjamin, *A History of Psychology: Original Sources and Contemporary Research* (Oxford: Blackwell, 2009), 421.

[3] Slavoj Žižek, *Enjoy Your Symptom! Jacques Lacan in Hollywood and Out* (New York: Routledge, 1992).

[4] On "metaphysical" detection, see Patricia Merivale and Susan Elizabeth Sweeney, eds. and introduction to *Detecting Texts: The Metaphysical Detective Story from Poe to Postmodernism* (Philadelphia: U of Pennsylvania P, 1999).

[5] See C. James Goodwin, *A History of Modern Psychology*, 3rd ed. (Hoboken, NJ: Wiley, 2008), 428.

[6] Ernst Bloch, "Philosophische Ansicht des Detektivromans," in *Der Kriminalroman I und II*, ed. Jochen Vogt (Munich: Fink, 1971), 332–33. Bloch's work on

the *Kriminalroman* also figures in Magdalena Waligórska's essay in this volume; the "darkness at the beginning" in her title is a clear reference to his work.

[7] Hanjo Berressem, "'Premeditated Crimes': The Dis-Solution of Detective Fiction in Gombrowicz's Works" in *Detecting Texts*, ed. Merivale and Sweeney, 231. In *Resisting Arrest: Detective Fiction and Popular Culture* (New York: Other, 2007), Robert A. Rushing also thoroughly examines, among other concepts, the "death drive" and "how detective fiction has typically been understood in a psychoanalytic context" (3–4). Susanne Knittel's essay in this volume also draws on the parallels between psychoanalysis and crime fiction.

[8] In addition, the novel's original hardcover featured a close-up of a suitcase.

[9] Rossmann's novels frequently include scenes of Valensky cooking; Heike Henderson explores the role of the culinary in two other novels in the Valensky series. See her essay in this volume.

[10] The novel's psychiatrist, Peter Zimmermann, himself is "gar kein Freund der klassischen Analyse" (78). On Freud's role in the history of psychology, see Goodwin, esp. 428–29. For a recent musing on Freud's continued relevance (to literary theory), see Jean-Michel Rabaté, "The Death of Freud: What Is to Be Preferred, Death or Obsolescence?" *qui parle* 19, no. 1 (2010): 37–63.

[11] Bloch 334, 341. This "light" continues the metaphoric use of light and darkness in Bloch's essay about crime fiction. See also Waligórska's essay in this volume.

[12] In another parallel between psychoanalysis and traditional detective fiction, Freud established himself as the lone genius and ultimate authority. See Goodwin on the "Freudian myth" (414). Historians generally agree that Freud saw himself as synonymous with psychoanalysis and had difficulty tolerating dissent in his field.

[13] Krajner also suggests that a cleaning woman with good relationships to other cleaning women could be essential to the investigation and her assertion is correct: her keen perspective is invaluable to solving the crime and her "Putzfrauenverbindungen," or cleaning-women-connections, open up new avenues of investigation and deliver vital clues. In her essay in this volume, Henderson also highlights Krajner's important role in Rossmann's novels and emphasizes the feminist import of the Valensky-Krajner relationship. Rossmann's nonfiction work could support a feminist analysis of her crime fiction. See Rossmann, *Heim an den Herd?* (Vienna: Folio, 1996).

[14] Dagmar C. G. Lorenz, "In Search of the Criminal—in Search of the Crime. Holocaust Literature and Films as Crime Fiction," *Modern Austrian Literature* 31, nos. 3–4 (1998): 37. The essays by Waligórska and Knittel in this volume also address this theme. See also Marieke Krajenbrink, "Unresolved Identities in Roth and Rabinovici: Reworking the Crime Genre in Austrian Literature," in *Investigating Identities: Questions of Identity in Contemporary International Crime Fiction*, ed., Krajenbrink and Kate M. Quinn (Amsterdam: Rodopi, 2009), 243–60.

[15] Susan Elizabeth Sweeney, "Crime in Postmodernist Fiction," in *The Cambridge Companion to American Crime Fiction*, ed., Catherine Ross Nickerson (Cambridge: Cambridge UP, 2010), 163.

[16] In "Formulations on the Two Principles of Mental Functioning (1911)," in *The Standard Edition of the Complete Psychological Works of Sigmund Freud*, vol. 7,

ed. and trans., James Strachey (London: Hogarth, 1958), 213–26, Freud argues "every neurosis has as its result ... a forcing of the patient out of real life, an alienating of him from reality" (218). Freud distinguishes between the "real" and the "pleasant" as the basis of the "reality principle" (219).

[17] Freud, "The Future of an Illusion (1927)" in *The Standard Edition of the Complete Psychological Works of Sigmund Freud*, vol. 21, ed. and trans. James Strachey (London: Hogarth, 1961), 54. See also Todd Dufresne, introduction to *Future of an Illusion* (Ontario, Canada: Broadview: 2012), 11–52.

[18] Sigmund Freud, "The Uncanny (1919)" in *The Standard Edition of the Complete Psychological Works of Sigmund Freud*, vol. 17, ed. and trans., James Strachey (London: Hogarth, 1955), 218–56. See also Bloch: "Etwas ist nicht geheuer, damit fängt das an" (322; Something is uncanny and this is how it begins). In her essay in this volume, Knittel works with the wordplay in Freud's concept "unheimlich" and applies it to the mysterious things at work in *Heimatkrimis*. "As a genre," she states, "the *Heimatkrimi* ... operates with a quasi-Freudian sense of the *unheimliche Heimat*" (125).

[19] Raymond Chandler, "Mord ist keine Kunst," in *Der Kriminalroman*, ed. Jochen Vogt, 164–84. See also Pierre Boileau and Thomas Narcejac, *Der Detektivroman* (Berlin and Neuwied: Luchterhand, 1967).

[20] Freud, "Construction," 258–59 (emphasis in original).

[21] Freud distinguished the task of the analyst in that "all of the essentials are preserved; even things that seem completely forgotten are present somehow and somewhere, and have merely been buried and made inaccessible to the subject" ("Construction," 260). Thus, while some detective novels may centrally locate chance as a way of building the limits of reason and knowledge into the genre, for Rossmann chance plays a role in the revelation of the connections, not in their existence.

[22] Freud, "Construction," 257.

[23] After the letter's revelations, there was much more evidence pointing to Mr. Bernkopf than to Ulrike (170). Subsequent to Valensky's trip, Ulrike disappears from the novel, having gone to visit her sister.

[24] The intertwining of personal life stories and history is also relevant to Knittel's analysis of *Heimatkrimis* and Germany's Nazi past. See Knittel's essay in this volume.

[25] Freud asserts that "Dora's reticule, which came apart at the top in the usual way, was nothing but a representation of the genitals, and her playing with it, her opening it and putting her finger in it, was an entirely unembarrassed yet unmistakable pantomimic announcement of what she would like to do with them—namely, to masturbate," in "Fragment of an Analysis of a Case of Hysteria (1905 [1901])," in *The Standard Edition of the Complete Psychological Works of Sigmund Freud*, vol. 7, ed. and trans. James Strachey (London: Hogarth, 1953), 77.

[26] Claire Kahane, Introduction: Part Two, *In Dora's Case: Freud—Hysteria—Feminism*, ed. Charles Bernheimer and Claire Kahane (New York: Columbia UP, 1985), 19.

[27] E. H. Erikson. "Reality and Actuality: An Address," *Journal of the American Psychoanalytic Association* 10 (1962): 456, emphasis mine.

[28] Ulrike's lawyer is Oskar Kellerfreund, Valensky's future husband.

[29] Freud, "A Case of Hysteria," 340.

[30] See Bice Benvenuto and Roger Kennedy, *The Works of Jacques Lacan: An Introduction* (London: Free Association Books, 1986), 91–102.

[31] Like Rushing, many postmodern analyses of detective fiction have Lacan at their theoretical roots. See Merivale and Sweeney; Žižek; Berressem. Many critics who analyze "metaphysical detective stories" share these viewpoints, even if they are not explicitly Lacanian. See Jeanne C. Ewert, "'A Thousand Other Mysteries': Metaphysical Detection, Ontological Quests," in Merivale and Sweeney, 179–98. For a failed "postfeminist" perspective, see Sonja Altnoeder, "Transforming Genres: Subversive Potential and the Interface between Hard-Boiled Detective Fiction and Chick Lit," in *The Millennial Detective: Essays on Trends in Crime Fiction, Film and Television, 1990–2010*, ed. Malcah Effron (London: McFarland, 2011), 88–89.

[32] Since I highlight a consideration of the "*che vuoi*" as essential to the "*che volgio?*" (Rushing 110), my reading of Rossmann's novel diverges significantly from more typical readings of crime fiction with psychoanalysis such as Rushing's. Such literary criticism tends to draw a straight line from Freud to Lacan as if such a line were inevitable. One could just as easily have moved on to, for example, Karen Horney with her *New Ways in Psychoanalysis* (New York: W. W. Norton, 1939) or Heinz Kohut with *The Restoration of the Self* (New York: International Universities Press, 1977) for models of developing psychoanalytic theory.

[33] Though the pursuit of this line of reasoning lies outside the scope of this essay, the connection is not as far-fetched as it might seem. Freud notes that "just as Kant warned us not to overlook the fact that our perceptions are subjectively conditioned and must not be regarded as identical with what is perceived though unknowable, so psycho-analysis warns us not to equate perceptions by means of consciousness with the unconscious mental processes which are their object. Like the physical, the psychical is not necessarily in reality what it appears to us to be" in "The Unconscious (1915)" in *The Standard Edition of the Complete Psychological Works of Sigmund Freud*, vol. 7, ed. and trans. James Strachey (London: Hogarth, 1957), 171. See also Alfred Tauber, "Freud's Dreams of Reason: The Kantian Structure of Psychoanalysis," *History of the Human Sciences* 22, no. 4 (2009): 1–29.

[34] This corresponds with Lorenz's observation about recent Austrian crime fiction that the victim now takes a place of central importance in the story (Lorenz, 39).

[35] The word, "Botschaft," or message, appears at other times when communication is difficult: when Valensky is speaking with a US journalist who is only partially understanding her, she remarks "die Botschaft schien nur teilweise beim Empfänger angekommen zu sein" (199); similarly, Dora Messerschmidt says wearily that it would be easier "die Botschaft bei mehr Menschen rüberzubringen" if the entire story were simpler and shorter (223).

[36] See note 34; also in the context of Holocaust poetics, Paul Celan's concept of *Flaschenpost* is useful: it involves a message being received and understood by another human being. See Gisela Dischner, "'Flaschenpost' and 'Wurfholz': Reflections on Paul Celan's Poems and Poetics," in *German and European Poetics*

after the Holocaust: Crisis and Creativity, ed. Gert Hofmann, Rachel MagShamhráin, Marko Pajević, and Michael Shields (New York: Camden House, 2011), 35–52; and Michael Eskin, *Ethics and Dialogue in the Works of Levinas, Bakhtin, Mandel'shtam, and Celan* (Oxford: Oxford UP, 2000).

[37] Ewert 181.

[38] I do not specifically address, as does William Donahue, the ethics of "Holocaust as fiction." See Donahue, *Holocaust as Fiction* (New York: Palgrave Macmillan, 2010). For an interesting discussion of this issue, see Waligórska's essay in this volume. Though she acknowledges potential problems with the incorporation of the Holocaust in a *Kriminalroman*, Waligórska underscores the potentially constructive nature of a reader's interaction with this theme.

Part III. Identity

9: Layered Deviance: Intersexuality in Contemporary German Crime Fiction

Angelika Baier

EVER SINCE ANTIQUITY, the western world has conceptualized the human body as being naturally either male or female, rendering as deviant those humans whose bodies display characteristics of both sexes. Today, the medical terms intersexuality[1] or DSD (Disorders of Sex Development)[2] encompass a wide range of what is considered an aberration of embryonic sex development.[3] Some of these conditions manifest themselves in a discrepancy between the genetic code, the gonadal tissue, and the phenotype of a human being. Other forms of intersexuality lead to an ambiguous phenotype of the external genitalia. Since the 1950s, intersexed children have been subject to surgical "corrections" of their bodies as a consequence of the attempt to render intersexuality invisible and to guarantee an outwardly homogenous body. Not until the end of the twentieth century has the so-called surgical fix been severely criticized for in fact mutilating the bodies and psyches concerned.[4] As a consequence, politically motivated activist groups formed in the 1990s in both the United States and in Europe with an agenda of publicizing the stories of intersex individuals and the stigmatization and discrimination they suffered.[5] The internet, in particular, served as an easily accessible platform for introducing the stories of intersex individuals to a wider public.[6] Since then, an increasing number of people have entered the public domain, telling previously withheld stories of psychic and physical wounds caused by the medical treatments.

Concurrent with these developments, twenty-first-century fiction has displayed a heightened interest in these stories, too.[7] In this chapter, I will elaborate on the discussion of intersexuality in twenty-first-century German crime fiction. Crime fiction that treats intersexuality revives the genre's centuries-old concern with gender deviance, and the link between deviant bodies, deviant psyches, and crime.[8] The gender deviance of the intersexed body, on the one hand, and the intersexed infant's difficult psychic situation resulting from the medical treatment and the often difficult and abusive relationships with doctors and parents on the other, contribute to a largely traumatic childhood.[9] Twentieth-century psychology, in turn, has associated childhood trauma with an adult's tendencies to engage in crime,[10] as the modern phenomenon of the "serial killer" illustrates. Mark Seltzer's analysis in his book *Serial Killers* follows the emergence of the concept of this special type of murderer during the course of the nineteenth century, interpreting it as the outcome of an academic "shift in focus from the criminal act to the character of the actor."[11] Through this development, Seltzer claims, the serial killer became "a type of person, a body, a case history, a childhood, an alien life form."[12] Thus, the cultural conceptualizations of serial killing and intersexuality represent an area of study that this chapter will further explore in regard to twenty-first-century German crime fiction.

From 2005 to 2011, in the German-speaking world alone, four thrillers treating intersexuality and serial killing were published.[13] This chapter takes a closer look at three of these:[14] Renate Kampmann's *Fremdkörper* (Foreign Body, 2005),[15] Andreas Winkelmann's *Tief im Wald und unter der Erde* (Deep in the Woods and below the Ground, 2009),[16] and Nané Lénard's *SchattenHaut* (ShadowSkin, 2011).[17] In what follows, I will focus on how the three crime novels treat the only recently widely discussed topic of intersexuality. First, I examine how crime fiction in general constructs reality. In this regard, I will introduce Sarah Dillon's concept of crime fiction's palimpsestic structure, which conceptualizes reality as a layered phenomenon consisting of a level of normalcy that overlies a hidden layer of criminal deviance. Accordingly, this chapter considers crime fiction's investigative process as it relates to Eve Kosofsky Sedgwick's notion of "paranoid reading" as an ever-vigilant attempt to expose the mysterious and hidden layer to the light of justice.[18] Next, I will study the ways by which the medical apparatus and an intersexed person's social surroundings, such as the family unit, force the intersexed's physical and psychic deviance into a dark, hidden realm, from where it may or may not surface and manifest itself in behavior. In my reading of the three novels, I will consider how the narrations display and treat these notions of layering, gender secrecy, and corporeal and psychic deviance. I will also explore the various ways the novels link intersexuality and serial killing. Finally, this essay examines the critical stance the novels take in regard to the approach of German society to intersexuality.

Crime Fiction, Intersexuality, and Layers of Reality

Crime novels often juxtapose norm-breakers and guardians of the law. Starting with a crime, usually a murder, a piece of crime fiction follows the investigators as they trace clues that the perpetrators have unwittingly left. The investigations can thus be described as a reading process that ends with the formation of a coherent, intelligible story put together from the formerly scattered signs. As a result of this process, the murderer is revealed and subsequently apprehended.

A typical crime-fiction plot holds a complex relation to temporality in that it focuses on solving a murder committed in the past so that theoretically such a crime cannot reoccur in the future. In this way, the process involved in reading crime fiction can be characterized as *paranoid* reading. According to Kosofsky Sedgwick, paranoia is "anticipatory," yet it "burrows both backward and forward because there must be no bad surprises. . . . [P]aranoia requires that bad news be always already known."[19] Crime fiction can accordingly be perceived as a paranoid "hermeneutics of suspicion" that is about the "exposure" of problematic events that shall not repeat themselves in the future.[20] As the terms "exposure" and "to burrow" suggest, crime fiction constructs reality as a layered phenomenon that acts as a palimpsest. Accordingly, Sarah Dillon notes that

> like a palimpsest, the classical detective whodunit contains two texts: the story of the "true" version of events which the perpetrator has erased, or attempted to erase; and the story of the ostensible version of events superimposed upon it. . . . The presence of the underlying text is announced by various clues visible in the overlying one, which, consequently both conceals and reveals the story of the crime. The task of the detective as palimpsest reader is to recognize these clues and to uncover and reconstruct the underlying story.[21]

In spite of the fact that both stories are present at the same time, crime fiction conceptualizes reality as a surface-depth phenomenon. The paranoid investigator digs out the layer of hidden deviance beneath a surface of normalcy, being in a state of constant vigilance since everyone is suspect and anything may turn out to be a crucial clue. The fact that each of a crime story's characters may be the perpetrator means that the characters as embodied entities within a specific societal realm also exhibit a palimpsestic sign structure that complies with crime fiction's topographic model of reality. The following two subchapters illustrate that exactly this notion of the human body and psyche as a layered phenomenon makes intersexuality particularly interesting for the study of contemporary crime fiction.

The Intersexed Body as a Palimpsest

Elizabeth Grosz emphasizes that "every body is marked by the history and specificity of its existence. It is possible to construct a biography, a history of the body, for each individual and social body."[22] The various parts of the body—its scars and dyed hair, for example—can be regarded as signs of a story left on and beyond its surface. The body's multitude of signs is to be interpreted alongside historically contingent frames of reference, such as gender, race, nationality, profession, or class.

As Western societies have been shaped by a hetero-normative system of gender dimorphism that acknowledges the human only as being exclusively male or female, this is especially true for the gendered body. Right from the moment of birth, a human being is addressed as either a girl or a boy.[23] Usually physicians and parents read the infant's body signs, giving them a gendered meaning. As Judith Butler has rightly emphasized, the infant's intelligibility within Western societies depends, in fact, on its readably gendered body.[24] Even to the present day, the reading process after or even before birth centers on visible body parts like penis or vagina, which are considered to unequivocally signify a person's sex. When a child is born with outwardly ambiguous genitalia, the search continues toward the inside and, depending on the historical period, the specialists' focus shifts toward gendered signs like gonads, chromosomes, or hormones. According to today's medical vernacular, forms of intersexuality or DSD that do not express themselves in ambiguous genitalia are most often not diagnosed at birth but in puberty when, for instance, an outwardly female person with XY chromosomal status and internal testicles does not menstruate or develop breasts.[25]

Each of the various medical intersex conditions in a given person's body unites allegedly female and male body signs. As all of these conditions depend on medical, or biological, definitions of masculinity and femininity, the persons concerned are entrusted into the hands of physicians, who, in collaboration with the parents, decide about the person's "true"[26] or "optimal"[27] sex. Since the 1950s, intersexed persons have mostly undergone surgical and hormonal treatment in order to homogenize the gendered body signs as far as possible.[28] Yet, as the assignment prioritizes some gendered body signs over others that are deemed irrelevant, the intersexed body can be conceived of as a *palimpsest* consisting of two layers, one of which is overwritten by the other. Importantly in regard to crime fiction, however, the "surgical fix" leaves behind physical and mental scars that simultaneously reveal and conceal the overwriting process. It renders it possible to homogenize a person's phenotype. Discrepancies between the gendered body signs, such as between a person's DNA status and phenotype, persist, however.

As will be shown, the crime fiction examined here treats the motif of the intersexed, palimpsestic body for mainly two reasons. First, the intersexed body renders the investigator's palimpsestic reading process more difficult. Usually, gender identification is a process that does not require conscious reflection. Encountering another person on the street, one instantly categorizes this person into one particular side of the gender binary or the other. By illustrating that this assignment process is commonly unquestioned even by the police, the crime novels challenge the allegedly natural and normal coherence of a person's various gender signs. Second, the layered nature of intersexuality intensifies the work of specialists, such as psychologists and forensic pathologists, as part of the investigation process depicted in contemporary crime fiction. Historically, investigators engage in professional readings of fingerprints, or the meaning of artifacts left at the site of crime. The recurrent analyses of DNA traces in contemporary crime fiction, however, demonstrate that the twenty-first-century examination process of human bodies and psyches involves technical skills of detection to an increasing extent. Accordingly, Christiana Gregoriou's analysis of *Deviance in Contemporary Crime Fiction* follows the emergence and development in the 1990s of the "medical examiner's crime genre,"[29] in which the police work on a specific case, often the case of a serial killer, in collaboration with a range of academically trained specialists, such as forensic pathologists, anthropologists, biologists, and psychologists. In two of the three novels examined here, forensic pathologists and their ways of reading dead bodies play a central role. In two of the texts, the analysis of traces of DNA is of major importance for the investigation process. Moreover, in each of the novels, interdisciplinary teams of investigators scrutinize the perpetrators' psychologically conspicuous profile. In this way, all three of the crime stories present the multifaceted search for a serial killer. In what follows, we will see that the personage of the serial killer not only brings "an urgency to the chasing of the murderer at hand," it also allows "the sense of there being a pattern."[30] Hence, in the end, the pattern-like murders in thrillers can be conceived of as signs of the serial killer's psychical constitution, which seemingly *drives* him or her to kill again and again. In this way, serial killers share core features with the intersexed, which makes both intriguing subjects for today's crime fiction. The traumatic childhoods of both groups lead to severe problems in their everyday lives as adults. In the following section, I will further explore the uncanny connections between the psychical condition of the serial killer and the intersexed individual.

The Intersexed's Psyche as a Palimpsest

In his analysis of today's Western therapy culture, Frank Furedi stresses that ever since the introduction and expansion of psychoanalysis and its narrative patterns in the nineteenth and early twentieth century, the period of childhood has come to be considered a critical factor for every individual's psychic and thus socially healthy development.[31] According to the therapeutic narrative, everyone is at risk, as from the moment of birth each of us is given over to a potentially abusive environment. Traumatic experiences during infancy and childhood are said to leave traces in the psychic apparatus of a person.[32] Furthermore, psychoanalysis has brought early-childhood sexuality and the significance of the suppression of deviant sexual desires into focus.[33] Psychoanalytic theory dictates that in order to guarantee an allegedly normal, heterosexual development of a person's stable gendered self, both traumatic experiences and socially deviant desires—that is, same-sex desires—have to be repressed to the unconscious, where they are, nevertheless, assumed to continually influence an adult person's well-being and actions.[34] In order to understand trauma, Christa Binswanger, Lotta Samelius, and Suruchi Thapar-Björkert take up the concept of the "cryptic incorporation" of an individual's "undigested" experiences that are "'alive inside,' though indecipherable."[35] In this context, the unconscious is often modeled as an "underlying region," as indicated, for example, by Freud's famous topographic model for the psychical apparatus, the *Wunderblock*[36] (Mystic Writing-Pad). Sarah Dillon, in turn, favors the term palimpsest over the Mystic Writing-Pad, because in contrast to the pad's endlessly blank surface, palimpsests continually keep their different layers present, yet in some cases undecipherable.[37]

With regard to intersexuality as a motif of crime fiction, it is of interest to understand the psyche as palimpsestic in various ways. According to the above-mentioned official guidelines for medical treatment of intersexuality, which were commonly accepted beginning in the 1950s, it is better that the hidden layers of the intersexed person's body remain concealed, particularly to the intersexed persons themselves. Nikki Sullivan claims that "bodies are often read as texts which bear an indexical relation to the psyches or souls that allegedly inhabit them. This is particularly the case with bodies that are marked in ways considered 'strange' or somehow inappropriate."[38] Accordingly, parents and physicians involved in the treatment of intersexuality have been expected to keep all the information on the treatment to themselves, out of concern for the intersexed's psychical well-being, with the assumption that physical ambiguity can lead to harassment and a general psychical instability of the person's gender identity.[39] Yet, because the process of physical, or surgical, and psychical gender assignment during infancy naturally runs the risk of "the wrong layer" being chosen to be of sole importance, the adolescent intersexed person is permanently subject to hypervigilant, paranoid gender readings. Child play, dress preferences, and, above all, sexual preferences at an older age are continually closely scrutinized in order to detect and prevent deviant behavior or desires as soon as possible. In this regard, statements by intersexed persons document that, in fact, the medical secrecy policy and the medical interventions themselves have been traumatic, and they report that the lack of information and the abusive medical examinations they had to endure during childhood and adolescence caused severe mental and physical problems at an older age.[40]

Ultimately, it is only a small step from the paranoid readings of the intersexed's palimpsestic body and psyche to another line of thought that connects corporeal and psychical, including behavioral, deviance with criminality. In the nineteenth century, physical abnormalities were prevalently associated with criminal deviance, as Cesare Lombroso's theories famously illustrate.[41] The same century, however, also provided a shift of focus for criminology, as Seltzer points out: "During the course of the nineteenth century, there is a radical shift in the understanding of crime, a shift in focus from the criminal act to the character of the actor: the positing of the category of the dangerous individual. And during the course of the nineteenth century, there is a shift in the understanding of desire, a shift in focus from sexual acts to sexual identity."[42]

With psychoanalysis, the unconscious, sexual deviance as a driving force, and a traumatic childhood have entered the realm of police work. According to Amy Yang, psychoanalysis "delved into the criminal's mind, teasing out the underlying driving force for murder, even if the criminal was not actively aware of it at the time of crime."[43] Correspondingly, Mark Seltzer maintains with respect to serial killers that "child abuse—wounded as a child, wounding as an adult—is one of the foundational scripts in accounting for the serial killer."[44] Seltzer emphasizes that the criminal is not the commonly assumed "antisocial individual" but rather represents the collapse of the social and the individual, of boundaries and distinctions, as the traumatic experience "'comes from within' but in the form of the breaking of an outside in."[45]

These observations establish parallels between the serial killer and the intersexed, such as trauma caused by social surroundings. In the novels I analyze here, I will take a closer look at the elaboration of motifs of deviant bodies and sexualities, childhood trauma, and the collapse of the social and the individual in regard to the intersexed characters.

Fremdkörper

Renate Kampmann's *Fremdkörper* was published in 2005 as the third novel in a series featuring forensic pathologist Leonie Simon; the series thus represents a German version of the US American medical examiner's crime genre that was established in the 1990s by Patricia Cornwell's Kay Scarpetta and Kathy Reich's Tempe Brennan series.

Fremdkörper combines three major story lines, the first being the series plot involving characters who play a role in every volume of the series. The second plot is conceptualized as a classic whodunit shaped by the discovery of a mysterious corpse at the beginning of the novel and the revelation of its murderer at the end. In the opening pages of Kampmann's novel, neighbors find the mummified corpse of Marlene Böttcher next to a tissue covered with traces of XY-DNA. As Marlene's death was caused by a ruptured aneurysm years before, the police believe that she has died of strictly natural causes. Dissecting and reading the body signs of her corpse, Leonie comes to a different conclusion and takes up the investigation by herself. She subsequently befriends Nicola Goerne, the victim's former best friend and part-time lover. The third story line follows the typical thriller plot.[46] At the time of the investigation surrounding the corpse within the whodunit plot, a serial killer shoots several other victims. In order to find the perpetrator before she or he strikes again, the police focus on the search for the serial killer whereas Leonie dedicates most of her time to her "private" case. It turns out that the two crime threads intersect in the character of Nicola in that the waitress becomes acquainted not only with Leonie but also with Axel Evert, whom the police eventually identify as the wanted serial killer.

Nicola, however, is secretly intersexed: she was born with XY chromosomes, but due to a mixed gonadal dysgenesis, her male phenotype did not develop according to medical norms.[47] During childhood she was surgically corrected to be female (417). Both Axel and Leonie are fascinated by Nicola, although they do not have the slightest idea of her secret. Instead, their interest and concern are predicated on explicit readings of Nicola's gendered body and behavior. In the following passage, Axel describes seeing Nicola for the first time: "Die Frau sah er zum ersten Mal, als er am späten Sonntagabend ... vor einer Baustelle hielt. ... Aber dann trat die Frau im obersten Stockwerk aus dem Schatten eines Gerüsts und setzte einen Fuß auf einen der T-Träger, die das Gerippe des Rohbaus bildeten. ... Die Frau hatte ihr Leben riskiert, und ihm schien, sie habe es genossen. Frauen taten so etwas nicht" (80–81; He saw the woman for the first time on late Sunday evening when he stopped at a building site. ... But then the woman appeared from the shadow of the scaffolding on the top story of the building and put her foot on one of the T-sections that formed the frame of the building's shell construction. ... The woman had risked her life, and it appeared to him that she had enjoyed this experience. For a woman that was unusual).[48]

Leonie, on the other hand, is captivated by Nicola's distinctive looks and voice: "Ohne großes Nachdenken hätte Leonie die junge Frau als attraktiv bezeichnet. Bei einiger Überlegung hätte sie allerdings einschränkend anmerken müssen, dass sie zu klein und stämmig war, ihre Nase zu groß und ihr Mund zu schmal, um als wirklich hübsch zu gelten. Ihre intensiv blauen Augen waren allerdings sehr beeindruckend, und den Klang ihrer warmen, ein wenig rauen Stimme fand Leonie aufregend" (116; Without much consideration, Leonie would have described the young woman as appealing. However, after reflecting more thoroughly, she would have had to concede that she [Nicola] was short and stout, her nose was too big and her mouth too narrow to be considered beautiful. Still, her intense blue eyes were certainly impressive, and Leonie found the sound of her warm, slightly hoarse voice exciting). However, Nicola's deviant gendered behavior and body signs hint at a hidden layer underneath the surface of female normalcy. Both Axel and Leonie are increasingly irritated in respect to the kind of sexual desire that Nicola evokes or does not evoke. Axel, for example, is confused because he does not fall in love with the attractive Nicola; he only desires to be friends with her (183). Leonie, in turn, is bewildered by her romantic feelings and sexual desire for Nicola that also do not correspond to the heterosexual image that Leonie claims for herself (256).

In regard to the crime plot, the description of Nicola's body, as well as the established structures of sexual desire, can be regarded as clues to her "real" sex according to her chromosomal status, which eventually identifies her as the "male" person present at the moment of Marlene's death. This revelation, however, is only possible after Leonie notices that, so far, her sympathetic relationship with the waitress has prevented a "proper" reading of Nicola's body signs. Up to this point, Leonie wanted to believe in Nicola's femininity and normalcy. Thus, she blames herself for confusion concerning her sexuality. But then Leonie realizes that "vom Offensichtlichen durfte man sich nicht täuschen lassen" (375; one shouldn't become misled by the obvious). Following this belief, she starts to assign meanings to all the small traces of deviance that she has previously refused to see in regard to Nicola's body and behavior. Eventually the forensic pathologist manages to force the underlying text of Nicola's palimpsestic body and biography into the open. In spite of the fact that Nicola's deviance had always been apparent, Leonie's now-paranoid approach to the deviant signs reveals the hidden secret:

> Langsam ging Leonie zurück in ihr Büro.... Der letzte Blick aus nächster Nähe hatte ihr enthüllt, dass Nicola Goerne Kontaktlinsen trug. Wie lange schon? Ihre besinnungslose Angst vor der Spritze. Die Narben an den Handgelenken. Eine Kindheit voller Krankheiten. Eine Allergie gegen Kirschen. Leonie ergriff das intensive Empfinden, dass all das eine Bedeutung hatte.... Mit einer Pinzette fischte sie die Tücher heraus [aus dem Abfalleimer], die rot von Nicola Goernes Blut waren und alle Informationen bereithielten—vorausgesetzt man verstand es, den Code der Chromosomen zu entschlüsseln. (398)

> [Slowly, Leonie returned to her office.... Her last look into Nicola's eyes had revealed that Nicola was wearing contact lenses. For how long? Her mindless fear of injections. The scars on her wrists. A childhood affected by diseases. An allergy to cherries. Leonie had the feeling that all this was of importance. With a pair of tweezers, she fished for the tissues, which were red from Nicola Goerne's blood and contained all the necessary information—provided that one was able to decipher the chromosomes' code.]

In the end, Nicola's deviant body signs match up with the story of her childhood trauma of being her parents' "Monster im Keller" (416;

monster in the cellar) and of having been examined by doctors, "die mich anglotzten, befummelten und mir wehtaten" (417; who stared at me, pawed at me, and hurt me). Leonie identifies Nicola as the probable murderer of Marlene and, indeed, also of Marlene's boyfriend Sven.

It turns out that Marlene and Nicola had been lovers until Nicola informed her about her intersexuality. Unable to deal with Nicola's gender deviance, Marlene ended the relationship and began a relationship with Sven. "Marlene war eine ungewöhnliche Frau. Sie gestattete mir eine Weile, sie zu lieben. Bis ich ihr sagte, *was* ich bin" (418; my emphasis; Marlene was an extraordinary woman. She allowed me to love her for a while. Until I told her, *what* I was). Leonie identifies jealousy and feelings of hurt as Nicola's motive for having left Marlene alone with a ruptured aneurysm and for stabbing Sven to death. However, besides the concurring traces of DNA found on the named tissues, there is no final proof that Nicola is responsible for these deaths, as she dies at the end of the novel during an explosion caused by Axel, in the course of which Nicola saves Leonie, but not herself.

Nicola's classic motive for murder stands in stark contrast to the motivation and the deeds of serial killer Axel. Typically in the case of serial killers, the police search for a perpetrator whose childhood indicates a problematic layer under the surface of normalcy. Hence, incongruent with Axel's apparent "super-normality"—"er . . . hielt sich gern sauber und ordentlich" (179; he liked to keep himself clean and proper), the police merge evidence from his psychological state, biography (368), and conduct as well as his body signs (336) into a coherent profile that in a way foreshadows his murders: "Ich vermute, wir haben es hier mit einem Mann zu tun, der über viele Jahre frustrierende Erfahrungen gemacht hat und diese irgendwann nicht mehr kompensieren konnte. Das extreme Bedürfnis nach Beherrschung der Situation, das sich in seinem Vorgehen erkennen lässt, kompensiert wahrscheinlich einen erlebten Kontrollverlust. Das können gescheiterte Beziehungen sein, Misserfolge in seiner beruflichen Laufbahn oder Ähnliches" (308; I assume we are dealing with a man who over the years experienced many frustrations and at some point was unable to compensate for these. Presumably, his extreme desire for control over a situation, revealed by his behavior, compensates for a prior loss of control. This could be a failed relationship, professional disappointments, or something similar).

By juxtaposing Nicola and Axel, Renate Kampmann's novel innovatively combines and contrasts two different types of murder and crime-novel traditions. In spite of the fact that both threads focus on the impact of society in the creation of murderers in the sense that the biographical, hidden layers of the characters' palimpsestically constructed bodies and psyches give a final explanation of their deeds, the two traditions allow different palimpsestic reading processes. In regard to Nicola as a classical murderer, her personality and body retain their layered structure of her personality, and she remains a fascinating, likeable character until the very end. Consequently, Leonie explicitly expresses her sympathy and sorrow with respect to Nicola's suicide. Because of Axel's monstrously motiveless deeds, however, his death at the end of the novel is not to be mourned; his character's palimpsestic structure is negated by a complete conflation of his person with the hidden, monstrous layer of his person and biography. The following reading will illustrate that this characterization is typical for serial killers.

Tief im Wald und unter der Erde

In 2009, Andreas Winkelmann published *Tief im Wald und unter der Erde* as the first novel in a series that centers around police chief inspector Nele Karminter and her team.[49] The thriller commences as four women, the last of whom is Nele's lover and police assistant Anouschka Rossberg, are kidnapped within four subsequent days. The police have to assume that a serial offender is responsible for the deeds.

In terms of narrative voice, Winkelmann's thriller frequently shifts narrative perspective. Through the eyes of the kidnappees, and subsequent murder victims, as well as through the eyes of the offender Karel Murow himself, the reader learns about the deeds and the perpetrator long before the police do. Here again, the reader becomes acquainted with Karel through repeated references to his physical deviance. Although Karel is consistently referred to as a man, it is his voice that first indicates a gender deviance:

> Der Mann verharrte. Sein Blick verdüsterte sich, so als würden seine Augen die Dunkelheit der Höhle aufsaugen. "Wenn du nicht still hältst, wirst du hier unten sterben." Seine Stimme klang ungewöhnlich hoch und fistelig und hatte für Jasmin einen unmenschlichen Klang. (54)

> [The man paused. His gaze darkened as if his eyes were sucking in the cave's darkness. "If you don't keep still you will die down here." The sound of his voice was high and shrill; for Jasmin it didn't sound human.]

The secret of his body and psyche, the hidden layer of the palimpsest, is revealed little by little, and eventually we find out that Karel was born as a boy without a penis. In order to conceal his lack of a phallus, he wears a huge dildo (297). This reference to psychoanalytical theory is by no means coincidental, as the novel holds traumatic childhood experiences within the so-called oedipal triangle responsible for Karel's psychical constitution. In diary-like insertions into the thriller narration (90–94,

158–66, 315–29), Karel depicts his father as a brute who repeatedly rapes his wife and humiliates his son because of his physical constitution.

After years of humiliation, teenaged Karel kills his father by castrating him. When confronted by the police, the mother assumes responsibility for the murder and goes to prison. Nevertheless, she neither appreciates the reprieve from her husband's violence, nor does she value her son's actions. Winkelmann's thriller thus presents the allegedly traumatic parental lack of recognition as a cause for Karel's drive to kill. In this way, Karel's development closely resembles Seltzer's description of the popular understanding of a serial killer's psychological constitution, according to which childhood trauma is seen as the experience of a self whose boundaries are constantly blurred by an abusive exterior. Consequently, the traumatized self overidentifies with its social surroundings, as its "interior states are nothing but outer or social forces and fantasies turned outside in: the subject as it were, flooded by the social and its collective fantasies."[50] Wishing to be "normal" like everyone else, his/her turning to serial killing can then be regarded as an attempt to finally melt into his/ her surroundings. Accordingly, the serial-killing self's continuing search for likeness and conformity with the expectations of its social surroundings leads to what Seltzer identifies as a "failure of distance with respect to context," that is realized "in the subject's absorption into 'background.'"[51] *Tief im Wald und unter der Erde* repeatedly spells out the suspension of boundaries as Karel's animal- and monster-like physicality seems to continually blend in with his environment:

> Da war doch was gewesen, am Waldrand! Vielleicht ein Reh? Aber was sich dann aus der Dunkelheit löste, als sei es ein Teil von ihr, war ganz gewiss kein Reh. Es war etwas Schwarzes, Großes, Unförmiges, das auf zwei Beinen lief. Ein Mensch, und doch auch wieder nicht. (11)

> [Something had been there at the edge of the wood. Maybe a deer? But the thing that detached itself from the darkness, as if it were part of it, wasn't a deer for sure. It was a big, black, bulky something, walking on two legs. It was a human being, and yet it wasn't.]

The blurred boundaries indicate that for Karel Murow, just as for Kampmann's Axel Evert, "the stakes of the murder are thus not finally the possession of an object of love or pleasure but *self*-possession: the repeated, and repeatedly failed attempt, to pass through identification to identity."[52]

As the serial killer is unable to distinguish between her/himself and the outer world, s/he also embodies the "mass in person," or the tendency not to stand out and to appear normal in social situations: the serial killer's "abnormality" is his/her "hypernormality."[53] Accordingly, in the years between the murder of his father and the slaughtering of the women, Karel's motivation only flourishes in the alleged underground of his psyche. For years, he leads a fairly normal life. When the police eventually enter his apartment after having followed his traces, they find in his closet "die gereinigte und ordentlich gebügelte Uniform eines Zugbegleiters der Deutschen Bahn" (258; the clean and neatly ironed uniform of a conductor of Deutsche Bahn). Karel's depiction as a palimpsestic person, displaying a normal surface on top of a layer of deviance, is also mirrored by the places in which he acts. His apartment, which is situated on the fourth floor of a building in Lüneburg, is "unauffällig" (258; inconspicuous), "eindeutig lebte hier ein Single, der zwar pedantisch Ordnung hielt, es aber nicht verstand, sich gemütlich einzurichten" (258; it was obvious that a bachelor was living here; a person, who knew how to keep a place meticulously clean, but had no feeling for making a place comfortable). The kidnapped women, on the other hand, are brought to a place "tief im Wald und unter der Erde"; in other words, to an old bunker in the woods where the Nazis manufactured ammunition. In this labyrinthine building without windows and light, which significantly contributes to the perpetrator's monstrous overcoding, Karel is able to move despite the lack of light: everyone else becomes disoriented. This can therefore be read as a representation of Karel's monstrously dark unconscious where his childhood traumas lay hidden.

Police officer and last kidnappee Anouschka Rossberg is the only one of the four women who manages to engage Karel in a dialogue about his childhood. At certain moments she feels empathy for him. In the end, however, the thriller thwarts the conception of Karel as a serial killer—that is, a "'Made Evil' criminal figure"[54]—by floating the idea that he may in fact be a "'Born Evil' criminal".[55]

> Anouschka betrachtete ihn fasziniert und ängstlich zugleich.... Seine Mutter hatte schon damals recht gehabt. In ihm hauste ein bösartiger Dämon, genauso wie in seinem Vater. Er würde niemals ein normaler Mensch sein, keine Therapie konnte diesem Mann helfen. Die Welt wäre ohne ihn besser dran. Er war gefährlich, weil er sein Inneres nicht kontrollieren konnte. Im ständigen Kampf mit sich selbst verlor er dauernd, und selbst wenn seine Mutter ihn damals nicht so gedemütigt hätte, wäre er trotzdem ein zutiefst asozialer Mensch geworden. Er war ohne Penis auf die Welt gekommen, und vielleicht fehlte ja noch mehr! Konnte es sein, dass Menschen ohne Seele zur Welt kamen? Anouschka wollte sich nicht mit solchen Gedanken belasten. Sie wollte auf keinen Fall Mitleid empfinden mit diesem Monstrum, das Tim [einen Kollegen] getötet hatte. (332)

> [Anouschka gazed at him, simultaneously fascinated and scared.... His mother had been right all along. There was an evil demon inside

him, just as there had been in his father. He would never be a normal human being, no therapy was able help him. The world would be a better place without him. He was dangerous because he was unable to control his inner life. In his fight against himself, he continuously lost; even if his mother had not humiliated him back in the day, he would have become a thoroughly antisocial person. He had been born without a penis, and maybe something else was missing! Was it possible that humans were born without a soul? Anouschka didn't want to strain herself with such thoughts. She didn't want to feel empathy for this monster, which had killed Tim.]

Engaging in an ever-more-paranoid palimpsestic reading process, the lesbian police officer Anouschka gives the absent penis one single denotation: it is read as an unambiguous sign for the absence of a "soul" or conscience. Thus conflating nineteenth-century notions of a deterministic deviant physiognomy with psychological explanations for the origins of crime, the thriller suggests that the secret of Karel's deviant behavior has lain all along in his hidden physical abnormity, against which no remedy is able to help. Similar to the reading of Axel in the previous section, Anouschka's understanding of Karel attempts to erase the palimpsestic structure of his person by only giving value to his monstrously dark depths. Consequently, she shoots him and it seems to her as if his demise had made the world "ein klein wenig heller" (408; a little bit lighter). In the end, his death is not mourned.

SchattenHaut

Nané Lénard's *SchattenHaut* (2011) presents the first volume of a crime-fiction series that features police inspectors Wolf Hetzer and Peter Kruse. Here again, the reader is confronted with an intersexed serial killer who is introduced in two different time frames. In recurrent episodes, we follow the 1960s and 1970s childhood of little Susi. The time frame set in the year 2010, on the other hand, divides the reader's attention between chapters that focus on the police's investigation, and chapters that describe the male perpetrator while he performs his patterned, murderous deeds. The two plot threads—of the male offender and a girl's childhood history—do not intersect until the very end of the novel, when forensic pathologist and police associate Mechthild Susanne "Mica" von der Weiden is identified as the wanted killer. The police are more than surprised, as they considered serial killing a male business (133). A thorough reading of Mica's physical gender signs confirms that assumption:

> Tut mir leid, Herr Hetzer, aber der Befund ist wirklich eindeutig.... Frau Dr. von der Weiden hat wahrscheinlich CAIS oder eine besonders ausgeprägte Form von PAIS.[56] Genetisch muss sie

als Junge auf die Welt gekommen sein, mit dem Erscheinungsbild eines Mädchens.... Diese "Jungen" können ihre eigenen männlichen Hormone nicht verwerten, darum bildet sich kein richtiger Penis aus. Eventuell zeigt sich eine etwas vergrößerte Klitoris. Die Hoden bleiben in den Leistenbeugen oder im Bauchraum stecken. Die Sache fällt erst in der Pubertät auf, weil diese Menschen keine Gebärmutter und Eierstöcke ausbilden. Es gibt daher keine Menstruation. (334)

[I am sorry, Mr. Hetzer, but the clinical evidence is clear.... Dr von der Weiden is suffering from CAIS or a very strong form of PAIS. Genetically, she must have been born a boy with the appearance of a girl.... The bodies of these "boys" cannot make use of their male hormones, that's why they are unable to grow normal penises. In some cases, they exhibit an enlarged clitoris. The testicles remain stuck in the groin or abdomen. Only during puberty do people start to notice that something is different, as the persons concerned have neither a uterus nor ovaries. Consequently, there is no menstruation.]

In the course of the narration, several clues that manifest themselves as signs of physical and psychical gender deviance lead to the realization that Susi, the supposedly male perpetrator, and Mica are, in fact, the same person. Mica possesses exceptional strength, as in the course of her first meeting with Wolf she "drückte Wolfs Hand so stark, dass er dadurch fast in die Knie ging" (24; pressed Wolf's hand so hard that he almost went down). The serial killer, on the other hand, is repeatedly characterized by his soft voice (13, 15, 68). But overall, Susi's childhood story introduces her as a palimpsestic person with layers of gender identity and physicality.

Susi grows up as a girl, but the narration tells us that she has the utmost interest in boys' toys, games, behavior, and clothes (50, 73, 121, 153, 202). As her parents do not want their daughter to be a misfit, they work strictly against every sign of gender deviance in her behavior or looks (52). Therefore, Susi's relationship to her parents, who want a perfect girl, is a difficult one. The usually speechless mother is dominated by the father, a generally unlikable person who repeatedly cheats on his wife and beats up his daughter. During puberty, Susi does not develop breasts or pubic hair. After an invasive and traumatic visit to a gynecologist, Susi's parents find out about her condition (277). The medical personnel do not, however, share the information with the teenaged Susi. Without her informed consent, her undescended testicles are surgically removed and her vagina is enlarged (340). In spite of, or maybe because of, these childhood experiences, Susi/Mica builds up an outwardly normal life. "Du hättest es nicht mal bemerkt, wenn du mit mir geschlafen hättest" (340; you wouldn't have noticed anything, even if you had slept with me), Mica tells Wolf Hetzer, indicating that grown-up Mica even looks physically norm-conforming. As a forensic pathologist, Mica furthermore performs a very professional and successful job. In the case of the victims of the wanted serial killer, Mica happens to be in the position of sophisticatedly reading her own criminal handwriting. In this sense, her job can also be considered a "mask of normalcy," as it provides her with the tools for both the investigative readings and the treatment of her victims.[57]

Mica's victims are the strongest indicator of her gender deviance. She kills three people, all of whom were part of the decision-making process in regard to surgically correcting her to an outwardly female and inwardly sexless person. A priest, a local politician and friend of her father, and an employee of the youth welfare service are slaughtered, but the police find Mica's father before he dies. As representatives of society and its rigid gender norms, these persons are held responsible for what happened to Mica:

> Sie gehören zu den Menschen, die mich zu dem gemacht haben, was ich bin. Es war Ihre Entscheidung, Ihr Rat. Sie sind Teil des Gerichts gewesen, das über mich geurteilt hat. In diesem Moment haben Sie meine Seele zerstört und darum ist sie jetzt auch nicht mehr zu retten. (15)
>
> [You belong to the group of people that has made me what I am now. It was your decision, your advice. You were part of the tribunal that passed judgment on me. Back then you destroyed my soul, that's why it can no longer be saved.]

Mica, however, not only kills these persons, but she also castrates them and severs their vocal chords. Because all the characters in *SchattenHaut*, including chief inspector Wolf Hetzer, equate the lack of adequate internal and external genitalia and gonads with being a "Kind, . . . ein Niemand ohne Stimme" (265; a child, . . . a nobody without a voice), Mica forms the victims into a "Neutrum. Ein Nichts" (83; a neuter. A nothing). She reverses her traumatic childhood by annulling the representatives of society in return.

They are made equal to the perception of herself, conflating Mica and her surroundings as described as typical for a serial offender. In this way, she is "Monster und Opfer zugleich" (338; both a monster and a victim), as Wolf Hetzer contends. According to the thriller's title *SchattenHaut*, being a monster and a victim at the same time illustrates Mica's palimpsestic structure. The fact that Mica commits the murders dressed up and passing as a man suggests that having been surgically forced to live as a woman, she has allegedly suppressed her male layer and the wounds of its attempted distinction. And now her "underlying" wounded male side seemingly drives her to kill the people by making them equal to herself.

However, as Mica kills for revenge and is not characterized as an uncontrollable, killing-machine like Axel Evert or Karel Murow, she doesn't completely fit the classical profile of a serial killer.

In the end, after a DNA test has proven her guilty of murder and kidnapping, Mica tries to commit suicide by provoking anaphylactic shock with the injection of bee venom. In spite of her murderous deeds, Hetzer still acknowledges Mica as a complexly layered, sympathetic person and tries to save her. Eventually, he is forced, however, to leave her in the hospital in a coma with an uncertain prognosis.

Reparative Readings?—A Conclusion

The crime novels by Kampmann, Winkelmann, and Lénard examined in this chapter ultimately leave the question unanswered whether they take a critical stance toward Western society's approach to intersexuality since the twentieth century. By incorporating intersexed characters, the thrillers doubtlessly engage in contemporary critical discussions about the paranoia of a society unable to deal with bodies that fail to comply with the established gender norms. Accordingly, the three protagonists are all affected by their upbringings and societal treatment: Winkelmann's Karel Murow is severely abused and humiliated by his parents; Kampmann's Nicola Goerne and Lénard's Mica von der Weiden suffer from the effects of a medical treatment that has left their bodies mutilated by surgically reinforcing upon them one single reading of their gendered body signs. In addition, both characters emphasize the difficulties in dealing with their parents' attempts to render intersexuality invisible.

The acknowledgment section in *SchattenHaut* mentions the German self-help group XY-Frauen (347), and *Fremdkörper* references intersex-researcher Hertha Richter-Appelt (431), and thereby illustrate that the books are directly involved in contemporary political discussions around intersexuality and the strongly requested revision of medical treatment procedures.[58] As a consequence, the fact that each of the three thrillers reveals the intersexed character to be the murderer can be interpreted as a critique of twentieth- and twenty-first-century German society for severely violating the psyches and bodies of intersexed persons. As the deeds of the characters can be considered a reflection of society's practices of violation and mutilation, in all three novels the psychically and physically wounded intersexed murderers at least momentarily encounter the investigators' sympathy, which expresses an understanding of the psychic conditions that have led to the murders.[59] However, regardless of these emphatic responses and the novels' references to the mirror effect of violence that at least to some extent blur the boundaries between the allegedly normal and the deviant, Western societies' legal systems demand that murderers are punished for their crimes. A closer look at the ways in which the intersexed murderers are penalized reveals a problematic side of these particular novels' depiction of intersexuality.

Ultimately, two of the intersexed murderers die and one remains in limbo; no outcome allows these characters much of a future. These endings can be interpreted as a result of crime fiction's typical paranoid reading process, in the scope of which the investigators in the role of palimpsest readers engage in finding a hidden truth under a surface of normalcy. In spite of illustrating gender assignment as a social, historically contingent reading process, Leonie Simon, Nele Karminter, and Wolf Hetzer indeed find a certainty in the supposedly layered gender signs of the criminals. In the course of the investigations, they discover that the offenders live in one gender, which the agents regard only superficially, and not as just one layer of a multilayered body and deviant personality. However, once the hidden layers of the palimpsest, or the allegedly underlying deviant gender signs, have been subject to a paranoid reading, they expose a secretly wounded and traumatized psyche. When signs like an XY-DNA structure or scars on the wrist are put together to form a story, they bring out the hidden truth that explains to the investigators seemingly all they need to know about the perpetrators' personalities, their behaviors, their gendered beings. The intersexed characters generally act as if their childhood stories determined who they were and would ever be. Thereby, the novels present no alternative way of dealing with childhood wounds besides depicting them as a latent driving force for murder. In all three novels, no other causalities for murder are of interest; none of the intersexed characters is eventually proven innocent.

All three works of crime fiction construct their narratives around a character-determining childhood, but to different degrees. In order to provide an understanding of their differences, an analysis of the affinity of the intersexed murderer to the figure of the serial killer in each of the works offers better insight. According to Seltzer's definitions, Winkelmann's Karel Murow embodies the prototypical serial killer. Without a classical motive, he takes lives randomly. In search of an identity, a stable notion of self, Karel violently absorbs his surroundings and their norms and expectations. Thus, his case illustrates any given society's difficulties in dealing with a person whose behavior is uncontrollably violent. The fact, however, that at the end of Winkelmann's narration, Karel is shot without ethical concerns remains highly problematic. It mirrors a society that sees itself in the uncontestable position to be able to judge what is right or wrong. Karel's execution marks him as an allegedly antisocial being as it ties him permanently to his deviant layers and the past of his deeds; he is not granted a future that allows for him to change. Thus, Winkelmann's thriller closely follows the above-described narrative pattern.

Lénard's and Kampmann's novels, in turn, provide an image of greater complexity. Mica von der Weiden is also a serial killer, but in contrast to Karel, she follows a mission and punishes only those persons who are responsible for what happened to her as a child. Hence, Mica is not depicted as the uncontrollable "drive in person," or the "'asocial' psycho," in Seltzer's words. On the contrary, the novel depicts her as a skilled forensic pathologist, a good teacher for her students, and a generally humorous person. Accordingly, Wolf Hetzer tries to save her in the end, still acknowledging Mica as a valuable member of society. Yet Mica's attempted suicide indicates that she does not envision a future for herself in this society that delivered a medical treatment that provided her with years of pain, loneliness, and despair. Consequently, she refuses to be disciplined once more by being brought to prison or a mental asylum. The attempted suicide, however, also ties Mica invariably to her past as victim, as it potentially forecloses the possibility for a future life that is not determined by childhood trauma.

The same applies to Kampmann's Nicola Goerne, who also takes her own life at the end of the story. In the course of the novel, Nicola is described as a fascinating person, far from embodying an uncontrollable serial killer. As the evidence suggests, she has killed one person out of jealousy, while in the case of Marlene's ruptured aneurysm, Nicola deliberately failed to render assistance. Kampmann's novel depicts these deeds as morally wrong but socially intelligible, and Leonie wants to prevent her from committing suicide. In contrast to serial killer Axel, whose motiveless deeds obviously preclude the possibility of saving him, Nicola is offered a future and a place within society. Like Mica, Nicola rejects the offer of inclusion into a community that has violated its duty to protect its most vulnerable members: its children. By solely identifying with her status as an intersexed victim, Nicola, in turn, also fails to assume responsibility for her own misdeeds.

Notwithstanding, *Fremdkörper* and *SchattenHaut* portray Nicola and Mica as complex personalities, who are, in contrast to the serial killers Axel and Karel, not completely determined by their deviant drive to kill. Consequently, both novels can be seen as attempts to acknowledge the fact that "although the process that creates palimpsests is one of layering, the *result* of that process, combined with the subsequent reappearance of the underlying script, is a surface structure."[60] The ways the novels represent their protagonists and their relationships with others provide suggestions for an alternative to the paranoid reading processes depicted in them: that psychic and physical wounds are there and that they have a meaning as signs in a story. But since meanings change over time and the significance of signs is subject to transformation, they do not refer to an unalterable underlying truth. Conversely, the metaphor of the palimpsest suggests that all layers remain of equivalent significance, as with time the layered structure opens itself to different readings. With regard to the intersexed body, Preves emphasizes that "perhaps the stigma or mark remains . . ., but the importance of the mark becomes transformed. Perhaps the stigma no longer serves as a source of core identity or master status."[61] Thus, in spite of the fact that, as Sara Ahmed has written, "when we face others, we seek to recognize who they are, by reading the signs on their body,"[62] the two novels suggest that we might remain open to what Sedgwick calls a "reparative reading" of the other. For Sedgwick

> to read from a reparative position is to surrender the knowing . . .; to a reparatively positioned reader, it can seem realistic and necessary to experience surprise. Because there can be terrible surprises, however, there can also be good ones. . . . Because the reader has room to realize that the future may be different from the present, it is also possible for her to entertain such profoundly painful, profoundly relieving, ethically crucial possibilities as that the past, in turn, could have happened differently from the way it actually did.[63]

Reparatively positioned readers regard wounds as merely one aspect of a person, which does not determine his or her future. Given that Mica, Nicola, and Axel are responsible for someone else's death, a judge might sentence them to some time in prison. The novels' narrative structures, however, eliminate this possibility. Mica and Nicola's attempted suicides as well as the depiction and treatment of serial killer Axel illustrate that Kampmann's and Lénard's novels do not adhere to a reparative way of reading the murderers' bodies and psyches until the very end. Yet, both stories reveal glimpses of a reparative potential that may influence future depictions of intersexuality in German or international crime fiction.

Notes

This research has been conducted as part of the project "Discursive Intersections in Literature on Hermaphroditism," funded by the Austrian Science Fund (FWF).

[1] The term intersexuality was introduced by Richard Goldschmidt in 1917, replacing the term hermaphroditism within the medical context throughout the twentieth century; see Alice Dormurat Dreger, *Hermaphrodites and the Medical Invention of Sex* (Cambridge, MA: Harvard UP, 2000), 31.

[2] The term DSD was introduced in 2005 in the course of the International Consensus Conference on Intersex, organized by the Lawson Wilkins Pediatric Endocrine Society and the European Society for Paediatric Endocrinology; see Peter Lee and others, "Consensus Statement on Management of Intersex Disorders," *Pediatrics—Official Journal of the American Academy of Pediatrics* 118 (2006): 488–500.

[3] For an overview of different forms of DSD, see Anne Fausto-Sterling, *Sexing the Body: Gender Politics and the Construction of Sexuality* (New York: Basic Books, 2000), 52.

[4] Fausto-Sterling, *Sexing the Body*, 56.

⁵ The first organization was the ISNA (Intersex Society of North America) founded in 1993.

⁶ See, for example, the autobiographical stories published on the website of the German self-help group XY-Frauen: http://www.xy-frauen.de/pers%F6nliche%20geschichten.htm (accessed February 11, 2013).

⁷ See, for example, Jeffrey Eugenides, *Middlesex* (New York: Picador, 2002); Ulrike Draesner, *Mitgift* (Munich: Luchterhand, 2002); Amanda Curtin, *The Sinkings* (Crawley: U of Western Australia P, 2008); Kathleen Winter, *Annabel* (Toronto: House of Anansi Press, 2010).

⁸ For further insights into this concern with gender deviance and its link to practices of cross dressing, see Marjorie Garber, *Vested Interests: Cross-Dressing and Cultural Anxiety* (London: Routledge, 1992), 186–209.

⁹ Sharon E. Preves, *Intersex and Identity: The Contested Self* (New Brunswick, NJ: Rutgers UP, 2003), 60–86.

¹⁰ Frank Furedi, *Therapy Culture: Cultivating Vulnerability in an Uncertain Age* (London: Routledge, 2004), 158.

¹¹ Mark Seltzer, *Serial Killers: Death and Life in America's Wound Culture* (London: Routledge, 1998), 4.

¹² Seltzer, *Serial Killers*, 2.

¹³ Besides the four German crime novels mentioned within this contribution, two recently broadcast episodes of the famous German-language TV crime series *Tatort* dealt with intersexuality: "Zwischen den Ohren" (Germany, broadcast first in 2011), and "Skalpell" (Switzerland, broadcast first in 2012).

¹⁴ The three selected novels can be considered realistic pieces of crime fiction. The fourth thriller, Ralf Isau's *Die Galerie der Lügen oder Der unachtsame Schläfer* (The Gallery of Lies or The Careless Sleeper, 2005), on the other hand, works with elements of the science-fiction thriller. Its story line is therefore not easily comparable to the other novels.

¹⁵ Renate Kampmann, *Fremdkörper: Ein Leonie Simon Roman* (Reinbek: Rowohlt, 2007).

¹⁶ Andreas Winkelmann, *Tief im Wald und unter der Erde* (Munich: Goldmann, 2009).

¹⁷ Nané Lénard, *SchattenHaut* (Hameln: CW Niemeyer, 2011).

¹⁸ Eve Kosofsky Sedgwick, *Touching Feeling: Affect, Pedagogy, Performativity* (Durham, NC: Duke UP, 2003), 130.

¹⁹ Kosofsky Sedgwick, *Touching Feeling*, 130.

²⁰ Kosofsky Sedgwick, *Touching Feeling*, 138–39.

²¹ Sarah Dillon, *The Palimpsest: Literature, Criticism, Theory* (London: Continuum, 2007), 65.

²² Elizabeth Grosz, *Volatile Bodies: Toward a Corporeal Feminism* (Bloomington: Indiana UP, 1994), 142.

[23] See Judith Butler, *Bodies that Matter: On the Discursive Limits of "Sex"* (London: Routledge, 1993), xvii. In times of ultrasound examinations and other prenatal diagnostic methods, this process already starts long before birth.

[24] Judith Butler, *Undoing Gender* (London: Routledge, 2004), 48.

[25] This happens for instance in the case of a Complete Androgen Insensitivity Syndrome (CAIS); see Fausto-Sterling, *Sexing the Body*, 52.

[26] The expression of one's "true sex" refers to Michel Foucault's introductory comment in the diary of Herculine Barbin, edited by Foucault himself; see Michel Foucault, introduction to Herculine Barbin, *Herculine Barbin: Being the Recently Discovered Memoirs of a Nineteenth Century French Hermaphrodite*, ed. Michel Foucault, transl. Richard McDougall (New York: Vintage, 1980), vii.

[27] For more information on the idea of a person's "optimal" sex, see Claudia Lang, *Intersexualität: Menschen zwischen den Geschlechtern* (Frankfurt: Campus, 2006), 105.

[28] Fausto-Sterling, *Sexing the Body*, 56–63.

[29] Christiana Gregoriou, *Deviance in Contemporary Crime Fiction* (New York: Palgrave Macmillan, 2009), 146.

[30] Gregoriou, *Deviance*, 142.

[31] Frank Furedi, *Therapy Culture*, 17.

[32] Furedi, *Therapy Culture*, 137–42.

[33] See Sigmund Freud, *Drei Abhandlungen zur Sexualtheorie* (Frankfurt: Fischer, 1991), 75–107.

[34] Sedgwick points out that according to Freud's theory, the suppression of same-sex desire leads to paranoia, *Touching Feeling*, 126.

[35] All quotes: Christa Binswanger, Lotta Samelius, and Suruchi Thapar-Björkert, "Palimpsests of Sexuality and Intimate Violence: Turning Points as Transformative Scripts for Intervention," *NORA—Nordic Journal of Feminist and Gender Research* 19 (2011): 27.

[36] Sigmund Freud, "Notiz über den 'Wunderblock.'" in *Texte zur Literaturtheorie der Gegenwart*, ed. Dorothee Kimmich, Rolf Günter Renner, and Bernd Stiegler (Stuttgart: Reclam, 1996), 171–76.

[37] Dillon, *Palimpsest*, 30.

[38] Nikki Sullivan, "Incisive Bodies: Lolo, Lyotard, and the 'Exorbitant Law of Listening to in Inaudible,'" in *Gender after Lyotard*, ed. Margret Grebowicz (Albany: SUNY Press, 2007), 47.

[39] Fausto-Sterling, *Sexing the Body*, 63–66.

[40] See Sharon E. Preves, *Intersex and Identity*, 60–86.

[41] For more information on Cesare Lombroso, see Gerhard Simson, *Einer gegen alle* (Munich: C. H. Beck, 1960), 151–219.

[42] Seltzer, *Serial Killers*, 4.

[43] Amy Yang, "Psychoanalysis and Detective Fiction: A Tale of Freud and Criminal Storytelling," *Perspectives in Biology and Medicine* 53 (2010): 597.

[44] Seltzer, *Serial Killers*, 4.

[45] Seltzer, *Serial Killers*, 160, 259.

[46] For a distinction between the typical thriller plot and the plot of detective fiction, see Peter Nusser, *Der Kriminalroman* (Stuttgart: Metzler, 2009), 23–68.

[47] Kampmann, *Fremdkörper*, 412.

[48] All translations of passages of the three novels presented in this essay are my own. I thank Helen Stringer for her help with the translations.

[49] Two years after *Tief im Wald und unter der Erde*, Winkelmann published a second thriller that features Nele Karminter and Anouschka Rossberg: *Bleicher Tod* (Munich: Goldmann, 2011).

[50] Seltzer, *Serial Killers*, 128.

[51] Seltzer, *Serial Killers*, 48.

[52] Seltzer, *Serial Killers*, 274.

[53] Seltzer, *Serial Killers*, 42, 127.

[54] Gregoriou, *Deviance*, 114.

[55] Gregoriou, *Deviance*, 111.

[56] Whereas the abbreviation CAIS refers to the so called Complete Androgen Insensitivity Syndrome, PAIS refers to the Partial Androgen Insensitivity Syndrome; for more information, see Kathrin Zehnder, *Zwitter beim Namen nennen: Intersexualität zwischen Pathologie, Selbstbestimmung und leiblicher Erfahrung* (Bielefeld: Transcript, 2010), 439.

[57] Seltzer, *Serial Killers*, 24.

[58] For an example of Richter-Appelt's publications on intersexuality, see Hertha Richter-Appelt, Katinka Schweizer, eds, *Intersexualität kontrovers: Fakten, Erfahrungen, Positionen* (Gießen: Psychosozial Verlag, 2012).

[59] See *SchattenHaut*, 346; *Fremdkörper*, 417; and *Tief im Wald*, 299.

[60] Dillon, *Palimpsest*, 3–4.

[61] Preves, *Intersex and Identity*, 141.

[62] Sara Ahmed, *Strange Encounters: Embodied Others in Post-Coloniality* (London: Routledge, 2000), 8.

[63] Sedgwick, *Touching Feeling*, 146.

10: Girls in the Gay Bar: Performing and Policing Identity in Crime Fiction

Faye Stewart

FEMINIST AUTHORS OF CRIME FICTION take several approaches to politicizing and queering the genre: recasting the traditionally male detective as a woman and assigning her agency in a male-dominated environment; stressing the implications of gender and sexuality in the crime and its investigation; and vesting the sleuth with sexual subject status.[1] Contemporary German writers Thea Dorn and Christine Lehmann combine these approaches, adapting and subverting the crime genre in novels that emphasize the interplay among literary conventions, reader expectations, and constructions of gender and sexuality. In so doing, these authors inflect their writing with critiques of stereotypes, discrimination, and privilege. Dorn and Lehmann do not stop there, however: they further demonstrate the ways in which the fluidity and malleability of their androgynous female detectives' genders can pose challenges to male-embodied authority, proposing that power lies in the performative intermingling of masculine- and feminine-gendered attributes. Dorn's Anja Abakowitz and Lehmann's Lisa Nerz style themselves according to the gender identities that serve their desired strategic purposes in specific situations, passing for male when necessary, as they do in order to enter the exclusive space of the gay men's bar. The female investigators' successful penetration of an establishment for men not only troubles gender norms but also furthers the crime plot. These gender-bending performances in the gender-specific spaces of Dorn's and Lehmann's crime novels queer mystery fiction conventions, directing our attention to sexism, homophobia, and other forms of discrimination—while also underlining the potential instability of social boundaries predicated on gender and sexual identity. They ask us to consider the enduring masculinity of social institutions such as academia and politics, which remain heavily male and less accessible to women, even at the turn of the twenty-first century.

This essay develops a reading of Thea Dorn's *Berliner Aufklärung* (Berlin Enlightenment, 1994) and Christine Lehmann's *Harte Schule* (School of Hard Knocks, 2005) as socially critical crime novels that take to task the persistence of gender and sexual discrimination in contemporary

Germany. The basis of this interpretation is the analysis of a key scene from each novel in which the female investigator masquerades as a man and goes to a men-only gay bar in order to interact with a suspect. In both texts, the cross-dressed detective's performance of masculinity is so successful that she easily passes the bouncer's examination at the bar's entrance, and once inside, she becomes an object of desire and flirtation for the club's homosexual patrons. The sleuth harnesses the position of power that comes with her performance of attractive yet sexually unattainable gay masculinity in order to gain a tactical advantage over the male suspects with whom she consorts. Perhaps most crucially, the detective's gender masquerade has a direct, positive consequence for her crime case: while in the bar, she learns information that advances her investigation. This study of *Berliner Aufklärung* and *Harte Schule* examines the dynamic effects of the bar space in concealing, revealing, and negotiating gender and sexuality in a literary genre that traffics in the investigation and uncovering of identities. Moreover, it interprets the bar scenes as crucial to an understanding of the novels' socially critical commentaries, because it is in these men-only bars that the cross-dressed female investigators, who initially seek only to solve a murder mystery, learn about further transgressions linked to gender and sexuality. These insights shed light on the larger contexts of discrimination and exploitation surrounding the murders. In Dorn's and Lehmann's novels, I read the gay bar as a stage for the performance of male privilege and masculine-embodied power. A comparative reading of these bar scenes, together with the many other attributes the two novels share, allows for an interpretation of these geographies as queer feminist incursions into contemporary social relations that seek to reveal and interrogate gender and sexual inequalities.

The gay bar scenes in Dorn's and Lehmann's novels call upon the crime-fiction convention of locating performances of male-embodied power and narrative authority in male-dominated spaces. The bar setting appears frequently in mystery fiction, from classic hard-boiled detective stories to contemporary feminist and lesbian texts, and Dorn and Lehmann take a critically queer approach to the tradition. Though the social dynamics of the taproom can vary depending on the type of locale it represents and the politics of the narrative in which it appears, the history of drinking establishments as male-dominated—if not implicitly for men only—is palpable in conventional crime fiction, a genre established by male authors of texts featuring macho male investigators. Anglo-American hard-boiled detective stories of the mid-twentieth century, for instance, prominently feature barrooms as backdrops for performances of virile heterosexual masculinities: to find examples of this, one need only read a few pages of virtually any novel by Raymond Chandler or Mickey Spillane.[2] The taproom scenery inscribes identity categories onto its occupants: social norms and expectations are the framework within which gendered and sexual positionalities become intelligible. An understanding of gender and sexuality as *positionalities* stresses both their locatedness within specific spatial contexts, and their mobility along a continuum of identity constructions.[3] Neither these positionalities nor their implications are fixed: gender and sexuality can have multiple and shifting connotations in changing sets of cultural constellations. Conventional literary representations of gender and sexuality in the bar space conform to specific expectations: men bond with one another by consuming alcohol and exchanging information, while women, if at all present or visible, represent threats to both the crime investigation and the dominant patriarchal order. These identity politics and power dynamics are heightened in the men-only gay club, a domain that is both gender-exclusive and oriented toward the sexual desires of gay men, and these dynamics are further emphasized when the focus is on women illicitly occupying this particular space. Dorn's and Lehmann's gay bar scenes thus playfully negotiate literary traditions and force a reckoning with the social implications of gender and sexuality.

By emphasizing the interplay between the crime-fiction genre and gender and sexuality, this study engages in a shared project with the two other essays in the "Identity" section of this volume. Like the criminals and investigators in the novels analyzed by Angelika Baier and Heike Henderson, Dorn's Anja Abakowitz and Lehmann's Lisa Nerz do not inhabit coherent gender identities; they thus embody critical reevaluations of gender norms and expectations in contemporary German-speaking society. Baier reads the high stakes of gendered normalcy as playing out on the bodies of intersexual murderers in crime fiction, whose transgressions point to the complicity of the society that expects gendered conformity and does not know what to do with the failure thereof. Unlike Baier's intersexual subjects, however, the boundary-crossing characters in the novels I discuss here are not murderers, but rather agents of justice, even if the reach and efficacy of such justice is limited. This distinction may have to do with the fact that Anja's and Lisa's affiliations with masculinity are chosen and strategic rather than inborn or identificatory. They elect to perform specific identities in specific places, such as masculinity in the gay bar. My study of the sexualized dynamics of bar space in feminist novels by Dorn and Lehmann demonstrates, like Henderson's exploration of gender, ethnicity, and the kitchen in Eva Rossmann's culinary mysteries, that contemporary fiction offers attractive, realistic, and nuanced alternatives to the stereotypically one-dimensional roles women traditionally played in crime novels. As Henderson suggests, feminist crime fiction vests female sleuths with authority, agency, and perhaps most significantly, complexity. Though they might on the surface seem quite different, the geographical microcosms of the kitchen and the gay bar therefore function as analogous settings for investigations of the politics of space and genre that reveal and contest the subtle workings and reverberations of sexism, domesticity, exploitation, and belonging.

Thea Dorn's *Berliner Aufklärung* and Christine Lehmann's *Harte Schule* can be assigned to the hybrid genre of the queer feminist crime novel, which critically focuses on identities, desires, and positionalities in the inquiries that lie at the heart of mystery fiction.[4] In Dorn's and Lehmann's mysteries, gender and sexuality become, together with crime, objects of investigation.[5] The novels' feminist worldviews are expressed in narrative perspectives that favor the experiences of amateur female investigators who circulate in professional spheres dominated by men: universities, law enforcement, journalism, and politics. The sleuths' amateur status is significant because it advances a radically democratic notion of participatory justice, stressing the necessary interventions of private citizens who pursue the truth and bring about justice when the state is unwilling or unable to do so. The investigators' female gender is also crucial to the political interventions they make into the workings of discrimination and oppression in the male-dominated worlds they explore.

As our female protagonists navigate traditionally patriarchal milieus, they investigate constructions and implications of gendered identities and their interplay with sexuality, class, age, race, profession, and cultural identity. Dorn's sleuth, Anja Abakowitz, is a former philosophy student who returns to the university to investigate the murder of Professor Rudolf Schreiner, a Nietzsche specialist. Anja's exploration of the circumstances behind Schreiner's death takes her into Berlin's gay subcultures and exposes the pervasive sexism, homophobia, and racism in the academic discipline of philosophy. Lehmann's detective, Lisa Nerz, is a journalist who covers the murder of Jürgen Marquardt, a popular teacher at a Stuttgart high school. As she sheds light on the dark secrets of Marquardt and his colleagues, Lisa discovers a political scandal and a conspiracy to cover up a pedophilic sex industry that exploits the school's students.

Just as the mysteries' feminist dynamics spin out along several axes—voice, characterization, setting, plot, and closure—so too do their queer facets engage multiple connotations of the term *queer*. In calling Dorn's and Lehmann's narratives queer, I draw attention to the means by which they dramatize identity as contingent, highlight marginal genders and sexualities, and destabilize literary conventions. In line with feminist and queer scholarship on the multiple meanings of *queer*, I demonstrate the versatility and critical value of the term by analyzing the various connections between queer texts and social critique.[6] First, Dorn's *Berliner Aufklärung* and Lehmann's *Harte Schule* take queer approaches to identity, which they stage as performative and contingent: identity is an effect of interpretation and can change according to cultural and spatial contexts. The novels thereby recall Michael Warner's understanding of *queer* as destabilizing notions of normalcy: they bring to the fore the violence that accompanies attempts to categorize and streamline social identities.[7] Second, the texts queer gender and sexuality in particular by presenting main characters that are both feminine and masculine and neither heterosexual nor homosexual. Dorn's and Lehmann's portrayals of androgynous bisexual detectives resonate with Judith Butler's and Eve Kosofsky Sedgwick's descriptions of *queer* as that which cannot inhabit conventional binary categories exclusively.[8] Dorn and Lehmann take this a step further in depicting boundary-crossing genders and sexualities as flexible positionalities that their amateur detectives actively and at times even defiantly occupy in order to achieve specific goals. These representations of queer detectives are quite unlike the intersexuals discussed by Baier and the transvestite analyzed by Jon Sherman in other contributions to this volume, whose sexual in-between-ness emerges as troubling and is linked to the status of victim or perpetrator of hate crimes, abuse, suicide, or murder. Rather than presenting indeterminacy as problematic, Dorn's and Lehmann's novels present it as a source of strength for the investigators. At the same time, sleuths Anja and Lisa must contend with the problem of the indeterminacy of others' identities in their efforts to decode the sexual desires and practices of their suspects, hermeneutical tasks that are fundamental to successfully solving the crime riddles.[9] And third, Dorn's and Lehmann's crime novels queer mystery genre conventions by going against the grain: they parody traditions, incorporate humor and eroticism, and challenge reader expectations. They thus take part in the gestures of *queering*—that is, challenging and subverting—narrative conventions that we find in other German texts, such as the films Alice Kuzniar analyzes in *The Queer German Cinema* and the various cultural forms featured in Christoph Lorey and John L. Plews's anthology *Queering the Canon*.[10] These writerly crime novels by Dorn and Lehmann do not offer ready-made solutions to the many mysteries they weave, but instead require their readers to do this interpretive work in order to make sense of the interconnected enigmas of crime, gender, and sexuality.[11]

Masquerades and deceptions are the building blocks of the crime genre, in which the survival and success of the criminals or of the detectives can depend largely upon the ability to hide their identities and pass for something else. As the chapters in this anthology by Sherman, Henderson, and Magdalena Waligórska also argue, the performance of identity—whether it is enabled by manipulating one's appearance, modifying one's behavior, adopting a new name, possessing false papers, or simply taking a different job—can have a profound effect on one's mobility, visibility, and access to information. Marjorie Garber demonstrates in her study of cross-dressing that gender masquerade is a classic strategy for disappearance in crime fiction.[12] It allows a sought-after suspect to vanish from the detective's (and the reader's) line of sight: since the investigation aims to catch a perpetrator with specific gender characteristics, the detective does not see the cross-dresser but rather overlooks her or him. Crime stories in which evasion becomes possible through cross-dressing reveal that a seemingly natural assumption about gender can become the central fallacy of an investigation, and emphasize the significance of the successful performance of gender, also called *passing*, to the criminal's survival.[13] Garber's study is symptomatic, however, of a tendency in scholarship on crime fiction to focus on the criminal's masquerade and to overlook the ways in which the detective can also harness this ruse as a tool in the investigation.[14] Mystery fiction provides ample evidence that the detective must also sometimes disappear in order to close a case: the sleuth's capacity to enter into certain spaces; access witnesses, information, or assistance; or evade a trap can have direct consequences for the closure of the crime riddle.

The bar as a social gathering place is common to late twentieth- and early twenty-first-century feminist, lesbian, and queer German detective fiction, where characters frequent the traditional and often male-dominated taproom[15] as well as another kind of locale, one that represents a safe space for women or homosexuals, or both. The latter category includes gender-specific and gender-inclusive establishments, such as women's cafés and queer-friendly clubs, which are settings for seductions, comings out, and exchanges of information among women.[16] This is a key location for the unfolding of the secondary plot common to lesbian and queer crime fiction: a romantic or erotic intrigue.[17] The representation of the gender-specific bar in particular differs from that of the unmarked heterosexual bar in one crucial way: a gatekeeper at the bar's entrance polices potential patrons for gender conformity. This is similar to the kind of policing typically performed by bouncers in many bars, especially in exclusive clubs where customers are screened for age, beauty, wealth, attire, or adherence to other standards. Policing both reads and produces the clientele's identity: in the men-only gay bar, policing constructs the patrons as conforming to accepted standards of maleness and masculinity, and to the concomitant expectation of homosexual desire. The bar scenes in Dorn's *Berliner Aufklärung* and Lehmann's *Harte Schule* stress the power and meaning of the bouncer's approval; as an effect of the bouncer's interventions, patrons who gain admittance are assumed to be gay men. The cross-dressers in these queer feminist crime novels simultaneously adhere to and subvert the bars' standards by looking masculine but being female-embodied. Their presence in a gender-specific locale exposes the constructedness of gender and sexuality, revealing the concurrent instability of any space predicated on culturally contingent norms. Policing also occurs through self-selection: customers frequent an establishment because they identify with or support its politics. Crime-novel protagonists, however, often go to places they might not otherwise frequent in order to solve mysteries, even if their positionalities do not align with the identity politics of such spaces, as is the case with Anja and Lisa. The men-only bar exemplifies an ironic reversal of the trend in the radical feminist movement to establish female spheres of influence by creating spaces for women only. Indeed, the men-only gay bar could be read as a metaphor for the failure of the feminist movement in attaining equal access for women to male-dominated institutions; this social and sexual sphere is seemingly impenetrable to women, whose presence there is undesirable and serves no ostensible purpose. By emphasizing gender policing, performance, and privilege, as well as the theatrical rendering of power relationships inflected by gender and sexuality in the bar, Dorn's and Lehmann's narratives subvert the conventions of crime fiction in order to condemn the occlusion of women from decision-making and public discourse. An analysis of these representations, in addition to contributing to a larger discussion of the ways in which texts construct identities and public spaces, can reveal their ideological underpinnings and the mechanisms by which queer crime narratives produce, naturalize, interrogate, and destabilize identities.

Titillating Transgressions in Tom's Bar: Thea Dorn's *Berliner Aufklärung*

Dorn's prize-winning debut novel overtly positions itself as a critique of academia and particularly the discipline of philosophy, with which the author, herself a former scholar, has personal experience.[18] *Berliner Aufklärung*'s parodic tone permeates the narrative: character names such as Hugo Lévi-Brune and Rebecca Lux and chapter titles such as "Das Kapital" (Capital), "Die Geburt der Tragödie" (The Birth of Tragedy), and "Speculum de l'autre femme" (The Speculum of the Other Woman) evoke theorists, concepts, and canonical works from various intellectual traditions.[19] The crime intrigue centers on the conflicts and power struggles among faculty and students in the philosophy department of the fictional Universität Berlin (University of Berlin) and begins with the gruesome murder of the closeted homosexual Rudolf Schreiner, a chauvinistic, antisemitic Nietzsche specialist. The director of the institute, Rebecca Lux, asks her friend and former student Anja, who left academia and founded a philosophical counseling practice, to investigate her colleague's mysterious death, in which the police identify Rebecca as a suspect.

No sooner has Anja begun working on the case than Rebecca too turns up dead. Anja's inquiry initially focuses on other faculty members and doctoral students, among whom Schreiner was widely despised, giving virtually everyone associated with the institute an apparent motive. However,

Anja ultimately identifies the murderer as her roommate Ulf's new lover Peer, a large, attractive, Aryan stereotype of a man who fits one philosophy student's description of the culprit as a Nietzschean *Übermensch* (superhuman). The gay bar scene comes near the novel's end and contains a moment of final suspense and the dramatic resolution of the crime story: disguised as a male leather fetishist, Anja seduces Peer, tortures him, and forces a confession while at the same time bringing him to orgasm.

Like other scenes in *Berliner Aufklärung*, the gay bar passage emphasizes the labor of making gender, whereby genderedness emerges not as raw material, but rather as a product of work. Dorn's text consistently stresses the actions Anja goes through in order to make her gender more masculine or feminine, and these portrayals link intelligibility with authority. Due to Anja's "eher maskulin" (*BA* 45; rather masculine) features and preference for cowboy boots and leather jackets, she is occasionally mistaken for a man, even when she does not seek to be read as such, but many scenes also show her donning skirts, lipstick, and heels in order to play the role of the confident career woman or the femme fatale. Anja's feminine masculinity is a changing and relational affiliation that entails a sense of play and tension: she actively manipulates her appearance in accordance with the strategic position she wishes to take in the crime investigation; however, though this grants her agency in many situations, Anja is not always entirely in control of the effects of these performances.[20]

Her gender ambiguity and the confusion that it can bring about for those who misread her are significant to the novel's finale because it is precisely in mobilizing her own androgyny that she is able to enter a men-only bar and bring closure to the crime story. Significantly, Anja chooses to perform a specific type of masculinity, the *Ledermann* (leatherman) who is often associated with gay male subcultures and typically occupies a position of sexual power in fetish play and scenarios of dominance and submission.[21] The leatherman disguise foreshadows Anja's sadistic exercise of power in the bar, where she subjugates Peer physically, emotionally, and sexually. The protagonist's labor in constructing gender, which receives emphasis elsewhere in the novel—for instance, Anja takes pleasure in changing clothes while driving, where she can shock other drivers and observe "ihr Werk" (*BA* 22; her handiwork) in the rearview mirror—is thematized in the gay club too, where Anja maintains her head-to-toe leather attire despite the humid heat, as if she must sacrifice comfort for the success of her masquerade. This scene links agency and power with the intelligibility of gender, while also constructing leather masculinity as a spectacle: Anja becomes the object of the gazes of gay men whose desire for her affirms her masculinity, and her rejection of sexual advances further intensifies her position of power within a setting where leather masculinity occupies a position of relative hegemony over other homosexual masculinities.[22]

The setting for this gender-bending scene is the real-life Berlin locale Tom's Bar, one of the oldest and most famous gay clubs in the city. Located in the colorful Motzstraße of the queer-friendly Schöneberg district, Tom's Bar has for decades been popular with young leathermen and is renowned for the pitch-black backrooms where patrons can cruise partners for anonymous sex. This sex scene and its participants are protected in part through the unofficial maintenance of the club as a space for men only. In accordance with article 3 of the *Grundgesetz* (Basic Law), gender discrimination is illegal in Germany, and women therefore cannot be barred from entering commercial establishments. Nonetheless, certain mechanisms of social policing coalesce to keep women from permeating the boundaries of gay sex clubs: prospective female patrons might be encouraged by bouncers to turn away or be jeered at by male patrons upon entering. Dorn's depiction of Tom's Bar emphasizes the selection process that takes place at its threshold, where those who do not fit the establishment's profile become victims of a collective attack: "Als zwei Frauen die Bar betraten, ging ein kurzer Ruck durch die Runde. Der Pockennarbige bezog Angriffsstellung, der Kellner knurrte 'keine Tussis hier!', und die beiden Frauen flohen verschreckt zurück ins Freie" (*BA* 187; When two women entered the bar, a quick twitch went through the group. The pock-faced man took an offensive position, the server snarled 'no chicks here!' and the two women fled, terrified, back outside). This policing has several noteworthy dimensions, beginning with a visual assessment that assumes a direct correlation between physical traits and biological sex.

In contrast with the presumably less-threatening public space outside to which the women flee, this bar is a confined area that imposes limitations on the bodies circulating within it—and the primary limitation is gender conformity. As if symptomatic of a pathological disturbance, a tangible physical reaction with aggressive undertones follows the women's entrance: the pock-marked man prepares for combat—as bouncer, his duty is to defend against intruders—while his colleague provides reinforcement with a battle cry. These figures literally embody the metaphor that philosopher Erika Faith Feigenbaum uses to describe privilege as a kind of policing with political implications: "Privilege functions best when doling out access, admitting and rejecting claims at whim like a burly bouncer at the gates of justice."[23] Dorn depicts Tom's Bar as the domain of male privilege while also parodying the notion of privilege by casting it as adamantly homosexual, as opposed to the heterosexual privilege that forms the critical focus of Feigenbaum's essay: here, ironically, it is gay men who gain respect, admission, and invisibility, and these privileges are unavailable to prospective female patrons. Like other social exclusions, male privilege is predicated on inequality and commonly entails violence. The ejection of the women from Tom's Bar demonstrates the centrality of femaleness to the establishment of men-only spaces, which find definition in the expulsion thereof. But because the women attempting to enter Tom's Bar comply with the men's demands, the violence is merely suggestive and does not rise to the level of physical expression. Violence and justice both become focal points in the remainder of this scene when a woman does indeed invade the bar and uses the privilege to which this gives her access. Anja's primary goal, however, is neither to pass nor to gain social acceptance as a man; rather, passing is the means by which she achieves other goals: to uncover the truth and to serve justice.

Despite the multiple and aggressive policing mechanisms at the threshold of Tom's Bar, the malleability of gender as laid out in Dorn's novel means that any boundary predicated on gender identity is necessarily unstable. *Berliner Aufklärung* plays with the notion of identity in flux by initially introducing Anja in disguise as an unidentified male bar patron, "ein Ledermann mit Glatze und hellem Schnäuzer" (*BA* 187; a leatherman with bald head and light mustache). The leatherman, who has ostensibly passed inspection and penetrated the guarded entrance, stands in a passageway between the front room, where patrons drink and flirt, and the back rooms, where men view pornography and have sexual intercourse: his liminal position suggests that the leatherman both belongs and is marginal to this space. When Peer enters the bar with his new lover Ulf, the leatherman addresses him by name, and neither man recognizes Anja behind the disguise. Both men become complicit in upholding the gender politics of the men-only bar by assuming that the leatherman is a homosexual interested in Peer and with whom Ulf must compete for attention. Anja's exercise of male-embodied power begins when she pries Peer away from Ulf and leads him into the bar's backrooms. In what might be read as a tacit affirmation of her femaleness, the detective in disguise steers her prey into the women's restroom, "das vermutlich noch nie eine Dame gesehen hatte" (*BA* 189; which had presumably never seen a lady). While this description suggests that women have not frequented a space that is, in other social contexts, usually reserved for their use, it leaves open the possibility of a female presence—like Anja's now—in male disguise; Anja therefore does not destabilize this gendered history because she presents as a *Ledermann* rather than as a *Dame* (lady). Throughout the scene, Anja continues to perform dominant male homosexuality to the extent that she ties Peer up and dictates the power dynamics of a sexual scenario that brings Peer to orgasm. This performance of gender and sexuality is in line with the sexual fetishism that, the novel suggests, typically takes place in this particular ladies' room, where the stench of old urine reveals that it is a stage for "Wasserspiele" (*BA* 189; water games), a euphemism for urine play.

The ensuing torture scenario serves a double function: it is an interrogation and a sadomasochistic seduction, both of which reveal the centrality of femininity and femaleness to the novel's social critique. Anja's ultimate transgression is indulging in "eine Sentimentalität" (*BA* 193; a sentimentality) by causing Peer to climax—even after he confesses to the murders and recognizes his torturer.[24] Because Anja never breaks character during her performance of masculinity, it is unclear how Peer comes to the realization that she is a woman. Peer addresses the leatherman with an epithet for female genitalia; this exclamation is the first indication of the leatherman's hidden identity, which otherwise remains implicit.[25] The text exposes the violence of chauvinism by placing these curse words in the mouth of the murderer, who reduces Anja's gender to the possession of negatively coded reproductive organs.

Femininity, however peripheral it may seem, is pivotal to this scene: it plays a crucial role in Peer's explanation of his motive for killing Professors Schreiner and Lux, whom he holds responsible for the suicide of his unnamed former lover, a master's degree candidate whose thesis both professors rejected. Significantly, the boyfriend's suicide takes the symbolic form of the disavowal of the feminine. Peer describes the costume his lover wore when he took his life: "Er hatte sich schön gemacht. Mit einem roten Korsett und roten Strapsen. Rote Netzstrümpfe. Rote Lackpumps. Er hatte sich eine blonde Lockenperücke aufgesetzt" (*BA* 191; He had made himself pretty. With a red corset and red garters. Red fishnet stockings. Red patent leather pumps. He had put on a curly blond wig). The representation of the lover who turns himself into the abject feminine before staging the ultimate act of self-negation, together with the revelation that the cause of his psychological deterioration was the repudiation of his intellectual work, invites a reading of this scenario as a metaphor for the marginalization of women in academia. The novel's philosophy institute is heavily masculine and includes only two female faculty members: Rebecca Lux, the second murder victim, and Petra Uhse, whose name recalls the actual sex-shop entrepreneur Beate Uhse and her eponymous commercial empire. That Petra is aligned with a stereotypical gender position, even in her scholarship—she is the department's token feminist, "eine Frau, die versucht, der Diskriminierung von Frauen entgegenzuarbeiten" (*BA* 130; a woman who tries to counteract discrimination against women)—and that she is not a professor but rather an *Assistentin* (assistant) draws attention to gender stereotypes and inequality. Though women graduate from German universities at approximately the same rates as men, the percentages of women who complete graduate degrees and enter academic professions, in particular professorships, still lag far behind those for men, and the numbers decrease with increasing rank.[26] Lux seems to be the exception to this trend, as she gains enough status and recognition in the profession to direct the institute, but her male colleagues have little respect for her work on classical antiquity, which they consider passé and uninteresting (*BA* 93). Dorn's novel alleges that women's scholarly contributions are undervalued or dismissed as typically feminine, and therefore inferior, intellectual work. According to Lux's male colleague, one reason for her professional success is the abjuration of anything traditionally feminine: she rises in a man's world because she plays a male part and sacrifices everything for her career (*BA* 112). The gay bar, with its men-only policy and policing mechanisms, thus functions as a poignant metaphor for male domination in the academic brotherhood, where men set standards for entrance into the world of scholarship and promotion to which their female colleagues can only rise by masculinizing themselves.

The suicide of Peer's cross-dressed lover and the murder of the closeted professor Schreiner can also be interpreted as a commentary on the marginalization of homosexuals. Published in 1994, the same year in which postunification revisions of the German *Grundgesetz* culminated in the abolition of Paragraph 175, the Prussian law making homosexual acts illegal, *Berliner Aufklärung* offers a vision of a world in which sexual equality is still a distant dream. Though Tom's Bar is not a particularly safe space, it nonetheless presumably welcomes all men regardless of sexual positionality. Academia, by contrast, is an unsafe space for homosexuals or for anyone who goes against the dominant theoretical trend. Despite his fame, Schreiner does not come out to his colleagues for fear of ruining the reputation he has built on antisemitic rhetoric and hatred; though a philosophy department should encourage debate, anything liberal or even pseudoliberal seems to have no place here. The institute is an exclusive institution, and those who are permitted to enter should be humbled and ought not to rock the boat.

Anja's performance in Tom's Bar demonstrates the way in which queerness and androgyny can serve as means of gaining power and authority. Passing as a man has a double function in this text: for the investigator, it is an effective vehicle for extracting a confession, while at the symbolic level, it exposes the potency of social mechanisms of inequality and oppression. In portraying Anja's completed penetration into a gender-specific space and her transgressive acts with Peer, the narrative calls attention to the constructedness and instability of gender and sexuality, and to the enduring influence of patriarchal structures that disenfranchise women and homosexuals. The Tom's Bar scene is also a playful rewriting of the perpetrator-victim dynamics typical of hate crimes: instead of falling victim to violence, the cross-dresser takes violent measures against a murderer to uncover the truth and punish him. Because Anja performs a hegemonic male homosexuality, she not only achieves a position of power less accessible to her as a woman, but also claims an authority to deliver justice that is usually reserved for the legal system.

Probing Politics and Pedophilia: Christine Lehmann's *Harte Schule*

The fourth book in an ongoing series featuring journalist and amateur detective Lisa Nerz, Lehmann's *Harte Schule* follows in the footsteps of her earlier mysteries with its dark humor and unflinchingly harsh perspective on the failings of contemporary society.[27] *Harte Schule* shares numerous characteristics with Dorn's *Berliner Aufklärung*, including an androgynous detective, an academic setting, and an intrigue involving revelations about the sexual desires and practices of suspects and perpetrators. The novel's critical focus is the sexual exploitation of minors, which is depicted as the basis of a pervasive and multifaceted industry protected by the collusion of politicians and law enforcement. Lisa's investigation begins when Hermann Elsäßer, the editor-in-chief of her newspaper, gives her an assignment that comes with a personal request: he asks her to write a tactful article about the mysterious murder of high school ethics teacher Jürgen Marquardt without making a stir, because Elsäßer's wife is a colleague and friend of the deceased. Marquardt, who is found butchered in the school's courtyard, at first appears to have sexually abused his students, yet Lisa learns that although he was aware of a child-pornography and prostitution ring at the school, he was uninvolved in it; rather, Marquardt sought to help the victims by educating them about the injustice of sexual exploitation and creating a safe space where they could talk about their experiences without fear. Lisa's inquiry unravels a conspiracy involving the school's headmaster Otter and other teachers; police officers, reporters, and media personalities; and going all the way up the political ranks to the Minister of Culture Bollach. *Harte Schule* concludes with Bollach's resignation from politics and Lisa's discovery that her own boss Elsäßer murdered Marquardt, whom he had wrongly suspected of having an affair with his wife, and assigned the story to Lisa in hopes that she would obey his request to report the story superficially and delve no further into the investigation.

Like Dorn's Anja, Lehmann's Lisa has androgynous features and actively manipulates her gender to emphasize masculinity or femininity, depending on which role gives her the desired tactical advantage in a particular setting. Lisa's ability to disappear from sight through gender masquerade is reminiscent of Garber's claim that the measure of the cross-dresser's success is being looked through rather than looked at.[28] In one scene, Lisa applies lipstick for an audience of male police officers in order to pass as an indifferent secretary, and in others, she wears men's suits in order to evade capture and persecution. Other characters perceive Lisa as both masculine and feminine, and she often fails—in their eyes—to inhabit either gender comfortably. For instance, when Lisa's on-again, off-again posttranssexual lover Richard Weber sleeps with a blonde bombshell named Isolde, the latter attributes Richard's infidelity to Lisa's lacking femininity: "Wahrscheinlich wollte er endlich mal mit einer richtigen Frau ins Bett" (*HS* 127; He probably just wanted to go to bed with a real woman for once).[29] With her sexual partners, Richard included, Lisa enjoys power play and prefers dominant positions, though she is also attracted to people who demand her submission. When uncontrolled, Lisa's penchant for sexual dominance can become violent, as it does when she rapes Krk, a queer man who is in love with her, in Lehmann's first crime novel, *Der Masochist* (The Masochist, 1997).[30] Lisa's performance of masculinity also comes across as incomplete: while at times characters alternately call her "Frau" and "Herr" (*HS* 90, 97, 168; Mrs. and Mr.), at other times they identify her not as a full-fledged man but rather belittle her masculinity by describing her instead as a "Junge" and a "Bürschchen" (*HS* 168–69; boy and young lad).

In the gay club, Lisa mobilizes her unfeminine features and boyishness to her advantage. The barroom scene appears in the first half of *Harte Schule* and signals a turning point in the investigation because not only does Lisa recognize two teenaged boys from the high school among the escorts who work in the exclusive locale, but she also encounters Otter and Bollach, who are in attendance as customers. With the assistance of Krk, who since the rape has not only become Lisa's friend but has also come out as gay, Lisa learns that her suspects are homosexual pedophiles and frequent a bar that caters to this illicit sexual practice. The unnamed establishment has two levels of gateways through which patrons must pass in order to gain access to its precious human commodities, and Lisa succeeds in entering partially because she is in the company of a man who knows the secret password. Though Krk is Lisa's ally here, acting in the name of justice to help her investigate sex crimes, he is an ambiguously positive figure at best: Krk's clarification that he knows the club because his boss regularly takes clients there indicates his complicity in supporting an industry that capitalizes on the sexual exploitation of children and protects the identities of its patrons (*HS* 93, 99).

This illegal establishment therefore requires more intense policing of potential clients than would a "regular" men-only gay club like the one in Dorn's text; it even has "ein exzellentes Frühwarnsystem" (*HS* 101; an excellent early warning system) in case of a police search. Due to its tight security, the club keeps operating despite repeated raids because law enforcement officials uncover no evidence of criminal wrongdoing; however, this system fails when it comes to Lisa. Having access to the club's codeword is a first step and opens the door for Lisa, who must also pass a visual inspection. The bouncer, a "Lederknecht vom Typ glatzköpfiger Frisör" (*HS* 91; leather servant of the bald hairdresser type), recalls Dorn's *Ledermann* but occupies a more liminal position: while Lehmann's bouncer unmistakably has the power to grant or refuse admission to the bar, this bouncer's status as *Knecht* (servant) communicates that he nonetheless defers to someone, if only in service of the establishment's management and regulations.

As the cross-dressed journalist enters the bar, the bouncer glances at her crotch: this is the first of several references in this scene alone to the physicality of Lisa's genital region, suggesting that the penis—or, in this case, the semblance thereof—is the primary sign of masculinity and gender difference.[31] Though the bouncer's gaze initially suggests that he reads the investigator as male, Lisa's ensuing confrontation with Bollach and Otter leads him to seek confirmation of masculinity by grabbing her groin; failing to locate palpable evidence of maleness, he ultimately ejects her from the club (*HS* 98–99). Upon entering the bar, Lisa considers the significance of her gender performance: "Hier kam es nicht darauf an, dass ich den Mann spielte" (*HS* 91; Here it didn't depend on whether I played the man). The implication is initially unclear: must Lisa now *be* the man instead of simply *playing* one, or must she take on another role altogether? The statement also poses an ironic counterpoint to other scenarios in which Lehmann's protagonist-narrator clarifies that it is to a woman's distinct advantage to play the man and to be perceived as doing so. At the novel's beginning, Lisa encounters a female police officer who performs masculinity for professional reasons: "sie [schien] seit Jahrzehnten erpicht darauf zu beweisen, dass sie der Abteilung bester Mann war" (*HS* 9; she seemed as though for decades she had been eager to prove that she was the department's best man). Entering the gay bar, which requires Lisa to embody masculinity, is a powerful metaphor for law enforcement—among other male-dominated professions—where success, especially for women, necessarily entails claiming masculinity and becoming legible as a man.

Lehmann's novel takes this critique of sexism a step further in using gender performances and gender inequality as vehicles for touching on other oppressions, in particular the sexual abuse of children, as well as racism and classism. As the gay bar scene unfolds, it becomes clear that Lisa must not in fact play the man, but rather the boy. In this space, "boys" like Lisa are coded as commodities and possessions, and Krk attempts to protect his veiled female companion from the predatory endeavors of other men by claiming that she belongs to him (*HS* 98). By presenting herself as a potential commodity and by extension a victim of sexual exploitation, Lisa gains admission for herself and her companion to the club's lower level, "ein rauer Kartoffelkeller für Herren mit Krawatte" (*HS* 94; a raw potato cellar for men with ties). The boy bar is a postcolonial playground for rich, influential men like Bollach and Otter who purchase safety and anonymity through its external policing, while inside they traffic in lads such as "ein verhungertes Mulattenjüngelchen" (*HS* 96; a starved young mulatto boy), a sexual object whose diminished physique is evidence of poverty and social inferiority.

While Lisa's race, like that of Krk, Bollach, Otter, and the other bar patrons, remains uncommented and thus unmarked, the biracial boy is one of two people in the bar who are identified primarily by racial markers; the other is "der lange Neger" (*HS* 95; the lanky black man) who serves beverages. The sexist, ageist, and classist power dynamics of the establishment develop along lines that reveal pronounced racist facets: the two nonwhite boys are clearly at the service of the bar's wealthy and presumably white clientele. These racially marginalized young men are also relegated to the margins of the dramatic action: they are decorative bystanders whose reactions—backing away from or smiling at the unfolding drama—convey the intensity and potential volatility of the confrontations among the scene's more central figures, Lisa and Krk, and Bollach and Otter. This racialized dynamic evokes the stereotype of the exotic other that is viewed from an ethnocentric perspective as intellectually or culturally inferior but nonetheless serves as a fetish object.[32] As sexual commodities and as part of the scenery, the dark-skinned young men serve primarily to bring into relief both the relative power of the other characters and the struggles among them. Lisa's investigation into the sex crimes uncovers two more ethnically marked victims, one of Turkish and the other of Croatian descent; these boys are symbolic for entire categories of German residents and citizens who still remain marginalized in many parts of social life today. Lehmann's portrayal of child prostitution and human trafficking opens up questions about racial and ethnic equality in an increasingly multicultural and yet also increasingly culturally divided German society in the early to mid-2000s, the last years of Gerhard Schröder's chancellorship.

Minister of Culture Bollach personifies abusive power, and Lisa's interaction with him in the boy bar is pivotal because it begins to expose the extent of his depravity. When Bollach asks the "boy" for his name, Lisa's stammered reply, "Li... Lie" (*HS* 96, ellipsis in the original), seems to be self-reflexive, suggesting that her masculinity is the real *lie*; such a reading would support Marjorie Garber's claim that crime novels often reveal gender masquerades through linguistic clues.[33] However, the developing characterization of Bollach as a violent chauvinist and pedophile who hides behind the façade of the dedicated liberal bureaucrat ultimately indicates that the *lie* to which Lisa's unprepared response points is actually Bollach's clean image. The politician's good reputation is due in part to the pretense of his "Fernsehbild" (*HS* 97; television picture) and in part to the protective supervision of staff who accompany him even to this locale: as soon as Otter identifies Lisa as a female reporter, Bollach's consultant jumps to shield his boss from the threat she represents. Though Bollach later orchestrates an assassination attempt against Lisa, in the bar he is surprisingly unfazed by the revelation of her gender; in fact, he continues to flirt with Krk's "boy" while offering to bribe the journalists and to buy Lisa from Krk.

By linking the negotiation of gender with the attempt to maintain control, this passage raises questions about sexism in politics. This association comes as no surprise for a novel published in 2005, the year in which Germany celebrated the election of its first female chancellor, Angela Merkel, and the hotly debated intersection of women and politics was under discussion in all areas of popular culture. The powerful minister of culture in Lehmann's novel embodies self-perpetuating chauvinism: Bollach surrounds himself with attractive, subservient young men and attacks anyone who threatens the integrity and gender-exclusivity of his enterprise. By stressing Bollach's blindness to his own participation in oppression, *Harte Schule* further suggests that such structures do not easily open themselves to challenges. The minister ultimately confesses to paying boys for sex and resigns from his position, although he declares that he has done nothing wrong, disavowing any association with the word *missbrauchen* (abuse): he glosses over the silent workings of power and privilege by claiming that, far from having forced boys to engage in sex acts, he had simply obliged their requests for sex and money (*HS* 242–43). Moreover, the pedophile's advances on Lisa in the bar belie his claims that he merely plays a passive role in sexual transactions. The revelation that a high-ranking politician is a producer, promoter, and consumer in this exploitative industry constructs politics as a boys' club, while also indicating that it thrives on the labor of racially and socially marginalized young men who are unlikely to have successful future careers in government or law enforcement. Lehmann's portrayal of Bollach's reign reminds readers of the political status quo: even in the twenty-first century and despite official gender-mainstreaming policies in Germany and the European Union, the sphere of political influence remains predominantly male.[34]

Though *Harte Schule*'s gay-bar scene ends with a loss of control for Lisa, who is banished from the club, this conclusion also demonstrates that Lisa's greater transgression is her profession as a journalist and not her female gender. Lisa's immediate reaction, to report the incident to her boss, to a lawyer, and to the police commissioner, confirms the fears of the bar's high-profile patrons that she would reveal the knowledge she had acquired there. Ultimately, the amateur investigator's success in bringing to light pedophilic prostitution and Bollach's corruption is thanks to her performance of masculinity in the boy bar, which gives her insight into these crimes. The novel's final revelation that Lisa's editor, Elsäßer, was the sought-after murderer and was motivated by marital jealousy is by contrast anticlimactic, but produces a narrative segue into a critique of the chauvinistic understanding of bourgeois marriage as a gendered ownership contract (*HS* 251–52). Despite this link between Elsäßer's crime and his sexist preconceptions, his isolated act of covetous violence seems almost unremarkable when compared with those social problems that *Harte Schule* constructs as far more pervasive and enduring: the sexual exploitation of minors and the abuse of political power.

Conclusion: Reading the Bar

The gay bar scenes in Thea Dorn's *Berliner Aufklärung* and Christine Lehmann's *Harte Schule* set the stage for negotiations of identity that lay bare the texts' feminist and antidiscriminatory messages. Although the gender-specific gay bar may take on idyllic contours in other literary and filmic genres, Dorn's and Lehmann's queer crime novels use this locale as a setting for performances of authority, violence, exploitation, and oppression. While Lehmann's boy bar is a site for the perpetration of sex crimes, Dorn's gay club sets the scene for solving the mystery and enacting vigilante justice. It can, however, become difficult to pin down the politics of these texts because they playfully juxtapose different and seemingly incoherent performances of identity, constructing the gender and sexuality of the queer investigator as malleable and strategic. Because Anja and Lisa render their femininity invisible and enter the gay bar through the empowered positions they access by passing as men, a reading of the bars' gender dynamics in isolation might encourage the misguided conclusion that these women are successful sleuths primarily because they perform masculinity. However, these bar scenes are part of the novels' larger parodies of gender roles altogether: numerous other passages in *Berliner Aufklärung* and *Harte Schule* show Anja and Lisa mobilizing performances of femininity and androgyny in order to disappear, find witnesses and suspects, and gain access to guarded spaces, all of which advances their investigations. Indeed, both texts expose the power, and its potential abuse, that accompanies hegemonic gender positionalities, like that of leatherman Anja, as well as the respective loss or absence of control and agency that these forces entail for others, such as the boys Lisa plays and encounters.

Representations of sex and sexuality are also pivotal to the novels' parodies: so successful are their masquerades that Anja and Lisa receive libidinal approval through homosexual flirtation, but they have ulterior motives for participating in such erotic exchanges. In contrast with the trend in feminist and lesbian crime fiction to highlight intimacy and romantic relationships, Dorn's and Lehmann's novels thematize detached sexual transactions that serve the goals of extracting confessions and gathering evidence. Both bar scenes conclude with the revelation of the sleuth's female gender, and thus form counterexamples to Garber's claim that in the detective genre, the truths hidden beneath masquerades are often exposed in bed.[35] In Dorn's and Lehmann's queer feminist mysteries, truths about gender and sexuality come out in the gay bar and include disclosures about the cross-dresser and about other patrons: in addition to the unmasking of the cross-dressing female detective, another crucial facet of these revelations is the cultural critiques they introduce by affirming the villainy and criminal transgressions of the male homosexual perpetrators who frequent these locales.

The depictions of gender masquerade in Dorn's and Lehmann's novels align transgressions of identity and space with social and sexual violence. Whether implied or actual, violence is a recurring theme that links the detective's work with the culprit's offences and suggests that everyone, even the protagonist, is guilty of participating in oppressive structures and thereby perpetuating social inequality. These scenarios underline the effects of aggression, abuse, and marginalization that accompany or ensue the enforcement of normative gender categories. By exposing mechanisms of inequality and representing androgyny as a source of performative power, Dorn's and Lehmann's queer feminist crime stories raise compelling questions about democracy, justice, and social change in a still deeply gendered world.

Notes

[1] These are the most common means of rewriting detective fiction with a feminist twist. For discussions of feminist approaches to the crime genre, see Sally R. Munt, *Murder by the Book? Feminism and the Crime Novel* (London: Routledge, 1994); Kathleen Gregory Klein, ed., *Women Times Three: Writers, Detectives, Readers* (Bowling Green, OH: Bowling Green State U Popular Press, 1995); Glenwood Irons, ed., *Feminism in Women's Detective Fiction* (Toronto: U of Toronto P, 1995); and Priscilla L. Walton and Manina Jones, *Detective Agency: Women Rewriting the Hard-Boiled Tradition* (Berkeley: U of California P, 1999).

[2] The classic fictional bar sets the stage for homosocial male bonding and heterosexual seduction, though the former often takes precedence over the latter. A bar scene typically begins with a lone male detective sitting at the counter of a dimly lit locale, drinking away his frustration over a complicated case. There he encounters either a man from whom he gathers information that helps his investigation, or a beautiful woman with whom a flirtation and seduction ensues. While women in the bar may be damsels in distress who require protection from threats of danger, more often they are femmes fatales with hidden agendas who use seduction to distract detectives from their complicity in the crimes under investigation. For instance, in Raymond Chandler's *The Long Goodbye*, gumshoe Philip Marlowe first lays eyes on femme fatale Eileen Wade in a hotel bar. Marlowe initially misreads Wade as a damsel in distress, but after he "rescues" her and nearly falls victim to her seduction, the detective finally discovers that she is the sought-after perpetrator of multiple crimes. Raymond Chandler, *The Long Goodbye* (1953; reprint, New York: Vintage, 1981), 87–96. Mickey Spillane's *Vengeance Is Mine!* features multiple bar spaces but diverges from hard-boiled traditions in including a gay bar among them. However, the politics of this representation are not gay-positive but rather misogynistic and homophobic. Mickey Spillane, *Vengeance Is Mine!*, in *The Mike Hammer Collection*, vol. 1 (New York: New American, 2001), 409–17. For

a discussion of the gender dynamics of hard-boiled crime fiction from a feminist perspective, see Gabriele Dietze, *Hardboiled Woman: Geschlechterkrieg im amerikanischen Kriminalroman* (Hamburg: Europäische Verlangsanstalt, 1997).

[3] The word *positionality* emphasizes the cultural construction of gender and sexuality and draws attention to the politics and interpersonal implications of identities and desires. Feminist scholar Linda Alcoff is credited with having first used the expression to denote gender and sexuality in 1988, and it lends itself particularly well to investigations of identity that are informed, as is mine, by queer theory. See Linda Alcoff, "Cultural Feminism versus Poststructuralism: The Identity Crisis in Feminist Theory," *Signs* 13, no. 3 (1988): 405–36.

[4] Elsewhere I define the queer feminist crime novel as a socially critical genre that mobilizes crime-fiction conventions and representations of queerly gendered and sexualized characters in order to develop commentary on cultural and political discourses. See Faye Stewart, *German Feminist Queer Crime Fiction: Politics, Justice and Desire* (Jefferson, NC: McFarland, 2014), especially 5–16.

[5] These are shared qualities of the related subgenres of feminist, lesbian, and queer crime fiction. On the characteristics of feminist and lesbian crime fiction, see Nicola Barfoot, *Frauenkrimi/polar féminin: Generic Expectations and the Reception of Recent French and German Crime Novels by Women* (Frankfurt am Main: Peter Lang, 2007); Phyllis M. Betz, *Lesbian Detective Fiction: Woman as Author, Subject and Reader* (Jefferson, NC: McFarland, 2006); Gaby Pailer, "'Weibliche' Körper im 'männlichen' Raum: Zur Interdependenz von Gender und Genre in deutschsprachigen Kriminalromanen von Autorinnen," *Weimarer Beiträge* 46, no. 4 (2000): 564–81; and Sabine Wilke, "Wilde Weiber und dominante Damen: Der Frauenkrimi als Verhandlungsort von Weiblichkeitsmythen," in *Frauen auf der Spur: Kriminalautorinnen aus Deutschland, Großbritannien und den USA*, ed. Carmen Birkle, Sabina Matter-Seibel, and Patricia Plummer (Tübingen: Stauffenburg, 2001), 255–71. On the defining facets of queer crime fiction, see Brigitte Frizzoni, *Verhandlungen mit Mordsfrauen: Geschlechterpositionierungen im "Frauenkrimi"* (Zurich: Chronos, 2009), 125–44; and Faye Stewart, "Dialogues with Tradition: Feminist-Queer Encounters in German Crime Stories at the Turn of the Twenty-First Century," in *Contemporary Women's Writing and the Return of Feminism in Germany*, ed. Hester Baer, special issue of *Studies in Twentieth and Twenty-First Century Literature* 35, no. 1 (2011): 114–35.

[6] On the versatility of queer meanings and queer methodologies, see David L. Eng, Judith Halberstam, and José Esteban Muñoz, eds., *What's Queer about Queer Studies Now?*, special issue of *Social Text* 23, nos. 3–4 84–85 (2005): 1–308.

[7] See Michael Warner, Introduction, in *Fear of a Queer Planet: Queer Politics and Social Theory*, ed. Michael Warner (Minneapolis: U of Minnesota P, 1993), vii–xxxi.

[8] For critical discussions of the meaning of the term *queer* that link it specifically to gender and sexuality and demonstrate its theoretical value, see Judith Butler, *Bodies That Matter: On the Discursive Limits of "Sex"* (New York: Routledge, 1993), 223–42; and Eve Kosofsky Sedgwick, *Tendencies* (Durham, NC: Duke UP, 1993), 1–20.

[9] For a discussion of the interplay between Dorn's novel's queer dimensions and the depiction of Anja's investigation, see Faye Stewart, "Of Herrings Red and Lavender: Reading Crime and Identity in Queer Detective Fiction," in *Lesbian Crime Fiction*, ed. Jacky Collins, special issue of *Clues* 27, no. 2 (2009): 33–44.

[10] See Alice Kuzniar, *The Queer German Cinema* (Stanford: Stanford UP, 2000); and Christoph Lorey and John L. Plews, eds., *Queering the Canon: Defying Sights in German Literature and Culture* (Columbia, SC: Camden House, 1998).

[11] For a definition of the readerly text and its counterpart, the writerly text, see Roland Barthes, *S/Z*, trans. Richard Miller, pref. Richard Howard (New York: Hill and Wang, 1974).

[12] Marjorie Garber, *Vested Interests: Cross-Dressing and Cultural Anxiety* (1992; reprint New York: Routledge, 1997), 186–209.

[13] Though here I focus on gender passing, the term is more versatile than my analysis may seem to imply. *Passing* can refer to the successful performance of gender identity as well as to other dimensions of identity such as race. See Elaine K. Ginsberg, *Passing and the Fictions of Identity* (Durham, NC: Duke UP, 1996); and María Carla Sánchez and Linda Schlossberg, eds., *Passing: Identity and Interpretation in Sexuality, Race, and Religion* (New York: New York UP, 2001).

[14] See also Linden Peach, *Masquerade, Crime, and Fiction: Criminal Deceptions* (Basingstoke: Palgrave, 2006). Peach discusses gender masquerade among other types of masquerade that criminals use to deceive investigators.

[15] Traditional bars appearing in feminist, lesbian, and queer crime fiction serve to emphasize the male genderedness of power and violence, bringing into relief the significance of the feminist intervention made by the novels' protagonists. See, for instance, the bar scenes in Claudia Wessel's *Es wird Zeit* (Gießen: Wemü, 1984) and Doris Gercke's *Weinschröter, du mußt hängen* (1988; reprint Munich: Goldmann, 2000).

[16] The representation of women's or gay bars in feminist crime writing often implies the necessity of gender-specific and queer-friendly space in empowering women and queer people and building communities. Such establishments feature prominently in Katrin Kremmler's *Die Sirenen von Coogee Beach* (Hamburg: Argument, 2003); Gabriele Gelien's *Eine Lesbe macht noch keinen Sommer* (Hamburg: Argument, 1993); Martina-Marie Liertz's *Die Geheimnisse der Frauen* (Munich: Goldmann, 1999); and several novels by Christine Lehmann, including, in addition to the one analyzed in this essay, *Der Masochist* (Reinbek: Rowohlt, 1997) and *Training mit dem Tod* (Reinbek: Rowohlt, 1998). For a scholarly analysis of representations of lesbian bars in the film genre, see Kelly Hankin, *The Girls in the Back Room: Looking at the Lesbian Bar* (Minneapolis: U of Minnesota P, 2002).

[17] On the lesbian and queer crime fiction as hybrid genres incorporating romance and the erotic, see Betz, *Lesbian Detective Fiction*; Stewart, "Dialogues with Tradition"; and Gill Plain, *Twentieth-Century Crime Fiction: Gender, Sexuality and the Body* (Chicago: Fitzroy Dearborn, 2001).

[18] Dorn's *Berliner Aufklärung* won the 1995 Marlowe prize for best German crime novel; subsequent novels have won other prizes as well. The author, whose given name is Christiane Scherer, uses a pseudonym that honors the Frankfurt

School philosopher Theodor Wiesengrund Adorno. Dorn has a master's degree in philosophy and had a brief engagement on the philosophy faculty at the Freie Universität Berlin (Free University of Berlin).

[19] Thea Dorn, *Berliner Aufklärung* (Munich: Goldmann, 1994). Subsequent references to this work are cited in the text using the abbreviation *BA* and page number. All translations from German to English are my own.

[20] I am working with Claudia Breger's concept of *feminine masculinity*, which "includes a sense of conflict between presumably contradictory elements, for example the interplay of 'butch' and 'femme' gestures or more generally of identity markers coded as distinctively masculine with others coded as distinctively feminine." Though the term *masculine femininity* could also be used to refer to this idea, I follow Breger's cue in fronting the concept of femininity in order to emphasize the tension between female embodiedness and performances of masculinity. Claudia Breger, "Hegemony, Marginalization, and Feminine Masculinity: Antje Rávic Strubel's *Unter Schnee*," *Seminar* 44, no. 1 (2008): 159.

[21] While the leatherman is indeed a stereotype of homosexual masculinity, it is not exclusive to this subculture; there are also straight leather cultures, such as biker communities. The leatherman is also an emblematic figure for BDSM subcultures, which comprise both gay and straight participants (BDSM is a common acronym for a range of sexual practices including bondage and discipline, dominance and submission, and sadomasochism). It is noteworthy in the context of this study that a similar type of character appears in the gay club scene in Lehmann's *Harte Schule*, though there it does not refer to the role that the investigator plays but rather to someone she encounters on her excursion to the gay bar.

[22] As Claudia Breger demonstrates, hegemonic masculinity is a relational category whose forms and meanings can change according to context ("Hegemony," 159).

[23] Erika Faith Feigenbaum, "Heterosexual Privilege: The Political and the Personal," *Hypatia* 22, no. 1 (2007): 7–8. Feigenbaum discusses her personal experience of heterosexual privilege and its significance in the political climate of the early 2000s during the marriage-equality debates in the United States. Her definition of privilege and its effects can also be applied to other kinds of privilege, including male privilege, white privilege, and middle-class privilege.

[24] That Anja should refer to Peer's orgasm as a sentimentality implies that it is an act from which she derives pleasure. However, what remains unclear is whether she takes pleasure in causing him pain, in the transgressive act of bringing a homosexual to orgasm, or in the power she has over him—indeed, perhaps these are all factors.

[25] Near the end of the restroom scene, Peer says, "Geh zum Teufel, verdammte Fotze!" (*BA* 192; Go to hell, damn cunt!). This is the only clear indication that the leatherman is not in fact a man; Anja's name never appears in the passage, which is narrated, like the rest of the novel, from an unembodied third-person perspective. The following chapter, the novel's closing passage, includes a reference to Anja's freshly shorn head, another indication that she was indeed Peer's gay bar torturer.

[26] A 2007 study by Rosalind Pritchard reported that the percentage of women in all ranks of professorship in Germany was 12.5 percent. Pritchard's article argues

that female professors have fewer opportunities for advancement, and less than 10 percent of those professors achieving promotion to the highest level are female. See Rosalind Pritchard, "Gender Inequality in British and German Universities," *Compare* 37, no. 5 (2007): 654.

[27] Christine Lehmann, *Harte Schule* (Hamburg: Argument, 2005). Subsequent references to this work are cited in the text using the abbreviation *HS* and page number. All translations from German to English are my own. Lehmann's Lisa Nerz series consists of ten novels thus far: a trilogy beginning with *Der Masochist* (1997) was published in the late 1990s, and the series continued in the 2000s with *Harte Schule* and six more novels in the feminist Ariadne crime series published by Ariadne, who also reissued the original first three "Lisa Nerz" books.

[28] See Marjorie Garber, *Vested Interests*, 187.

[29] Though Richard Weber is a recurring character in the Lisa Nerz series, only the second novel mentions his transsexuality and past identity as a woman. See Christine Lehmann, *Training mit dem Tod*, 140–43.

[30] Lehmann, *Der Masochist*, 120–21. The name *Krk* appears to be a journalistic pseudonym. In *Der Masochist* the rape scenario is portrayed as a biological inevitability due to the participants' relative gender positionalities, Lisa's dominance and her victim's submission: Lisa is the "Beschäler" (121; stud) while Krk is the "heiße Weibchen" (121; female in heat). The depiction of the forced sexual act as animalistic and therefore natural has the effect of sidestepping the problematic issue of Lisa's culpability.

[31] This resonates with feminist and transgender theories about gender difference. See, for instance, Luce Irigaray, *This Sex Which Is Not One*, trans. Catherine Porter (Ithaca, NY: Cornell UP, 1985); and Suzanne J. Kessler and Wendy McKenna, "Toward a Theory of Gender," in *The Transgender Studies Reader*, ed. Susan Stryker and Stephen Whittle (New York: Routledge, 2006), 165–82.

[32] See, for instance, Anne McClintock, *Imperial Leather: Race, Gender, and Sexuality in the Colonial Contest* (New York: Routledge, 1995); and Edward W. Said, *Orientalism* (1978; reprint New York: Vintage, 2004).

[33] Garber, *Vested Interests*, 190–91.

[34] One noteworthy exception to this trend is the Green Party, which has made gender equality a guiding principle since it was first established. For historical contextualizations of gender and politics in Germany and the European Union, see R. Amy Elman, ed., *Sexual Politics and the European Union: The New Feminist Challenge* (Providence, RI: Berghahn, 1996); and Silke Roth, ed., *Gender Politics in the Expanding European Union: Mobilization, Inclusion, Exclusion* (New York: Berghahn, 2008).

[35] See Marjorie Garber, *Vested Interests*, 202.

11: Eva Rossmann's Culinary Mysteries

Heike Henderson

CULINARY MYSTERIES ARE one of the most flourishing subgenres of crime fiction today. As J. Madison Davis contends, "the world of haute cuisine provides lots of opportunities for odd, colorful characters obsessed with perfecting their work."[1] It is therefore not surprising that culinary mysteries have enjoyed wide popularity and commercial success both in the United States and in Europe.[2] The Austrian capital Vienna even features a special bookstore for mysteries and culinary arts: Thrill and Chill: Spezialbuchhandlung für Krimi und Kulinarik.[3]

One of the most compelling series of culinary mysteries, written by Eva Rossmann, takes place in Vienna. The protagonist of Rossmann's mystery series, which comprises fifteen titles to date, is Mira Valensky, a journalist and passionate cook.[4] Together with her Bosnian sidekick, Vesna Krajner, she solves cases that take place in restaurant kitchens, supermarkets, wineries, and on the sets of cooking shows. Both Mira and Vesna are strong female characters who, true to Rossmann's feminist leanings, defy gender expectations and try to right the social wrongs they encounter.[5] In these culinary mysteries, a reevaluation of cooking as a gendered activity thus goes hand in hand with a critical examination of gender roles in contemporary Austrian society.

In her Mira Valensky series, Rossmann invites her readers to contemplate the implications of diverse issues like food safety and working conditions in restaurants and supermarkets. She is also sensitive to gender, ethnic, and disability discourse, and expands limiting notions of "Austrianness" by including protagonists from many different subsections of society. While none of these topics is purely Austrian—which could account for the mysteries' appeal across the German-speaking world—they are certainly important issues in Austria today. Food has always played a significant role in Austria, and, not coincidentally, Austria is widely known for its many culinary delicacies. It is also a country with a fairly traditional society that has experienced some recent upheaval in regard to gender roles, specifically in regard to women taking leadership positions and entering the political realm.[6]

My analysis of Rossmann's fiction explores how her focus on social issues allows her to comment on a wide variety of topics and to question traditional stereotypes about women and minorities. I will also show how culinary mysteries with strong female characters reconcile female readers' contradictory desires for feminine domesticity and feminist action. I believe this is one of the main reasons for their popularity and commercial success. While these culinary mysteries do not challenge heteronormative gender roles, they attempt, from a feminist perspective, to reclaim traditional feminine domains like cooking.

Culinary Mysteries as a Subgenre of Crime Fiction

Although there is no clear-cut definition for what constitutes a culinary mystery, most mysteries in this subgenre exhibit common characteristics. Usually the protagonist is a nonprofessional detective with culinary aspirations (often a chef, caterer, or journalist), and the crime takes place within a culinary milieu. The majority of these mysteries are so-called cozies, mysteries that are light on violence, sex, and rough language. Contrary to the genre conventions of the police procedural or hard-boiled detective fiction, crime solving in culinary mysteries is generally "less about police procedures than about understanding relationships within a small community."[7] Readers think of the sleuth as a friend and enjoy tagging along on the adventure.

One of the main reasons for this subgenre's vast commercial success is its strong appeal to female readers. Natalee Rosenstein, a senior executive editor of the Penguin publishing group, contends that the overwhelming majority of culinary mystery readers are women: "They see their own lives reflected in these characters."[8] While not exclusively a female or even feminist genre, many culinary mysteries are written by women, and have a female investigator as the main character. Besides providing entertainment, these mysteries quite often also deal with important social and cultural issues like sexism, working conditions, and gender roles. In addition to these topical considerations, many culinary mysteries also include recipes, and almost all have a strong regional focus.[9]

In 2009, Nieves Pascual Soler published the first book-length investigation of culinary detective stories. Although her study fills an important gap in the scholarship of crime fiction, it unfortunately does not include any German-language culinary mysteries. The reason for this is undoubtedly the lack of translations. Although culinary mysteries by Eva Rossmann and other German-language authors have been extremely popular in German-speaking countries, as of 2013 none of them has been translated into English. In her study, Soler identifies the "gourmandization" of society and the postfeminist movement as some of the main factors that have contributed to the success of the culinary mystery.[10] She states that, more than ever, we are preoccupied with what we put into our mouths, and quotes Mike Featherstone's assessment that a "calculating hedonism," in which "discipline and hedonism are no longer seen as incompatible," has become a feature of the new middle classes.[11]

Beth Kalikoff sees an even-stronger feminist potential in culinary mysteries. She contends in "Killer Cupcakes: Food, Feminism, and Murder in Mystery Fiction by Women," that "food mysteries are ultimately about female independence and sustaining the self."[12] According to Kalikoff, one of the main reasons for the genre's appeal, especially to female readers, is the fact that the culinary mystery "values the daily domestic skills of women who cook, bake, serve, and eat."[13] Their protagonists "embrace and transform conventional gender roles . . . through their relationships to cooking, baking, and eating."[14]

Rossmann's Mira Valensky Series

For the purpose of this chapter on Rossmann's culinary mysteries, I have chosen to focus on two of her novels that have a strongly food-related topic: *Kaltes Fleisch* (2002) and *Ausgekocht* (2003).[15] These mysteries focus on meat sold in supermarkets and gourmet restaurants, respectively, and will provide the basis for my discussion. Two other noteworthy mysteries in this context are *Wein & Tod* (2005), which takes place at a winery in the *Weinviertel*, the wine-growing area close to Vienna where Rossmann lives, and *Millionenkochen* (2007), which focuses on televised cooking shows.[16] Due to popular demand for recipes by readers who wanted to recreate Mira's feasts, Rossmann also published a cookbook, *Mira kocht* (2007).[17] This cookbook includes recipes from all of Rossmann's prior mysteries.

Kaltes Fleisch, Rossmann's fourth Mira Valensky mystery, deals with the timely, food-related topic of food safety. The title, which could be translated as "cold meat" or "cold flesh," already invokes a multitude of associations caused by the text's being imbedded in both the culinary and the mystery genre. In a literary treatment of real-life occurrences, the mystery exposes unsavory practices in supermarkets and meat-distribution companies. In the novel, supermarkets repackage meat once it gets close to its expiration date, and meat distribution companies switch fresh meat with previously frozen meat and sell it online for a large profit. The mystery also treats the bovine spongiform encephalopathy crisis that swept Europe in the late 1990s and early 2000s.[18]

Although the mystery was published in 2002, this topic's relevance has only increased in recent years. For evidence, one only needs to consider the German meat scandal in 2005–06 that caused the word *Gammelfleisch* (rotten meat) to appear in fifth place in the 2005 *Wort des Jahres* (word of the year) list, chosen by the *Gesellschaft für deutsche Sprache* (Society for German language), and to be officially accepted into the definitive German dictionary Duden in 2006.[19] Even today, despite new EU guidelines that make it harder to repackage meat once it is past the expiration date, there are still many reports of unsavory and dangerous practices concerning the food industry.

Besides its explicit focus on meat safety, *Kaltes Fleisch* highlights working conditions in a supermarket. The novel features a wide variety of victims: supermarket employees who are being exploited, consumers who are being duped, and two people who end up getting killed. Gender roles figure prominently, as does the role of foreigners in Austria today.

Rossmann's fifth mystery, *Ausgekocht*, has the strongest culinary focus of all the books in the series, and takes place in the world of gourmet cooks and culinary critics.[20] The title itself is a play on words: *ausgekocht* means both being done with cooking (i.e., one cannot cook anymore when one is dead), and it also means clever or hard-boiled. Its plot deals with a series of pranks and sabotage that escalate to assault and finally murder. All of the weapons are also kitchen-related and range from a thrown watermelon to poison mushrooms, knives, a meat tenderizer used as a bat, and, in its gruesome finale, the hand of a murdered TV chef run through the restaurant's meat grinder.

This mystery highlights stressful working conditions in restaurants, sexism, and the bitter competition in the restaurant scene. The hunt for culinary distinction and public recognition mixed with inflated egos and a high-pressure environment causes tempers to fly and people to get hurt. Cooking for pleasure competes with the business of cooking.

In both of these mysteries, Rossmann employs a similar strategy. She uses real-life occurrences like the meat scandal or the relentless competition in the restaurant scene as a springboard and background for her mysteries. She is thus able to explore important social topics in a fictional form. In my discussion of these culinary mysteries, I will focus on the following aspects of her narrative investigations: Rossmann's critique of working conditions in supermarkets and restaurant kitchens, the role of the culinary in these novels, narrative devices, the main character Mira, Rossmann's multifaceted representation of women, her portrayal of the role of foreigners and other minorities in Austria, and the culinary mysteries' specific appeal to female readers. I don't attempt to provide an exhaustive analysis of these two mysteries; my focus instead is on highlighting aspects that I find particularly relevant.

Rossmann's Critique of Working Conditions

One of the major accomplishments of both *Ausgekocht* and *Kaltes Fleisch*, besides providing fast-paced entertainment, is the realistic description of working conditions in restaurant kitchens and supermarkets. The profit margin in the grocery business is slim, and many supermarkets do not treat their low-wage employees very well. In *Kaltes Fleisch*, a union representative who notices the inferior quality of the meat and asks too many questions is threatened and ultimately killed, and a general atmosphere of fear prevents employees from speaking up against injustices.

Ausgekocht highlights the strict hierarchies and underlying sexism in restaurant kitchens. It also shows the stressful working conditions in professional kitchens. There is a lot of hidden prep work that needs to be done before guests arrive, and during the dinner rush, it is easy to get overwhelmed. The atmosphere is harsh, jokes quite often deteriorate into profanities, and especially female chefs face tough working conditions: "Die meisten Köche sind Männer, gerade in Großküchen ist das so. Stress und ungesundes Leben und jede Menge Hormone, die verrückt spielen." (58; Most chefs are men, especially in large kitchens. Stress and an unhealthy lifestyle and a lot of hormones that go crazy). In some kitchens, disagreements are not restricted to verbal sparring, but might involve throwing silverware and plates. When Mira wonders if Billy, the female chef at the center of events in *Ausgekocht*, was too harsh with her sous-chef, the chef responds "Ach du liebe Güte, das ist normal, man muss eben etwas Druck machen, was glauben Sie, wie es in anderen Küchen zugeht? . . . Der Ton ist bei uns eben manchmal—na ja, etwas rau, aber wo er vorher gearbeitet hat, da sind ab und zu sogar Teller und Messer geflogen." (43; Oh my gosh, that's normal, one has to apply some pressure, you have no idea what happens in other kitchens. The tone is sometimes— well, a little bit rough, but where he worked before, occasionally even plates and knives were thrown).[21]

Within the context of the plot, Billy uses the professional kitchen's harsh environment as an excuse for the way she treats her subordinates. On a narrative level, this works to draw the readers' attention to the way female chefs struggle to establish their authority in a traditionally male-dominated space. In real life as in the novel, most top chefs are men, and within the strict hierarchies of restaurant kitchens, many women have a difficult position establishing their authority when dealing with subordinates: "Die einen glauben, sie brauchen dir als Frau nicht zuzuhören, die anderen wollen mit dir ins Bett und damit vor ihren Kumpels prahlen" (58; Some believe they don't have to listen to you because you are a woman, others want to have sex with you and boast about it in front of their peers). Even Mira, who prides herself on her enlightened position in regard to gender equality, wonders:

> Ob es sich die beiden Männer auf Dauer gefallen lassen, von ihrer jungen Chefin so behandelt zu werden? Klar bin ich grundsätzlich der Meinung, dass es nicht vom Alter und schon gar nicht vom Geschlecht abhängen kann, wer der Chef ist. Aber gelernt haben wir es alle nun einmal anders. (37)

> [If in the long run the two men will accept being treated like that by their young, female boss? Of course I generally believe that who is

the boss cannot depend on age or, even worse, gender. But unfortunately we all learned it differently.]

Ausgekocht also spotlights the shady practices of some restaurant critics who offer to write positive reviews in exchange for free meals and paid-for advertising in the magazines that they write for:

> Bachmayer [the food critic who ends up getting murdered] hat mich sogar höchstpersönlich angerufen und vor einer nicht so guten Kritik gewarnt. Dabei hat er mir gleich über die supergünstigen Inseratpreise für das 'Fine-Food'-Magazin und den 'Fine-Food'-Gastronomieführer erzählt, ganz nebenbei, versteht sich. Er hat gemeint, dass es gerade nach einer Neuübernahme sinnvoll wäre, etwas Werbung zu betreiben. Vielleicht könne er mir auch noch einmal einen Testesser vorbeischicken, um ganz sicherzugehen, dass der erste richtig geurteilt hat. (73)

[Bachmayer even called me himself and warned me about a not-so-positive review. At this point he also mentioned the super special rates for advertising in the *Fine Food Magazine* and *Culinary Guide*, just as an aside, of course. He pointed out that after a change in ownership it would be useful to engage in advertising. And maybe he could send over another tester to make sure that the first one judged correctly.]

This episode highlights the huge financial impact of restaurant reviews and culinary awards. While Mira repeatedly insists that she only cares about the quality of a restaurant and not whether it has a Michelin star or any other official award, many other guests choose the restaurants they frequent based on these awards and critiques.

The Role of the Culinary in These Mysteries

In all of the mysteries in this series, Mira occasionally takes time out from her investigation to cook multicourse meals. This is both a literary strategy and an integral part of the plot. Mira thinks about the case while cooking; action thus gets interspersed with reflection. Sometimes these cooking intermezzos are quite involved; even when she talks about preparing a "simple meal," it usually involves multiple courses and delicacies whose preparation requires significant skills. She also uses cooking to extract favors from friends and acquaintances—a rather successful strategy that Vesna terms *einkochen* (literally: to boil down or preserve). In *Kaltes Fleisch*, when Mira needs a favor from her boyfriend Oskar, who later on in the series becomes her husband, Vesna suggests "Dann du kochst ihn ein und bittest ihn um kleinen Gefallen" (242; Then you cook him down and ask him for a small favor, 242).[22]

The most interesting function of the culinary within theses mysteries, however, is its intimate and intricate connection to crime solving. Cooking and solving crimes both require a similar set of skills. They are intuitive, creative, and at the same time analytical endeavors. Gourmet cooking in particular is an expression of both skill and art, of knowledge and creativity. Mira rarely follows recipes. Instead, she surveys the available ingredients and follows her inspiration. Her menus are often centered on one main ingredient, and include many different variations on a theme. She uses a similar approach in her professional life as a journalist and when solving crimes: circling in on the topic from many different angles. She combines both culinary and professional skills with creative experimentation. Her approach to crime solving includes critical analysis of the facts, insights into human behavior, and intuition.

The elaborate descriptions of cooking adventures also add to the popularity of culinary mysteries, an aspect that I will consider further in my subchapter on the strong appeal of these mysteries to female readers. In a 2007 interview marking the publication of *Mira kocht*, Rossmann described how readers repeatedly asked her for recipes, because they wanted to cook for themselves what Mira was cooking (the mysteries describe the general cooking process, but do not give any quantities of ingredients or exact instructions).[23] In recent years, this strategy of publishing a cookbook to go with a popular book, film, or TV series has been very successful; and it is a good example of innovative marketing strategies that explore synergies between separate customer bases, like those who buy crime fiction and those who buy cookbooks.

Narrative Devices

Rossmann's strongest narrative device is the use of culinary metaphors and associations. She also skillfully plays with readers' expectations and stereotypes. *Ausgekocht*, for example, starts with a scene that invokes a crime scene: "Ein Knall. Und dann überall Rot. Decke und Arme, Kopf und Spülbecken. Ich taumle und wische mir mit dem Handrücken über die Stirn. Zwecklos. Da Rot, dort Rot." (7; A bang. And then red everywhere. Ceiling and arms, head and sink. I stumble and use the back of my hand to wipe across my forehead. Useless. Red here, red there). It turns out that the scene is caused by a cooking disaster instead of a crime, and not blood, but tomatoes that were left too long in an old pressure cooker are responsible for the mess. In this first scene of the novel, Rossmann plays with the conventions of crime fiction (a vivid description of a crime scene is a very typical beginning), and thus with her readers' expectations.

In addition to her use of culinary associations, Rossmann employs many other typical conventions of crime fiction: foreshadowing, plot twists, red herrings and an escalation of crimes. There are also side stories and other possible suspects. In *Ausgekocht*, Billy's sous chef Peppi disappears after the murder of the food critic, thus causing fears that he also got murdered or was otherwise involved in the crime. Mira and Vesna finally find him cooking under a different last name in his native Czech Republic, where Billy's former boss, Demetz, who turns out to be the perpetrator, helped him get a job. Demetz knows that it is hard to find good cooks, and his successful attempt to lure Peppi away from Billy was yet another way to hurt his former protégée who he feels has "forgotten to be thankful to him" (246). In a final showdown in Billy's restaurant kitchen, Demetz attacks the protagonist Mira and tries to stuff her arm into the meat grinder. This, of course, follows another typical convention in crime fiction: the investigator's own life gets threatened just as she or he pieces together the evidence and successfully concludes the investigation.

The Main Character Mira

All of Rossmann's mysteries unfold from the protagonist Mira's perspective and are filtered through her liberal-leaning morality. Mira is wary of oppressive traditions and values equal opportunities for women and minorities. Since she is the main character and first-person narrator, readers are most likely to identify with her. It is therefore especially important to evaluate how Mira performs her different, overlapping roles as woman, investigator, journalist, and hobby cook.

Mira is portrayed as a strong, independent woman who critically reflects upon women's role in society. A recurrent theme in the mystery series is Mira's worry that her enjoyment of cooking dinner for Oskar reduces her to the role of a subservient housewife who cooks for her man and waits for him to come home from work, the way it used to be in her family when she was growing up:

> Selbstverständlich war es so gewesen, dass sich meine Mutter als Gattin eines Landesrates um den Haushalt kümmern musste. Der Vater brachte das Geld nach Hause und legte dafür Wert auf gute Bedienung. Wann immer er heimkam, sollte das Essen fertig sein, seine Frau fröhlich, entspannt und bereit, ihm zuzuhören. (*Kaltes Fleisch*, 78)

> [Of course my mother, as the wife of a state government official, had to take care of household matters. Father brought home the money and in return he expected good service. Whenever he came home, food was supposed to be ready, and his wife cheerful, relaxed, and ready to listen to him.]

Mira rejects and criticizes these traditional gender roles that she still sees as prevalent in contemporary Austrian society. This makes her hesitant to move in with Oskar, since she fears that she will lose her independence. In all of the mysteries, she repeatedly reflects on her conflicting desires for close connections and independence, as this example from *Kaltes Fleisch* demonstrates: "Jedenfalls liebte ich nicht nur ihn, sondern auch meine Unabhängigkeit." (133; Anyway, I did not only love him, but also my independence.)

Despite her apprehensions about falling into the traps of traditional gender roles, Mira appreciates domesticity and home-cooked meals. She is wary of people who do not care about what they eat (like her former boyfriend Joe in *Ausgejodelt*—not surprisingly, this relationship is short-lived). One of the reasons she gets along so well with Oskar is that they both love food; as Rossman writes in *Kaltes Fleisch*: "Wir harmonierten eben gut miteinander. Besonders, wenn es ums Essen ging." (25; We were really in synch. Particularly in regard to food). She enjoys cooking for her friends, and especially Oskar, but at the same time she repeatedly needs to reassure herself that she is not just a stereotypical housewife performing domestic duties. These conflicting desires make her relatable to her readers who may be similarly torn between a longing for domesticity and an awareness of its pitfalls—a topic that I will discuss in more detail in the section on the culinary mysteries' appeal to female readers.

Like many of her readers, Mira is also forced to negotiate between her enjoyment of food and social pressures on women to be thin:

Warum kommt ein Mensch, der so gerne isst und kocht wie ich, auch auf die Idee, zehn Kilo abnehmen zu wollen? . . . Ich hatte auch bisher mit der Tatsache, dass ich dem klassischen Schönheitsideal nicht vollkommen entsprach, gut leben können. Ein paar Kilo mehr, warum nicht? Besser als magersüchtig und unglücklich.[24]

[Why does somebody who enjoys eating and cooking as much as I do get the idea to lose ten kilo? . . . Up to now, I have been able to live well with the fact that I don't fully adhere to traditional beauty ideals. A few kilos more, why not? Better than anorexic and unhappy.]

This defiant attitude toward contemporary beauty ideals validates readers who themselves might be struggling with a few pounds too many. According to Kaufman and Kaufman, who in "Food, Anger, and the Female Detective" analyze fictional female detectives from contemporary American crime series, this kind of rebellious attitude is reflective of a general rejection of traditional sex role expectations for women, specifically the taboo on women's open expression of anger and the severe social pressure on females to be thin. They assert that "the degree to which a woman challenges traditional sex roles is reflected in her attitude and behavior toward food."[25] This correlates with Rossmann's narrative strategy of questioning social conventions.

Mira has no rigid behavioral code, and sometimes grapples with contradictory desires. Her biggest moral dilemma is that she wants to both live the good life, which for her mainly consists of good food and plenty of leisure time, and be a feminist and stand up for social justice and equal opportunities for all members of society. Despite having earned a law degree, she makes her living as a lifestyle journalist. Like most professionals, she is occasionally forced to compromise between her personal convictions and her professional obligations. She has to accept directives from her boss, who is concerned with the financial survival of the newspaper and encourages her to report in a sensationalist manner, as evidenced in *Kaltes Fleisch*: "Ohne Skandal keine Geschichte" (68; Without scandal no story). He also warns her not to step on the toes of readers or advertisers (90–91). Through her main character, Rossmann thus questions journalistic integrity and the limits of personal involvement.

Rossmann's Multifaceted Representations of Women

The most important secondary female character is Mira's sidekick and best friend Vesna. At the beginning of the series, she starts out as an illegal cleaning lady who works for Mira. She is feisty, outspoken, and adventurous, and the fact that she works for Mira does not stop her from contradicting or admonishing her: "Ich putze deinen Dreck und ich denke, was ich will. Und es ist gut für dich, mir zuzuhören." (I clean your dirt and I think what I want. And it is good for you to listen to me).[26] Her Bosnian background is an important aspect of her personality and quite often proves helpful in solving the cases. I will further discuss this in the next part on the role of foreigners and other minorities in Rossmann's mysteries. Later on in the series, Vesna opens her own cleaning company, with an unofficial side business for investigations: "Sauber! Reinigungsarbeiten aller Art" (Clean! Housekeeping of all kinds).[27]

In addition to Mira and Vesna, all of Rossmann's mysteries feature a wide variety of female characters. In my discussion of working conditions in restaurants, I have already mentioned the sexism that *Ausgekocht*'s female chef, Billy, encounters. There are two additional women who play a prominent role in *Kaltes Fleisch*: the very outspoken union representative Karin and the shy, insecure cashier Grete, whose experience ends up being very helpful in solving the crime. The initial depiction of Karin and Grete as opposites encompasses their personality, their respective level of strength and independence, and their physical appearance. Karin is tall, heavyset, and has bright-red hair. She is feisty and quick witted, and fights for what she believes in, whether for workers' rights or consumers' rights. When Grete is first introduced, her appearance is very unflattering. Due to a botched dye job that she undertook to please her husband who likes blond hair, she has yellow, permed hair that looks like hay. She desperately tries to please everybody and suffers from low self-esteem.

During the course of the investigation, the readers' impression of Grete changes. This is due to the fact that Mira discovers aspects of Grete's personality that were previously hidden from the casual observer, partly because Grete's contact with Mira and Vesna—both of them strong women—helps her open up and gain a certain degree of self-confidence. In *Kaltes Fleisch*, as the case draws to a close, Grete's insights into the uneven relationship between the main perpetrator and his wife prove invaluable in getting the suspect's wife to testify against her husband (310). At the end of the novel, Grete's life has changed and she has started to gain more confidence in her skills. This is once again expressed through her physical appearance: she cuts her hair and colors it reddish-brown.

Grete's transformation, culminating in the stereotypical cutting of her hair, could be decried as cliché-laden. To a certain extent, this assessment also applies to other characters in the series, including the heroine. What differentiates the Mira Valensky series from cookie-cutter serial fiction, however, is the wide variety of characters that Rossmann depicts, plus an awareness of the systematic nature of the problems that Mira encounters. Yes, change is possible, but one woman's transformation does not change society, as this observation from *Kaltes Fleisch* confirms: "Frauen würden weiterhin um zu wenig Geld arbeiten und nicht aufmucken, weil sie es eben nicht gewohnt waren aufzumucken oder glaubten, sich das nicht leisten zu können." (314; Women will continue to work for too little money and not complain because they are not used to complaining or believe they cannot afford to do so).

The Role of Foreigners and Other Minorities in Rossmann's Mysteries

Rossmann's mysteries show both the plight of foreigners and minorities—for example, poor working conditions in supermarkets and restaurant kitchens—and innovative ways in which stereotypes and preconceived notions about minorities can be used against those who hold them. Mira's fearless sidekick Vesna is especially skilled in this endeavor. She quite often uses her role as a foreign cleaning lady (partly true, partly employed as a ruse) to get in and out of buildings, unnoticed, to gather information. Mira's colleague Droch, who uses a wheelchair, also occasionally employs a similar strategy by playing into others' preconceived notions about people with disabilities. By showing how Vesna and Droch are able to use existing stereotypes to their advantage, Rossmann accomplishes two things: She points to existing stereotypes in a society that at least officially considers itself antidiscriminatory, and she shows ways to deal with these stereotypes that go beyond complaining and finger-pointing.

In *Kaltes Fleisch*, Vesna goes undercover to help solve the mystery. She starts working in the supermarket, restocking shelves. As a foreigner, it is easy for her to pretend that she understands very little German, and thus she is able to spy on people and learn about what is happening behind the scenes. Other workers with a migrant background are also more willing to talk to her than they would be with Mira or the police. When Mira insists on talking to one of the other temporary workers herself, Vesna reminds her that this would not be a feasible strategy: "Sie wird nicht mit dir reden, Mira Valensky. Du bist nicht vom Supermarkt. Du bist nicht aus Bosnien." (169; She won't talk to you, Mira Valensky. You are not from the supermarket. You are not from Bosnia). The outsider Vesna has become the quintessential insider, and without her help, Mira would not be able to solve the case.

In *Ausgekocht*, Vesna also contributes to the solution of the crime through undercover work. She takes a job as a dishwasher in the restaurant where the prime suspect works[28]—rightfully pointing out that nobody would believe the well-educated Austrian citizen Mira would be willing to work as a dishwasher for four euro an hour. This once again accomplishes two things: it points to the common exploitation of foreign labor—as a foreigner without a work permit, Vesna endures stereotyping, poor working conditions, and low hourly wages—and it shows how, as a minority member, Vesna has access to parts of society that are inaccessible to Mira.

Vesna also has a wide network of family and friends on whom she can call for favors to help with the investigation. In *Ausgekocht*, she knows the wife of the hospital director, who, as a fellow refugee from Yugoslavia, used to work with Vesna. With one short phone call, Vesna is able to convince her friend to persuade her husband to overrule hospital policies and let Mira talk to the injured octogenarian waiter. This episode is one of many that testifies to the importance of personal relationships in contemporary Austria—it is important to know the right people to help navigate the bureaucratic maze of hospitals and administrative offices. It also spotlights the plight of refugees like Vesna's friend who, despite being a professor in her home country, had to work as a cleaning lady when she first arrived in Austria.

The Culinary Mysteries' Appeal to Female Readers

In her daily life, Mira faces many contradictions to which readers can relate. She wants to solve the case and bring about social change, but she also wants to make a living and enjoy life. This makes her relatable to her readers, who face similar struggles and challenges. The serial character of the novels helps in this identification process. Priscilla L. Walton, in her discussion of feminist paradigms and racial interventions in hard-boiled women's detective fiction, has argued that the series structure of popular mysteries, which encourages identification with the main characters, "helps to open the texts (and their political message) to readers who might otherwise not read 'social problem' works."[29] Specific concerns and social issues can thus "be addressed and then assimilated by readers who would not necessarily read about them in other venues."[30]

The ease with which mainly female readers can relate to Rossmann's protagonist is a typical characteristic of the *Frauenkrimi*. According to Nicola Barfoot, who in her 2007 text *Frauenkrimi/polar feminine* has provided a thorough examination of German and French women's crime novels, the *Frauenkrimi* is supposed to contain "eine starke bis vorbildhafte feministische Frau" (a strong to exemplary feminist woman), providing a heroine as "Identifikationsangebot und Wunschbild" (positive role model and ideal), as "Projektionsfläche für Wünsche und Sehnsüchte" (a projection plane for wishes and desires).[31] The overturning of traditions and clichés is often seen as the main constitutive element of the *Frauenkrimi*.[32] As Brigitte Frizzoni, in her 2009 analysis *Verhandlungen mit Mordsfrauen: Geschlechterpositionierungen im 'Frauenkrimi'* has pointed out, it also usually goes hand in hand with gender-specific marketing to women.[33]

The culinary part in culinary mysteries adds another component to the widespread appeal of serial crime novels. Especially readers who like to cook get hooked through the description of culinary adventures and relate to the culinary-expert characters. The transformative power of cooking and the tendency of protagonists in culinary mysteries to resort to food preparation to ease their problems have been well established.[34] Many readers, especially if they themselves like to use cooking (or at least envision themselves engaging in cooking) to relieve stress, can relate to this. Rossmann goes one step further by adding a critical examination of gender roles. She invites her readers to identify with the gourmet sleuth and envision themselves as a feminist domestic goddess who enjoys life and also fights for the greater good of society.[35]

Joanne Hollows, in her examination of the significance of television cook and cookbook writer Nigella Lawson, argues that Lawson's work "negotiates a form of feminine identity between the frequently polarized figures of 'the feminist' and 'the housewife,'"[36] I believe this is an apt analogy for the appeal of culinary mysteries like Rossmann's Mira Valensky series to female readers. Similar to Lawson, Rossmann's heroine offers a choice that encompasses both feminism and domestic femininity. Instead of viewing cooking as a chore, Mira revalues cooking and extracts pleasure from the cooking process. As Hollows argued for Lawson, Mira represents "a mode of femininity that is based around cooking and eating as pleasure, rather than servitude and denial."[37] This provides an alternative means of representing women's relationship with food to that offered by mainstream society or feminist criticism, which tends to focus on an analysis of cooking as servitude to others.

Although it might not be possible for readers to follow in Mira's footsteps and solve crimes while whipping up gourmet meals, Rossmann offers a fantasy that holds immense appeal to women who are trying to negotiate their sometimes conflicting desires for feminine domesticity and feminist change. At least in our imagination, Rossmann allows us to be just like Mira and feel like a crime-solving domestic goddess.

Notes

[1] J. Madison Davis, "Mystery Meat, Beverage, and Your Choice of a Just Desserts," *World Literature Today* (January–February 2009): 9.

[2] See Ashley Strickland, "Dig In: Food with a Side of Murder," *CNN*, April 13, 2011, http://www.cnn.com/2011/LIVING/04/13/culinary.mysteries.gain.popularity/index.html; and Holly Hibner, "Culinary Mysteries," *Books & Authors Blog* December 3, 2011, http://booksandauthorsblog.com/archives/1924. In regard to the popularity of German-language culinary mysteries, see Robert Kropf, "Tatort Küche: Kulinarische Krimis," *Die Presse*, October 25, 2007, http://diepresse.com/home/leben/ausgehen/339309/Tatort-Kueche_Kulinarische-Krimis (all accessed February 15, 2013).

[3] The grand opening of this bookstore in November 2006 featured food, a wine tasting, and a reading by Eva Rossmann. For more information on this innovative specialty bookstore, see http://www.thrillandchill.at/ (accessed February 15, 2013).

[4] Not all of the mysteries in Rossmann's Mira Valensky series can be categorized as culinary mysteries per se. Some of the novels primarily deal with other topics like social security, plastic surgery, or energy politics. Even in these texts, however, significant space is devoted to the description of their protagonist Mira's cooking and enjoying food.

[5] Prior to writing mysteries, Rossmann published five nonfiction books that deal with the situation of women in politics and society.

[6] Rossmann's first mystery, *Wahlkampf* (Vienna: Folio, 1999), was inspired by the author's experiences working as a coordinator of presidential candidate Gertrude Knoll's political campaign. Instead of writing a nonfiction treatise about her experiences, as originally planned, she used them as background for her mystery. See Eva Rossmann, "Interview mit Christian Lehner, 2011," http://www.eva-rossmann.at/index,13.html; for further data on women in Austrian society and politics, see http://www.bka.gv.at/site/6811/default.aspx and http://www.parlament.gv.at/PERK/FRAU/ (all accessed June 7, 2013).

[7] Davis, "Mystery Meat," 10.

[8] Strickland, "Dig In."

⁹ See, for example, these other culinary mystery series with a regional focus: Brigitte Glaser's Katharina Schweitzer series *Leichenschmaus* (Cologne: Emons, 2003), *Kirschtote* (2004), *Mordstafel* (2005), *Die Eisbombe* (2007), *Bienenstich* (2009), and *Himmel un Ääd* (2012); Ella Danz's Georg Angermüller series, especially *Kochwut* (Meßkirch: Gmeiner, 2009) and *Geschmacksverwirrung* (2012); Carsten Sebastian Henn's Julius Eichendorff series starting with *In Vino Veritas* (Cologne: Emons, 2002), and, to a somewhat lesser extent, Pierre Emme's Vienna-based Mario Palinski series starting with *Pastetenlust* (Meßkirch: Gmeiner, 2005). There are also many anthologies of short stories with a strong regional focus.

¹⁰ Nieves Pascual Soler, *A Critical Study of Female Culinary Detective Stories: Murder by Cookbook* (Lewiston, NY: Mellen, 2009), 24.

¹¹ Mike Featherstone, "The Body in Consumer Culture," in *The Body: Social Process and Cultural Theory*, ed. Mike Featherstone, Mike Hepworth, and Bryan S. Turner (London: Sage, 1991), 171.

¹² Beth Kalikoff, "Killer Cupcakes: Food, Feminism, and Murder in Mystery Fiction by Women," *The CEA Critic* 69, nos. 1–2 (Fall 2006–Winter 2007): 75.

¹³ Kalikoff, "Cupcakes," 74.

¹⁴ Kalikoff, "Cupcakes," 75.

¹⁵ Eva Rossmann, *Kaltes Fleisch* (5th ed. Bergisch Gladbach: Bastei Lübbe, 2009, originally Vienna: Folio, 2002) and *Ausgekocht* (5th ed. Cologne: Bastei Lübbe, 2010, originally Vienna: Folio, 2003). Subsequent references to these works are cited in the text using the page number. All translations are my own.

¹⁶ Eva Rossmann, *Wein & Tod* (Cologne: Bastei Lübbe, 2007, originally Vienna: Folio, 2005) and *Millionenkochen* (Bergisch Gladbach: Bastei Lübbe, 2009, originally Vienna: Folio, 2007).

¹⁷ Eva Rossmann, *Mira kocht* (Vienna: Folio, 2007).

¹⁸ See http://www.spiegel.de/politik/ausland/rinderseuche-die-chronologie-der-bse-krise-a-105210.html (accessed February 18, 2013).

¹⁹ See http://www.gfds.de/aktionen/wort-des-jahres/ and http://www.duden.de/rechtschreibung/Gammelfleisch; for a detailed description of the meat scandal, see http://www.spiegel.de/spiegel/print/d-43301961.html (all accessed February 18, 2013).

²⁰ In 2002, while doing research for this novel, Rossmann herself started working in the kitchen of her favorite Weinviertel restaurant, Manfred Buchinger's *Zur alten Schule*. What started as a research project has since turned into a part-time job for Rossmann. In 2004, the author-cook passed the cooking exam with distinction, and she still cooks there on a regular basis. For more background information on Rossmann, see Mirjam Reither, "Eva Rossmann," http://www.ichkoche.at/eva-rossmann-artikel-768 (accessed December 22, 2012).

²¹ This description of tough language, pranks, and exaggerated manliness mirrors the conditions made famous by Anthony Bourdain in his best-selling exposé *Kitchen Confidential: Adventures in the Culinary Underbelly* (New York: Bloomsbury, 2000). In the context of *Ausgekocht*, Mira and Billy establish a professional connection with each other, and with the informed reader, by referring to

Bourdain's text. For two other culinary mysteries that excel in their description of working conditions in restaurant kitchens, see Renate Möhrmann, *Die Frau, die kocht* (Passau: Schenk, 2009) and Glaser, *Leichenschmaus* (2003).

[22] While this is a traditional strategy for women, to use cooking to please a man and get what they want, in the Mira Valensky series it is not limited to a domestic setting.

[23] Eva Rossmann, "Hörprobe—Eva Rossmann spricht über *Mira kocht*," http://audio.evarossmann.at/mira-kocht.mp3 (accessed December 22, 2012).

[24] Eva Rossmann, *Ausgejodelt*, 6th ed. (Cologne: Bastei Lübbe, 2010, originally Vienna: Folio, 2000), 15–16.

[25] Natalie Hevener Kaufman and Susan Kaufman, "Food, Anger, and the Female Detective," *Clues: A Journal of Detection* 20, no. 1 (1999): 49–50.

[26] Eva Rossmann, *Freudsche Verbrechen*, 7th ed. (Cologne: Bastei Lübbe, 2010, originally Vienna: Folio, 2001), 23. For a discussion of *Freudsche Verbrechen*, see Traci O'Brien's contribution in this volume.

[27] Rossmann, *Millionenkochen* 30.

[28] In addition to Vesna, Mira also goes undercover in *Ausgekocht*. After Billy's sous chef Peppi disappears, Mira starts working in Billy's kitchen. This allows her to get an intimate view of the scene of the crime, and also to learn more about what is happening in restaurant kitchens in general. In contrast to Vesna's work as unskilled laborer, however, Mira is able to indulge in her passion for cooking while solving the crime.

[29] Priscilla L. Walton, "Bubblegum Metaphysics: Feminist Paradigms and Racial Interventions in Mainstream Hardboiled Women's Detective Fiction," in *Multicultural Detective Fiction: Murder From the "Other" Side*, ed. Adrienne Johnson Gosselin (New York: Garland, 1999), 265.

[30] Walton, "Bubblegum Metaphysics," 268. See also Phyllis M. Betz who, in her analysis of women as authors, subjects and readers in the context of lesbian detective fiction, points to the "ability of genre literature to balance tradition and innovation." Phyllis M. Betz, *Lesbian Detective Fiction: Woman as Author, Subject and Reader* (Jefferson, NC: McFarland, 2006), 24.

[31] Nicola Barfoot, *Frauenkrimi/polar feminine* (Frankfurt am Main: Peter Lang, 2007), 78, 82, and 85.

[32] Barfoot, *Frauenkrimi* 89.

[33] Brigitte Frizzoni, *Verhandlungen mit Mordsfrauen: Geschlechterpositionierungen im 'Frauenkrimi'* (Zurich: Chronos, 2009), 9.

[34] See, for example, Christine A. Jackson, *Myth and Ritual in Women's Detective Fiction* (Jefferson: McFarland, 2002), 31.

[35] Of course, the genre's fantasy could be considered a "safety valve" that allows things to go on pretty much unchanged, as one of the readers of this article suggested, but then again I believe that holds true for most forms of entertainment.

[36] Joanne Hollows, "Feeling Like a Domestic Goddess: Postfeminism and Cooking," *European Journal of Cultural Studies* 6, no. 2 (2003): 179.

[37] Hollows, "Domestic Goddess," 197.

Works Cited

Alcoff, Linda. "Cultural Feminism versus Poststructuralism: The Identity Crisis in Feminist Theory." *Signs* 13, no. 3 (1988): 405–36.
Alewyn, Richard. "Anatomie des Detektivromans." In Vogt, *Der Kriminalroman*, 67–68
———. "Anatomie des Detektivromans." In Vogt, *Der Kriminalroman II*, 375.
Althans, Birgit, and Antke Tammen. "Das Begehren am Kriminalroman." In *Von Freud und Lacan aus: Literatur, Medien, Übersetzen. Zur "Rücksicht auf Darstellbarkeit" in der Psychoanalyse*, edited by Tanja Jankowiak, Karl-Josef Pazzini, and Claus-Dieter Rath. Bielefeld: 2006.
Altnoeder, Sonja. "Transforming Genres: Subversive Potential and the Interface between Hard-Boiled Detective Fiction and Chick Lit." In *The Millennial Detective: Essays on Trends in Crime Fiction, Film and Television, 1990–2010*, edited by Malcah Effron, 82–96. London: McFarland, 2011.
Applegate, Celia. *A Nation of Provincials: The German Idea of Heimat*. Berkeley: U of California P, 1990.
Auden, W. H. "The guilty vicarage: Notes on the detective story by an addict." *Harpers*, May 1948. Available at: http://harpers.org/archive (April 12, 2012).
Bachmann, Ralf. *Ich bin der Herr. Und wer bist du? Ein deutsches Journalistenleben*. Berlin: Dietz, 1995.
Baier, Eckhart. "Mord in der Heimat." *Börsenblatt* no. 27 (July 5, 2007): 44–46.
Barbin, Herculine, and Michel Foucault. *Herculine Barbin: Being the Recently Discovered Memoirs of a Nineteenth Century French Hermaphrodite*. Introduced by Michel Foucault and translated by Richard McDougall. New York: Vintage, 1980.
Barfoot, Nicola. *Frauenkrimi/polar féminin: Generic Expectations and the Reception of Recent French and German Crime Novels by Women*. Frankfurt am Main: Peter Lang, 2007.
Baron, Ulrich. "Markt & Totschlag: Regio regiert (nicht)," *Crimemag, Kolumnen und Themen* (blog), May 21, 2011 (7:12), http://culturmag.de/crimemag/markt-und-totschlag-regio-regiert-nicht.
Barthes, Roland. *S/Z*. Translated by Richard Miller. Preface by Richard Howard. New York: Hill and Wang, 1974.
Bauer, Matthias. "Der unheimliche Fall der Psychoanalyse. Wie Sigmund Freud im historischen Kriminalroman erst als Detektivfigur eingesetzt

und dann des 'Seelenmords' verdächtigt wird." In *Geschichte im Krimi. Beiträge aus den Kulturwissenschaften*, edited by Barbara Korte and Sylvia Paletschek, 59–76. Köln: Böhlau Verlag, 2009.

Baumann, Manfred. *Zauberflötenrache*. Pößneck, Germany: Gmeiner, 2012.

Baßler, Moritz. *Der deutsche Pop-Roman*. Munich: C. H. Beck Verlag, 2006.

Benjamin, Ludy T. *A History of Psychology: Original Sources and Contemporary Research*. Oxford: Blackwell, 2009.

Benvenuto, Bice, and Roger Kennedy. *The Works of Jacques Lacan: An Introduction*. London: Free Association Books, 1986.

Betz, Phyllis M., *Lesbian Detective Fiction: Woman as Author, Subject and Reader*. Jefferson: McFarland, 2006.

Binswanger, Christa, Lotta Samelius, and Suruchi Thapar-Björkert. "Palimpsests of Sexuality and Intimate Violence: Turning Points as Transformative Scripts for Intervention." *NORA—Nordic Journal of Feminist and Gender Research* 19 (2011): 27.

Blickle, Peter. *Heimat: A Critical Theory of the German Idea of Homeland*. Rochester, NY: Camden House, 2002.

Bloch, Ernst. "A Philosophical View of the Detective Novel," *Discourse* 2 (Summer 1980).

———. "Philosophische Ansicht des Detektivromans." In Vogt, *Der Kriminalroman*, 38–51.

Bloching, Maria. "Freiheit des Autors stößt auf Kritik." *Alb Bote*, 29 Oct. 2007.

Boa, Elizabeth, and Rachel Palfreyman. *Heimat. A German Dream: Regional Loyalties and National Identity in German Culture, 1890–1990*. Oxford Studies in Modern European Culture. Oxford: Oxford UP, 2000.

Boileau, Pierre and Thomas Narcejac. *Der Detektivroman*. Berlin and Neuwied: Luchterhand, 1967.

Bollhöfer, Björn. *Geographien des Fernsehens—Der Kölner Tatort als mediale Verortung kultureller Praktiken*. Bielefeld: Transcript Verlag, 2007.

Bollmann, Doreen. "Deutschsprachige Kriminalliteratur im Wandel der Zeit." In *Lesekultur: Populäre Leststoffe von Gutenberg bis zum Internet*, edited by Petra Bohnsack and Hans-Friedrich Foltin, 111–24. Marburg: Universitätsbibliothek Marburg, 1999.

Brandt, Sabine. *Vom Schwarzmarkt nach St. Nikolai: Erich Loest und seine Romane*. Leipzig: Linden, 1998.

Breger, Claudia. "Hegemony, Marginalization, and Feminine Masculinity: Antje Rávic Strubel's *Unter Schnee*." *Seminar* 44, no. 1 (2008): 154–73.

Breznik, Melitta. *Das Umstellformat*. Munich: Luchterhand, 2002.

"Bruchsal, 26. Juni." *Heidelberger Zeitung* 152, July 2, 1861. Accessed August 4, 2012. http://digi. ub.uni-heidelberg.de/diglit/hdtz1861a/0001?sid=b599a5bbaac33b93cc37869c 7b3aefe1.

Bruckmüller, Ernst. *The Austrian Nation: Cultural Consciousness and Socio-Political Processes*. Riverside: Ariadne Press, 2003.

Butler, Judith. *Bodies That Matter: On the Discursive Limits of "Sex."* London: Routledge, 1993.

———. *Undoing Gender*. London and New York: Routledge, 2004.
Buttler, Monika. *Dunkelzeit*. Meßkirch: Gmeiner Verlag, 2006.
Capote, Truman. *In Cold Blood*. New York: Random House, 1965.
Cawelti, John. *Adventure, Mystery and Romance*. Chicago: U of Chicago P, 1976.
Cawelti, John G. "*Chinatown* and Generic Transformation in Recent American Films." In *Mystery, Violence & Popular Culture*, 193–209. Madison, WI: The U of Wisconsin P, 2004.
Chambers, Helen. "'Bestialisch dahingeschlachtert': Extreme Violence in German Crime Fiction." In *Violence, Culture and Identity: Essays on German and Austrian Literature, Politics and Society*, edited by Helen Chambers, 401–15. Oxford: Peter Lang, 2006.
Chandler, Raymond. *The Long Goodbye*. 1953, New York: Vintage, 1981.
———. "Mord ist keine Kunst." in Vogt, *Der Kriminalroman*, 164–84.
Cobley, Paul. "The Reactionary Art of Murder: Contemporary Crime Fiction, Criticism and Verisimilitude." *Language and Literature* 21, no. 3 (2012): 286–98.
Confino, Alon. *The Nation as a Local Metaphor: Württemberg, Imperial Germany, and National Memory, 1871–1918*. Chapel Hill: U of North Carolina P, 1997.
Curtin, Amanda. *The Sinkings*. Crawley: U of Western Australia Press, 2008.
Dankwart, Paul Zeller. *Das Geheimnis der Partisanen-Tora: Eine Theologische Kriminalgeschichte*. Albstadt: C. M. Brendle Verlag, 2009.
Dapp, Hans-Ulrich. *Emma Z. Ein Opfer der Euthanasie*. Stuttgart: Quell, 1990.
Detre, Laura A. "Wolf Haas: The Weather Fifteen Years Ago (Review)." *Modern Austrian Literature* 43, no. 3 (2010).
Dietze, Gabriele. *Hardboiled Woman: Geschlechterkrieg im amerikanischen Kriminalroman*. Hamburg: Europäische Verlangsanstalt, 1997.
Dillon, Sarah. *The Palimpsest: Literature, Criticism, Theory*. London, New York: Continuum, 2007.
Dischner, Gisela. "'Flaschenpost' and 'Wurfholz': Reflections on Paul Celan's Poems and Poetics." In *German and European Poetics after the Holocaust: Crisis and Creativity*, edited by Gert Hofmann, Rachel MagShamhráin, Marko Pajević, and Michael Shields, 35–52. Rochester, NY: Camden House, 2011.
Donahue, William Collins. *Holocaust as Fiction: Bernhard Schlink's "Nazi" Novels and their Films*. New York: Palgrave, 2010.
———. "The Popular Culture Alibi: Bernhard Schlink's Detective Novels and the Culture of Politically Correct Holocaust Literature." *German Quarterly* 77, no. 4 (2004).
Donnenberg, Richard. "Kurze Geschichte des österreichischen Krimis." Last modified 2005. Accessed December 15, 2012. http://www.krimiautoren.at/geschichte_krimi.html.
Dorn, Thea. *Berliner Aufklärung*. Munich: Goldmann, 1994.

Dove, George N. *The Reader and the Detective Story*. Bowling Green, OH: Bowling Green State University Popular Press, 1997.
Doyle, Sir Arthur Conan. *Sherlock Holmes: The Complete Novels and Stories*, Vol. 1. NewYork: Random House, 1986.
Draesner, Ulrike. *Mitgift*. Munich: Luchterhand, 2002.
Dreger, Alice Dormurat. *Hermaphrodites and the Medical Invention of Sex*. Cambridge, MA: Harvard UP, 2000.
Dufresne, Todd. *Future of an Illusion*. Ontario: Broadview: 2012.
Dunker, Michael. *Beeinflussung und Steuerung des Lesers in der englischsprachigen Detektiv- und Kriminalliteratur: eine vergleichende Untersuchung zur Beziehung Autor-Text-Leser in Werken von Doyle, Christie und Highsmith*. Frankfurt am Main; New York: Peter Lang, 1991.
Dürrenmatt, Friedrich. *Das Versprechen*. Zürich: Verlag der Arche, 1958.
Eco, Umberto. *The Role of the Reader: Explorations in the Semiotics of Texts*. Bloomington: Indiana UP, 1979.
Effron, Malcah. *The Millenial Detective: Essays on Trends in Crime Fiction, Film and Television, 1990–2010*. Jefferson, NC: McFarland, 2011.
Eigler, Friederike. "Critical Approaches to Heimat and the 'Spatial Turn.'" *New German Critique* 39, no. 1 (2012): 27–48.
Eigler, Friederike, and Jens Kugele. *Heimat: At the Intersection of Memory and Space*. Media and Cultural Memory. Berlin: De Gruyter, 2012.
Elman, R. Amy, ed. *Sexual Politics and the European Union: The New Feminist Challenge*. Providence: Berghahn, 1996.
Eng, David L., Judith Halberstam, and José Esteban Muñoz, eds. *What's Queer about Queer Studies Now?* Spec. Issue of *Social Text* 84–85, 23, nos. 3–4 (2005): 1–308.
Erdmann, Eva. "Nationality International: Detective Fiction in the Late Twentieth Century." In *Investigating Identities: Questions of Identity in Contemporary International Crime Fiction*, edited by Mareike Krajenbrink and Kate M. Quinn, 11–26. Amsterdam: Rodopi, 2009.
Erikson, E. H. "Reality and Actuality: An Address." *Journal of the American Psychoanalytic Association* 10 (1962): 451–74.
Eskin, Michael. *Ethics and Dialogue in the Works of Levinas, Bakhtin, Mandel'shtam, and Celan*. Oxford: Oxford UP, 2000.
Eugenides, Jeffrey. *Middlesex*. New York: Picador, 2002.
Falkenstein, Sigrid. *Annas Spuren: Ein Opfer der NS-'Euthanasie.'* Munich: Herbig, 2012.
Feigenbaum, Erika Faith. "Heterosexual Privilege: The Political and the Personal," *Hypatia* 22, no. 1 (2007): 1–9.
Finke, Edmund. "Über den Kriminalroman." *Das deutsche Wort* 12 (1936): 419–22.
Fitzel, Thomas. "Heimatroman mit Leichen: Regional-Krimis verkaufen sich ausgezeichnet." Accessed April 12, 2013. http://www.dradio.de/dkultur/sendungen/fazit/2072786/.
Forshaw, Barry. *Death in a Cold Climate: A Guide to Scandinavian Crime Fiction*. Basingstoke: Palgrave Macmillian, 2012.

Freud, Sigmund. "Construction in Analysis (1937)." In *The Standard Edition of the Complete Psychological Works of Sigmund Freud*, Vol. 23, edited and translated by James Strachey, 255–69. London: Hogarth, 1964.

———. "Fragment of an Analysis of a Case of Hysteria (1905 [1901])." In *The Standard Edition of the Complete Psychological Works of Sigmund Freud*, vol. 7, edited and translated by James Strachey, 3–122. London: Hogarth, 1953.

———. "The Future of an Illusion (1927)." In *The Standard Edition of the Complete Psychological Works of Sigmund Freud*, vol. 21, edited and translated by James Strachey, 3–56. London: Hogarth, 1961.

———. *Konstruktionen in der Analyse: Studienausgabe. Ergänzungsband*. Frankfurt am Main: Fischer, 1982.

———. "Notiz über den 'Wunderblock.'" In *Texte zur Literaturtheorie der Gegenwart*, edited by Dorothee Kimmich, Rolf Günter Renner, and Bernd Stiegler, 171–76. Stuttgart: Reclam, 1996.

———. *Die Traumdeutung*. Frankfurt am Main: Fischer, 1991.

———. "The Uncanny (1919)." In *The Standard Edition of the Complete Psychological Works of Sigmund Freud*, Vol. 17, edited and translated by James Strachey, 218–56. London: Hogarth, 1955.

———. *Writings on Art and Literature*, ed. James Strachey. Meridian: Crossing Aesthetics. Stanford: Stanford UP, 1997.

Frizzoni, Brigitte. *Verhandlungen mit Mordsfrauen: Geschlechterpositionierungen im "Frauenkrimi."* Zurich: Chronos, 2009.

Furedi, Frank. *Therapy Culture: Cultivating Vulnerability in an Uncertain Age*. London, New York: Routledge, 2004.

Garber, Marjorie. *Vested Interests: Cross-Dressing & Cultural Anxiety*. London: Routledge, 1992.

———. *Vested Interests: Cross-Dressing and Cultural Anxiety*. New York: Routledge, 1997.

Gelien, Gabriele. *Eine Lesbe macht noch keinen Sommer*. Hamburg: Argument, 1993.

Gercke, Doris. *Weinschröter, du mußt hängen*. Munich: Goldmann, 2000.

Gerhards, Sascha. "Ironizing Identity: The German Crime Genre and the Edgar Wallace Wave of the 1960s." In *Generic Histories of German Cinema: Genre and its Deviations*, edited by Jaimey Fisher, 133–55. Rochester, NY: Camden House, 2013.

———. "Zeitgeist of Murder: The Krimi and Social Transformation in Post-1945 Germany." PhD Diss., U of California, Davis (2013).

Gerlach, Franziska. "Der Boom der Regionalkrimis." Goethe Institute, last modified November 2011. Accessed December 15, 2012. http://www.goethe.de/kue/lit/aug/de8129560.htm.

———. "The Boom of the Regional Crime Novel." Goethe Institute, last modified November 2011. Accessed December 15, 2012, http://www.goethe.de/kue/lit/aug/en8129560.htm.

Gerlach, Gunter. "Keine Tränen." In *Mörderisches Ländle*, edited by Gudrun Weitbrecht, 3–15. Stuttgart: Theiss, 2008.

Gilman, Sander L. *Smart Jews: The Construction of the Image of Jewish Superior Intelligence*. Lincoln: U of Nebraska P, 1996.
Ginsberg, Elaine K. *Passing and the Fictions of Identity*. Durham, NC: Duke UP, 1996.
Giritzhofer, Katrin. "Mörderisch und Kulinarisch: Eva Rossmanns Frauenduo Mira und Vesna zwischen Wien, Wein und Veneto." Master's thesis, U of Vienna, 2008.
Goodwin, C. James. *A History of Modern Psychology*. 3rd ed. Hoboken, NJ: Wiley, 2008.
Gorrara, Claire. "Reflections on Crime and Punishment: Memories of the Holocaust in Recent French Crime Fiction" *Yale French Studies* 108 (2005).
Gregoriou, Christiana. *Deviance in Contemporary Crime Fiction*. New York: Palgrave Macmillan, 2009.
Grella, George. "Murder and Manners: The Formal Detective Novel." *NOVEL: A Forum on Fiction* 4, no. 1 (1970): 30–48.
Griem, Juliaka, ed. *Tatort Stadt—mediale Topographien eines Fernsehklassikers*. Frankfurt: Campus, 2010.
Grimm, Thomas, ed. *Wolfgang Harich: Ahnenpass. Versuch einer Autobiographie*. Berlin: Schwarzkopf & Schwarzkopf, 1999.
Gross, Rainer. *Grafeneck*. Bielefeld: Pendragon, 2007.
Grosz, Elizabeth. *Volatile Bodies: Toward a Corporeal Feminism*. Bloomington: Indiana UP, 1994.
Gutknecht, Günther, Günter Krapp, and Cornelia Zenner, eds., *Grafeneck: Schülerheft*. Rot a. d. Rot: Krapp & Gutknecht, 2011.
Haas, Franz. "Aufklärung in Österreich. Die erhellenden Kriminalromane von Wolf Haas." In *Mord als kreativer Prozess: Zum Kriminalroman der Gegenwart in Deutschland, Österreich und der Schweiz*, edited by Sandro Moraldo, 127–44. Heidelberg: Universitätsverlag Winter, 2005.
Haas, Wolf, *Auferstehung der Toten*. Reinbek b. Hamburg: Rohwolt, 1996.
———. *Brenner und der liebe Gott*. Reinbek b. Hamburg: Rohwolt, 2009.
———. *Das ewige Leben*. Reinbek b. Hamburg: Rohwolt, 2003.
———. *Der Knochenmann*. Reinbek b. Hamburg: Rohwolt, 1997.
———. *Komm, süßer Tod*. Reinbek b. Hamburg: Rohwolt, 1998.
———. *Silentium!* Reinbek b. Hamburg: Rohwolt, 2000.
———. *Wie die Tiere*. Reinbek b. Hamburg: Rohwolt, 2001.
Hall, Katharina. "The Crime Writer as Historian: Representations of Natinal Socialism and its Post-War Legacies in Joseph Kanon's The Good German and Pierre Frei's Berlin." *Journal of European Studies* 42, no. 1 (2012): 50–67.
Hankin, Kelly. *The Girls in the Back Room: Looking at the Lesbian Bar*. Minneapolis: U of Minnesota Press, 2002.
Harich, Wolfgang. *Keine Schwierigkeiten mit der Wahrheit. Zur nationalkommunistischen Opposition 1956 in der DDR*. Berlin: Dietz, 1993.
Haycraft, Howard. *Murder for Pleasure: The Life and Times of the Detective Story*. New York and London: D. Appleton-Century Company, 1947.

Heiland, Henrike. *Blutsünde*. Bergisch Glattbach: Bastei Lübbe, 2007.
Heim, Uta-Maria. *Feierabend*. Meßkirch: Gmeiner, 2011.
Heißenbüttel, Helmut. "Spielregeln des Kriminalromans." In Vogt, *Der Kriminalroman II*, 356–71.
Herzog, Todd. *Crime Stories: Criminalistic Fantasy and the Culture of Crisis in Weimar Germany*. New York: Berghahn, 2009.
———. "The *Krimi*." In *The Directory of World Cinema: Germany*. Edited by Michelle Langford. London: Intellect Books, 2013.
Heuner, Almuth. "Germany's Crime and Mystery Scene." *World Literature Today* 85, no. 3 (May–June 2011): 16–17.
Hitzig, Julius Eduard, and William Häring. *Der neue Pitaval: Eine Sammlung der interessantesten Criminalgeschichten aller Länder und Völker*. Frankfurt am Main: Insel Verlag, 1986.
Holzweißig, Gunter. *Zensur ohne Zensor. Die SED-Informationsdiktatur*. Bonn: Bouvier, 1997.
Höpcke, Klaus. *Probe für das Leben. Literatur in einem Leseland*. Leipzig: Mitteldeutscher Verlag, 1982.
Hügel, Hans-Otto. *Die Leiche auf der Eisenbahn: Detektivgeschichten aus deutschen Familienzeitschriften*. Darmstadt: Luchterhand, 1981.
———. *Untersuchungsrichter, Diebsfänger, Detektive: Theorie und Geschichte der deutschen Detektiverzählung im 19. Jahrhundert*. Stuttgart: Metzler, 1978.
Inglorious Basterds. Dir. Quentin Tarantino. Universal, 2009.
Irigaray, Luce. *This Sex Which Is Not One*, translated by Catherine Porter. Ithaca, NY: Cornell, 1985.
Irons, Glenwood, ed., *Feminism in Women's Detective Fiction*. Toronto: U of Toronto Press, 1995.
Irwin, John. *The Mystery to a Solution: Poe, Borges, and the Analytic Detective Story*. Baltimore: Johns Hopkins UP, 1994.
Irwin John T. "Mysteries We Reread, Mysteries of Rereading." In *Detecting Text: The Metaphysical Detective Story from Poe to Postmodernism*, edited by Patricia Merivale and Susan Elizabeth Sweeney, 27–54. Philadelphia: U of Pennsylvania Press, 1999.
Iser, Wolfgang. "Indeterminacy and the Reader's Response." In *Twentieth-Century Literary Theory*, 2nd ed., edited by K. M. Newton. New York: St. Martin's Press, 1997.
Jahn, Reinhard. "Was ist ein Regionalkrimi." Presentation, Thomas Morus-Akademie, Bergisch-Gladbach, Bensberg, January 9, 2000. Republished online at *Krimiblog*, September 29, 2009, http://krimiblog.blogspot.com/2009/09/was-ist-ein-regionalkrimi-eine-autopsie.html.
James, P. D. *Talking About Detective Fiction*. New York: Alfred A. Knopf, 2009.
Janka, Walter. *. . . bis zur Verhaftung. Erinnerungen eines deutschen Verlegers*. Berlin: Aufbau, 1993.
———. *Spuren eines Lebens*. Berlin: Rowohlt, 1991.

———. *Die Unterwerfung. Eine Kriminalgeschichte aus der Nachkriegszeit*. Munich: Hanser, 1994.

Jones, Christopher. "Images of Switzerland in Swiss Crime Fiction." In *German-Language Literature Today: International and Popular?*, edited by Arthur Williams, Stuart Parkes, and Julian Preece, 85–98. Oxford: Peter Lang, 2000.

Just, Gustav. *Die fünfziger Jahre in der DDR*. Berlin: Buchverlag Der Morgen, 1990.

Kahane, Claire. "Introduction: Part Two." In *Dora's Case: Freud—Hysteria—Feminism*, edited by Charles Bernheimer and Claire Kahane, 19–32. New York: Columbia UP, 1985.

Kahn, Daniel. "Six Million Germans." *Partisans and Parasites*. Oriente Musik, 2009.

Kessler, Suzanne J., and Wendy McKenna. "Toward a Theory of Gender." In *The Transgender Studies Reader*, edited by Susan Stryker and Stephen Whittle, 165–82. New York: Routledge, 2006.

Klein, Kathleen Gregory, ed. *Women Times Three: Writers, Detectives, Readers*. Bowling Green, OH: Bowling Green State University Popular Press, 1995.

Klinkner, Tina. "Der deutsche Regionalkrimi." *media mania*, n.d., http://www.media-mania.de/index.php?action=artikel&id=51.

Knight, Stephen. *Crime Fiction 1800–2000. Detection, Death, Diversity*. New York: Palgrave Macmillan, 2004.

Knittel, Susanne, "Beyond Testimony: Nazi Euthanasia and the Field of Memory Studies." *The Holocaust in History and Memory* 5 (2012): 85–101.

———. "Bridging the Silence: Towards a Literary Memory of (Nazi) Euthanasia." *Edinburgh German Yearbook* 4 (2010).

Komarek, Alfred. *Zwölf mal Polt. Kriminalgeschichten*. Innsbruck-Vienna: Haymon, 2011.

Korte, Barbara and Sylvia Paletschek. *Geschichte im Krimi. Beiträge aus den Kulturwissenschaften*. Cologne: Böhlau, 2009.

———. "Geschichte und Kriminalgeschichte(n)—Texte, Kontexte, Zugänge." In *Geschichte im Krimi: Beiträge aus den Kulturwissenschaften*, edited by Barbara Korte, 7–27. Cologne: Böhlau, 2009.

Kracauer, Siegfried. "Detektiv." In Vogt, *Der Kriminalroman II*, 345.

Kracauer, Siegfried. *Der Detektiv-Roman—Ein philosophischer Traktat*. Frankfurt am Main: Suhrkamp Taschenbuch Wissenschaft, 1979.

Krajenbrink, Marieke. "Unresolved Identities in Roth and Rabinovici: Reworking the Crime Genre in Austrian Literature." In *Investigating Identities in Contemporary International Crime Fiction*, edited by Marieke Krajenbrink and Kate M. Quinn, 243–60. Amsterdam: Rodopi, 2009.

Kramlovsky, Beatrix. "Show Your Face, oh Violence." *World Literature Today* 85, no. 3 (May–June 2011): 13.

Kremmler, Katrin. *Die Sirenen von Coogee Beach*. Hamburg: Argument, 2003.

Kretschmer, Ernst. "Abgründe in der Provinz. Alfred Komareks Kriminalromane." In *Mord als kreativer Prozess*, edited by Sandro M. Moraldo. Heidelberg: Universitätsverlag Winter, 2005, 111–26

Kutch, Lynn Marie. "'Die lange blutige Literatursitzung': Veit Müller's Interrogation of the Writing Process in Regional Detective Fiction." *Modern Language Studies* 41, no. 2 (2012).

Kutscher, Volker. *Goldstein*. Köln: Kiepenheuer & Witsch, 2011.

Kuzniar, Alice. *The Queer German Cinema*. Stanford: Stanford UP, 2000.

Labroisse, Gerd, and Ian Wallace, eds. *DDR-Schriftsteller sprechen in der Zeit. Eine Dokumentation.* German Monitor 27. Amsterdam: Rodopi, 1991.

Lang, Berel. "Holocaust Memory and Revenge: The Presence of the Past." *Jewish Social Studies* 2, no. 2 (1996).

Lawson, Mark. "Crime's Grand Tour: European Detective Fiction." *The Guardian*, October 26, 2012. http://www.guardian.co.uk/books/2012/oct/26/crimes-grand-tour-european-detective-fiction.

Lee, Peter, et al. "Consensus Statement on Management of Intersex Disorders." *Pediatrics—Official Journal of the American Academy of Pediatrics* 118 (2006): 488–500.

Lehmann, Christine. *Harte Schule*. Hamburg: Argument, 2005.

———. *Der Masochist*. Reinbek: Rowohlt, 1997.

———. *Training mit dem Tod*. Reinbek: Rowohlt, 1998.

Lénard, Nané. *SchattenHaut*. Hameln: CW Niemeyer, 2011.

Leseland DDR. Aus Politik und Zeitgeschichte 11 (2009).

Liertz, Martina-Marie. *Die Geheimnisse der Frauen*. Munich: Goldmann, 1999.

Loest, Erich. *Als wir in den Westen kamen*. Stuttgart: DVA; Leipzig: Linden Verlag, 1997.

———. *Durch die Erde ein Riß*. Munich: dtv, 1990.

———. *Prozesskosten. Bericht*. Göttingen: Steidl, 2007.

———. *Der Zorn des Schafes*. München: dtv, 1993.

———. "Zu von mir begangenen Fehler nach dem 17. Juni 1953." Adk SV (neu) 313, Bl. 70–71.

Lorenz, Dagmar C. G. "In Search of the Criminal—in Search of the Crime. Holocaust Literature and Films as Crime Fiction." *Modern Austrian Literature* 31, no. 3–4 (1998): 35–48.

Lorenzer, Alfred. "Zum Beispiel 'Der Malteser Falke': Analyse der psychoanalytischen Untersuchung literarischer Texte." In Vogt, *Der Kriminalroman*, 298–415.

Lorey, Christoph, and John L. Plews, eds., *Queering the Canon: Defying Sights in German Literature and Culture*. Columbia, SC: Camden House, 1998.

Lützen, Wolf Dieter. "Der Krimi ist kein deutsches Genre. Momente und Stationen zur Genregeschichte der Krimiunterhaltung." In *Der neue deutsche Kriminalroman: Beiträge zu Darstellung, Interpretation und Kritik eines populären Genres*, edited by Karl Ermert and Wolfgang Gast, 162–81. Loccumer Kolloquien 5. Rehburg-Loccum: Evangelische Akademie Loccum, 1985.

Mandala, Susan. "Crime Fiction as Regional Fiction: An Analysis of Dialect and Point of View in Sheila Quigley's *Bad Moon Rising*." *Style: A Quarterly Journal of Aesthetics, Poetics, Stylistics, and Literary Criticism* 46 (2): 177–200.

Marsch, Edgar. *Die Kriminalerzählung: Theorie, Geschichte, Analyse*. Munich: Winkler, 1972.

Martens, Gunther. "'Aber wenn du von einem Berg springst, ist es wieder umgekehrt.' Zur Erzählerprofilierung in den Meta-Krimis von Wolf Haas." *Modern Austrian Literature* 39, no. 1 (2006): 66.

Mattson, Michelle. "Tatort: The Generation of Public Identity in a German Crime Series." *New German Critique* 78 (1999): 161–81.

McClintock, Anne. *Imperial Leather: Race, Gender, and Sexuality in the Colonial Contest*. New York: Routledge, 1995.

Meid, Volker. *Sachwörterbuch Zur Deutschen Literatur*. Stuttgart: Reclam, 1999.

Merivale, Patricia and Susan Elizabeth Sweeney, eds. *Detecting Texts: The Metaphysical Detective Story from Poe to Postmodernism*. Philadelphia: U of Pennsylvania Press, 1999.

"Miscellen." *Berliner Gerichts-Zeitung*, October 1, 1853, Nr. 1 edition, sec. Beilage zur Berliner Gerichts-Zeitung, 6, Staatsbibliothek zu Berlin Preußischer Kulturbesitz. http://zefys.staatsbibliothek-berlin.de/list/title/zdb/24332471.

Mittermayer, Manfred. "Das Schweigen der Salzburger: Zur Verfilmung des Romans *Silentium!* von Wolf Haas durch Wolfgang Murnberger." In *Gegenwartsliteratur* 7 (2008): 138–59.

Mohr, Heinrich. "Spurensicherung. Erich Loests Versuch, die eigene Wahrheit zu schreiben." In *Probleme deutscher Identität. Zeitgenössische Autobiographien. Identitätssuche und Zivilisationskritik*, edited by Paul Gerhard Klussmann and Heinrich Mohr, 1–17. Bonn: Bouvier, 1983.

Moltke, Johannes von. *No Place Like Home: Locations of Heimat in German Cinema*. Berkeley: U of California P, 2005.

Moretti, Franco. *Graphs, Maps, Trees—Abstract for a Literary History*. London: Verso, 2005.

Morris-Keitel, Peter. *Die Verbrechensthematik im Modernen Roman: Untersuchungen und Analysen zur Motivstruktur in der Deutschsprachigen Literature nach 1970 anhand kriminologischer Theorien*. New York: Peter Lang, 1989.

Munt, Sally R. *Murder by the Book? Feminism and the Crime Novel*. London: Routledge, 1994.

Muny, Eike. "Erzählen ohne Ewigkeit: Strategien der Aussparung bei Wolf Haas." In *Schrift-Zeichen: Poetologische Konstellationen von der Frühen Neuzeit bis zur Postmoderne*, edited by Jan Broch and Markus Rassiller, 223–37. Cologne: Kleine Schriften der Üniversitäts- und Stadtsbibliothek, 2006.

Nindl, Sigrid. "Jetzt wird schon wieder was analysiert . . ." In *Gesprochen—Geschrieben—Gedichtet*, 103–15. Berlin: Erich Schmidt Verlag, 2009.

———. *Wolf Haas und sein kriminalliterarisches Sprachexperiment.* Berlin: Erich Schmidt Verlag, 2010.
Nusser, Peter. *Der Kriminalroman.* Stuttgart: Metzler, 2009.
Otte, Björn. *Das Milieu im Fernsehkrimi: Am Beispiel der Krimi-Reihe "Tatort."* Tectum Verlag, 2013.
Pailer, Gaby. "'Weibliche' Körper im 'männlichen' Raum: Zur Interdependenz von Gender und Genre in deutschsprachigen Kriminalromanen von Autorinnen." *Weimarer Beiträge* 46, no. 4 (2000): 564–81.
Partner, Nancy F. "Historicity in an Age of Reality-Fictions." In *A New Philosophy of History,* edited by Frank R. Ankersmit and Hans Kellner, 21–39. London: 1995.
Pascual Soler, Nieves. *A Critical Study of Female Culinary Detective Stories: Murder by Cookbook.* Lewiston, NY: Edwin Mellen Press, 2009.
Peach, Linden. *Masquerade, Crime, and Fiction: Criminal Deceptions.* Basingstoke: Palgrave, 2006.
Plain, Gill. *Twentieth-Century Crime Fiction: Gender, Sexuality and the Body.* Chicago: Fitzroy Dearborn, 2001.
Plener, Peter. "404 Ding. Über die Kriminalromane von Wolf Haas." In *Neues: Trends und Motive in der (österreichischen) Gegenwartsliteratur,* edited by Friedbert Aspetsberger. Innsbruck: StudienVerlag, 2003.
Polheim, Karl Konrad, ed., *Wesen und Wander der Heimatliteratur am Beispiel der österreichischen Literatur sein 1945.* Bern: Peter Lang, 1989.
Poore, Carol. *Disability in Twentieth-Century German Culture.* Ann Arbor: U of Michigan Press, 2007.
Preves, Sharon E. *Intersex and Identity: The Contested Self.* New Brunswick, New Jersey, London: Rutgers UP, 2003, 60–86.
Pritchard, Rosalind. "Gender Inequality in British and German Universities." *Compare* 37, no. 5 (2007): 651–69.
"Prospect." *Berliner Gerichts-Zeitung,* October 1, 1853, Nr. 1 edition, 1, Staatsbibliothek zu Berlin Preußischer Kulturbesitz, http://zefys.staatsbibliothek- berlin.de/list/title/zdb/24332471.
Quinn, Kate M., and Marieke Krajenbrink. *Investigating Identities: Questions of Identity in Contemporary International Crime Fiction.* Amsterdam: Rodopi, 2009.
Rabaté Jean-Michel. "The Death of Freud: What Is to Be Preferred, Death or Obsolescence?" *qui parle* 19, no. 1 (2010): 37–63.
Rainer Gross. *Grafeneck.* Bielefeld: Pendragon, 2011.
———. *Kettenacker.* Bielefeld: Pendragon, 2011.
Reimer, Paul. "Kultusgemeinde kritisiert Stolpersteine" *Die Tageszeitung.* July 22, 2006. Accessed March 6, 2013. http://www.taz.de/1/archiv/archiv/?dig=2006/07/22/a0268.
Reiterer, Albert F., ed. *Nation und Nationalbewusstsein in Österreich.* Vienna: Verband der wissenschaftlichen Gesellschaften Österreichs, 1988.
Ritzel, Ulrich. *Der Schatten des Schwans.* Lengwil: Libelle, 1999.

Roland, Jürgen. "Time doesn't move forward . . ." In *Out of the Dark: Crime, Mystery and Suspense in the German Cinema 1915–1990*, translated by Leslie Ann Pahl, 5. Munich: Goethe Institut, 1992.
Rossmann, Eva. *Ausgejodelt.* Cologne: Bastei Lübbe, 2010.
———. *Ausgekocht.* Bastei Lübbe, 2010.
———. *Freudsche Verbrechen.* Cologne: Bastei Lübbe, 2010.
———. *Heim an den Herd?* Vienna: Folio, 1996.
———. "Hörprobe—Eva Rossmann spricht über Mira kocht." http://audio.evarossmann.at/mira-kocht.mp3.
———. *Kaltes Fleisch.* Bergisch Gladbach: Bastei Lübbe, 2009.
———. *Millionenkochen.* Bergisch Gladbach: Bastei Lübbe, 2009.
———. *Mira kocht.* Vienna: Folio, 2007.
———. *Wahlkampf.* Vienna: Folio, 1999.
———. *Wein & Tod.* Cologne: Bastei Lübbe, 2007.
Roth, Gerhard. *The Lake*, translated by Michael Winkler. Riverside, CA: Ariadne, 2000.
———. *Der See.* Frankfurt am Main: S. Fischer, 1995.
Roth, Silke, ed., *Gender Politics in the Expanding European Union: Mobilization, Inclusion, Exclusion.* New York: Berghahn, 2008.
Rushing, Robert A. *Resisting Arrest: Detective Fiction and Popular Culture.* New York: Other Press, 2007.
Rußegger, Arno. "'Alte Regel, solange du liest, bist du nicht tot' Wolf Haas' *Silentium!* Und die Didaktik des Kriminalromans." *Informationen zur Deutschdidaktik*, 1 (2003): 75.
———. "Ortspiele. Wortspiele. Aspekte kriminalistischen Erzählens in der österreichischen Literatur." In *Mord als kreaktiver Prozess*, edited by Sandro M. Moraldo, 75–98. Heidelberg: Universitätsverlag Winter, 2005.
Said, Edward W. *Orientalism.* New York: Vintage, 2004.
Sánchez, María Carla, and Linda Schlossberg, eds., *Passing: Identity and Interpretation in Sexuality, Race, and Religion.* New York: New York UP, 2001.
Sänger, Florian. *Literatur und Film im Feld narrativer Theorien.* Aachen: Shaker Verlag, 2009.
Saupe, Achim. *Der Historiker als Detektiv—der Detektiv als Historiker. Historik, Kriminalistik und der Nationalsozialismus als Kriminalroman.* Bielefeld: Transcript, 2009.
Schäfer, Jörgen. "'Neue Mitteilungen aus der Wirklichkeit.' Zum Verhältnis von Pop und Literatur in Deutschland seit 1968." In *Text + Kritik: Pop-Literatur*, edited by Heinz Ludwig Arnold and Jörgen Schäfer, 14–17. Munich: Richard Boorberg Verlag, 2003.
Schiller, Friedrich. "Vorrede zur Pitaval-Ausgabe von 1792–1795." In *Schillers Pitaval: Merkwürdige Rechtsfälle als ein Beitrag zur Geschichte der Menschheit, verfaßt, bearbeitet und herausgegeben von Friedrich Schiller*, edited by Oliver Tekolf, 75–76. Frankfurt am Main: Eichborn Verlag, 2005.
Schneider, Kerstin. *Maries Akte.* Frankfurt am Main: Weissbooks, 2008.

Schönert, Jörg. "Kriminalgeschichten in der deutschen Literatur zwischen 1770 und 1890: Zur Entwicklung des Genres in sozialgeschichtlicher Perspektive." In Vogt, *Der Kriminalroman*, 322–27.

Schreckenberger, Helga. "The Destruction of Idyllic Austria in Wolf Haas's Detective Novels." In *Crime and Madness in Modern Austria*, edited by Rebecca S. Thomas, 424–33. Newcastle, UK: Cambridge Scholars Publishing, 2008.

Schubert, Helga. *Die Welt da drinnen. Eine deutsche Nervenklinik und der Wahn vom "unwerten Leben."* Frankfurt am Main: Fischer, 2003.

Schütz, Erich. *Judengold*. Meßkirch: Gmeiner Verlag, 2009.

"Schwurgericht." *Berliner Gerichts-Zeitung*, October 1, 1853, Nr. 1 edition, 3, Staatsbibliothek zu Berlin Preußischer Kulturbesitz. http://zefys.staatsbiblio- thek-berlin.de/list/title/zdb/24332471.

Sedgwick, Eve Kosofsky. *Tendencies*. Durham: Duke UP, 1993.

———. *Touching Feeling: Affect, Pedagogy, Performativity*. Durham, London: Duke UP, 2003.

Segev, Tom. *The Seventh Million: The Israelis and the Holocaust*. New York: Henry Holt, 2000.

Seidman, Naomi. "Elie Wiesel and the Scandal of Jewish Rage" *Jewish Social Studies* 3, no. 1 (1996).

Seltzer, Mark. *Serial Killers: Death and Life in America's Wound Culture*. London: Routledge, 1998.

———. *Serial Killers: Death and Life in America's Wound Culture*. London: Routledge, 2004.

Snell, K. D. M. "The Regional Novel: Themes for Interdisciplinary Research." In *The Regional Novel in Britain and Ireland. 1800–1900*, edited by K. D. M. Snell, 1–58. Cambridge: Cambridge UP, 1998.

Snyder, Sharon L., and David T. Mitchell. *Cultural Locations of Disability*. Chicago: U of Chicago P, 2006.

Spillane, Mickey. *Vengeance Is Mine!* 1950. In *The Mike Hammer Collection*. Vol. 1. New York: New American, 2001.

"Der Staatsgefangene und seine Tochter." *Münsterberger Wochenblatt*, January 4, 1839, 1st ed., Staatsbibliothek zu Berlin Preußischer Kulturbesitz. http://zefys.staatsbibliothek-berlin.de/list/zdb/24335642.

Staudte Wolfgang, dir. *Die Mörder sind unter uns*. (DEFA, 1946).

Stewart, Faye. "Dialogues with Tradition: Feminist-Queer Encounters in German Crime Stories at the Turn of the Twenty-First Century." In *Contemporary Women's Writing and the Return of Feminism in Germany*, edited by Hester Baer, Spec. issue of *Studies in Twentieth and Twenty-First Century Literature* 35, no. 1 (2011): 114–35.

———. *German Feminist Queer Crime Fiction: Politics, Justice and Desire*. Jefferson: McFarland, 2014.

———. "Of Herrings Red and Lavender: Reading Crime and Identity in Queer Detective Fiction." In *Lesbian Crime Fiction*, edited by Jacky Collins, special issue of *Clues* 27, no. 2 (2009): 33–44.

———. "Queer Investigations: Genre, Geography, and Sexuality in German-Language Lesbian Crime Fiction." PhD. Diss., Indiana University, 2007.
Stone, Susan. "Why German Crime Fiction Fails to Thrill US Readers." *PRI's The World: Global Perspectives for an American Audience.* December 28, 2012. http://www.theworld.org/2012/12/why-german-thrillers-are-not-popular-in-us/
Stowe, William W. "Critical Investigations: Convention and Ideology in Detective Fiction." *Texas Studies in Language and Literature* 31, no. 4 (1989): 570–91.
Sweeney, Susan Elizabeth. "Crime in Postmodernist Fiction." In *The Cambridge Companion to American Crime Fiction*, edited by Catherine Ross Nickerson, 163–77. Cambridge: Cambridge UP, 2010.
Symons, Julian. *Bloody Murder: From the Detective Story to the Crime Novel.* New York: Mysterious Press, 1992.
Tannert, Mary W. *Early German and Austrian Detective Fiction: An Anthology.* . Jefferson, NC: McFarland and Company, 2007.
Tauber, Alfred. "Freud's Dreams of Reason: The Kantian Structure of Psychoanalysis." *History of the Human Sciences* 22, no. 4 (2009): 1–29.
Teraoka, Arlene. "Detecting Ethnicity: Jakob Arjouni and the Case of the Missing German Detective Novel." *German Quarterly* 72, no. 3 (1999): 265–89.
Uta-Maria Heim, *Wem sonst als Dir.* Tübingen: Klöpfer & Meyer, 2013.
Vogt, Jochen. "Alles total groovy hier—Oder: Wie das Ruhrgebiet im Krimi zu sich selbst kam." *Der Deutschunterricht* 2 (2010): 20–28.
———. "Krimi—international." *Der Deutschunterricht: Beiträge zu seiner Praxis und wissenschaftlichen Grundlegung* 2 (2007): 2–6.
———, ed. *Der Kriminalroman: Poetik, Theorie, Geschichte.* Munich: Fink, 1998.
———, ed. *Der Kriminalroman II.* Munich: Fink, 1971.
———. *Medien Morde: Krimis intermedial.* Paderborn: Fink, 2004.
———. "Tatort—der wahre deutsche Gesellschaftsroman. Eine Projektskizze." In *Medien-Morde: Krimis intermedial*, edited by Jochen Vogt, 112–29. Munich: Wilhelm Fink, 2005.
Walton, Priscilla L., and Manina Jones. *Detective Agency: Women Rewriting the Hard-Boiled Tradition.* Berkeley: U of California P, 1999.
Wanninger, Klaus. *Schwaben-Ehre.* Hillesheim: KBV, 2009.
Warner, Michael. "Introduction." In *Fear of a Queer Planet: Queer Politics and Social Theory*, edited by Michael Warner, vii–xxxi. Minneapolis: U of Minnesota Press, 1993.
Watson, Colin. *Snobbery with Violence. Crime Stories and Their Audience.* London: Eyre and Spottiswoode, 1971.
Weitbrecht, Gudrun, ed. *Henker, Huren, Mordgesellen: historische Schwabenmorde.* Mannheim: Wellhöfer, 2009.
———. *Mörderisches Ländle.* Stuttgart: Theiss, 2008.
———. *Tödliche Kehrwoche.* Stuttgart: Theiss, 2007.
———. *Tod unterm Tannenbaum: Weihnachtskrimis aus dem Ländle.* Stuttgart: Theiss, 2012.

Wenzel, Eike, ed. *Tatort—Recherchen und Verhöre, Protokolle und Beweisfotos.* Berlin: Bertz Verlag, 2000.
Wessel, Claudia. *Es wird Zeit.* Gießen: Wemü, 1984.
Westermann, Stefanie, Richard Kühl, and Tim Ohnhäuser, eds. *NS-'Euthanasie' und Erinnerung: Vergangenheitsaufarbeitung—Gedenkformen—Betroffenenperspektiven.* Medizin und Nationalsozialismus. Münster: LIT, 2011.
Wigbers, Melanie. *Krimi-Orte im Wandel: Gestaltung und Funktionen der Handlungsschauplätze in Kriminalerzählungen von der Romantik bis in die Gegenwart.* Würzburg: Königshausen & Neumann, 2006.
Wilke, Sabine. "Wilde Weiber und dominante Damen: Der Frauenkrimi als Verhandlungsort von Weiblichkeitsmythen." In *Frauen auf der Spur: Kriminalautorinnen aus Deutschland, Großbritannien und den USA,* edited by Carmen Birkle, Sabina Matter-Seibel, and Patricia Plummer, 255–71. Tübingen: Stauffenburg, 2001.
Wilson, Anna. "Death and the Mainstream: Lesbian Detective Fiction and the Killing of the Coming-Out Story," *Feminist Studies* 22, no. 2 (1996): 251–78.
Wiltenburg, Joy. "True Crime: The Origins of Modern Sensationalism." *The American Historical Review* 109, no. 5 (2004): 1377–1404.
Winkelmann, Andreas. *Tief im Wald und unter der Erde.* Munich: Goldmann, 2009.
Wittkowski, Joachim. *Auf Streife im Revier—Der Krimi im Ruhrgebiet.* Bottrop: Verlag Henselowsky Boschmann, 2009.
Wolfe, Tom. "Mauve Gloves & Madmen, Clutter & Vine." In *Mauve, Gloves & Madmen, Clutter & Vine and Other Stories, Sketches, and Essays,* 163–64. New York: Picador, 1990.
Wright, Willard Huntington. *The Great Detective Stories: A Chronological Anthology.* New York: Charles Scribner's Sons, 1927.
Yarbrough, Trisha. "The Cultural Work of Regional Mysteries." *Clues: A Journal of Detection* 22, no. 1 (2001 Spring-Summer 2001): 13–20.
Zeller, Dankwart Paul. *Das Geheimnis der Partisanen-Tora: Eine Theologische Kriminalgeschichte.* Albstadt: C. M. Brendle Verlag, 2009.
Žižek, Slavoj. *Enjoy Your Symptom! Jacques Lacan in Hollywood and Out.* New York: Routledge, 1992.
"Zur Chronik des Kreises Münsterberg." *Münsterberger Wochenblatt,* January 4, 1839, 1st ed., Staatsbibliothek zu Berlin Preußischer Kulturbesitz. http://zefys.staatsbibliothek-berlin.de/list/zdb/24335642.
Zwerenz, Gerhard. *Der Widerspruch. Autobiographischer Bericht.* Frankfurt am Main: Fischer, 1974.

Contributors

Dr. Angelika Baier is a project assistant at the Department of German Studies at the University of Vienna. She is currently working on the project *Discursive Intersections in Literature on Hermaphroditism* (P 22877 G-20), funded by the Austrian Science Fund (FWF). Her research interests are twentieth and twenty-first century literature, popular culture, affect studies, gender studies, and cultural analysis. Recent publications include "Affective Encounters and Ethical Responses in Robert Schneider's *Die Luftgängerin* und Sybille Berg's *Vielen Dank für das Leben*," in *Ethical Approaches in Contemporary German-Language Literature and Culture* (Edinburgh German Yearbook 7), edited by Emily Jeremiah and Frauke Matthes (2013); and *Affekt und Geschlecht: Eine einführende Anthologie*, co-edited with Christa Binswanger, Jana Häberlein, Eveline Yv Nay, and Andrea Zimmermann (2014).

Carol Anne Costabile-Heming is a professor of German and Chair of the Department of World Languages, Literatures, and Cultures at the University of North Texas. She received her PhD in German from Washington University in St. Louis and has distinguished herself as a scholar of twentieth- and twenty-first-century German literature and culture. She has published widely on *Wende* literature and post-*Wende* Berlin, including *Textual Responses to German Unification: Processing Historical and Social Change in Literature and Film* (2001) and *Berlin, The Symphony Continues: Orchestrating Architectural, Social, and Artistic Change in Germany's New Capital* (2004). She has also published essays and book chapters on Volker Braun, F. C. Delius, Jürgen Fuchs, Günter Grass, Günter Kunert, Peter Schneider, and Christa Wolf. She is the former president of the American Association of Teachers of German and currently is vice president and president-elect of the Southern Conference on Language Teaching (SCOLT). In 2012, she was named the Outstanding German Educator for the Post-Secondary level by the American Association of Teachers of German.

Kyle Frackman is an assistant professor of Germanic Studies at the University of British Columbia in Vancouver, where he teaches in both German and Scandinavian subject areas. He has a PhD in German Studies from the University of Massachusetts Amherst. His teaching and research interests include eighteenth- to twentieth-century German literature, German and Scandinavian film, music history, GDR studies, and gender and sexuality studies.

SASCHA ANDREAS GERHARDS is a visiting assistant professor of German at Miami University in Oxford, OH. He completed his dissertation, entitled "Zeitgeist of Murder: The Krimi and Social Transformation in Post-1945 Germany," in 2012. In the 2012–13 school year he held a Max Kade Distinguished Fellowship in German Studies at the University of California, Davis. Sascha received his BA equivalent in English and social sciences from the University of Cologne, Germany, and his Master of Arts degree in comparative literature from the University of Rochester, NY. He has published an interview with acclaimed linguist Claire Kramsch on her book *The Multilingual Subject,* and a chapter about the postwar Edgar Wallace films in Jaimey Fisher's *Generic Histories of German Cinema: Genre and its Deviations* (2013). Sascha is currently reworking his dissertation into a monograph, tentatively entitled "Tatort Deutschland: Representations of Social Change in Germany's Oldest Crime Show." In a journal article soon to be completed, he analyzes the crime genre's standing in East Germany with particular attention to the pressure of the country's political elite.

HEIKE HENDERSON is a professor of German and associate chair of the Department of World Languages at Boise State University. She holds a PhD in German Literature with a Designated Emphasis in Feminist Theory and Research from the University of California, Davis. Her research expertise is in contemporary German and Austrian literature. She has published on food in literature, minority discourse, and representations of cannibalism. Her current work focuses on mystery novels with a culinary slant.

TODD HERZOG is a professor and Head of the Department of German Studies at the University of Cincinnati, where he also directs the Center for Film and Media Studies. He is co-editor of the *Journal of Austrian Studies*. His books include *East, West, and Centre: Reframing Post-1989 European Cinema* (2014, with Michael Gott), *Crime Stories* (2009), *Rebirth of a Culture* (2008, with Hillary Hope Herzog and Benjamin Lapp) and *A New Germany in a New Europe* (2001, with Sander Gilman).

SUSANNE C. KNITTEL is an assistant professor of comparative literature at Utrecht University in the Netherlands. Her book, The Historical Uncanny: Disability, Ethnicity, and the Politics of Holocaust Memory will be published in December 2014 by Fordham University Press. In it, she presents a comparative study of German and Italian memory culture after 1945. Her current project, supported by a grant from the Netherlands Organization for Scientific Research (NWO), revolves around the representation of perpetrators in literature, film, and at sites of memory in Germany and Romania since 1989.

LYNN M. KUTCH is a professor of German in the Modern Language Studies department at Kutztown University of Pennsylvania. She has published on drama pedagogy to teach difficult texts, the comic book humor of *Sonnenallee* and media images of Angela Merkel. She also has presented extensively on a curriculum and assessment model for the graphic novel version of *Die Verwandlung*. She also created and maintains the internationally recognized The German Graphic Novel web resource that indexes and reviews contemporary German language graphic texts.

ANITA MCCHESNEY is an assistant professor of German at Texas Tech University. She earned her PhD from the Johns Hopkins University. She has several authored articles on constructions of truth in detective stories by authors such as E. T. A. Hoffmann and Peter Handke, and on intersections of media, narration and Austrian history in the novels of Gerhard Roth and Christoph Ransmayr. Her current research examines contemporary Austrian crime fiction as a tool for socio-historical critique.

TRACI S. O'BRIEN is an associate professor of German at Auburn University. In her book, *Enlightened Reactions*, she focuses on the articulation of (feminine) autonomy via racializing metaphors in German women's writing of the nineteenth-century. In addition, O'Brien has published on the novelist and travel writer, Ida von Hahn-Hahn, as well as on twentieth-century Austrian poet and literary critic Ernst Schönwiese. Forthcoming is a piece on nineteenth-century German journalist Ottilie Assing. O'Brien's research also has a significant focus on pedagogical topics. She has published in the *Unterrichtspraxis/Teaching German* on "bridging the gap" between students' proficiency levels in upper-level content courses and has a forthcoming book chapter on the importance of assessment strategies for graduate student teachers.

JON SHERMAN is an assistant professor of German at Northern Michigan University. He teaches German language courses, and occasionally "The Legends of King Arthur" and "Viking Mythology." His research focuses primarily on medieval German literature, especially Arthurian narratives, and more recently on the modern adaptation and reimaging of these medieval texts in popular culture. He has published on the Middle High German Arthurian romance *Wigalois* and is currently working on a project examining the BBC's adaptation of the Arthurian legends in the series *Merlin*.

FAYE STEWART is an assistant professor of German at Georgia State University in Atlanta, Georgia. Her research interests include crime fiction, feminist and queer literature, and film and popular culture. She is the author of *German Feminist Queer Crime Fiction: Politics, Justice and Desire* (2014).

MAGDALENA WALIGÓRSKA is an assistant professor of East European History and Culture at the University of Bremen, Germany. She is the author of *Klezmer's Afterlife: An Ethnography of the Jewish Music Revival* (2013).

Index

Ahmed, Sara, 195–96
ALV (*Amt für Literatur und Verlagswesen*), 140
Applegate, Celia, 45, 124
Auden, W. H., 101, 107
Auden, W. H., works by: *If I Could Tell You*, 104

Baier, Angelika, 12, 202, 204
Barfoot, Nicola, 235
Benjamin, Walter, 1
Berndorf, Jacques, 26, 35, 46
Bernhard, Thomas, 9, 62, 102
Berressem, Hanjo, 156, 160
Binswanger, Christa, 182
Bitterfeld Conference, 140
Blickle, Peter, 123, 128
Bloch, Ernst, 1, 82, 102, 107, 156, 158, 160, 161, 168
Börsenblatt für den deutschen Buchhandel, 26, 142
Borst, Meta, 147–48
Brecht, Bertolt, 1, 2
Bruckmüller, Ernst, 84–85
Butler, Judith, 180, 204
Buttler, Monika, works by: *Dunkelzeit*, 102, 105, 108, 111–12, 115

Cawelti, John G., 2–3, 11, 43–44
Confino, Alon, 124
Costabile-Heming, Carol Anne, 11
crime fiction, 1–14, 23–24, 25, 26, 28–29, 42, 44, 46, 50–51, 62–63, 64–65, 75, 76, 81, 101–3, 106, 107–8, 110, 112, 113, 116, 117, 139, 145, 151, 158–59, 160, 166, 178, 178–79, 180–81, 182, 190, 194, 200, 201, 223, 224–25, 229–30; Austrian, 43, 82; French, 103; German, 1–14, 51, 56, 102, 103, 106, 116, 145, 177–96; high/low art, 1, 103; and *Vergangenheitsbewältigung*, 112–17
criminal justice system, 28–30, 32
criminality, 10, 102, 105, 183
cross-dressing, 201, 204–5, 211–12, 214, 217–18

Davis, J. Madison, 223
deportation: and Freudian trauma, 164; and Grafeneck, 127–28
detective fiction, 1, 5, 11, 25, 27–28, 62–63, 64, 65, 92–93, 166, 205, 224; English language, 5; feminist, 200, 205; lesbian, 12, 205; and psychoanalysis, 156; women's, 234–35
Detre, Laura, 62
deviance: corporeal, 178; criminal, 178, 182–83; psychic, 178
Dillon, Sarah, 178–79, 182
discrimination, 177, 200, 201, 203, 208, 210
Donahue, William Collins, 102–3, 110, 112, 117
Donnerstag Club, 143
Dorn, Thea, 200
Dorn, Thea, works by: *Berliner Aufklärung*, 200–206, 212–13, 217–18
Dove, George N., 27–28
Duty, Helga, 150

Eco, Umberto, 27–28
Effron, Malcah, 4
English-language crime fiction, 5, 26
Enlightenment, 23–24, 156; enlightenment rationality, 160–61
entertainment literature, 103, 148–49
Erdmann, Eva, 6–7, 24, 84, 95

Erikson, Erik, 164
ethnicity, 61, 71–73, 202
euthanasia, and *Grafeneck*, 10, 120–38
exile, 156, 164

Falkenstein, Sigrid, works by: *Annas Spuren*, 121
Fallgeschichte, 8, 23
Familienzeitschriften, 29–30
Featherstone, Mike, 224–25
Feigenbaum, Erika Faith, 208
Finke, Edmund, 5
Foucault, Michel, 12
Frackman, Kyle, 8, 9
Freud, Sigmund, 12, 156–69; "Dora," 156, 164, 165; Freud Museum, 155, 156, 157, 168; Freudian theory, 123–25, 164, 182; repression and psychoanalytic theory, 155, 157–58, 160, 162, 163, 164, 169
Freud, Sigmund, works by: *Interpretation of Dreams*, 155
Friedrich, Cäcilia, 147–48
Frizzoni, Brigitte, 235
Furedi, Frank, 181

Gammelfleisch, 225
Gärnter-Scholle, Carola, 147
Gauss, Karl-Markus, 81
gender: identity, 73–75, 182, 191, 209; roles, 12–13, 217, 223–25, 226, 230–31, 235; secrecy, 178
genocide, 101, 105
Gerhards, Sascha, 8–9
Gerlach, Gunter, 33–36
German Democratic Republic (GDR, DDR), 10–11, 139–52; as *Leseland* and *Literaturgesellschaft*, 140
Giritzhofer, Katrin, 83, 85
Gombrowicz, Witold, 160
Gombrowicz, Witold, works by: *Diary*, 101
Gorrara, Claire, 103
Grafeneck, 10, 120–38
Gross, Rainer, works by: *Grafeneck*, 120–38
Grosz, Elizabeth, 179

Haas, Wolf, 9–10, 61–76
Haider, Jörg, 94
hard-boiled, 162, 226; detective, 5, 64; detective fiction, 201, 224, 235
Harich, Wolfgang, 143
Häring, Wilhelm, 29
Haycraft, Howard, 5, 24–25
Heiland, Henrike, works by: *Blutsünde*, 102, 105
Heimat, 6, 8–10, 14, 42–43, 45–47, 55–56, 92, 121–36
Heimatfilm, 42, 45, 46, 47
Heimatkrimi, 120–36
Heimatkunde, 90, 92
Heimatliteratur, 26, 124
Heimatroman, 7, 83, 133
Heimattheater, 90, 92
Heißenbüttel, Helmut, 63
Henderson, Heike, 13, 202, 204
Herzog, Todd, 110
historical crime novel, 47, 50, 52
Historischer Kriminalroman, 47, 50, 52
Hitzig, Julius Eduard, 29
Hoheiser, Horst, works by: *Monument of the Grey Buses* (memorial), 121
Hollows, Joanne, 235
Holocaust, 6, 10, 93, 101–19, 121–22, 133–34, 160, 170
Huby, Felix, 46–47
Hügel, Hans-Otto, 51

international crime fiction, 5, 13
intersexuality, 12, 177–99
Irwin, John T., 1
Iser, Wolfgang, 27

Jauß, Hans Robert, 27
journalism, 30–31, 203
Joyce, James, 143

Kafka, Franz, 143
Kahane, Claire, 164
Kalikoff, Beth, 225
Kampmann, Renate, works by: *Fremdkörper*, 178, 183, 186, 188, 193–96
Karr, H. P., 46–47

Kaufhold, Marianne, 146
Klub der jungen Künstler (Young Artists Club), 143
Korte, Barbara, 50, 55–56
Knittel, Susanne C., 10–11
Knitz, Andreas, works by: *Monument of the Grey Buses* (memorial), 121
Knopp, Guido, works by: *Hitlers . . .*, 52–53
Komarek, Alfred, 81, 85–88, 89, 92–95
Komarek, Alfred, works by: *Zwölf Mal Polt*, 81, 85–88
Kovner, Abba, leader of Nakam, 111
Kracauer, Sigfried, 1, 55
Krajenbrink, Marieke, 4, 24, 93–94
Kramblovsky, Beatrix, 85
Kretschmer, Ernst, 87–88
Kriminalliteratur, 2, 23, 50
Kündiger, Robert, 146
Kutch, Lynn Marie, 25
Kutcher, Volker, 51–52
Kutcher, Volker, works by: *Goldstein*, 102–4, 110; *Der nasse Fisch*, 52–55; *Der stumme Tod*, 52–55

Lang, Berel, 110
language, as a literary device, 62, 72, 76, 89 128
law enforcement, 28, 30, 73, 203, 212–14, 216
Lawon, Mark, 6
Lawson, Nigella, 235–36
layering, 178, 195
Lehmann, Christine, 200
Lehmann, Christine, works by: *Harte Schule*, 200–206, 212–18; *Der Masochist*, 213
Lénard, Nané, works by: *SchattenHaut*, 178, 190–93, 194, 196
lesbian, 190; crime fiction, 12, 205; detective fiction, 12, 217; texts, 201
linguistics, 215; in Wolf Haas's novels, 67–71
Loest, Erich, 11; the case of, 139–54; and Eulenspiegel Verlag, 151; and

HV Verlage (Hauptverwaltung Verlage), 146–48, 150; and Linden Verlag, 152–53; and Mitteldeutscher Verlag, 141, 143–47, 150–51; pseudonym Hans Walldorf, 145–46, 151
Lokalkolorit, 43, 45–47, 47–48
Lombroso, Caesare, 182–83
Lorenz, Dagmar, 160

Marsch, Edgar, 35
McChesney, Anita, 9–10, 43, 52
modernity, 23, 45, 88
Moltke, Johannes von, 45, 46, 47
Moretti, Franco, 43–44, 85
motive, 24, 87, 92, 120, 135, 157, 158, 162, 186–87, 194–95, 206, 210; Holocaust as, 105–6, 109, 111, 117
Muny, Eike, 63
mystery fiction, 106, 200, 201, 203, 205

National Socialism, 6, 12, 50–52, 92, 102, 105, 107, 110, 116
Nazism, 102
Neuhaus, Volker, 51
New German crime novel, 42–45, 85
Nietzsche, Friedrich, 161, 203, 206–7
Nindl, Sigrid, 65–67
Noglik, Gert, 145–48
Nuremberg laws, political correctness vis-à-vis Jews, 112, 132
Nusser, Peter, 28

O'Brien, Traci S., 11
Otte, Björn, 7

Paletschek, Sylvia, 50, 55–56
Pasikowski, Władysław, 103
Petöfi Circle, 140
philosemitism, 116–17
Pitaval, François Gayot de, 29
Plener, Peter, 63
Poe, Edgar Allan, 106
Poe, Edgar Allan, works by: *The Purloined Letter*, 166
Polanski, Roman, 43–44

political correctness, 103, 111–12
political identity, 9, 56
Preves, Sharon E., 195–96
privilege, 200–201, 206, 208–9, 216
Proust, Marcel, 143
psychoanalysis, 11, 124, 156, 158, 160, 165, 181–82, 183; and detection (of crime/criminality), 11, 165, 183; and fiction (crime/detective), 156

queer: crime fiction, 200, 203, 205, 206, 217, 218; detective fiction, 204, 205; general fiction, 203; mystery fiction, 200, 204, 217; sexuality/identity, 203–4, 208; theory, 12, 201 217
Quinn, Kate M., 4, 24

realism, 24, 140
Regiokrimi, 8, 10, 41–47, 50
regional crime fiction, 4, 8–10, 23–40
regionalism, 6, 42, 45, 49, 55
Reinhold, Conrad, 143
Richter-Appelt, Hertha, 193
Rossman, Eva, 11–12, 13, 202, 223–38
Rossman, Eva, works by: *Ausgekocht*, 225–34; *Freudsche Verbrechen*, 155–74; *Kaltes Fleisch*, 225–34; *Millionenkochen*, 225; *Mira kocht*, 225; *Wein & Tod*, 225
Roth, Gerhard, 51–52
Roth, Gerhard, works by: *Der See*, 81–82, 92–95
Rushing, Robert, 1, 14

Samelius, Lotta, 182
Sänger, Florian, 67
Saupe, Achim, 122
Schätzing, Frank, works by: *Tod und Teufel*, 50
Schiller, Friedrich, works by: *Vorrede zur Pitaval-Ausgabe 1792–1795*, 25, 29
Schlink, Bernhard, works by: *Selbs Betrug; Selbs Justiz; Selbs Mord*, 102, 110
Schreckenberger, Helga, 66, 88–89

Schröder, Gerhard, 215
Sedgwick, Eve Kosofsky, 178, 179, 196, 203–4
Seidman, Naomi, 110
serial killer, 190–96
Seltzer, Mark, 12, 178, 183, 188, 194–95
sexual identity, 12, 14, 183, 200
Shaw, George Bernard, 5
Sherman, Jon, 9–10, 204
Siebenstädt, Ingeburg, 146
Snell, K. D. M., 8
Soler, Nieves Pascual, 224–25
Stasi (Staatsicherheit), 139–40, 143–46, 151
stereotype, 11, 13, 24, 73, 81, 84–85, 95, 108–9, 110, 200, 210, 224, 229, 233–34
Stewart, Faye, 12–13
Stolpersteine, 105–6, 115
Stowe, William W., 4
Sullivan, Nikki, 182
Sweeney, Susan Elizabeth, 160
Symons, Julian, 25, 30

Tatort, 2, 6, 8–9, 10, 23, 27, 55–56; "Der Weg ins Paradies," 41–49
Teraoka, Arlene, 6
terrorism, 4, 47, 104; Sauerland Gruppe, 48
Thapar-Björkert, Suruchi, 181–82
Third Reich, 4, 10, 50, 105, 108, 127, 132
thriller, 24, 45–46, 103–4, 110, 178, 181, 184, 187–94
totalitarianism, 10

Unterhaltungsliteratur, 103, 148–49

Verarbeitungskrimi, 9, 47, 49–51, 56
vengeance, as a motive, 109; *Nakam*, 111
Vergangenheitsbewältigung, 112–17
Vienna, 11, 64, 65, 82, 88, 155–57, 159, 162–63, 165, 223, 225
Vogt, Jochen, 1–2, 45–46, 84, 85

Waligórska, Magdalena, 10, 204
Wallace, Edgar, 44
Wallace Films, 44, 47
Wanninger, Klaus, 27, 33–35
Warner, Michael, 203
Watson, Colin, 82–83
Weimar, 47, 50–53
Weitbrecht, Gudrun, 27, 33, 34
Wessel, Horst, 53–54
Wiesel, Elie, 110
Wigbers, Melanie, 7
Winkelmann, Andreas, works by: *Tief im Wald und unter der Erde*, 178, 187–88, 193–94

Witte, Gunter, 46–47
World War I, 124
World War II, 5, 6, 42, 45, 56, 94, 103, 105, 115, 124, 141
Wright, Willard Huntington, 5

Yang, Amy, 183

Zeller, Dankwart Paul, 113
Zeller, Dankwart Paul, works by: *Das Geheimnis der Partisaner-Tora*, 102, 112
Žižek, Slavoj, 155, 166
Zwerenz, Gerhard, 143

www.ingramcontent.com/pod-product-compliance
Lightning Source LLC
Chambersburg PA
CBHW021659230426
43668CB00008B/671